COVENTRY LIBRARIES

Please return this book on or before the last date stamped below.

2004

2017

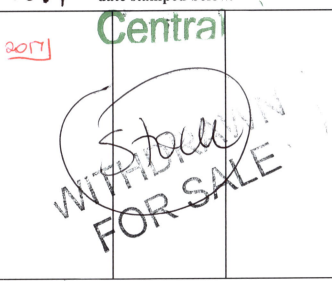

Central

WITHDRAWN FOR SALE

To renew this book take it to any of
the City Libraries
before the date
due for return

Coventry City Council

SIKH COINAGE
Symbol of Sikh Sovereignty

SIKH COINAGE

Symbol of Sikh Sovereignty

SURINDER SINGH

MANOHAR
2004

First published 2004

© Surinder Singh, 2004

ISBN 81-7304-533-X

Published by
Ajay Kumar Jain. for
Manohar Publishers & Distributors
4753/23 Ansari Road, Daryaganj
New Delhi 110002

Typeset by
A J Software Publishing Co. Pvt. Ltd.
New Delhi 110005

Printed at
Lordson Publishers Pvt. Ltd.
Delhi 110007

To
the everlasting memory of our
beloved son CHANDER MOHAN SINGH,
who left for his heavenly abode
on 15 January 2002 in a fatal road accident.

A wise man of learning in Israel once said that there is no end to the writing of books. Adding one more would therefore be pointless, unless it broke fresh ground.

LEWIS BROWNE in *Wisdom of Israel*

These words weighed very heavily on my mind when I considered the desirability of getting this book published. I believe that my study does break fresh ground and reveals authentic historical evidence, hitherto untraced, which helps in removing some of the cobwebs of ignorance and the moss of disinformation about Sikh coinage. I hope my contribution to this field will bring out the pristine beauty of Sikh coinage, the true symbol of Sikh sovereignty. The integration of numismatics, a hitherto neglected subject, with history has provided a fresh perspective on Sikh history.

SURINDER SINGH

Contents

Illustrations

Preface

Towards the close of my tenure lasting over three decades in the civil service (Indian Defence Accounts Service), I was posted at Jullandhar (Punjab) in 1979. While at Jullandhar, I became acquainted with a schoolteacher of Hoshiarpur who was a keen collector of ancient and medieval coins, and he introduced me to the fascinating world of old coins. In his collection, there were some coins pertaining to the Sikh period. These coins, inscribed with legends in praise of the Sikh Gurus in the Persian language, greatly fascinated me. I also started collecting Sikh coins and in a period of about ten years I had collected about eight hundred such coins.

With the dismemberment of the Mughal Empire in the eighteenth century, besides the Mughal and Afghan coins then in circulation the larger states both Hindu and Muslim also struck their own coins. Similarly, the European trading companies started striking their own coins in those areas where they were well entrenched. These various coins bore the name of the ruler, the year and the place of striking, with some ornamentation and even the legends of God's grace. Besides being used in trade and commerce, these coins were the symbol of the sovereignty of the ruler over his territory and the people under his authority.

Sikh society emerged mainly from the lower strata of Hindu society and developed under the guidance of the Sikh Gurus, from Guru Nanak to Guru Gobind Singh (AD 1469 to 1708), a period of over two centuries. Under the guidance of the Gurus, the Sikhs, hitherto oppressed by caste distinctions and Brahminical rituals and tyrannized by foreign rulers, were transformed into a self-reliant community, breathing the spirit of freedom, democracy, and sacrifice.

Shortly before his demise, Guru Gobind Singh abolished the institution of the personal Guruship and placed his spiritual authority in the holy book of the Sikhs, thereafter called the *Guru Granth Sahib*. He placed his temporal authority in the hands of the Khalsa, thereafter called the Khalsa Panth. The Sikhs, in spite of the Guru's instructions, treated their Gurus as the temporal sovereigns also and carried out the administration as a sacred trust. Thus, the Sikhs were the de-facto temporal sovereigns and their Gurus were the de-jure temporal sovereigns. This aspect is very aptly depicted in their daily salutation, '*Wahe Guru Ji ka Khalsa, Wahe Guru Ji ki Fateh*', meaning that the Khalsa belongs to the Guru and so does the victory belong to the Guru. Sikh coins are unique since they were struck in the name of the Sikh Gurus from the very first day in 1710 to the very last day, 29 March 1849, when the Sikh state was annexed by the British. Shiploads of Nanak Shahi coins were sent to the Bombay and Calcutta mints in order to be converted into British currency.

By the time I had collected a few hundred coins of silver and copper, I started contacting local coin collectors in the region to help me decipher and understand the legends inscribed on these coins and other features about which I was ignorant. Not only were these coin collectors unwilling to share their expertise, but even their knowledge was superficial and was based neither on any proper study of historical accounts nor on any numismatic investigation. My discussions with them were soon narrowed down to topics such as the rareness of the coins and the consequential increase in their sale/purchase value. The depth of their understanding of Sikh coinage was primarily confined to bazaar gossip and hearsay.

I finished my M.A. in history in 1952 and earned M.A. degree in political science in 1954, and was engaged on a study of the Indian Constituent Assembly when I was selected in the Allied Services in 1956. I thus drifted away from academic study and became busy with my mundane life as a government official. The study of Sikh coins and Sikh history once again rekindled in me the desire to pursue gainful knowledge which had been lying dormant in some forgotten chamber of my mind. I retired in 1987 and after sorting out my post-retirement problems, I became fully engaged in the study of Sikh coins and Sikh history related to this subject. By then I had collected about a thousand coins and possessed a reasonably decent collection of books on Sikh history as well.

The study of Sikh coins encompasses three disciplines of the social sciences, viz., numismatics, history, and political science; it also demands proficiency in the Punjabi and Persian languages. I wished to pursue a Doctoral degree in the subject but was unable to secure admission to a nearby university primarily due to my failure to persuade a university teacher conversant with my subject to be my guide. Since I was not willing to drop my passionate interest in this study, I continued with my work on my own.

I soon discovered that the study of Sikh coinage has been a greatly neglected subject, both by historians and numismatists. What little fragmentary work had been done was primarily in the field of cataloguing and even less work existed in the field of any serious analytical study. It was only after the mid-twentieth century that some numismatic work was carried out by a few scholars. Historians have made fanciful remarks regarding Sikh coins based on very meagre evidence and at times even non-existent evidence in support of their claims. They have commented on Sikh coins without even physically examining those coins which were otherwise readily available.

This negligence on the part of historians often resulted in baffling situations. The accounts in the books gave out a particular story about certain coins, but the imprints of the legends and other inscriptions on those very coins revealed a different story. Hence, arriving at the correct assessments about these coins became very difficult and time consuming. I recalled a carpentry lesson from my school days which taught that when two pieces of wood are to be joined together in a firm grip, these should be cut and joined in a manner popularly called dovetailing. This lesson proved to be very handy to me in dovetailing the historical data with the numismatic investigation; where the two sides led to the same conclusion my doubts were clarified and where the two sides did not agree I detected some form of historical disinformation. I started writing research papers on issues I was able to understand and presented my findings at conferences, seminars, and talks at nearby universities and at other institutions. In a decade or so, wrote over twenty-five research papers covering almost all important aspects of Sikh coins. My work was appreciated by other scholars and I gained sufficient confidence to pursue further study. I received a Ph.D. from the Rabindra Bharati University, Calcutta on my dissertation, 'Studies in Sikh Coinage', and this book is by and large based on my Doctoral thesis.

I seek the indulgence of my readers as a certain extent of unavoidable repetition has occurred at certain places. In order to counter the disinformation repeatedly recorded by several historians, every piece of available evidence has to be marshalled to establish the correct position. Thus, certain pieces of vital evidence which form the framework of the Sikh ethos were repeated while examining the issues under discussion in their correct perspective.

I had the opportunity to visit Himachal University a couple of times as a resource person in the refresher course for university teachers. One day, after I had delivered a lecture on Sikh coins, as we were dispersing, somebody remarked that I was changing history. This remark did hurt me and set me thinking. Suddenly I realized that I was in fact changing the recorded history so far as Sikh coins are concerned. My analytical examination of Sikh coins has given a new dimension to the study of Sikh history so far as events connected with the coins and the concept of Sikh sovereignty are concerned. Disinformation regarding these coins has been exposed and the pristine beauty of these coins has been brought out. I hope that some scholars will further pursue the study of this subject so that whatever aspect I have not been able to take up or whatever I have not been able to fully establish or clarify can be brought to light.

During this period of fifteen years while I carried out my work, my family has all along been a source of great assistance and encouragement to me, especially my younger son Chander Mohan Singh. I have sought guidance and assistance during this period from a wide range of teachers, scholars, librarians, numismatists, linguists, and others, some of whom went out of their way to help me.

I felt myself like a bird, collecting straws of knowledge from all around to build a nest of wisdom. I have felt the warmth of knowledge, secure in my nest, and I am now ready to take up my next project on the concept of Sikh sovereignty. I express my deep gratitude to all those persons from whom I was able to secure bits of knowledge to build my nest of wisdom.

November 2003   SURINDER SINGH

Introduction

The study of Sikh coinage has been a greatly neglected subject and very little work, both historical and numismatic, in this field has been carried out.[1] The earlier descriptions of the coinage of the Sikhs, who succeeded the Durranis in the Punjab, are by C.J. Rodgers, Lepel Griffin, and R.C. Temple.[2]

V.A. Smith was the first historian who argued that in ancient India, coins, especially the punch-marked coins, were the private issue of guilds and silversmiths and were produced with the permission of the ruling authorities.[3] Coins became a state issue with the rise of mercantilism and the formation of strong monarchies during the Buddhist period, nay, even earlier, towards the close of the Vedic period. With social stability, increasing urbanization, the growth of trade and commerce and an expansion in the activities of the state, the rulers required sufficient amounts of cash. Hence, the growth of imperialist practices is related to the development of the coinage system.[4] Kautilya's *Arthashastra* reveals that the state exercised complete control over the coinage system. The coins most often mentioned in the *Arthashastra* are the *pana*. Coins in circulation were silver coins of one, half, quarter, and one-eighth *pana*, copper coins of one *mashaka*, half *mashaka*, one *kakani*, and half *kakani*.[5] There was an elaborate system of minting and penalties were imposed for making or using counterfeit coins.[6]

The Mughal Emperors were not content with issuing coins from their capital cities and important provincial towns. They also possessed mobile mints which moved with the imperial armies and struck coins as and when a major city or territory was conquered.[7] The earliest Muslim mint in India was at Lahore, which was named Mohammadpur by Mohammad Ghaznavi. In the time of Farrukh Siyar, the system of farming was introduced for the mints, i.e. the right of minting coins was given to persons who guaranteed a certain amount of annual revenue to the royal exchequer.[8] The native states, particularly during the days of the declining Mughal Empire, had their own mints and did not issue coins in their own names but in the names of the Mughal emperors; they were content to place some distinct mark of their own on these coins.[9] Near about one hundred native states claimed the right to strike coins after they came under British rule, but this right was given only to thirty-four states by the British. After the country gained independence in 1947, all state mints were abolished by the Government of India.[10]

Numismatics was recognized as a primary source for the study of history and was utilized as a historiographical tool of analysis in India as early as the twelfth century by Kalhana, the chronicler of the history of Kashmir. But in the modern concept of historiography, in the development of which the West has played an important part, it became an auxiliary service to the discipline of history at a relatively late date.[11] The first notice on the subject of numismatic research appeared in 1790, when the discovery of Roman coins and medals was referred to in the second volume of the *Asiatic Researches*.[12] At the beginning of the twentieth century, there emerged a group of numismatists who were not only very keen collectors of coins but who were also ardent students of the subject. They were keenly interested in coordinating the results of their research studies and sought to systematize and encourage the further development of this emerging field of study by offering a common platform to coin collectors and students of Indian numismatics.[13]

The Numismatic Society of India was formed on 28 December 1910 in Allahabad by six persons, four of whom were ICS officers, one was a preacher, and one an Indian.[14] Although coin collecting was quite popular in India, the activity was pursued in a haphazard manner. The society intended to be a coordinating body, assisting and propagating the study of Indian numismatics. This society has grown with the passage of time; it has assisted in the large-scale cataloguing of coins, numerous monographs on coins have been brought out under its aegis, and an annual journal is regularly issued. The society is now permanently located in the Banaras Hindu University, Varanasi.[15] Numismatics is now a subject of study and research in various Indian universities. A specialized institution, the Indian Institute of Research in Numismatic Studies, located in Anjaneri (Nasik, Maharashtra), has also been established for promoting the study of numismatics.

Sikh coinage has been erroneously treated by numismatists as merely one of the many currencies of the native states which emerged in the chaotic conditions which accompanied the downfall of the Mughal Empire.[16] While the currencies of some native states continued to exist until India gained independence in 1947, Sikh coinage went out of circulation with the annexation of Punjab in 1849 and the declaration of Sikh coinage as dead currency.[17] Sikh coins have some very unique and fascinating features defining the concept of Sikh sovereignty, but the study of Sikh coins has virtually remained a neglected subject till recent times; no significant research on this subject has taken place in Indian universities. The only study carried out prior to my own thesis was by Madanjit Kaur of the Guru Nanak Dev University, Amritsar. Madanjit Kaur was kind enough to send me a copy of her study, which has not yet been published. Her study deals with the coins issued by Ranjit Singh and his successors, and her views and deductions are based on the drawings of Sikh coins by C.J. Rodgers.[18] Rodgers's account of Sikh coins and their drawings suffers from various discrepancies, which I have discussed in detail elsewhere.[19] Madanjit Kaur's study, largely based on secondary sources which suffer from quite a few deficiencies, has not been considered to be useful for research purposes.

The available sources of information on Sikh coins are largely fragmentary accounts in various books on Sikh history and occasional articles in a few journals. These accounts are by and large of an elementary nature, in which the Sikh coins have not been examined and, even if examined, no proper analysis of their significance has been carried out. There are also some accounts of an elementary nature in books on Indian coins and also some articles on Sikh coins, more so in recent times. There have also been some attempts to catalogue Sikh coins in some museums, and recently a detailed catalogue of Sikh coins compiled by the German scholar, Hans Herrli,[20] has proved to be quite useful in numismatic examinations of Sikh coins. The catalogue has generated a lot of interest in the collection of Sikh coins, and consequently the prices of these coins have shot up two to three times their value in northern India. Besides my own personal collection, Sikh coins are also available with other private collectors and in certain museums in India and Pakistan.

Some of the important sources for the study of Sikh coins in the initial stages are the writings of William Irvine, Karam Singh, and Ganda Singh. Gulshan Lall Chopra, D.C. Sharma, R.K. Parmu, Bhagat Singh, Madanjit Kaur, Ranjit Singh Kharag, and Hari Ram Gupta have written about Sikh coins of the later period. Short notes on numismatics have been written by C.J. Brown, W.H. Valentine, and Parmeshwari Lal Gupta in their books. C.J. Rodgers, C.K. Panish, J.S. Dyell, Ken Wiggins and S. Goron have published articles in various journals, of which C.J. Rodgers's account is relatively more comprehensive than that of the others. Some accounts are available in various catalogues, such as the following:

1. *Catalogue of Coins in the Government Museum Lahore*, by C.J. Rodgers, Calcutta, 1891.
2. *Catalogue of Coins (Miscellaneous Coins)*, by C.J. Rodgers, 1895.
3. *Coins of Dal Khalsa and Lahore Darbar*, by Parmeshwari Lal Gupta and Sanjay Garg, Chandigarh: Punjab Government, 1989.
4. *Coins of the Sikhs*, by Hans Herrli, Nagpur: Indian Coin Society, 1993.
5. *Copper Coins of India*, by W.H. Valentine, New Delhi: Inter India Publications, 1914.
6. *Archaeological and Numismatic Section, Sri Pratap Museum, Srinagar*, by R.C. Kak, Calcutta, Spink & Co., 1923.
7. *World Coins Standard Catalogue*, 21st edn., Wisconsin, USA: Krause Publications, 1994.
8. *Standard Guide to South Asian Coins and Paper Money Since 1956 AD*, 1st edn., Wisconsin, USA: Krause Publications, n.d.

All these sources are referred to in various sections of this book where necessary.

The interplay between the history of ancient India and the contemporaneous coins has been of a very restricted nature; for instance, the location of coins in a given area in large numbers frequently leads to certain conclusions about the ruler of that area if indications about his name or his period are available on the coins.[21] The discovery of coins issued by a particular ruler in a distant land corroborates the existence of trade and commerce between these two areas.[22] In the case of Sikh history and Sikh coins, well-documented books, manuscripts, and coins in almost their entire range are also readily available for scholarly examination. Hence, the study of the interplay of history and the coins of both the ancient and the post-medieval periods require different parameters. This interplay of history writing and numismatics has a rather limited role to play in the study of ancient history, but it can have a more significant impact on the study of medieval and even modern history.

A major lacuna in the historical records and in numismatic investigations of Sikh coins has been that historians have by and large written about the coins without actually examining the evidence, and numismatists have similarly examined the coins without locating the proper historical context where available and without understanding and appreciating the traditions and ethos of the people involved.

The sudden rise of the Sikhs from relative obscurity to political and military power, their pushing back the Afghan invaders beyond the Khyber Pass, and establishing their rule over north-western India were the subjects addressed by British and European travellers moving through the Punjab and the neighbouring Muslim countries. Their travelogues describing Sikh coins and related incidents are based on bazaar gossip and hearsay, emphasizing their unique and romantic elements. Unfortunately, later historians have taken such accounts as authentic historical records, without carrying out independent investigations of their own.[23] The unreliability of these accounts as historical sources could not have been revealed had the Sikh coins been no longer available, and their investigation, both historical and numismatic, not been taken up.[24]

Proper evidence is a prerequisite for the study of history. This observation is equally valid for the study of coins. The interpretation of history may be subjective, and even incorrect, but the recordings on the coins cannot be doubted and may be taken as essentially authentic. The study of Sikh coinage both by historians and numismatists has suffered due to the lack of proper historical evidence and its proper use in numismatic investigation; in this process a number of discrepancies, even distortions, have taken place. A few of the important ones are the following:

(1) John Dyell based his account of the initial Sikh coins on Hadi Kamwar Khan's *Tazkirat-i-Salatin-i-Chughtaiya*, whereas there is no reference to the Sikh coins in this manuscript.

(2) Hans Herrli identified the initial Sikh coinage struck during Banda Bahadur's time as having been struck in the time of Kapur Singh or even Jassa Singh Ahluwalia, but he did so without basing this claim on any evidence whatsoever.

(3) The claim regarding Jassa Singh Ahluwalia having struck a coin in his own name, but this claim is also made without establishing the existence of any such coin as corroborating evidence.

(4) The claim that Ranjit Singh struck coins in the name of a courtesan called Moran has been stated by many historians and even numismatists but without any proper evidence.

(5) Hari Singh Nalwa is stated to have struck coins in his own name from Kashmir and Peshawar but this claim is made without any proper supporting evidence.

(6) Ranjit Singh's attempt to strike coins depicting himself sitting with Guru Nanak has been incorrectly identified as Guru Nanak sitting with Mardana.

(7) Incorrect nomenclature of Sikh coinage and its illogical differentiation into Nanak Shahi and Gobind Shahi coins.

(8) Various theories have been put forward regarding the leaf motif on Sikh coins but without any convincing evidence.

(9) I had the occasion to meet learned Sikh historians, viz., Ganda Singh, Hari Ram Gupta, Bikramjit Hasrat, Gopal Singh, Avtar Singh Sandhu, and R.K. Parmu who have written about Sikh coins in their books. I asked them to what extent had they been able to examine actual Sikh coins as the source of evidence in support of the facts stated by them. It was a great surprise for me to learn that none of them had actually examined Sikh coins. Bhagat Singh, who wrote his Ph. D. thesis on the Sikh polity and who devoted a chapter to Sikh coins, had also not examined any actual coins. The inaccurate details recorded by many Sikh historians did create certain problems in establishing their inaccuracy and bringing out their correct position.

(10) A fairly accurate and detailed catalogue of Sikh coins was published by Hans Herrli in 1993 from Nagpur. The coin collectors rely on this catalogue, and in fact with the issue of this catalogue the prices of Sikh coins have risen two to three fold. But in recent publications, the historians mentioned hereunder do not seem to have taken note of this catalogue and are still repeating the mistakes committed by earlier writers.

(11) Patwant Singh's book *The Sikhs* states that Banda engraved an official seal and coins to celebrate Sikh rule. These were dedicated to the Gurus and the Persian inscription on his seal read:

Degh O Tegh O Fateh O Nasrat-i-bedirang
Yaft uz Nanak Guru Gobind Singh.

The inscription eulogized the kettle (representing the Sikh commitment to feed the poor), the sword (the symbol of power), victory and unqualified patronage as attributes bequeathed by Nanak to Guru Gobind Singh'.

Patwant Singh further states, 'A silver coin was issued to announce their assumption of political power and declaring Amritsar as the mint city.' But this is an incorrect statement as Sikh coins were first struck from the Mughal mint at the capital city of Lahore dated 1822 Sambat, i.e. AD 1765. The first Sikh coin minted from Amritsar was dated Sambat 1832, i.e. AD 1775. He further states that the coins minted on the occasion of Ranjit Singh's coronation bore a verse in Persian that had appeared on Banda Bahadur's seal and offers the following translation:

My largesse, my victories, my unalloyed fame
I owe to Guru Nanak and Guru Gobind Singh.[25]

It is very strange that Patwant Singh gives two different translations of the same legend discussed by him in his Chapter II and Chapter III, with a wide range of variation, whereas in the earlier translation, the recipient of Guru Nanak's benediction was Guru Gobind Singh, but in the later translation, the recipient of these benedictions is Ranjit Singh. In order to understand and appreciate the spirit behind these legends, the translations have to be literal and not wayward.

This is a fairly incorrect rendering of the legend 'Degh Tegh Fateh Nusrat Baidrang, Yaft uz Nanak Guru Gobind Singh', which means that the economic power, the strength of arms and the resultant victory with unrestrained help was received from Nanak Guru Gobind Singh and the recipient of this benediction was the entire Khalsa Panth and not only Ranjit Singh.

(12) J.S. Grewal, the eminent Sikh historian, has laid down a standard for the collection of evidence and its interpretation:

The modern student of history aims at interpreting the past modes of life and processes of change in rational and human terms . . . he demands evidence in support of every statement made about the past and insists on the application of valid techniques and methods in interpreting evidence. He accepts nothing on faith.[26]

In an international seminar on Maharaja Ranjit Singh, Grewal read out the keynote address, stating at the outset 'that this seminar was meant·to be a serious academic event and that my words could set the tone'.[27] The address brought out certain claims or interpretations which do not reach the standard laid down by J.S. Grewal himself, nor do these stand the scrutiny of the touchstone of numismatic investigation and evidence connected with it.

On page 4 of the keynote address, Grewal states that Banda Bahadur struck a coin with the following inscription:

Sikka zad bar har do alam Tegh-i-Nanak wahib ast.
Fateh Gobind Singh Shah-i-Shahan fazl-i-Saccha Sahib ast.

He further states that this inscription was used on the coins struck at Lahore in 1765 when the city was occupied by a few Sikh leaders. This coin was known as Gobind Shahi. The above statement is incorrect as the coin struck from Lahore was inscribed with a different legend. The legend on the above-mentioned coin minted in Lahore in 1765 was: *Degh Tegh Fateh.* (For details, see Chapter II.) Grewal has confused the two legends which appeared on coins struck from Lahore and Amritsar and thus a number of discrepancies have crept into his account. The legend mentioned by J.S. Grewal pertaining to the coin of 1710 has an inaccuracy. The coins struck by Banda Bahadur for the second year (the first year's coin has not been located so far) had the word 'Gobind' and not 'Gobind Singh'. The phrase 'Gobind Singh' has been used on the third year's coin only (see Plate I). The legend used on the obverse and the reverse of the Lahore coins of 1765 was:

Obverse   *Degh Tegh Fateh O Nusrat Baidrang*
             Yaft uz Nanak Guru Gobind Singh
Reverse   *Zarb Dar-ul-Saltanate Lahore mainminat*
             Manoos Jalus Sambat 1822.[28]

J.S. Grewal's characterization of this coin as Gobind Shahi is incorrect. All Sikh coins have the names of both Nanak and Gobind Singh on their obverse. There are no coins on which only Guru Gobind Singh's name is given. Hence, Sikh coinage can only be called Nanak Shahi coinage. The British called Sikh coins Nanak Shahi coins after the annexation of the Punjab in 1849. The earlier traders, without any knowledge or evidence, did call the Lahore coins inscribed with the '*Degh Tegh Fateh*' legend as Gobind Shahi coins and this characterization was repeated by some historians, again without any examination or evidence.[29] (For details, see Chapter II.) J.S. Grewal states that 'Ranjit Singh's seal bore no reference to him; his government was called *Sarkar Khalsaji*, and his court *Darbar Khalsaji*'. The seal used by Ranjit Singh was 'Akal Sahai Ranjit Singh'. This type of seal bearing the Akal Sahai and the individual's name was prevalent amongst the Sikh sardars who preceded Ranjit Singh. The Gurmukhi impression on this seal is reproduced on the top of the title page of the book *Civil and Military Affairs of Maharaja Ranjit Singh* by J.S. Grewal and Indu Banga, 1987, Amritsar. The Urdu impressions of this seal are also given in *From Guru Nanak to Maharaja Ranjit Singh* by J.S. Grewal, 1982, Amritsar, pp. 154-5 and 164-5. All these seal impressions are *Akal Sahai Ranjit Singh*. Page 3 of the keynote address is mainly taken from Khushwant Singh's book *The*

Sikhs, vol. I, 1963, New Delhi, pp. 200-1. Khushwant Singh's account of Sikh coinage is sketchy and partially incorrect, and the same mistake has occurred in J.S. Grewal's account.

The translation of the '*Degh Tegh Fateh*' legend is not correct and is at variance from what J.S. Grewal has stated in his earlier studies. He has stated that festivity (abundance), sword, victory without delay, Guru Gobind Singh received from Nanak.[30] In his keynote address, Grewal translates the same passage as follows: 'The victory, the sword, and the deg are stated to be the gifts received from Guru Nanak'.[31] The name of Guru Gobind Singh has been left out, for which no reason has been given nor have the recipients of the Guru's benediction been identified.

(13) Jean-Marie Lafont in his recent book on Ranjit Singh devotes a page to the coins of the Sikh kingdom, assisted by a local coin collector, Jyoti Rai.[32] The statement that Sikh coins were struck from Lahore in 1765 and 1772 is incorrect as Sikh coins were first struck from Lahore in 1765 and continued without any break and the coins of most of the years after 1765 are available. It is further stated that the Persian inscription on the Amritsar coin was in the name of Guru Nanak and hence it was called Nanak Shahi coinage. The legend quoted on the same page has the names of both Guru Nanak and Guru Gobind Singh and the statement made is incorrect. In the legend '*Degh Tegh Fateh*', the meaning of '*Yaft uz Nanak Guru Gobind Singh*' has been given as 'Guru Gobind Singh received from Guru Nanak, whereas the correct meaning is 'the Khalsa received from Nanak Guru Gobind Singh' thus encompassing the entire period of the Gurudom (see Chapter II). The interpretation or claim that 'at times people became linked with a particular symbol on a coin or a certain legend connected with it' is not correct. The Sikh coins from Kashmir from the Hari Singh period, i.e. 1820 to 1821, and during the rest of the period of Sikh rule upto 1846 were not called the *Hari Singhji* but the *Harisinghee rupia* in a derogatory sense, as the Kashmiris are notorious for their habit of distorting names. As regards the Moran Shahi coins said to be struck in the name of the courtesan Moran, this is a misnomer (see Chapter III). Similarly, the name of the Peshawar coins as '*Peshawari Naunihal Singhji*' is also an incorrect construction as most historians consider that these coins had been struck by Hari Singh Nalwa.

Such statements, especially those regarding coins and the notion of Sikh sovereignty, are based on incorrect evidence and thus create historical distortions. When these errors are made by learned historians, they are easily accepted by the general readership, and hence awkward and difficult to set the record straight. All these issues are fully discussed, with references to the available evidence, in various chapters of this book.

Guru Nanak, having witnessed the social discrimination practiced by the upper-caste Hindus against the rest of the society and the Lodhi rulers' inability to defend themselves against the Mughal onslaught, envisioned a self-reliant society devoid of any fear and based on righteous conduct. Guru Nanak preached an equal and just social order amongst his followers, and his successors made further contributions to his original teachings. Guru Arjan realized the inherent dangers of the hostility of the Mughal rulers and thought of arming the nascent Sikh community for self-defense. The cruel persecution of Guru Arjan and Guru Tegh Bahadur deepened Sikh apprehensions and accelerated the pace of their resistance.[33] The hostility of and persecution by the Mughals and the self-defence undertaken by the Sikhs established a cycle of action and reaction which continued until Mughal rule was finally rooted out from the Punjab and the surrounding areas by the Sikhs in the mid-eighteenth century.

Guru Gobind Singh who bore the major brunt of Mughal wrath in the Punjab created the Khalsa (in 1699), a body of self-sacrificing saint-soldiers. While serving the *Khanda Pahul* to the five beloved ones (*Panj Piaras*), he himself took the same *pahul* from them, thereby making them his equals and the co-sharers of his sovereignty.[34] Shortly before his demise in Nander, he abolished the institution of the personal Guruship and placed his spiritual sovereignty in the *Guru Granth Sahib* and vested his temporal sovereignty in the entire Khalsa community. The temporal sovereignty so bequeathed by Guru Gobind Singh has all along been held by the Khalsa as a sacred trust. The most remarkable feature of the Sikh coinage struck after the demise of Guru Gobind Singh and the formation of the Sikh state has been that it was struck in the name of the Gurus as a symbol of their sovereignty in an age in which coins were struck in the name of the actual temporal rulers.

This book is an attempt to correct the distorted interpretation of the Sikh coins and seeks to bring out their uniqueness as a testimony to the Sikh concept of sovereignty in the feudal age.

The objectives of this study are:

(1) To identify the discrepancies, distortions, and other weaknesses in the existing accounts on Sikh coinage.
(2) To investigate and analyse the reasons for these distortions.
(3) To present the correct position as emerging from the study of relevant Sikh history and the investigation of the Sikh coins of that period.
(4) To highlight the uniqueness of the Sikh coins as a symbol of Sikh sovereignty.

This study has been divided into four periods. The first period is that of the initial Sikh coinage issued under Banda Bahadur's command and his control of Subah Sirhind and the surrounding territories from 1710 to 1713. With the capture of Banda Bahadur and his followers in 1715 in Gurdas Nangal and the extreme persecution of the Sikh community by the Mughal rulers, an attempt was made to literally annihilate the entire Sikh community and the Sikh state was eclipsed from 1715 till 1765. The second period was the period of the confederacy of the Sikh *misls* which occupied Lahore and issued Sikh coins from the city in 1765 and continued to do so not only from Lahore but also from the other mints of Amritsar and Multan till 1800. The third period began with the emergence of a single leader in the person of Ranjit Singh in 1800 and the striking of Sikh coins till 1837. The fourth period deals with the coinage struck by his successors from 1837 till the annexation of the Sikh state by the British in 1849.

The study is confined to gold and silver coins which were state issues. Although copper coins were also used in great abundance, these were farmed out to individual bankers and traders due to the non-availability of sufficient quantities of copper from the Jagadhari traders who were not very cooperative with the Lahore Darbar. However, the general pattern of issuing a large number of small legends on copper coins in the name of the Sikh Gurus is also seen in the case of these coins. These coins too did not bear the name of any *sardar* or ruler. Hence, these have not been taken up for examination here. A large number of religious tokens, somewhat similar to the coins, have long been in circulation. Although these are neither coins nor state issues, yet these tokens create a certain amount of confusion among the unknowing public.

Appendix A deals with Sikh religious tokens.

Appendix B deals with certain discrepancies in the recently published *Encyclopaedia on Sikhism*, 1995-8. While attending the thirty-first Punjab History Conference at Punjabi University, Patiala in March 1999, I came across the recently published *Encyclopaedia on Sikhism*, vol. IV, in which an entry on Sikh coins appears on pp. 136-8. The entry suffers from a number of discrepancies and inaccuracies that have, by and large, been dealt with in various parts of this study and the correct positions been established. Subsequently, I also examined the earlier volumes and found discrepancies in the information given there regarding coins and seals. Since a great deal of importance is given to the facts as recorded in encyclopaedias, I consider it desirable to give a consolidated critique of these entries found in the vols. I to IV of the *Encyclopaedia on Sikhism*.[35]

Appendix C deals with the first, rather lengthy article on Sikh coins written by C.J. Rodgers in 1881, in which his bias against the Sikhs, their Gurus, and their doctrines has been brought out. I have also discussed other inadequacies and distortions in his account.

Appendix D deals with the chronological dates with special reference to the Sikh coins.

NOTES

1. P.L. Gupta, 'A survey of Indian numismatography (coinage from the decline of the Mughal empire to 1947)', *Golden Jubilee Volume, 1910-1960,* Varanasi: Numismatic Society of India, 1961, p. 84.

2. (i) C.J. Rodgers, 'On the Coins of the Sikhs', *Journal of Asiatic Society of Bengal.* Calcutta, 1881, pp. 71-93.

    (ii) C.J. Rodgers, 'Some Coins of Ranjit Dev, King of Jammu', *Journal of Asiatic Society of Bengal,* Calcutta, 1885, pp. 60-7.

    (iii) Lepel Griffin, 'Rajas of Punjab', vol. II, Punjab: Languages Department, 1970, pp. 285-9.

    (iv) R.C. Temple, 'The Coins of the Modern Chiefs of the Punjab', *Indian Antiquary,* vol. XVIII, Bombay, 1893, pp. 21-41.

3. Lallanji Gopal, 'The right of minting coins in Ancient India', *Journal of the Numismatic Society of India,* vol. XXII, 1960, p. 98.

4. Ibid., p. 38.

5. Kautilya, *The Arthashastra,* tr. L.N. Rangarajan, New Delhi: Penguin Books India Ltd., 1992, pp. 75, 228, 328.

6. Ibid., p. 75.

7. Upendra Thakur, 'Mints and Minting in India', *Golden Jubilee Volume, 1910-1960,* Varanasi: Numismatic Society of India, 1961, p. 193.

8. Ibid., p. 195.

9. Ibid., p. 197.

10. Ibid., p. 197.

11. J.N. Tiwari, 'A Survey of Indian Numismatography', *Golden Jubilee Volume 1910-1960,* Varanasi: Numismatic Society of India, 1961, p. 21.

12. A.K. Narain, 'Fifty Years of the Numismatic Society of India', *Golden Jubilee Volume, 1910-1960,* Varanasi: Numismatic Society of India, 1961, p. 1.

13. Ibid., p. 1.

14. Ibid., p. 1.

15. Ibid., p. 19.

16. A.N. Lahiri, 'Numismatography of Indian Princely States', Platinum Jubilee Session, *Journal of Numismatic Society of India,* vol. XLIX, 1987, p. 192.

17. Foreign Department, General Report, *Administration of Punjab Territories, 1949-51,* Calcutta, 1856, p. 34.

18. Madanjit Kaur, 'A Study of Sikh Numismatics with Special Reference to the Coins of Maharaja Ranjit Singh and his Successors'. A summarized version of this study is published in *Maharaja Ranjit Singh: Politics, Society and Economy,* in Fauja Singh and A.C. Arora, eds, Patiala: Punjabi University, 1984, pp. 327-50.

19. Surinder Singh, 'A Critique on "the Coins of the Sikhs" by C.J. Rodgers', *Panjab Past & Present,* vol. XXV, pt. II, October 1991, Patiala: Punjabi University, pp. 40-55.

20. Hans Herrli, *The Coins of the Sikhs,* Nagpur: Indian Coin Society, 1993.

21. J.N. Tiwari, 'A Survey of Indian Numismatography', op. cit., p. 21.

22. A.K. Narain, 'Fifty Years of the Numismatic Society of India', op. cit., p. 1.

23. (i) Baron Hugel, *Travels in Kashmir and Punjab,* Languages Department, Punjab (rpt), 1970, pp. 123, 254, 384.

    (ii) V. Jacquemont, *Journey through India, Tibet, Lahore and Kashmir* (translated from the French), Edward Charten, 26 Molless Street, 1834, p. 55.

(iii) Ali Shahamat, *Sikhs and Afghans*, Punjab: Languages Department, rpt., 1970, p. 53.

(iv) W. Moorcraft, *Travels in the Himalayan Provinces of Hindustan and Bokhara from 1819-1825*, Punjab: Languages Department, rpt., 1970, pp. 53, 546.

(v) Major Leech, *Survey 1943*, Revenue of Kashmir, Foreign Section, New Delhi: National Archives of India, nos. 13-17 S.C.

(vi) G.T. Vigne, *Travels in Kashmir, Ladakh and Skardu*, Punjab: Languages Department, · rpt., 1970, p. 57.

(vii) Ganeshi Dass, *Siyahat-i-Kashmir*, Chandigarh: Punjab Itihas Prakashan, 1976, p. 39.

(viii) Mohan Lal, *Travels in Punjab, Afghanistan and Turkestan*, Punjab: Languages Department, 1970, p. 49.

24. Patwant Singh, *The Sikhs*, New Delhi: Harper Collins India, 1999, pp. 75, 91.

25. Ibid., p. 105.

26. J.S. Grewal, *From Guru Nanak to Ranjit Singh*, Amritsar: Guru Nanak Dev University, 1982, p. 82.

27. J.S. Grewal, 'Keynote Address at the International Seminar on Maharaja Ranjit Singh', 10-11 April 2002, Centre for Defence and National Security Studies, Panjab University, Chandigarh, p. 2.

28. See note 80 in Chapter II, where various references to the striking of the *Degh Tegh Fateh* Legend coins from Lahore in 1765 are given.

29. A detailed account is given in Chapter II, pp. 66-7.

30. J.S. Grewal and S.S. Bal, *Guru Gobind Singh*, Chandigarh: Panjab University, 1967, p. 239.

31. J.S. Grewal, 'Keynote Address', op. cit., p. 5.

32. Jean-Marie Lafont, *Maharaja Ranjit Singh: Lord of the Five Rivers*, New Delhi: Oxford University Press, 2002, pp. 92-3.

33. A.C. Banerjee, *Sikh Gurus and Sikh Religion*, Delhi: Munshiram Manoharlal, 1983, pp. 273 and 280-1.

34. Ibid., p. 310.

35. *Encyclopaedia on Sikhism*, edited by Harbans Singh, Patiala: Punjabi University (4 vols.), 1995-8:

  (i) *Entry on Akal Purakh*, vol. I, p. 58.

  (ii) *Entry on Hari Singh Nalwa*, vol. II, p. 252.

  (iii) *Entry on Moran*, vol. III, p. 123.

  (iv) *Entry on Coins or Numismatics*, vol. IV, pp. 136-8.

CHAPTER I

The Initial Sikh Coinage
AD 1710-1712

Guru Gobind Singh wrote to the Sikhs of Dhaul on 2 October 1707 that his negotiations with the Mughal emperor were in progress and that he would soon return to the Punjab.[1] But for reasons not fully known, he accompanied Bahadur Shah, the Mughal emperor, towards the Deccan and, in the words of Khafi Khan, 'Gobind, leader of the infamous community, with two to three hundred armed horsemen and infantry moved alongwith the emperor'.[2] The *Tarikh-i-Bahadur Shahi* also states that the Guru was in the habit of constantly addressing worldly persons, religious families, and all sorts of people.[3] Although the emperor was quite friendly towards the Guru, the entire Mughal camp and the courtiers were hostile towards him. They wholeheartedly sided with Wazir Khan, the faujdar of Sirhind, who was responsible for most of the travails of the Guru.[4] Guru Gobind Singh, realizing the gravity of the situation and the unlikelihood of Bahadur Shah siding with him over Wazir Khan's crimes, moved from the Mughal camp and shifted his establishment to a nearby area, which he named Abchalnagar.[5]

Establishment of the Sikh State

Guru Gobind Singh came in contact with a *bairagi* (an ascetic) named Madhodas in early September 1708, and in an extremely short period he became the Guru's ardent disciple.[6] He was named Banda Bahadur or Banda Singh Bahadur and was made commander of the Sikh forces and was sent to the Punjab to lead and guide the Sikhs in their struggle against the Mughal authorities. Banda Bahadur was given an advisory council of five devoted Sikhs and a contingent of twenty-five soldiers. He was given *hukamnamas* for the Sikhs of Majha, Malwa, and Doaba to join him in this struggle and also some temporal symbols, including the Guru's own sword, green bow, and arrows, and the party moved towards the Punjab by the close of September 1708.[7]

Not much is known about the early period of Banda Bahadur's life. He is said to belong to a Rajput family from the Shivalik Hills. He was a good hunter and about four years younger to Guru Gobind Singh. When he was around 20 years of age, he renounced the worldly life and became an ascetic. He settled at Nander at the time Guru Gobind Singh went there.[8] There are quite a few controversial accounts dealing with the question of whether he was baptized a Khalsa by Guru Gobind Singh or whether he was deliberately not baptized lest he may put a claim to the Guruship,[9] and whether he was asked by the Guru to live a chaste life and whether he subsequently violated the Guru's orders by marrying.[10] These controversies are not based on any reliable corroborative evidence and may be attributed to the partisan attitudes of many writers. We have no confirmed account duly corroborated by contemporary evidence. It is presumed that Banda Bahadur's selection and move may have been kept secret from the Mughal court, and no detailed account in this regard is readily forthcoming. What is true is that Guru Gobind Singh selected Banda Bahadur as the commander of his Sikhs, thus recognizing Banda's abilities and placing his confidence in him. It is also a fact that Banda's devotion to Guru Gobind Singh till his last day is unmatched in the annals of Sikh history. These controversies have no relevance to the subject of our study. It seems plausible that Guru Gobind Singh and Banda might have known each other during their younger days in the Shivalik Hills as otherwise such a great decision was not likely to have been taken so casually and in so short an association. Contemporary historians are silent on this aspect.

Banda Bahadur left for the Punjab with his associates in September 1708.[11] The distance between Nander and Hissar, about 1,600 kms, was normally covered in about three months, but Banda and his associates took almost a year to travel between the two towns. They seem to have travelled in disguise and by circuitous routes across Maharashtra and Rajasthan, avoiding contact with the Mughal forces and other government agencies.[12] The Mughal espionage system was most elaborate in the time of Aurangzeb and that might have contributed to the circumspect manner of his selection and his move to the Punjab. No detailed account of such a momentous decision is forthcoming and it is presumed that it may have been deliberate in order to avoid detection by the Mughal camp. Shortly after his departure, Banda Bahadur received the news of the demise of Guru Gobind Singh on 18 October 1708 and hence became more careful in his movements. Banda Bahadur emerged in Narnaul and helped the local people in suppressing dacoits and robbers in their area; he won the confidence of the common people of the local area and became their leader.[13]

When Banda Bahadur had passed on the Guru's orders to his Sikhs, they started assembling under his banner, and thus commenced his real mission, with a following of about 500 men.[14] He looted the government treasury at Sonepat and distributed the booty amongst his followers; likewise he raided other treasuries at Kaithal and Bhiwani. He subdued Samana and the nearby towns.[15] The next big town subdued was Sadhura, where he raised a mud fort for his forces and also occupied Lohgarh, a small fortress in the Shivalik foothills, and the surrounding areas. By now Banda's army had become fairly large, swollen by a larger number of camp followers who were more interested in loot rather than in mere victory. In May 1710, the famous Battle of Chappar Chiri was fought between Banda Bahadur and Wazir Khan, the faujdar of Sirhind, in which the Mughal forces were totally routed and the entire territory of the Subah of Sirhind and large parts of the surrounding areas came under the control of the Sikhs.[16] A Sikh state was established in the true sense, with its *thanas* and *chowkis*, and the large landholdings were distributed amongst the tillers. The Sikhs assumed sovereignty over the conquered territories and struck their own coinage.[17]

The Sikhs considered Sirhind, the largest town, to be accursed and hence they treated it only as a base depot for their supplies.[18] The Sadhura fort was strengthened with an extra mud wall and a moat, and the Lohgarh fortress, about 10 miles distant (the entire area covered with streams and forests), was also strengthened. I have visited the site a number of times and on my report, the Shiromani Gurudwara Parbandhak Committee, Amritsar is planning to raise a suitable memorial to Banda Bahadur at Lohgarh. Lohgarh was originally called Mukhlispur, named after a hunting lodge raised by Mukhlis Khan, governor of Sirhind. Lohgarh, located on a perpendicular mountain cliff about 700 ft. high, lies on the border of a thickly forested area (which even after three centuries is still a reserved forest with virtually no human habitation). Banda Bahadur used Lohgarh as a base for tactical retreat or rearguard action with much success. When he could not repulse the onslaught of the combined Mughal forces along with the Rajputs and the Jats which heavily outnumbered his forces at Sadhura, and further fighting appeared suicidal, he would suddenly withdraw his forces overnight to Lohgarh and after undertaking a day's rearguard action to stall the enemy forces, he would escape into the forests beyond Lohgarh along with his forces. He employed this strategy successfully in both the battles of Lohgarh in AD 1710 and 1713.[19]

The claim by many historians that Banda Bahadur established his capital at Lohgarh does not seem to be based on any concrete evidence but rather on historical hearsay, as the small fortress covering hardly an acre could not have accommodated a state capital, howsoever small the state may have been. The basic characteristics of a capital, such as its central location, its easy accessibility, and sufficient area for habitation, are totally lacking at the Lohgarh site, and an examination of the area clearly establishes that the capital of the Sikh state could not have been Lohgarh. Banda Bahadur gives the likely salient features of the capital of the Sikh state on the reverse of the initial Sikh coin but no name of any city, whether Sirhind or Lohgarh, has been recorded after the word 'zarb'. He calls the capital of the Sikh state '*ba aman al dahar*' or '*ba aman al din*', i.e. 'coined at the refuge of the world' or 'the most protected place', which in the next coin appears as 'the protection of the faith', '*masawar-at shahr zinat*', the picture of a beautiful city, '*Altakht Khalsa Mubarak Bakht*', where the fortunate throne of the Khalsa state is located (see Plate I). This legend does indicate that the Khalsa state had only established base camps, fortresses, and *thanas*. In fact, one is inclined to believe that the Sikhs never had sufficient time to set up a state capital, and that all their time was spent in an attempt to retain their acquired territories and hence there is no name of the capital city on the coins.

Historians have described Banda Bahadur as the successor of Guru Gobind Singh, Sacha Padshah, and so on. More informed scholars have called him a false Guru and a rebel Guru, but most experts state that he took on regal authority. Khushwant Singh calls him an emperor. Ganda Singh calls him a king except in name, a characterization based on the prevailing medieval concept of kingship and the absolute hold of the ruler over his subjects. This has not been true of the Sikh social organization. The spirit of democracy had deep roots in the very foundations of the Sikh society established by their Gurus and the spirit of collective leadership bequeathed to the Khalsa by the tenth master was so deeply ingrained amongst the Sikhs that no one person could think of abrogating it to himself, much less of assuming it.[20] This was equally true even after half a century when the Sikhs occupied Lahore in 1765 under the leadership of Jassa Singh Ahluwalia, who had successfully led the Sikh forces for over a quarter century. Banda Bahadur was the first among equals but he was certainly not the absolute ruler nor was he the leader in the contemporary sense. He had not only given due consideration to the opinion of the senior Sikhs who came with him from Nander, but he also gave them all the senior commands and governorships of territories. This is further attested to by the fact that all the symbols of sovereignty were in the name of the state and the Sikh Gurus and that Banda Bahadur did not adopt any epithet, howsoever minor, for himself. C.H. Payne has correctly stated that Guru Gobind Singh had nominated Banda Bahadur as his successor, not as the Guru, but as a commander of the forces of the Khalsa.[21]

Historical Accounts of the Initial Sikh Coinage

The earliest accounts of Sikh coins and the Sikh seal pertain to the period of Guru Gobind Singh. Khushwaqt Rai, a Persian chronicler and an official newswriter of the East India Company, wrote *Tarikh-i-Sikhan* in AD 1811. He states that Guru Gobind Singh issued a coin with the legend '*Deg Tegh Fateh Nusrat Baidrang Yaft uz, Nanak Guru Gobind Singh*', but he provides no source reference for this claim.[22]

Khushwaqt Rai's statement is not supported by any other historian nor has any such coin been located. He gives a similar account about Ranjit Singh having struck coins in his own name on the day of his coronation and having distributed these among the poor; but this statement is apparently incorrect as no historian shares his views nor has any such coin been located anywhere in the Punjab or elsewhere. Similarly, Muhammad Latif in his *History of Punjab* states that Guru Gobind Singh had a personal seal inscribed with the above legend which the *pujaris* used to affix on his *hukamnamas*.[23] We have quite a few *hukamnamas* issued by Guru Gobind Singh but none of them bears the imprint of any seal, nor is there any imprint of any seal on the *Zafarnama* written by Guru Gobind Singh to Emperor Aurangzeb. These facts make it highly likely that both the accounts of Khushwaqt Rai and Muhammad Latif are imaginary and hence unreliable. Contemporary historians and newswriters mention the striking of Sikh coins with the establishment of the first Sikh state after the fall of Sirhind in AD 1710 to the Sikh forces under the leadership of Banda Bahadur, the commander of the Khalsa army. For a long time, these historical accounts either remained unnoticed or were not given credibility by numismatists, presumably on account of the nonavailability of such coins. But since 1967 a couple of such coins have been located and it appears reasonable and logical to assume that the initial Sikh coinage was struck during 1710-12 with the formation of the Sikh state over the province of Sirhind and the surrounding territories under Sikh occupation.[24]

Before we take up the numismatic investigation that commenced from 1967, we will examine the historical backdrop against which these coins were struck. The first account of Sikh coins occurs in the account of newswriters of January 1710 in the *Akhbar-i-Darbar-i-Mualla*.

The Khalsa Sikhs have strange practices amongst themselves. They call one person as an army. In their dispatches, they write that an army of Sikhs has arrived. Some say they have struck coins and in their 'hukamnamas', the year '*Ahad*' is written. In the villages the produce is divided between them and the tillers of the land, two parts to the tiller and one part to them. The land has been given to the tiller. They want all this to be made known to the emperor. Elephants, cash and grain of Wazir Khan of Sirhind have fallen into their hands in large quantities. They have made their own 'mohar' seal.

> *Azmat-i-Nanak Guru ham zahir O Ham Ghaib ast,*
> *Badshah din O duniya aap sachcha sahib ast.*

> (The greatness of Guru Nanak is both patent and latent and the true lord himself is the king of both the spiritual and the temporal worlds.)

> (There is a great cry amongst the people. They are astonished at the decree of God.)[25]

The word '*ghaib*' is a distortion of the correct word '*batin*', meaning inner, and the same word is given in the newsletter dated 6 July 1710.[26] This is corroborated by the recording of the same couplet by another contemporary historian in the *Hadiqat-i-Aqalim*.[27] The use of this legend on the state seal is not authenticated by the availability of its imprint on any state document. These reports clearly bring out the abolition of the existing feudal society and its replacement by land-holding peasants free from feudal domination as preached by the Sikh Gurus. The seal impressions that have been located are:

> *Deg Tegh Fateh O Nusrat Baidarang,*
> *Yaft uz Nanak Guru Gobind Singh.*

meaning that the kettle to feed, the sword to defend, and the resultant victory have been achieved with the spontaneous help received from Guru Nanak to Guru Gobind Singh. The Arabic word '*nusrat*' means 'help'; it is also translated as 'victory' in some Persian dictionaries. This legend appears as a seal imprint on the *hukamnamas* issued by Banda Bahadur, for instance, on 12 December 1710 to the *Sangat* at Jaunpur and another (undated) to Bhai Dharam Singh.[28] Half a century later, this legend was being widely used by the Sikhs on their coins struck regularly from Lahore, Amritsar, Multan, Kashmir, Peshawar, and some other towns as well.[29]

William Irvine in *Later Mughals* writes: 'At Lohgarh Banda Bahadur tried to assume something of a regal state. He was *Sacha Padshah*, the veritable sovereign; the coin was struck in the new sovereign's name.' It bore the following legends:

Obverse   *Sikka zad bar har do alam, Tegh-i-Nanak wahib ast.*
           Fateh Gobind Shah-i-Shahan, Fazal Sachacha Sahib ast.
Reverse   *Zarb ba aman-al-dahar, masavarat shahr zinat altakhat mubarak bakht.*

meaning 'Fateh Gobind, King of Kings, struck coin in the two worlds, the sword of Nanak is the granter of desires, by grace of god he is the veritable lord. Coin at refuge of the world, the walled city, ornament of the fortunate throne.'[30] Irvine is incorrect in stating that Banda Bahadur was the new sovereign and was called '*Sacha Padshah*' and that the coin was struck in his name. Apparently the coins were struck in the name of the Gurus as sovereignty with all its symbols belonged to the Sikh Gurus. Irvine is known for giving copious references from original manuscripts, of which he had a very large collection, to establish the authenticity of the factual portion of his accounts. There are, however, no footnotes giving the primary or contemporary accounts from which Irvine took the above legends and drew his impressions quoted above. Irvine could not complete *Later Mughals* due to his ill-health, and the manuscript was entrusted to Jadu Nath Sarkar for editing and completion by Irvine's daughter. Jadu Nath Sarkar is stated to have carried out a severe compression of the copious footnotes and the references made by Irvine.[31] A doubt arose as to whether footnotes/ references, if any, about the legends may have been struck down under the editor's pen, and the opportunity to compare the recorded legends with the imprinted legends on the coins was lost for ever. This is especially not correct since there are certain discrepancies between the two versions.

Fortunately, some earlier portions of *Later Mughals* had been published in various journals. The portion pertaining to the striking of the Sikh coin was reproduced in the *Journal of the Asiatic Society of Bengal* in 1894,[32] but even here no footnotes or references have been given regarding these coins. Irvine, however, appears to have taken the material on the coins from an 'anonymous fragment' of a manuscript, folio no. 141 (from his own collection). This seemed to be a part of Mir Muhamad Ahsan Ijad's manuscript of which another fragment

FIGURE I: BANDA SINGH BAHADUR

is in the British Museum Library, MS OR 25; Ijad's manuscript not being available in the important research centres in India, I requested a friend in London to locate it with the British Museum. The curator of the Persian Section at the British Museum reported that a careful checking of folios nos. 14 to 16 of Ijad's manuscript did not reveal any mention of Sikh coins.[33] A long search is needed to identify the library which holds Irvine's manuscript.

Almost the entire portion on the Sikhs given in *Later Mughals* was published by Irvine in the *Journal of the Asiatic Society of Bengal*, no. 3 (1884), pp. 112-43 under the heading 'Guru Gobind Singh and Banda', and the two accounts are identical in every way, without any editing having been done by Jadu Nath Sarkar. Hence, Jadu Nath Sarkar's remark that if he had 'not used his discretion in omitting much of what Irvine had written against the Sikh community he would have by that time become a martyr' is an apparent distortion of the facts and is totally unwarranted.[34] Similar misinterpretations of the history of nations and events detract from the stature of Jadu Nath Sarkar as an unbiased historian.

Around this period, Karam Singh, a scholar in the employ of the Patiala State, wrote a couple of books on Banda Bahadur. He was fully conversant with the Persian language. His first book on Banda Bahadur, written in 1907, makes no reference to the coins having been struck by the Sikhs,[35] nor is there any reference to *Farrukhsiyar Nama* by Ahsan Ijad in the bibliographical notes. His second book *Banda Kaun See* (1929) has details about *Farrukhsiyar Nama* by Ahsan Ijad and the special features of his work in the bibliographical notes.[36] Based on Ijad's authority, Karam Singh had recorded the striking of coins by Banda Bahadur and the obverse legend on these coins (no specific page is cited for this claim). Ijad was a court chronicler who wrote *Farrukhsiyar Nama* under the orders of Farrukh Siyar in Hijri 1131, i.e. AD 1715. Some of his accounts of the period of Banda Bahadur are not available in any other Persian manuscript.[37] Karam Singh also gives a second reference, *Hadiqat-i-Aqalim*, for these Sikh coins, but this statement is incorrect as the legend mentioned therein is a different one.[38] Both writers were contemporaries but apparently never met or exchanged views. The complete manuscript of Ahsan Ijad, located at the Aligarh Muslim University, unfortunately also does not mention these coins, and the volume ends much before the reign of Farrukh Siyar. The legend mentioned by Karam Singh is exactly the same as that mentioned by Irvine, giving the impression that both these scholars might have taken the above legends from some other account of Ahsan Ijad.

In his book on Banda Bahadur (1935), Ganda Singh states that Banda Bahadur struck a coin in the name of his saviours, Guru Nanak and Guru Gobind Singh. The legends mentioned by Ganda Singh are the same as those noted by Irvine except that he has inserted the word 'Singh' after 'Gobind'.[39] Ganda Singh's rendering of the Persian legends into English is slightly different. In fact, he changed his rendering in his next piece of writing on Banda Bahadur. However, the Roman English rendering of the legends is exactly the same as that done by Irvine and some minor mistakes committed by Irvine are also repeated by Ganda Singh, viz., the word '*al*' between '*aman*' and '*dahar*' and before '*takht*' has been written as '*ud*'. Ganda Singh quotes Persian extracts and references at great length but does not give any source reference on the coin and its legends. Ganda Singh wrote another booklet on Banda Bahadur in 1976 in which he also mentions the coin and its legends as in the earlier footnotes, viz., Ijad's *Farrukh-siyar Nama* and *Hadiqat-i-Aqalim*. He does not give the page number of Ijad's work nor its location.[40]

Hadiqat-i-Aqalim is available at the Aligarh Muslim University, besides other places, and it is recorded that the successors of the sect of Nanak Shah have struck a coin in their own name with the legend exactly as mentioned in *Akhbar-i-Darbar-i-Mualla*,[41] but not the one recorded by Ganda Singh and thus this is an incorrect inference. A similar mistake has been made by Karam Singh and it is quite likely that Ganda Singh reproduced the error from Karam Singh's account. I contacted Ganda Singh twice at his Patiala residence in 1982-3 to enquire about the source reference for these said legends but he could not cite any specific reference for them. In another long article, 'Banda Singh Bahadur, his achievements and the place of his execution', Ganda Singh gives the same legends and the same incomplete and incorrect references as in the case of his earlier booklet.[42]

Hari Ram Gupta merely states that Banda Bahadur struck coins and issued orders under his own seal,[43] without giving any source reference for this claim, although he has otherwise been as meticulous as Irvine in giving references and footnotes. Khushwant Singh notes in this context:

Thus Banda the bairagi-hermit who as a military commander had become Banda Bahadur—the brave—assumed his third incarnation as Banda Padshah, the emperor. He introduced a new calendar year dating from his capture of Sirhind. He had also got new coins struck to mark his reign bearing the names of Guru Nanak and Gobind.[44]

The legends mentioned by Hari Ram Gupta in the footnotes are those mentioned by Ganda Singh, without giving his source reference or acknowledging Ganda Singh's accounts. Gupta's comments are apparently incorrect.

G.S. Deol, a fairly recent biographer of Banda Bahadur, acknowledges that the coins and their legends have been taken from Ganda Singh's account.[45] Giani Gian Singh in his book *Shamsher Khalsa Alharof Guru Khalsa* gives a fairly detailed account of Banda Bahadur but here again there is no mention of the coin or its legends.[46]

J.S. Grewal states that Banda Bahadur adopted Mukhlispur, an imperial fort now called Lohgarh, as his capital and struck a new coin in the names of Guru Nanak and Guru Gobind Singh. Adopting a similar inscription he started using a seal on his orders (*hukamnamas*).[47] Although Grewal cites Ganda Singh on the matter of the seal on the *hukamnamas*, he does not give any reference/footnote about the coin or the legends inscribed on it.

From the above accounts, it emerges that the legends on the coins said to have been struck by Banda Bahadur were apparently recorded by Ahsan Ijad in a manuscript of his which appears to have been scrutinized by Irvine and Karam Singh. Karam Singh carried out most of his research in Lahore libraries and hence Ijad's manuscript is likely to be available in some library in this city. I have not been able to secure any access to these archives so far in spite of repeated requests to various authorities in Lahore. The manuscript examined by Irvine was his own copy; I have not been able to determine the library in Britain to which this manuscript was donated. Ganda Singh seems to have taken the account of the legends from the works of Irvine and Karam Singh without acknowledging them; nor does he appear to have examined any original source reference. The historians who wrote on the initial Sikh coinage apparently did so without examining the coins; hence their analyses are based on inadequate evidence, especially when the most important and reliable source of evidence, i.e. the actual coins which being available for scrutiny were not located and taken into account.

Repeated reading of Ijad's *Farrukhsiyar Nama* seems to indicate that the author included the description of the coins in some other of his works or in that of some other chronicler, as the volume available in the British Museum and the photocopy with the Aligarh Muslim University virtually close before the Sikh period and hence this document is not pertinent to our study. About half a century after the fall of the first Sikh state, it arose again in AD 1765 and the legend adopted on the coins was the same one which appeared on the seal, and a few years later the same one on the coin. Hence, based on circumstantial evidence also one may believe with a reasonable amount of certainty that the Sikh coins were struck during 1710-13.

Numismatic Investigation of the Initial Sikh Coinage

Numismatic investigation of Sikh coins was pioneered by C.J. Rodgers in the second half of the nineteenth century, when he collected Sikh coins and wrote the first article on the subject in 1881.[48] He seems to have been unaware of the extent of the available historical accounts of Banda Bahadur's coins as well as of the existence of any actual coins. After mentioning the elusive coin alleged to have been struck in the name of Jassa Singh Ahluwalia, Rodgers dealt with the coin of AD 1765, i.e. Sambat 1822, from Lahore with the legend appearing on the Khalsa seal under Banda Bahadur. This coin is readily available in various museums and even with private collectors. Rodgers's understanding of the Sikh ethos and history was very superficial and quite a few of his assertions on Sikh coinage are incorrect.[49] J.D. Cunningham and N.K. Sinha, on the whole, share Rodgers's assessment with slight variations in emphasis.[50]

Colonel Charles Panish came across a silver rupee coin which closely resembled the coin legends mentioned by Irvine. Although there were certain minor variations, Panish was inclined to consider it as the legendary issue of Banda Bahadur. He brought the coin to the notice of the numismatic world in an article published in 1967.[51] Over a decade later, John Dyell, a numismatist of international repute, came across a somewhat similar coin and wrote an elaborate article in 1980 on various aspects of both his and Panish's coins.[52]

Dyell's detailed and careful numismatic investigation is a pioneering work on the initial Sikh coinage. He notes that the recitation of the legends on the obverse and the reverse of the coin, fairly accurately by various historians, intrigued him and led him to trace a long chain of secondary references back to what appeared to be the source of the testimony of Banda's coinage, which is the manuscript *Tazkirat-i-Salatin-i-Chughtaiya* by Mohammed Hadi Kamwar Khan.[53] Dyell contends that Kamwar Khan was personally present at the first siege of Lohgarh in 1710 and that it was at that time that the coin was first witnessed, presumably by Kamwar Khan himself. While comparing his coin with Panish's coin, Dyell states that the literature soon revealed that his coin was the very issue recorded by Kamwar Khan and that his coin fully corroborates the testimony of Kamwar Khan.[54] Dyell's assertions—that he traced a long chain of secondary references back to what appeared to be the source of the testimony of this coinage and that his delving into the literature soon made it apparent that his coin was the very issue recorded by Kamwar Khan—are incorrect and did not actually come from any source reference. Dyell has not given any account of the alleged long chain of secondary references which led him to Kamwar Khan's account. It seems that Kamwar Khan's account has been pressed into Dyell's narrative to lend the weight of authenticity to his arguments which are otherwise lacking in evidence. In fact, the entire basis of his argument rests on Kamwar Khan's account which he seems to have located but does not appear to have examined. Numismatic investigations are partly scientific in nature and hence an examination of correct and detailed primary references is essential; any dependence on presumptions can lead to grievous errors and misinterpretations, as has happened in Dyell's case study under examination here. In fact, the history of the study of the initial Sikh coinage is a long list of various historians and even numismatists who depended on secondary sources without going to the primary sources. This negligence is particularly unfortunate since some of these primary sources are readily available. This has led to the repeated spread of disinformation rather than any enlightening information.

Puzzled by the non-availability of Ijad's account, I made efforts to examine Kamwar Khan's account. Kamwar Khan was a Hindu convert named Chandidas who was neither commissioned by the emperor nor sponsored by any nobleman and who wrote of his own volition. Although he had been an eyewitness to some of the events that took place during the period of his record, his work is almost entirely based on information received from daily court records and abstracts. The *Tazkirat-i-Salatin-i-Chughtaiya* is one of the three books he wrote during his stay in Delhi.[55] There are more than fifteen manuscripts present in different libraries, nine of which have been consulted by Muzaffar Alam who has prepared an edited version of these with an introduction.[56] I have examined Muzaffar Alam's work, the manuscript with the Aligarh Muslim University and the Khalsa College, Amritsar and observed that there is no mention of any Sikh coin and its legends in these manuscripts. Hence, the numismatic investigations, the delving into the literature and the long list of secondary sources carried out by Dyell prove to have been a purposeless pursuit and this has produced incorrect assertion. Unfortunately, the study of Sikh coins by historians has been marred by the scholars' tendency to comment on Sikh coins without personally having examined these coins; hence, they frequently arrived at incorrect conclusions and repeatedly spread misinformation. Numismatists have also succumbed to the temptation of accepting such misinformation or reaching certain conclusions without first examining the available primary references and hence they have also arrived at incorrect inferences.

It appears rather strange that Dyell, a numismatist of international repute, chose to base his entire thesis on a reference which he did not consult, although it was readily available, and which has no relevance to the subject at hand. Dyell, by his detailed analysis based on incorrect evidence, has done more harm than good to the study of the initial Sikh coinage. By uncritically citing Dyell's incorrect inferences and assertions, the later historians/numismatists, some of them even without acknowledging him, became equally responsible for spreading misinformation.

Parmeshwari Lal Gupta, Director, Indian Institute of Research in Numismatic Studies, has prepared a catalogue of Sikh coins with the Sheesh Mahal Museum at Patiala. He describes the coins:

For long, coins issued by Banda Bahadur had not come to light. Mohammed Hadi Kamwar Khan, the author of *Tazkirat-i-Salatin-i-Chughtaiya* as the only source of information. He had seen the coins and had mentioned them in his work and had quoted their inscriptions from them. The information about the coins was borrowed by all the subsequent writers of Sikh history. Only recently, two coin collectors—Charles K. Panish and John S. Dyell—discovered this coinage and substantiated the authenticity of Kamwar Khan's words.[57]

Since I have also not been able to locate any specific contemporary reference from *Tazkirat-i-Salatin-i-Chughtaiya*, I requested Parmeshwari Lal Gupta to specify the exact part of Kamwar Khan's work dealing with the Sikh coin and its location. I was greatly surprised at the reply I received from Parmeshwari Lal Gupta, who wrote that 'as regards the Persian sources, I must frankly admit that I do not know Persian; and having full faith in those scholars who mentioned them, I have used their material'.[58]

Hans Herrli prepared an extensive catalogue of Sikh coins with drawings in

1993, a revised version of his earlier work of 1986. He was kind enough to share with me copies of his various manuscripts. The catalogue covers almost the entire spectrum of Sikh coinage, with over four hundred drawings and an elaboration of the legends; Herrli's book is a definite contribution to the study and collection of Sikh coins, and has contributed to the surge in the prices of Sikh coins among the coin collectors in northern India. But his descriptions are at places quite incorrect and his understanding of the Sikh ethos, history and culture inadequate. With reference to Dyell's and Panish's coins he writes:

The manuscript of Kamwar Khan's account has not been seen by scholars in recent years and not much is known about its reliability or even about the exact contents of its report on the subject of Banda's coinage. I think the rupees were not struck by Banda but around 1734 AD by Nawab Kapur Singh or even still later in 1765-66 AD as a reaction of the Sarbat Khalsa to Jassa Singh Ahluwalia's rupee. In this case, the era used to date the Khalsa rupees could well be connected with Sirhind, but with the occupation of Sirhind and the destruction of the town in December 1763 and not with the sack of 1710 AD.[59]

Hans Herrli's comments on Kamwar Khan's account and the coins struck under Banda Bahadur are more fanciful than objective and are not based on any historical analysis nor on any proper numismatic investigation.

Ken Wiggins and Stan Goron have written a number of articles on Sikh coins in the *Newsletter of Oriental Numismatic Society*, Surrey, United Kingdom from 1981 to 1985. Their examination is based on the foundations laid in C.J. Rodgers's work and hence their account, although of an elementary nature, offers a correct assessment of Sikh coinage to some extent, although their record is incomplete and unauthenticated at many places.[60] The first step in the location of the initial Sikh coinage was made by Charles Panish in 1967 when he published his findings on the Sikh coin struck by Banda Bahadur. But unfortunately no Indian scholar has pursued this topic for further investigation. Sadly, none of the three initial coins located so far remain in the country of their origin.

From the above historical and numismatic accounts we now turn to the numismatic analyses of these coins. The available coins are:

1. *John Dyell's Coin*: The details are given by Dyell in his article quoted above. The drawings and photograph of this coin also appear in Hans Herrli's *Catalogue of Sikh Coins* and in the *Standard Guide to South Asian Coins*. However, I have not been able to secure a photograph of this coin from Dyell, or from Saran Singh who purchased Dyell's collection some years back.
2. *Charles Panish's Coin*: In addition to the information given by Panish, the drawings are given by Hans Herrli and the *Standard Guide to South Asian Coins*. I have also received a tinfoil of the coin with its details from Panish (see Plate I).
3. *Mrs Norma J. Pudderster's Coin*: Mrs Pudderster works for the Canadian High

Commission in Hong Kong and is a keen collector of Sikh coins. Her coin is the same die struck as that of Panish except that the size of the disc is a little larger. A photograph of the coin with its details, since long awaited from Mrs Pudderster, has not been received. Since her coin and that of Panish are similar and of the same year, the numismatic investigation is confined to the first two coins only.

Although Dyell has incorrectly based his historical investigations on Kamwar Khan, the other aspects of his investigation have been carried out quite logically and correctly. Dyell is correct in his assessment that his coin is an earlier issue than that of Panish's as it carries the numeral 2 and the other coins carry the numeral 3 as the years of their striking. He is, however, incorrect in saying that his coin is the first issue of Banda Bahadur.[61] The prevailing practice on contemporary coinage was to use the word 'ahad' on first issues instead of the numeral 1 and there is evidence that the Sikhs were using the word 'ahad' on their state correspondence in the first year of their new era.[62] The first coin has yet to be located along with the account of Ahsan Ijad or any other contemporary historical account for a complete examination of the initial Sikh coinage.

Dyell states that Ganda Singh's addition of the word 'Singh' to 'Gobind' on the obverse legend has hopelessly muddled the rhyme.[63] In his writings Ganda Singh has added 'Singh' to the names of historic Sikh personalities who lived after the creation of the Khalsa by Guru Gobind Singh, since 'Singh' is deemed an integral part of the name and is not regarded as a surname or a sub-caste. One is inclined to agree that Ganda Singh may have added the word 'Singh' to 'Gobind' without its having been based on any historic evidence, but the third year's coin has the word 'Singh' added to 'Gobind', thus establishing that the Sikhs themselves made this change in AD 1712, assuming that the simple word 'Gobind' as such was not in full reverence to their Guru who had made 'Singh' an essential part of his and the Sikh names. The question as to why and how Ganda Singh added the word 'Singh' becomes irrelevant since the word 'Singh' actually appeared on the third year's coin. How Dyell missed noticing this on Panish's coin is rather inexplicable.

According to our understanding, the meaning of the legends, based on the Sikh ethos, should be as follows:

Obverse   The coin has been struck in both the worlds herein and hereafter. With the guarantee of Guru Nanak's double-edged sword or guaranteed by Guru Nanak under the strength of his sword. The victory of Guru Gobind Singh, King of Kings, has been achieved with the grace of Sachcha Sahib, the God Almighty. Sikhs have a firm belief in the absolute supremacy of God and their ten Gurus as having one identity and all these saviours, God and Nanak to Gobind Singh, stand encompassed in this couplet on the obverse of the coin as the sovereign of the Sikh state.

Reverse   Differing literal meanings have been given by various historians. To our understanding,

PLATE I: INITIAL SIKH COINAGE

SECOND YEARS COIN

OBVERSE: SIKKA ZAD BAR HAR DO ALAM TEGH-I-NANAK WAHIB AST
FATEH GOBIND SHAH-SHAHAN FAZAL SACHCHA SAHIB AST.

REVERSE: ZARB BA-AMAN-UL-DAHAR MASAWARAT SHAHR ZINAT-
AL-TAKHT KHALSA MUBARAK BAKHT.

THIRD YEAR'S COIN

THE WORD GOBIND IS CHANGED AS GOBIND SINGH ON THE OBVERSE.

THE WORD AMAN-UL-DAHAR IS WRITTEN AS AMAN-AL-DIN ON THE REVERSE.

it should be *Zarb-ba-aman-ul-dahar*, coined at the refuge of the world, the most protected place, safe and peaceful, the emphasis being primarily on the security of the place; *Masawarat-Shahr-Zinat*, the picture of a beautiful city; the word *'Zinat'* should appropriately be linked with *'Shahr'* and not with *'Altakht' (Altakht Khalsa Mubarak Bakht)*, where is the auspicious throne of the Khalsa. With the addition of the word *'Khalsa'* this would mean: where the auspicious throne of the Khalsa is located. Thus, the meaning is: coined at the place of peace and security, picture of a beautiful city, where the auspicious throne of the Khalsa is located.

Dyell was the first to assert, based on logical arguments, that Sikh coins need not have been minted at Lohgarh, but at the place where it was convenient or where the main strength of the Khalsa army was located. He further states that from the elegance of his coin pertaining to the second year, it can be assumed that it was minted in more secure and peaceful circumstances than the second coin pertaining to the third year which is rather crude and dumpy. There is a change on the reverse legend of the second coin and the words *'aman-al-dahar'* have been changed to *'aman-al-din'*, i.e. from 'the security of the place', it has been changed to 'under protection of the faith', which also in a way indicates the disturbed conditions at the time of minting. This view is further supported by the fact that when the Sikhs had established their firm hold on the Punjab territories by 1765, they started including the names of various mint towns on the reverse of the coins. We share the views of Dyell that the Sikh coins may not have been minted from Lohgarh as the facilities required for the establishment of a capital city could hardly exist in and around this small fortress. The changes on the coins indicate the changes in the political situation faced by the newly risen nation. Although there no longer exist any doubts regarding the existence of the initial Sikh coinage of 1710-12, still the study of the initial Sikh coinage will remain somewhat incomplete and partially inconclusive till the first year's coin and until the account of Ijad or of any other contemporary writers which mentions these coins or any other contemporary historical reference are traced and examined by scholars and numismatists.

It is now firmly established on the basis of the historical accounts and numismatic investigation of the coins located so far that the initial Sikh coinage was started by Banda Bahadur in AD 1710. This also throws light on a very important feature of the Sikh concept of sovereignty shortly after the demise of Guru Gobind Singh and the institution of the first Sikh state. The two legends, both on the coin and on the seal, give a true depiction of the concept of temporal sovereignty as bequeathed by the tenth Master to the Khalsa Panth. It is noteworthy that Banda Bahadur, although belonging to a different religion, became a staunch disciple of Guru Gobind Singh and within a short span of only a month or so was selected as the commander of the Khalsa army and was sent to the Punjab where he spent all his energies and time in creating and defending the infant Sikh state. Yet in this short time he understood and expressed the Sikh concept of sovereignty in such simple, lucid, and meaningful words that no Sikh authority has ever suggested any modification or any improvement on his original description. He certainly had a profound insight into the Sikh ethos and traditions, and he was also an extraordinary commander of the Sikh army.

The development of the initial Sikh coin offers evidence of the democratic spirit prevalent in Sikh society as laid down by their Gurus even in the feudal age. The legend on the initial coin was composed in praise of Guru Nanak only. It is presumed that some Sikhs would have desired the inclusion of the name of the tenth Guru also. Hence, the above legend with the names of both the first and the tenth Gurus was decided upon. Thereafter the name of Guru Gobind Singh was written as Gobind only, and some Sikhs would have desired the recording of his full name and hence in the third year's coin the name given is Gobind Singh. This shows the use of democratic measures regarding even the most sensitive issues.

Note: It was noticed in the book *Banda Singh Bahadur and Sikh Sovereignty* by Harbans Kaur Sagoo, a Reader in History, University of Delhi, published by Deep & Deep Publications (P) Ltd., New Delhi, that page after page covering over 3,000 words from an article on 'Initial Sikh Coinage', published in *Oriental Numismatic Studies*, 1996 have been copied. The matter was taken up with H.K. Sagoo and the Publisher for serious violation of the Copyright Act, 1957 vide letter No. SS/Plagiarism/1 dated 1 August 2002, the substance of which is re-produced as under:

It has come to my notice that you have carried out extensive copying of complete paragraphs and even complete pages including drawings from the article 'Intital Sikh Coinage' published in Oriental Numismatic Studies, vol. I, 1996, in the Chapter 'Establishment of Sikh State' in your book Banda Singh Bahadur and Sikh Sovereignty.

The above mentioned plagiarism by you and your publisher, by merely changing the order of the paragraphs or some minor changes etc., has come to me as a great shock. This large-scale copying cannot be deemed as a brief quotation in a critical article or review. It is downright a literary crime to steal and purolin the thoughts or words of another person in a literary composition. . . . I am amazed at your and your publisher's audacity to virtually copy out the entire portion of my research on Intial Sikh Coinage and on top of it claim copyright to the work which is not your and infact is a stolen property of somebody else.

I hereby request you and your publisher to intimate to me as to why you have carried out the above large-scale theft unbecoming of a research scholar and a teacher as well as by a publisher of merit. Your reply should reach me within ten days of the receipt of this letter failing which I shall take administrative as well as legal action against you and your publisher over the same.

After some discussion and correspondence, both the authors and the publisher submitted an unconditional apology vide their letter dated 23 August 2002. The relevant substance thereof is reproduced as under:

In our recently published book, Banda Singh Bahadur and Sikh Sovereignity, we have quoted very liberally from your article "Initial Sikh Coinage", published in the journal of the Oriental Munismatic Studies, vol. I, New Delhi, 1996. It being a subject not having researched earlier, we took a very large extent of the subject matter from your article. On receipt of your letter accusing us of large-scale copy of several pages, which is violation of the Copyright Act, 1957, we have realised the gravity of the same and are greatly regretful thereof.

We, Dr. Harbans Kaur Sagoo (the author) and G.S. Bhatia (Publisher, Deep & Deep Publications (P) Ltd.), offer to you, Sir, our unqualified apology for the above-said violation of the Copyright Act 1957.

Sd/- G.S. Bhatia, Publisher,   Sd/- Dr. Harbans Kaur Sagoo, Author
Deep & Deep Publications (P) Ltd.,   198, Kadambiri, Sector 9, Rohini,
F-159, Rajouri Garden, New Delhi   New Delhi

This has been brought to the notice of the readers to avoid any confusion as the Sagoo's book has been published about 2 years earlier than the publication of this book.

NOTES

1. Hari Ram Gupta, *History of Sikh Gurus*, New Delhi: U.C. Kapoor & Sons, 1973, p. 228.
2. Khafi Khan, *Muntakhab-ul-Lubab*, Elliot and Dowson, New Delhi: Low Priced Publications, rpt., 1990, vol. 7, p. 413.
3. *Tarikh-i-Bahadur Shahi, History of India*, Elliot and Dowson, New Delhi: Low Priced Publications, 1990, vol. 7, p. 566.
4. Max Arthur Macauliffe, *The Sikh Religion*, New Delhi: S. Chand & Co., 1985, vol. V, pp. 235-6.
5. Hari Ram Gupta, *History of Sikh Gurus*, op. cit., p. 232.
6. Macauliffe, p. 238; Hari Ram Gupta, op. cit., p. 233; J.S. Grewal and S.S. Bal, *Guru Gobind Singh*, Chandigarh: History Department, Panjab University, 1967, p. 154; Ganda Singh, *Banda Singh Bahadur*, Amritsar: Khalsa College, 1935, pp. 13 to 19, wherein Ganda Singh cites from over forty sources.
7. Ganda Singh, op. cit., p. 4; Karam Singh, *Banda Bahadur* (Punjabi), Amritsar: Chief Khalsa Diwan, 1807, p. 21.
8. Hari Ram Gupta, op. cit., p. 232.
9. Ganda Singh, op. cit., p. 25; Macauliffe, op. cit., p. 238.
10. Ganda Singh, op. cit., p. 25; Hari Ram Gupta, *History of Sikhs*, vol. II, New Delhi: Munshiram Manoharlal, 1978 edn., p. 5.
11. Hari Ram Gupta, op. cit., pp. 6 and 7.
12. Hari Ram Gupta, op. cit., p. 7; Ganda Singh, op. cit., p. 27.
13. Bhai Parmanand, *Bir Bairagi*, Delhi: Rajpal & Sons, 1984 edn., p. 56.
14. Hari Ram Gupta, op. cit., p. 9.
15. Hari Ram Gupta, op. cit., p. 9.
16. William Irvine, *Later Mughals*, Delhi: Taj Publications, 1989, p. 103; Hari Ram Gupta, op. cit., p. 13; Ganda Singh, op. cit., p. 66; J.D. Cunningham, *A History of Sikhs*, New Delhi: S. Chand & Co., 1972, p. 72.

17. William Irvine, op. cit., p. 110; Ganda Singh, op. cit., p. 82; Hari Ram Gupta, op. cit., p. 10.
18. Ganda Singh, *Life of Banda Singh Bahadur*, op. cit., p. 72.
19. Ibid., pp. 138-45 and 187-90.
    The author has visited the site of Lohgarh and the ground conditions clearly establish the above position. The last few kilometers of the distance do not have even a cart road to the fortress and the surrounding area is totally unsuited for habitation. There are remains of rearguard action, fortifications all around the fortress to stall enemy advance by suicidal squads and these are stated to be fifty two in number.
    The Shiromani Gurudwara Parbandhak Committee has decided to raise a suitable memorial to Banda Bahadur at Lohgarh. The author has been appointed the convenor of the above-mentioned committee.
20. (i) N.K. Sinha, *Rise of Sikh Power*, Calcutta: A. Mukherji & Co., 1973, footnote 3, pp. 54-6.
    (ii) Ganda Singh, *Jassa Singh Ahluwalia*, Patiala: Punjabi University, 1990, p. 110.
    (iii) Ganda Singh, *Life of Banda Singh Bahadur*, op. cit., pp. 69-70.
21. C.H. Payne, *A History of Sikhs*, Punjab: Language Department, 1970, p. 43.
22. Khushwaqt Rai, *Tarikh-i-Sikhan*, MS SHR, 1274, Amritsar: Khalsa College, p. 46.
23. Muhammad Latif, *History of Punjab*, Ludhiana: Kalyani Publishers, rpt., 1989, p. 270.
24. Charles K. Panish, 'First Sikh Trans-Sutlej Coinage', *Journal of the Numismatic Society*, Banaras, vol. XXIX, pt. II, 1967, pp. 88-90. The first coin pertaining to Banda Bahadur's period was located by Charles Panish in 1967.
25. *Akhbar-i-Darbar-i-Mualla*. Old historical records, Jaipur. Newsletter dated 9 January 1711 (photocopy received from Ganda Singh). Translated and edited version available in *Panjab Past & Present*, vol. XVIII, no. II, October 1984, Patiala: Punjabi University, p. 51.
26. Ibid., p. 39 and p. 30 of the above quoted *Panjab Past & Present*.
    Hidayat Kesh, the chief new writer, presented the Emperor the following verse of the rebel Guru. '*Azmat-i-Nanak Guru ham Zahir O ham batin ast. Padshah-i-din-o-duniya aap Sacha Sahib ast.*'
27. *Hadiqat-al-Aqalim* (MS), Murtaza Hussain, Aligarh: Aligarh Muslim University, p. 148.
28. *Hukamnama*, dated 12 December 1710 and another addressed to Bhai Dharam Singh (undated), reproduced in *Hukamnama* by Ganda Singh, Patiala: Punjabi University, 1985, pp. 925.
    I visited the *dera* of Banda Bahadur on the bank of the River Chenab near Riasi and close to the Pakistan border. While Banda Bahadur's family (wife and son) were taken as prisoners to the Mughal court at Delhi, his second wife escaped since she had gone to her parents' house in Jammu for her confinement. Her son was the first *gaddinashin* of the *dera* and the present Baba, Jatinder Pal Singh, is the tenth descendent of Banda Bahadur. I was shown a seal at the *dera*, which belonged to Banda Bahadur's period, and the impression of this seal matches the seal impression on the *hukamnamas* of Banda Bahadur (see Plate I).
29. Hans Herrli, *The Coins of the Sikhs*, Nagpur: Indian Coin Society, 1993, pp. 31-3.
30. William Irvine, *Later Mughals*, Delhi: Taj Publications, 1989, p. 110.
31. Ibid., p. xxviii.
    The editor (J.N. Sarkar) has considered it advisable to subject Mr Irvine's copious footnotes to a severe compression. These notes were written by him more for his own satisfaction, i.e. as a means of verifying his statements and giving an outlet to his overflowing miscellaneous but extremely accurate information, the garnered harvest of a long and

studious life, than as a means of instructing the reader. His notes as he left them would have buried his narrative under their ponderous load.

32. William Irvine, 'Guru Gobind Singh and Banda', *Journal of the Asiatic Society of Bengal*, pt. I, no. 3 (1894), p. 134. The name of the journal is incorrectly given as *Calcutta Review* on p. xxx of *Later Mughals*.

33. Letter dated 25 October 1990, from M.I. Walay, Persian and Turkish Section, British Library, London to Dr B.S. Bagga:

'Your inquiry regarding a reference in Ijad's *Farukhsiyar Nama* to Banda Bahadur's coins of 1710 to 1712. I have to report that in checking carefully through folios 14 to 16 of our MS OR 25 I found no word at all on that subject—possibly a MS in some other library was intended.'

34. H.R. Gupta, *Life and Letters of J.N. Sarkar*, Chandigarh: Panjab University, 1958, p. 62.

35. Karam Singh, *Banda Bahadur* (Punjabi), Amritsar: Chief Khalsa Diwan, 1907.

36. Karam Singh, *Banda Bahadur Kaun See* (Punjabi), Amritsar, undated, p. 34.

37. Ibid., p. 35.

38. Ibid., p. 36. See note 21.

39. Ganda Singh, *Life of Banda Bahadur Singh*, Amritsar: Khalsa College, 1935, pp. 82-3.

40. Ganda Singh, *Baba Banda Bahadur*, Sirhind: Sirhind Historical Research Society, 1997, p. 9.

41. *Hadiqat-ul-Aqalim* (MS), Aligarh: Aligarh Muslim University, p. 148.

42. Ganda Singh, 'Banda Singh Bahadur' *Panjab Past & Present*, Patiala: Punjabi University, vol. XXII, pt. II, October 1988, p. 123.

43. Hari Ram Gupta, op. cit., p. 10.

44. Khushwant Singh, *History of Sikhs*, vol. I, Delhi: Oxford University Press, 1987, p. 107.

45. G.S. Deol, *Banda Bahadur*, Jullandhar: New Academic Publishing House, 1972, pp. 57, 58.

46. Gian Singh Giani, *Shamsher Khalsa Alharof: Twarikh Guru Khalsa* (Urdu), published from Sialkot, 1892, Sec. 2, pages 1 to 23 deal with Banda Bahadur but there is no mention of Sikh coins.

47. J.S. Grewal, *The Sikhs of Punjab*, The Cambridge History of India, vol II, no. 3, New Delhi: Orient Longman, 1990, p. 83.

48. C.J. Rodgers, 'The Coins of the Sikhs', *Journal of the Asiatic Society of Bengal*, vol. L, 1881, pp. 71-93.

49. Surinder Singh, 'A Corrigendum, "On the Coins of the Sikhs" by C.J. Rodgers', *Panjab Past & Present*, Patiala, vol. xxv, pt. II, October 1991, p. 40

50. (i) J.D. Cunningham, *History of the Sikhs*, New Delhi: S. Chand & Co., rpt., 1972, pp. 935.
    (ii) N.K. Sinha, *Rise of Sikh Power*, op. cit., p. 55.
    (iii) Gulshan Lall Chopra, Hoshiarpur: V.V. Research Institute, 1960, pp. 152-4.

51. Charles K. Panish, 'The First Sikh Trans-Sutlej Coinage', op. cit., pp. 88-90.

52. John S. Dyell, 'Banda Bahadur and the First Sikh Coinage', *Numismatic Digest*, vol. IV, pt. I, June 1980, Bombay, pp. 59-67.

53. Ibid., p. 61.

54. Ibid., p. 65.

55. Muzaffar Alam, edited version with an introduction to *Tazkirat-i-Salatin-i-Chughtaiya* by Mohammed Hadi Kamwar Khan, Delhi, Asia Publishing House, 1980, p. 247.

56. Ibid., p. 2.

57. Parmeshwari Lal Gupta and Sanjay Garg, *Coins of Dal Khalsa and Lahore Darbar in Sheesh Mahal Museum, Patiala*, Chandigarh: Government of Punjab, 1989, pp. 12-13.

58. Extract from P.L. Gupta's letter dated 12 December 1989 in reply to my communication.
59. Hans Herrli, *The Coins of the Sikhs*, op. cit., p. 46.
60. Ken Wiggins and Stan Goron, 'Gold and Silver Coinage of Sikhs', International Colloquium, Nasik: Indian Institute of Research in Numismatic Studies, 1984, pp. 125-6.
61. John Dyell, 'Banda Bahadur and the First Sikh Coinage', op. cit., p. 65
62. *Akhbar-i-Darbar-i-Mualla*, Newsletter dated 9 January 1711, op. cit.
63. John Dyell, 'Banda Bahadur and the First Sikh Coinage', op. cit., p. 62.

CHAPTER II

The Coinage of the Misl Period
AD 1765-1799

Brief Account of the Sikh Struggle upto 1765

Banda Bahadur established Sikh rule in Subah Sirhind and the surrounding areas in 1710 and established the Sikh state on the principle of Sikh sovereignty.[1] Large landholdings were taken over from zamindars and distributed amongst the tillers of those lands, giving rise to peasant proprietorships.[2] Land revenue was fixed on a half-yearly basis, at one-third to the government and two-thirds to the peasants, which could be paid either in cash or in kind. The caste system and social distinctions were abolished and democratic institutions were set up, a noteworthy achievement in that feudal age. The Sikh forces also made incursions right upto Lahore and the Upper Ganga Doab.[3] William Irvine states:

a low scavenger or leather dresser, the lowest of the low in Indian estimation, had only to leave home and join the Guru, when in a short space of time he would return to his birth place as its ruler, with his order of appointment in his hand. As soon as he set foot within the boundaries, the well born and the wealthy went out to greet him and escort him home. Arrived there, they stood before him with joined hands, awaiting his orders. . . . Not a soul dared to disobey an order, and men, who had risked themselves in battle fields, became so coward that they were afraid even to remonstrate.[4]

The phenomenal rise of Sikh power greatly alarmed Bahadur Shah, the Mughal emperor, and he hurriedly settled terms with the rebellious Jats and Rajputs and moved towards the Punjab in mid-1710. He was so greatly worried that he did not enter the capital Delhi, and all governors in northern India were asked to join him with their forces.[5] The Sikh forces could not stand against the might of the imperial army which was assisted by several governors and Rajput chiefs. They fought for a few days at Sadhaura and then shifted to Lohgarh, where again they fought a day's rearguard action to stem the tide of the imperial forces and retreated into the jungles of the Shivalik Hills in December 1710.[6]

Banda Bahadur reorganized his forces and returned to the plains in September 1711 and occupied Pathankot and Gurdaspur. He built a fortress in Gurdaspur where he collected stores and munitions. Bahadur Shah, who was ailing, died at Lahore in February 1712, and a war of succession broke out amongst his sons.[7] Banda Bahadur once again recovered Sirhind and Lohgarh in March 1712.

Farrukh Siyar, who succeeded to the throne, sent a large army under Abdus Samad Khan and Zakariya Khan to chastise the Sikhs. The Mughal armies camped at Sadhaura and fighting continued for a few months. According to Khafi Khan, 'Sikhs showed greatest boldness and daring and made nocturnal attacks on the imperial forces and exhibited great courage and daring.'[8] When the stocks of supplies and munitions were exhausted, Banda Bahadur and his troops once again took refuge in the Shivalik Hills in October 1713 as they had done in 1711.

Banda Bahadur once again reorganized his forces and became active in the areas north of Amritsar, close to Gurdaspur, from where he could also retreat to the nearby jungles. The Mughal forces in a surprise move converged on the Sikh forces from three sides; on the fourth side was the Ravi in spate it was not possible to ford the river. Banda Bahadur took shelter in Gurdas Nangal where he was surrounded by Mughal forces in April 1715.[9] The siege lasted for eight months. The Sikhs could not break the siege although they fought very bravely. Banda Bahadur with 740 followers was captured and sent in chains to Delhi where the captives were executed in batches in June 1716.[10] Thus the short-lived Sikh struggle to carve out an independent state once again ended in a fiasco.

The Sikh resurgence had been completely crushed and the Mughal emperor issued orders for the complete annihilation of the Sikh community. A prize money of Rs. 25 was placed on the head of every Sikh and Rs. 100 for every Sikh captured alive. Pretty girls were to be made concubines and elderly women were to be used as maid servants. The Sikhs were in a critical position; they faced extreme persecution and they had no leader to guide them.[11] The Sikhs simply disappeared from the Mughal dominions. Those who had escaped capture fled to the Shivalik Hills, the Malwa desert, and the Lakhi jungles.[12] Once the shock of their defeat wore off and they had adjusted to the changed circumstances, the Sikhs once again began organizing themselves and dreaming of regaining the independence which they had tasted for a short while. The zeal and courage which Guru Gobind Singh had engendered among the Sikhs made itself manifest. The Sikhs continued their struggle until they were finally able to regain the Sikh state in 1765. The half century from 1715 to 1765 had been a long-drawn out struggle against the might of the Mughal Empire and the Afghan invaders, marked by ebbs and flows, defeats and successes, in which about 2,00,000 brave Sikhs lost their lives, but their spirit remained unbroken. Each defeat served to inspire them to greater effort and resolve until they finally achieved their goal. This half century has been the golden period of Sikh struggle.

The Sikhs emerged from their hideouts and attacked government officials and hostile villages located close to the foothills and jungles. Samad Khan could not suppress the Sikhs and he was shifted to Multan and a very tough and able governor, Zakariya Khan, was posted in his place in 1727.[13] Zakariya Khan recruited 20,000 troops, half to be located at the capital and the rest in columns of 1,000 each, provided with very effective guns called *zambukahs*, as well as camels and horses for speed and mobility.[14] They were to track down the Sikhs in their hideouts and exterminate them. These troops worked quite effectively for some time but soon the Sikhs adapted themselves to the changed situation and resorted to guerrilla tactics which permitted them to make successful intrusions into Mughal territories. The situation has been very aptly described as 'the government ruled during the day and the Khalsa at night'.[15]

Zakariya Khan, a great commander, was also an able politician. Having failed to exterminate the Sikhs and crush their insurgency, he took to placating the Sikhs by offering them *jagirs*, nawabships, and peaceful residence at Amritsar among other incentives. The Sikhs were not willing to accept any favours. However, the offer of a nawabship was jokingly thrust on the young Sikh, Kapur Singh, who at that time, in 1731, looked after the animals and kitchen.[16] By dint of faith and hard work Kapur Singh became the leader of the Sikh forces in a short time; he was the only nawab who never attended the Mughal court or ever waited on the emperor.[17] The Sikhs were not amenable to living a life of servility and continued to create problems for the government. Zakariya Khan in 1753 made an offer to recruit Sikhs into his forces, which was declined by the Sikhs and the *jagir* was confiscated; the Sikhs left Amritsar for their hideouts once again.[18] Nadir Shah's invasion in January-May 1739 placed the government in north India in very difficult circumstances and made it totally ineffective. This was a great opportunity for the Sikhs who now emerged from their hideouts and spread all over the Punjab under their leaders Kapur Singh, Jassa Singh Ahluwalia, and others. They erected mudforts as places of retreat and to store their booty. The Sikhs had become so bold that they attacked the rear of Nadir Shah's army and relieved the invaders of a part of their booty plundered from the imperial capital Delhi.[19] Nadir Shah in a conversation with Zakariya Khan made certain prophetic remarks about the Sikhs.

NADIR: Who are these mischief makers?
ZAKARIYA: They are a group of *faqirs* who visit their Guru's tank twice a year, and after bathing in it, disappear.
NADIR: Where do they live?
ZAKARIYA: Their homes are their saddles.
NADIR: Take care. The day is not distant when these rebels will take possession of thy country.[20]

After the return of Nadir Shah, Zakaria Khan again resorted to the use of mobile columns to persecute the Sikhs and the Sikhs once again retreated to their hideouts. Zakariya Khan desecrated the Sikh temple at Amritsar and killed any Sikh found visiting the holy place. Zakariya Khan died in July 1745 and no capable governor came in his place due to court rivalries. The Sikhs once again got the opportunity to come out and organize themselves. They had already arranged themselves into the Budha Dal and the Taruna Dal. They assembled at Amritsar on Diwali in October 1745 and arranged themselves into 25 groups of about 100 persons each. The organization of the Sikhs into regular bands to engage in guerrila warfare was most suited to meet their needs given their existing circumstances. These groups later on led to the establishment of a regular army called the Dal Khalsa.[21] These groups raided hostile villages and killed those Muslims and Hindus who were responsible for the killing of innocent Sikhs. One such daring party raided a part of Lahore, the state capital, in the dead of a cold January night, looted the shops and houses, and killed those responsible for killing Sikh captives.[22] The Sikhs received a severe beating from Lakhpat Rai and Yahiya Khan in June 1746. But the civil war between Zakariya Khan's sons took away the heat from them and once again they started visiting Amritsar.[23] After celebrating Baisakhi in April 1747 at this city, they decided to build a fort at Amritsar which was named Ram Rauni (God's Shelter); this new settlement could accommodate about 500 persons.[24]

Nadir Shah was killed in June 1747 and his place was taken by Ahmad Shah Abdali. The Sikhs who were now better organized found a leader in Jassa Singh Ahluwalia who combined all these bands into a wellorganized army called the Dal Khalsa. The smaller groups were leagued together into a dozen divisions, which later on came to be known as *misls*, each placed under a particular *sardar*. The Dal Khalsa was organized on the principle that the military system of the Sikhs was not established by a king or a chief. The Sikh *sardars* did not create and endow their followings, but were instead created and endowed by them. In fact, they were elected by their soldiers.[25] The foundation of the Dal Khalsa was a step of great significance in Sikh history because it united them once again into a compact body for the third time. The first time was when the army was created by Guru Gobind Singh in 1704, the second time was by Banda Bahadur in 1710, and this third creation of the Dal Khalsa endured for almost half a century.

The Mughal government, realizing the serious danger posed by the Afghan attacks and the Sikh insurgency, posted their most capable commander, Muin-ul-Mulk, popularly called Mir Mannu, as the governor of the Punjab in April 1748. The Sikhs who had been lying low got an opportunity to retaliate against the imperial forces in 1749, during the second invasion of Ahmad Shah Abdali. They raided Lahore and looted part of the city.[26] Muin-ul-Mulk reacted by beginning the persecution of the Sikhs. Ahmad Shah Abdali again invaded India in December 1751 and the pressure on the Sikhs was somewhat eased. Muin-ul-Mulk had to fight alone against Ahmad Shah Abdali without help from the emperor. After a siege of four months, Muin-ul-Mulk surrendered to Ahmad Shah. Ahmad Shah annexed the Punjab and appointed Muin-ul-Mulk as his governor.[27] During this hiatus of about six months, the Sikhs laid waste to most of the Bari Doab and the Jullandhar Doab.

Having become free from danger from both Delhi and Kabul, Muin-ul-Mulk again started putting pressure on the Sikhs. Mir Mannu, a notorious bigot, killed every Sikh captured by his troops; he also committed unspeakable atrocities against Sikh women and children.[28] Out of the ashes of their martyrs, the Sikhs arose phoenix-like with greater glory and splendour. The harsher Mir Mannu grew, the bolder they became. The Sikhs would sing:

Mir Mannu sadi datri
Asin Mir Mannu de soe.
Jiyuon Jiyuon sanun wadhde,
Asin sau sau dune hoe.[29]

(Mir Mannu is our sickle and we are his grass blades.
As he cuts us we grow hundredfold.)

Between March 1752 and November 1753 about 30,000 Sikhs lost their lives but the Dal Khalsa became increasingly stronger. Muin-ul-Mulk died of poisoning in November 1753.

After the death of Muin-ul-Mulk, virtual anarchy reigned for the next three years and the Sikhs and their institutions prospered. The Sikhs rebuilt the Ram Rauni fort and renamed it Ram Garh. They ravaged the suburbs of Lahore, Ambala district, and Sirhind. They introduced the *rakhi* system. The villagers who gave the Sikhs one-fifth of their income twice a year were given protection against revenue farmers, government troops, and other raiders, and most of the Punjab soon came under the indigenous revenue system of the Sikhs. The farmers by and large preferred Sikh protection to that of the government revenue officials.[30]

Ahmad Shah Abdali's fourth invasion in November 1756–April 1757 did not do much damage to the Sikhs due to an outbreak of a cholera epidemic in his camp and he had to rush back. He reached Delhi and carried out a systematic plunder of the city, and on his return journey annexed Sirhind. Ala Singh, the Malwa *sardar* of Patiala, accepted Ahmad Shah's suzerainty, a step which was greatly disliked by the Dal Khalsa, but the matter was patched up with the intervention of Jassa Singh Ahluwalia. The Sikhs, however, barred the passage of the Afghans with their booty from Delhi at Sunam and looted half their treasure. They again attacked Ahmad Shah's troops at Malerkotla and several times between Delhi and the Chenab river. Ahmad Shah attacked Amritsar, pulled down the temple, and filled the tank with refuse and dirt.[31] The contest with Ahmad Shah resulted in great adversity to the Sikhs. Time and again the holy temple was pulled down and polluted and the Sikhs faced terrible persecution all over the Punjab. But with every defeat, the Sikhs rose with unabated vigour, heroically seizing every opportunity, and ultimately emerged triumphant in their struggle against one of the mightiest rulers of the age.

From late 1757 to early 1761, i.e. the next invasion of Ahmad Shah, the Sikhs increased their hold over the Punjab and further stabilized their *rakhi* system. The Sikh *misls* became well established and mudforts were raised all over the Punjab for their defense. The dispute between Jahan Khan, governor of Lahore, and Adina Beg, governor of Jullandhar, in addition to the Maratha invasion of the Punjab, gave the Sikhs the opportunity to raid and loot Lahore again and again. Taimur Khan and Jahan Khan left without a fight and their baggage and property were looted by the Sikhs and the Marathas. The Afghan soldiers were taken prisoners in chains by the Sikhs and employed to clean the desecrated temple at Amritsar. Ahmad Shah Abdali defeated the Marathas at Panipat in January 1761, which led to the breaking up of the Maratha confederacy. The Sikhs greatly harassed Ahmad Shah as he was returning with the loot from Delhi and the Doab. They released a number of captive women and children at the ferry of Goindwal and sent them to their homes. After following Ahmad Shah upto the Indus, the Sikhs returned to the Punjab, defeated Mirza Khan of Char Mahal, defeated Nur-ud-din sent by Ahmad Shah at Sialkot, defeated Khawaja Abed Khan at Gujranwala, and attacked and occupied Lahore for a short while.

Ahmad Shah's sixth invasion was in January 1762, primarily against the Sikhs. He made a surprise move and had a straight fight with the Sikhs at Kupp (Malerkotla), in which about 20,000 Sikhs lost their lives. This is called '*Wadda Ghalu Ghara*', the bloody carnage. Ahmad Shah destroyed the Sikh temple at Amritsar and razed it to the ground with ammunition. When the Sikhs recovered from the great shock, they treated the defeat as if the alloy had been removed and only the pure Khalsa remained to carry on the work of their Gurus.[32] In May 1762, when Ahmad Shah was camped at Kalanaur, the Sikhs attacked Zain Khan, *faujdar* of Sirhind, and defeated him. The Dal Khalsa under Jassa Singh Ahluwalia invaded the towns and villages of Jullandhar which were hostile to the Sikhs, and all this greatly troubled Ahmad Shah. The Sikhs marched towards Amritsar in October 1762 and engaged Ahmad Shah in another battle. Ahmad Shah who was camping at Lahore marched to Amritsar to face the Sikhs. A fierce battle took place on 17 October between the two armies and Ahmad Shah escaped back to Lahore under cover of darkness.[33] He left for Afghanistan in December 1762 and was harassed by the Sikhs on his way back home.

After the departure of Ahmad Shah, the Sikhs emerged from their hideouts, refuges, and places of safety and virtually occupied the entire Punjab. They sacked Kasur, a stronghold of the Afghans, in May 1763. Jahan Khan, the Afghan commander of the Durrani forces, was defeated and killed in November 1763. Malerkotla was laid waste in December 1763. The Sikhs attacked Sirhind in January 1764, defeated and killed Zain Khan, and looted and destroyed the city. They invaded Lahore and forced Kabuli Mal to pay tribute. In March 1764, they captured Rohtas and made Sarbuland Khan, governor of Kashmir, a prisoner. The

Sikhs crossed the Yamuna and plundered Saharanpur and the surrounding towns of present-day western Uttar Pradesh. Najib-ud-daula paid eleven lakh rupees as hush money to the Sikhs. Hari Singh Bhangi plundered Multan and other towns in Derajat.

Ahmad Shah made his seventh invasion in December 1764, and advanced on Amritsar from Lahore in January 1765. He destroyed the holy temple and the Sikhs continued to attack his flanks. There were seven pitched battles, with heavy casualities on both sides; Ahmad Shah at last returned to Afghanistan in May 1765. Ahmad Shah's eighth and ninth invasions in 1767 and 1768 ended in his defeat and the entire Punjab came under the control of the Sikhs. Ahmad Shah died on 14 April 1772, the day on which the Sikhs crossed the Indus and plundered Peshawar.

The first sixty years of the eighteenth century had thus been for the self-reliant Sikh community, nursed by their ten Gurus, a period of great struggle against unprecedented persecution.

The Sikhs were so drunk with courage and devotion to the word of their Gurus that even this relentless persecution only served to fuel their resistance and to strengthen their resolve. They were determined to rule their own destiny in their own land, to obtain and retain the sacred trust of temporal sovereignty bequeathed to them by Guru Gobind Singh shortly before his demise. They did achieve temporal sovereignty in 1765 at a sacrifice of over 2,00,000 Sikh lives in a period of about half a century, fulfiling the oft-repeated *shloka* 'Raj Karega Khalsa' as a part of their daily prayers.

The Most Controversial Sikh Coin

The coin alleged to have been struck in the name of Jassa Singh Ahluwalia in Lahore in 1758 or 1761 has been the most controversial Sikh coin, more so because no such coin is actually forthcoming. The controversy regarding this coin started fairly soon after its alleged striking, a claim which has been picked up by almost every historian of the *misl* period and by every numismatist studying Sikh coins. The real significance of this coin at this stage does not lie in its having been struck or not, or whether it was struck with Jassa Singh's approval or otherwise, or whether it was an act of mischief by the local *qazis* and *mullahs* aimed at instigating the Afghan invaders against the Sikhs, or whether it was the result of a momentary euphoria among the victorious Sikh army over the capture of Lahore after a period of nearly 750 years of foreign occupation, or whether it was an aberrant act,[34] or whether it was the gift of a small number of coins as a *nazrana* presented by the notable citizens of Lahore to the Sikh commander for withholding his forces from sacking the town. The real importance of this coin as well as the controversy surrounding it lies in its violation of the concept of Sikh sovereignty, which was held sacrosanct by the

Sikhs in the eighteenth century, the period during which this coin is alleged to have been struck.

Ahmad Shah, after defeating the Marathas in the Third Battle of Panipat in January 1761, departed for Afghanistan in May 1761, leaving behind Khawaja Obed Khan as the governor of Lahore and Zain Khan as the governor of Sirhind. Immediately after Ahmad Shah's departure, the Sikhs started occupying the areas which were under the Afghan governors. Mirza Khan, in-charge of Char Mahal, came out to fight the Sikh forces but was defeated and killed.[35] Bikram Khan of Malerkotla was defeated and the town sacked. On receiving this disturbing news, Ahmad Shah sent a trusted general, Nur-ud-din, with a well-trained force to chastise the Sikhs, but he was defeated at Sialkot by Charat Singh; Nur-ud-din fled, leaving his army at the mercy of the Sikh forces.[36] Khawaja Obed Khan invaded Gujranwala in September 1761 and laid siege to the fort. In the meantime, other *sardars* came to the help of Charat Singh and they in turn besieged Obed Khan. Obed Khan beat a hasty retreat, leaving behind huge quantities of arms and ammunition, camels, horses, and other camp equipment which the Sikhs claimed.[37] Thus, in a short span of about four months, the Sikhs had subdued all the Afghan chiefs set up by Ahmad Shah and practically the entire Punjab came under their control.

In October 1761 the Sikhs assembled at Amritsar to celebrate Diwali. They held a meeting of the Sarbat Khalsa and passed a *gurmata* to punish Aqil Das of Jandiala, who belonged to the Niranjani sect, and who was a persistent enemy of the Sikhs and a steadfast friend of the Durranis; the assembly also voted to occupy Lahore and establish Sikh supremacy all over the Punjab.[38] The Sikhs marched to Lahore under the leadership of Jassa Singh Ahluwalia and laid siege to the city. Obed Khan, the governor, shut himself in the fort and would not face the Sikh forces. He was later killed in a skirmish with the Sikhs. The leading citizens, appreciating the delicate situation created by the weakness of the governor, negotiated with the Sikh commander; they then opened the city gates to the Sikh forces, thus saving Lahore from sack and plunder. The jubilant Sikh forces entered Lahore and are said to have occupied the royal mint and are alleged to have struck a coin in the name of their leader:

> *Sikka zad dar jehan bafazal-e-Akal*
> *Mulk-e-Ahmad garift Jassa Kalal.*[39]

meaning that the coin is struck in the world by the grace of Akal, the God, the country of Ahmad held by Jassa Kalal. Of all those who claim that the coin was struck, none actually provides any details regarding the legend on the reverse, the name of the mint, and the year of its origin, which are essential features establishing the authenticity of any coin. Besides the question of the actual striking of this coin, the date of its striking is also disputed. James Browne believes that the Sikhs expelled Timur Shah and Jahan Khan from Lahore, occupied the city, and struck a coin in the name of their leader Jassa Singh Ahluwalia in 1758.[40] Browne bases his account on the *Risala-i-Nanak* which he received from Budh Singh Arora and Ajaib Singh of Malerkotla,[41] whom he met in Delhi in 1783 during his stay at the Mughal court from 1782-5.[42] A number of later historians, including Lt. Col. Malcolm, Elphinstone, Cunningham, Latif, and Narang,[43] base their accounts on the observations made by James Browne but these scholars do not put forth any new or contemporary evidence nor have they made any attempt to locate and examine this coin. Hari Ram Gupta, the foremost historian of the period of the Sikh *misls*, states that in 1758 the Punjab was leased out to Adena Beg by the Marathas for an annual tribute of seventy-five lakh rupees[44] and that the Sikhs could not have assumed control of the state capital, Lahore. Hari Ram Gupta assigns the date for this event as November 1761.[45] In November 1760, about 10,000 Sikhs invaded Lahore but left after receiving a *nazarana* of 30,000 rupees from the governor of Lahore for *karah parshad*.[46] He primarily bases his inference on Ghulam Ali Khan Azad's account *Khazana-i-Amira*, written in 1762, deeming it to be the most reliable record. The *Khazana-i-Amira* states that the Sikhs killed the Durrani, governor of Lahore, captured the capital, and issued this coin and that it was due to these doings of the Sikhs that Ahmad Shah invaded India in early 1762 and inflicted a severe defeat on the Sikhs, massacring about 20,000 of them.[47] N.K. Sinha does not accept the above evidence as satisfactory. Taking into account all the facts of the past few years, we are inclined to agree with Hari Ram Gupta that the date of striking the coin, if at all it had been struck, in all probability should be taken as 1761, and not 1758 as recorded by Browne and others. However, this aspect concerning the date of the striking of the coin is a minor part of the controversy.

The real issue is the alleged striking of the coin by Jassa Singh Ahluwalia. Browne states that in 1757 Jassa Singh Ahluwalia expelled the *amils* of Ahmad Shah from the city and the Subah of Lahore, and he became so popular that he ventured to strike rupees at the mint of Lahore in his own name.[48] But after these had been in circulation for fifteen years, the Grand Diet of the Sikh chiefs called the *gurmata* determined to recall all those rupees and have them struck in the names of Guru Nanak and Guru Gobind Singh.[49] Browne further states that he had several of these coins in his possession.[50]

First, Browne's presumption that the coin was struck in 1758 does not seem to be correct. Second, his statement that the Grand Diet withdrew it after it had been in circulation for fifteen years is not supported by any other evidence. The Sikh commonwealth decided in 1765 to occupy Lahore and strike a coin in the name of their Gurus as a symbol of their sovereignty. Had this coin been in circulation for seven years, as stated by Browne, it would certainly have drawn adverse comments and criticism, which are not forthcoming in the historical record; this lack of evidence regarding the coin raises serious doubts about its ever having actually been struck. It has been universally admitted by all historians that in the prevailing circumstances only a small number of coins would have been struck. The occupation of Lahore by the Sikhs in 1758 was for a very short spell and that too was done along with the Marathas. Browne's statement that several of these coins were in his possession evokes our skepticism. Even if we believe that he did secure several of these coins in 1783-5 from Delhi, at a time when the hobby of coin collecting as such had not become prevalent in India, he was immediately thereafter recalled and returned to England. It is likely that he would not have given away these coins and it is possible that some of them might have been acquired as part of the collections of some museums; but no such coin has been located anywhere in the world. Browne's account is at best only speculative, without any authentic evidence in its support. Banda Bahadur struck Sikh coins in small numbers during 1710-12 while he was at war and the state administration was still in its infancy, yet a few coins have been located. In the case of the coins struck in 1758 by Jassa Singh, if these were in circulation for fifteen years, some of these should certainly have been traced.

Hari Ram Gupta emphatically asserts that coins were struck by Jassa Singh Ahluwalia in 1761:

. . . in a fit of enthusiasm and delight the Sikhs fulfilled the wishes of their revered leader the late Nawab Kapur Singh by declaring Jassa Singh Ahluwalia as Padshah, then seizing the royal mint they struck the second Sikh rupee. In the heat of passion of having attained this glory, after the hardest struggle for more than half a century, bubbling over with their success and flushed with the pride of victory, they let them pass beyond the bounds of reasons and thus they glorified the victor who had led them from one conquest to another for about a dozen years past. That the mistake, made in the highest excitement of the hour, was realized in saner, cooler and calmer moments is evident beyond all doubts.[51]

There is of course the contemporary account of the *Khazana-i-Amira* which does lend some support to his assertion. Hari Ram Gupta's explanation, however, takes recourse to strong emotions rather than to hard evidence. His reference to the wishes of the late Nawab Kapur Singh is not relevant to the issue and cannot be a part of the evidence. His assertion that the decision to strike the coin was due to momentary jubilation undermines the authority behind the issuing of the coin; indeed, he himself deems it to be against the Sikh ethos and the principle that sovereignty belonged to the Khalsa and not to any single individual. He locks horns with N.K. Sinha in a rather unpleasant debate.[52] Sinha denies that such an event ever occurred.[53]

Hari Ram Gupta writes, 'The Sikhs seem to doubt the striking of these coins, because no Sikh writer except Gian Singh has mentioned this fact in his work.'[54] He thereafter constructs half a dozen imaginary Sikh doubts and then tries to demolish them with his arguments.[55] This attempt at first raising strawmen and then pushing them down is rather uncharitable on his part. There cannot be a Sikh view and a Hindu view on this issue of history. Certain Sikh historians such as S.S. Bal and G.S. Chhabra also share Hari Ram Gupta's views.[56] No further discussion of Hari Ram Gupta's doubts is necessary since it does not contribute to the solution of the controversy. Since no such coin has as yet been located, evidence from the *Khazana-i-Amira*, which does not mention the incident, cannot be taken as authentic and final, as instances do exist where such evidence from contemporaneous sources has proved to be incorrect. A contemporary chronicler, Ahmad Yadgar, states that before the Second Battle of Panipat, Hemu threw off his allegiance to his master Adil Shah and struck coins in his own name. No such coin has survived and in the light of modern research Ahmad Yadgar's statement stands disproved.[57] A newswriter of the Jaipur court wrote in 1710 that the Sikhs under Banda Bahadur had minted a coin with the following legend:[58]

> *Azmt-e-Guru Nanak, ham zahir o ham batin ast,*
> *Badshah-i-Din-o-Duniya ap Sacha Sahib ast.*

> (The greatness of Guru Nanak is both patent and latent and the true Lord himself is the king of both the spiritual and the temporal worlds.)

Another contemporary account, *Hadiqat-ul-Aqalim*[59] by Murtaza Hussain, states that Banda Bahadur struck coins with the above legend, whereas the actual seal imprint and the few coins of Banda Bahadur that have been located use different legends.[60] In view of these instances, the account in *Khazana-e-Amira*[61] cannot be relied upon to establish the striking of the coin by Jassa Singh and the contention of Hari Ram Gupta cannot be given credibility beyond its being an emotionally charged assumption at least until such a coin is located. I have been meeting Hari Ram Gupta from 1980 onwards, both at his residence at Ferozepur and at my residence at Jullandhar. During our discussions of Sikh history, Hari Ram Gupta stated that he had neither seen nor studied Sikh coins and my collection was the first that he had examined.

Ganesh Das Badhera in *Char Bagh-i-Punjab*[62] states that the local *qazis* and *mullahs* struck 21 such coins and sent them to Ahmad Shah to instigate him against the Sikhs. This view contradicts the argument that Jassa Singh himself or the Sikhs struck this coin in his name. Ganesh Das has not given any contemporary evidence in support of his claim and thus it is merely another presumption. Later historians have taken Ganesh Das's view into account and thus further roiled the controversy but they have not made any new contribution to the debate. Khushwaqt Rai in *Kitab-i-Tarikh-i-Punjab*[63] states that this coin was short lived because its circulation was stopped on account of the disaproval of the Sikhs regarding the use of the half names of their leaders, which were inscribed on the coin in question. This statement too is not supported by contemporary evidence. It is primarily a reiteration of Browne's view with some modification. Ahmad Yadgar in his *Tarikh-i-Salatin-i-Afghana*,[64] written in 1835, states that the Sikhs felt distressed that the credit of their victory was being given to an individual and not to the Gurus. Consequently, they stopped the circulation of the coin and struck another coin in the name of their Gurus. There is also no evidence that the coin was restruck in the succeeding years after its initial issue. Ahmad Yadgar has not cited any contemporary evidence in support of his allegation. The accounts of Khushwaqt Rai and Ahmad Yadgar suffer from the same weakness as that of Browne's narrative regarding the withdrawal of the coin by the Sikh authorities.

Ganda Singh, another noted historian of the Sikhs, has written a detailed biography of Jassa Singh Ahluwalia,[65] but has not paid any attention to the controversy regarding this coin. He dismisses the debate as not deserving any further discussion in view of the disinclination of the Sikhs regarding the use of the half name of any *sardar*. Lepel Griffin states that these coins must have been struck in very small numbers.[66] He further states that the raja of Kapurthala did not possess any such coin, nor could he contact anyone who had seen this coin. The matter was taken up with the present head of the house of Kapurthala, Brigadier Sukhjit Singh, who stated in 1980 that 'with regard to the coins purported to have been struck by Baba Jassa Singh there was, to the best of my knowledge, one such coin in the former Kapurthala treasury'.[67] Since this coin is no longer traceable, this raises doubts about Griffin's assertion and hence does not lead us any nearer to a solution.

However, there is one other possible explanation which no historian has considered so far. In late 1761, the Sikhs had besieged Lahore city and the governor had locked himself in the fort; since there were no opposing forces, the fall of the city to the Sikhs was imminent. Keeping in view the impending sack of the city and the threat of plunder by the conquerors, the leading citizens began negotiations with the Sikh commander and opened the city gates to the Sikh forces, thus saving the city from ruination.

In November 1760 also, about 10,000 Sikhs besieged Lahore city and Mir Mohammad, the governor, shut himself in the fort. The Sikhs had cut off all means of communication and were going to break the city walls. Facing the imminent fall of the city and its sack by the Sikhs, the leading citizens persuaded the governor to pay 30,000 rupees from the state revenues to the Sikhs for *karah parshad* and thus persuaded the Sikh forces to withdraw.[68] It is probable that cash *nazranas* were paid to the victorious Sikh army in accordance with the prevailing practice. It is our presumption that the leading citizens might have struck a small number of coins, may be 21 coins as a token of their gratitude and in acceptance of the suzerainty of the great Sikh commander over Lahore. The number 21 does not seem to have any special significance. The legend is in fair conformity to the existing Mughal and Afghan legends on their respective coins, wherein the use of half names was a common practice. The alleged couplet under discussion seems to be the work of some Mughal mint master and was quite appropriate to the occasion, and its being in violation of Sikh traditions may not have been known to the mint officials. Jassa Singh may have accepted the coins and got them broken down later on. In a similar case, Sultan Muhammad

Khan bin Musa Khan states in his *Tarikh-i-Sultani* that Shah Shujah got a presentation coin made in honour of Alexander Burnes and the English East India Company with the following couplet inscribed on it:[69]

Sika zad bar simmotilla Shah Shujah Armini,
Nur-i-Chashm Lord Burnes Khak-i-pa Kampani

meaning that coins of silver and gold were struck by Shah Shujah, the Armenian, the light of the eyes of Lord Burnes and the dust under the feet of the Company. Shah Shujah was the protege of the British and was being set up as the ruler of Afghanistan under the protection of the British forces sent under Alexander Burnes (who was later assassinated by the rebel Afghans in 1841 at Kabul). The coin was obviously aimed at pleasing and humouring Alexander Burnes and the British in a manner most derogatory and humiliating to the sovereign Afghan king.

In a somewhat similar situation, Allard presented fifty silver coins to Ranjit Singh on the festival of Dussehra in 1836 which he had got made while on leave in France; these coins bore Ranjit Singh's name and the title 'Wali of Punjab'.[70] What happened to these coins is not known, nor have any of these coins surfaced so far. Hence, it is quite likely that the leading citizens of Lahore may have got these coins prepared from the royal mint as a *nazrana* to the Sikh commander, and with the passage of time the incident assumed different hues and colours. This interpretation of events seems to be more appropriate than the other probable versions of the incident, but it cannot be deemed as proper historical evidence till the coin is located and analysed.

The most analytical and articulate assessment has been made by N.K. Sinha, although he is unable to dispute with certainty the striking of the coin. He is quite convinced that Jassa Singh Ahluwalia would never have struck the coin in his own name in violation of Sikh traditions and the concept of Sikh sovereignty. The suggestion that Jassa Singh imprinted on the coins of the Khalsa the legend '*Mulk-e-Ahmad garift Jassa Kalal*' is highly absurd and unlikely.[71] N.K. Sinha further states:

The theocratic zeal and democratic spirit were far too deep rooted to allow any individual to do such a highly objectionable thing. Sikh democracy was such a living force in those days of the Sikh struggle against the Durranis, that no Sikh, howsoever highly placed, would dare flout the Khalsa in such a way. Jassa Singh Ahluwalia, the ideal democratic leader, conspicuous for his spirit of self sacrifice, was too faithful a follower of the commonwealth and too wholesale a patriot to attempt to distinguish himself in a way so revolting to a Sikh.[72]

Khushwant Singh has not given any cognizance to the striking of the coin and makes only a passing reference to it. He speaks of the 1765 coins in the name of the Gurus as having been issued on the occasion of the victorious entry of Jassa Singh Ahluwalia at the head of the Khalsa forces into Lahore city.[73]

The chances of tracing the coin are becoming increasingly remote with the passage of time; the controversy over whether it was struck or not amounts to the flogging of a dead horse. The true position can be ascertained only with the finding of an actual coin. And here the matter must rest at present.

Were these coins the authorized issue of the Khalsa commonwealth? This very important question remains unanswered in all the historical accounts. From the above analysis of the controversy it becomes abundantly clear that there existed an unmistakable and persistent trend in the Sikh polity during the period of Jassa Singh Ahluwalia and thereafter which rested on the fundamental principle that Sikh sovereignty belonged to the entire Khalsa Panth and its principal symbol, the coin, could not be struck in the name of just anybody, howsoever mighty he may be. This privilege was vested exclusively in the names of the Sikh gurus.

Assumption of Sovereignty by the Sikhs and the Striking of Sikh Coins in AD 1765

'The defacto sovereignty of the Sikhs was practically established in the Punjab. They also asserted de jure authority, although this clashed with the Afghan claim. In those days no assertion of authority could be held as valid unless it was accompanied by an issue of coin', writes N.K. Sinha.[74]

With the departure of Ahmad Shah, the Sikhs retired to Amritsar to celebrate Baisakhi on 10 April 1765. They cleaned and repaired the entire complex. The *sarowar*, tank of nectar, was cleared of debris and repaired. The Harimandir and other buildings were reconstructed; the Sikh *sardars* spent large sums of money on this project. Leaders of about half a dozen *misls*, which formed the commonwealth, appointed their representatives in the temple, thus setting up an establishment. *Granthis* were appointed to regularly carry out the religious ceremonies, which continue to the present day.[75] The *Guru ka Langar* was set up on a larger scale than ever before.[76]

The jubilation over their victories and the festivities of Baisakhi went on for about a month and thereafter the *sardars* sat down at the Akal Takht to attend to the common problems faced by the community. Historians have called these gatherings general assemblies and national councils, which were held during Baisakhi and Diwali every year. Here the pressing problems faced by the community were discussed and decisions were taken collectively in the form of *gurmatas*. The *gurmata*, literally meaning the advice or counsel of the Guru, had developed into an important institution to determine the general will of the community by consensus. It helped to provide unity and cohesion amongst the independent *sardars* and to take collective action against their persecutors. *Gurmatas* were introduced by Guru Gobind Singh to ascertain the views of his followers, and there are instances where he accepted the will of the general body over his own views. European travellers such as John Malcolm and George Forster have given detailed accounts of an independence of expression of views by every member in such assemblies, where their personal and private feuds were forgotten and they rendered extreme devotion and service to their religion and the commonwealth.[77]

The Sikh *sardars* assembled at the Akal Takht in April 1765 passed the *gurmata* of their complete independence and the assumption of sovereignty and resolved to regain their old territories and acquire new ones wherever possible. They also decided to issue a coin in the name of the Gurus as a mark of their sovereignty.[78] The presence of a Muslim governor of Lahore, hardly 30 miles from Amritsar, appeared offensive to their newly formed sense of independence. The Bhangi chiefs, Lehna Singh and Gulab Singh, joined by Sobha Singh marched on Lahore and occupied the city without any serious resistance and parcelled the town amongst themselves in May 1765.[79] The triumphant Sikhs struck the first coin of good, pure silver with the inscription '*Degh Tegh Fateh*' from the Lahore mint in May 1765, i.e. 1822 Sambat. Thus was publicly proclaimed the establishment of Sikh sovereignty.[80] These coins are readily available with collectors and various museums in India and abroad. Although Sikh coins were struck by Banda Bahadur in AD 1710-12[81] and a widely debated coin is alleged to have been that of Jassa Singh Ahluwalia, yet the Sikh coins for regular use really commenced with the coin of AD 1765.

The legend selected for the coin was the same one selected by Banda Bahadur for the state seal in AD 1710 and is found embossed on some of his *hukamnamas*.[82] A seal of Banda Bahadur's time is preserved at the *dera* of Baba Banda Bahadur at Riasi. The legend on the seal is the same as on the *hukamnamas*. Since the seal had no reverse side, the Sikhs took the existing legend found on the reverse of the Mughal coins issued from the Lahore mint. The legends are:

Obverse *Degh Tegh Fateh O Nusrut Baidarang*
         Yaft uz Nanak Guru Gobind Singh.
Reverse *Zarb Dar-ul-sultanat Lahore Sambat 1822*
         Maiminat Manus Jalus.

'*Degh*' (the cooking pot) represents food, prosperity, and economic power in the wider sense; '*Tegh*' (the sword) represents strength of arms and military power; and '*Fateh*' means the resultant victory. *Nusrat*; is an Arabic word meaning 'help' '*Baidarang*' means 'without restraint' or 'spontaneous'; and '*Yaft uz*' means 'received from'. The couplet thus means: the food and the arms with the resultant victory have been achieved with the spontaneous help received from Guru Nanak to Guru Gobind Singh. The reverse means: minted at the capital city Lahore, auspicious and prosperous Sambat 1822.

The Sikhs also issued a coin from Amritsar later on but the exact year is not known. Numismatists have located the earliest such coin for the year 1832 Sambat. Hence, the earliest coin available from Amritsar pertains to the year AD 1775, i.e. 1832 Sambat.[83] The legend on the coin is that used by Banda Bahadur on his coins during AD 1710 to 1712 and it runs as follows:

Obverse   *Sikka Zad Bar Har Do Alam, Tegh-i-Nanak Wahib Ast.*
            Fateh Gobind Singh Shah-i-Shan Fazal, Sachcha Sahib Ast.
Reverse   *Zarb Sri Amritsar Jeo,*
            Sambat 1832 Jalus Takht Akal Bakht.
            Maiminat Manus Jalus

The meaning of the obverse legend is explained in detail in Chapter I. The meaning of the reverse legend is: 'minted at *Amritsar Jeo*' (the city which was held in great reverence). The words *'Jalus Takht Akal Bakht'* mean the reign of the Akal Takht, and *'maiminat manoos'* auspicious and prosperous, whereas on the reverse of the Lahore coin, the Sikhs copied the legend from the Mughal coins. On Amritsar coin, the Sikhs called it the reign of the Akal Takht, from which Guru Hargobind launched his temporal authority.

The first couplet was used regularly and appears on the majority of the available Sikh coins; the second couplet was used on the initial Sikh coins and thereafter on the coins from Amritsar and on some coins from the Lahore and Multan mints (see Plate II).

The couplet *'Degh Tegh Fateh'* on the Sikh coins has been given various interpretations; it has also been treated as a mere Persian couplet in praise of the Gurus. J.D. Cunningham, Muhammad Latif, G.C. Narang, G.L. Chopra, J.S. Grewal, and a few other historians are incorrect in translating *'Degh'* as 'Grace'. They are also wrong in treating *'Yaft uz Nanak Guru Gobind Singh'* as 'received by Guru Gobind Singh from Guru Nanak'.[84] The correct meaning is 'received from Guru Nanak to Guru Gobind Singh'. Cunningham is also wrong in treating *'Degh Tegh'* as the *'miri* and *piri'* of Guru Hargobind.[85] H.R. Gupta has incorrectly drawn a similarity between *'Degh Tegh Fateh'* and the Hindu holy trinity of Brahma, Vishnu, and Shiva.[86] It appears that historians have not given due attention to these couplets and thus have not appreciated the true meaning and spirit of this couplet. Their assumptions, besides being incorrect, also go against the concept of Sikh sovereignty.

The concept of *'Degh Tegh'* was inherent in Guru Nanak's teachings of community service and self-reliance, meaning that the nonacceptance of tyranny was to be resisted later on with the help of the sword against the sword. These two aspects—service to the community and resistance to injustice and tyranny—took an increasingly visible form with the increase in the number of Sikh devotees and the increased tyranny of the rulers of the Punjab. The execution of the Sikh Gurus and other forms of persecution of the Sikhs only served to deepen and strengthen the concept, which became an integral part of the Sikh ethos and culture. Guru Gobind Singh, the tenth Guru, fully institutionalized and concretized this principle. He states in the *Krishan Avtar*: *'Degh Tegh Jag me duon chalen, Rakh lo Ap mohe, awar na dalen'*, meaning that 'My free community kitchen and my sword should prevail supreme in the whole world. Grant me your protection and none else will be able to trample upon me.'[87] He carried out

PLATE II: EARLY COINS, 1765 ONWARDS

LAHORE COIN 1822 SAMBAT

OBVERSE: DEG TEG FATEH NUSRAT O BAIDARANG YAFT UZ NANAK GURU GOBIND SINGH

REVERSE: ZARB DAR-UL-SALTANAT LAHORE MAIMINAT MANUS JALUS.

AMRITSAR COIN 1832 SAMBAT

OBVERSE: SIKKA ZAD BAR HAR DO ALAM TEGH-NANAK WAHIB AST
FATEH SAHI GOBIND SINGH SHAH SHAHAN FAZAL SACHCHA SAHIB AST

REVERSE: 'ZARB SRI AMRITSAR JEO' SAMBAT 1832 MAIMINAT MANUS JALUS TAKHT AKAL BAKHT

FIGURE II: JASSA SINGH AHLUWALIA

various measures in the short span available to him to strengthen his *Degh* and *Tegh*, i.e. the economic and financial resources and the strength of his armies and weapons. He abolished the debased and corrupt institution of the *masands*.[88] The devotees were ordered to come fully armed. Guru Gobind Singh created the Khalsa in AD 1699[89] and engendered such a spirit of devotion and sacrifice in his Khalsa that they could take up resistance even against vastly superior forces.[90]

'*Degh Tegh Fateh*' appears on the top of the *hukamnamas* issued by Mata Sahib Devi, wife of Guru Gobind Singh, to the Sikhs after she settled down in Delhi.[91] '*Degh Tegh Fateh*' was framed into a Persian couplet in Banda Bahadur's time and was used on the state seal in AD 1710. This couplet was used by the Lahore Darbar on its coins and continued till the annexation of the Punjab by the British and the declaration of Sikh coinage as a dead currency in 1850.[92] '*Degh Tegh Fateh*' is also part of the daily *ardas*, the prayer read out after every Sikh religious ceremony. This couplet has also been used by the Nabha State on its coinage and the Patiala State on its *nazrana* coins struck for *puja* purposes, which continued till the accession of these states to the Union of India in 1948.[93]

The Early Lahore Coins, Incorrectly Called the Gobind Shahi Coins

The Sikhs were the most harassed and persecuted community in India in the first half of the eighteenth century, but during the second half of the eighteenth century their rise was meteoric. They established a firm hold over almost the entire Punjab after defeating the Mughal rulers and pushing back the Afghan invaders beyond the borders of the subcontinent. Under the able stewardship of Ranjit Singh, the Sikhs ruled over the entire Punjab and the surrounding territories of Kashmir, the frontier tribal areas, and Derajats, for half a century. Even the East India Company treated the Sikhs with restraint and respect.

Under the monetary system prevailing in northern India in the eighteenth and nineteenth centuries, various currencies such as those of the Mughals, Afghans, numerous native states, the British, and other European settlers were operative. There was no system for the withdrawal of obsolete currencies from circulation. The revenues and taxes were largely paid in the currencies of the rulers then in power and these were regularly minted; the earlier currencies gradually went out of circulation as their minting ceased and some of these were melted and restruck by the new rulers. The Sikh currency was first nominally issued in AD 1710-12 when the first Sikh state was formed, encompassing Subah Sirhind, under the command of Banda Bahadur.[94] Thereafter, the Sikhs were defeated by the Mughal forces under Farukh Siyar and continued to be hunted and persecuted by the Mughal rulers and the Afghan invaders. In 1765 the Sikhs occupied Lahore, the state capital, and the surrounding areas, and Sikh coinage was issued regularly from Lahore in AD 1765 (1822 Sambat) and onwards and from Amritsar AD 1775 (1832 Sambat) and onwards.[95] By 1800 Ranjit Singh came to power and within a decade he had consolidated the Sikh territories into a strong Sikh state. With the establishment of political stability and under the leadership of a capable ruler, trade and commerce prospered and increased. This led to the increased minting of Sikh coins. Thanks to the steadfast maintenance of the purity of the metal during Sikh rule, Sikh coinage became the premier currency in north-western India. The Sikh state was annexed to the British Indian territories in 1849 AD and the issue of Sikh currency came to a close.

The annexation of the Sikh state was deemed an act of naked aggrandizement by the British.[96] Its administration was controlled and guided by the British Resident from 1846 to 1849 and the child ruler Dalip Singh was their ward. To justify the annexation, a spate of historical accounts on the Sikhs was brought out by European writers, many by British administrators in India and their Indian *munshis* who were commissioned for this task. These historical accounts contain occasional references to Sikh coins, primarily based on *bazaar* gossip and hearsay rather than being based on any historical analysis. However, recent numismatic investigations of Sikh coinage have revealed a number of fallacies, which have often been repeated as a matter of fact by later historians. One such fallacy concerns the nomenclature of the Sikh coins, as Gobind Shahi and Nanak Shahi, without any critical examination of the historical accounts or any proper numismatic investigation.

Rulers the world over have struck coins as a symbol of their sovereign power over the territories under their control and the people over whom they rule. These coins generally bear the name of the ruler, the place and year of minting, and some legend proclaiming the greatness of the ruler or perhaps a religious invocation. This was also the existing practice in the Indian subcontinent. The Sikh coinage which came into existence in the eighteenth century had a distinctive feature. The Sikh religious traditions exercise a tremendous influence over the entire life of a Sikh, viz., the religious, social, and political aspects of an individual's life are to be based on certain moral values enunciated in the holy scriptures. Guru Gobind Singh, shortly before his demise, abolished the institution of the personal Guruship and vested the spiritual aspect of his sovereignty in the *Granth*, thereafter called the *Guru Granth Sahib*, and the temporal sovereignty of his Gurudom in the entire Sikh community.[97] These two fundamental aspects of the Sikh way of life or the Sikh ethos are enshrined in the prayer, which all Sikhs recite every day, and in fact on every occasion before they take an important decision in their life. Political sovereignty thus stood vested in the entire Sikh community and not in any one Sikh. This was an extreme form of a democratic institution in the feudal world of the early eighteenth century. This aspect of the Sikh tradition has been aptly described by Murray as 'Lahore and Sirhind being ruled by seventy thousand sovereigns when the provinces came under Sikh dominion.'[98]

The Sikhs selected two couplets for their coins and their seal in 1710:

(i)   *Sikka Zad bar har do alam, Tegh-i-Nanak Wahib ast*
        Fateh Gobind Singh Shah-i-shahan, fazal Sacha Sahib ast.

meaning that 'a coin has been struck in both the worlds, herein and hereafter under the guarantee of Guru Nanak's sword. The victory of Gobind Singh, King of Kings, has been with the grace of the true Lord, the Akal Purakh.'

(ii)   *Degh Tegh fateh-o-nusrat baidrang,*
        Yaft uz Nanak Guru Gobind Singh.

meaning '(*Degh*) the economic prosperity, (*Tegh*) the strength of the sword arm, *fateh* the resultant victory, *nusrat* (an Arabic word meaning 'help') and *baidrang* meaning 'without restraint' or 'spontaneously' received from Nanak to Guru Gobind Singh.[99]

Both these legends, recorded on the obverse of the coins, denote the basic concept of Sikh sovereignty bequeathed to them by their Gurus. Guru Gobind Singh had developed the concept of '*Degh Tegh Fateh*' as an elaboration of the concept of *Miri Piri* enunciated by Guru Hargobind, the sixth master, wherein the spiritual and the temporal powers of the Guru were exercised from two different places, viz., the Harimandir and the Akal Takht respectively. Ranjit Singh called himself the servant of the Gurus and deemed them to be the true sovereigns.[100] In the period after 1765 both the above mentioned legends were used on the obverse of the Sikh coins. The reverse legends are similar to those given on the Mughal/Afghan coins but with slight modifications. Most European historians and even some Indian historians have incorrectly interpreted the later part of the second legend, i.e. '*Yaft uz Nanak Guru Gobind Singh*' as 'Guru Gobind Singh received from Guru Nanak'.[101] In accordance with Sikh traditions and ethos, all the ten Gurus were the reincarnations of Guru Nanak, representing one ideology, and the phrase '*Nanak Guru Gobind Singh*' covers the entire period of gurudom. Both legends speak of the first and the tenth Masters by name, thus giving the benediction of all the ten Gurus to the Sikh Panth. Some later Indian historians have brought out the correct translation.

J.D. Cunningham in his book *History of the Sikhs* states that the Sikhs after their occupation of Lahore struck a rupee coin with the legend '*Degh Tegh Fateh*' and this coin was called the Gobind Shahi rupee.[102] He has not, however, given any reason or evidence explaining why it was called the 'Gobind Shahi'. His translation of the second line of the couplet is incorrect as he states that the benediction was received by Guru Gobind Singh from Guru Nanak, whereas the benediction was received by the Sikhs from their Gurus.

Lepel Griffin in his book *Rajas of Punjab* states that after the occupation of Lahore, the capital, in 1765 the Sikhs struck the first national coin with the '*Degh*

Tegh' legend and it was called the Nanak Shahi coinage.[103] He explains in a footnote that it was sometimes called Nanaki or Nanak Shahi and was current at the time of his writing his book. He disagrees with Colonel Sleeman and Cunningham over the translation of *Degh* but makes the same mistake in translating the second line as was made by Cunningham.

C.J. Rodgers in his article on Sikh coins states that at this time (AD 1765/1822 Sambat) they struck, in Lahore, the political capital of the Punjab, the first Sikh rupee. They were called Gobind Shahi and not Nanak Shahi as stated by Griffin.[104] He has not given any reason or evidence explaining the grounds for his disagreement with Griffin. He calls the Amritsar rupees struck at Amritsar from 1835 Sambat and onward as Nanak Shahi because these contain the words 'Shah Nanak'. The Persian rendering of the legend on the coins is, however, incorrect, as is the translation of the second line of the '*Degh Tegh Fateh*' legend. Rodgers seems to have based his historical analysis on the stories and gossip he collected from the shopkeepers, money changers, and petty bankers in the bazaars of Amritsar and some other towns of the Punjab and not from any actual historical records.[105]

C.J. Brown in his book *Coins of India* states that the Sikhs struck the Gobind Shahi rupees from Lahore in 1765 onward and the Nanak Shahi rupees from Amritsar in 1777 with a different legend.[106] Brown does not explain the legends but states that they were called Gobind Shahi because the name of Guru Gobind Singh was included in the Persian couplet which formed the inscription. His explanation, although the only explanation given by a historian/numismatist, is incorrect as the names of both Guru Nanak and Guru Gobind Singh occur on every Sikh silver coin bearing either of the two legends.

Gulshan Lall Chopra in his book *The Punjab as a Sovereign State* gives an account of Sikh coins stated to be based on historical data and his personal examination of the coins with the British Museum, London and the Government Museum, Lahore. He writes:

Coins were struck for the second time in Sambat 1822 (AD 1765) after the Sikh conquest of Lahore in that year. These were called 'Gobind Shahi' and not 'Nanak Shahi' as stated by Griffin. The coins struck from Amritsar in Sambat 1835 and onwards are stated to be called Nanak Shahi. His translation of the couplet is also incorrect as in the case of the others.'

Chopra appears to have simply taken Rodgers's statement without acknowledging it nor giving any evidence in support of his contention.[107] His claim is certainly not based on any historical analysis or numismatic investigation. Hari Ram Gupta in his book *History of the Sikhs* writes: 'They struck in Lahore a Sikh rupee, which came to be called "Gobind Shahi" and not "Nanak Shahi" as stated by Griffin.'[108] This assertion too has apparently been taken from Rodgers without any acknowledgement, and nor has Hari Ram Gupta given any reason or argument in support of his belief. Hari Ram Gupta has, however, correctly translated the second line of the legend as 'having been received from Guru Nanak and Guru Gobind Singh'.[109] Parmeshwari Lal Gupta in his book *Coins* mentions only the 1835 coins struck in Amritsar as the 'Nanak Shahi' coins and is somewhat confused over the AD 1765 coins struck in Lahore.[110] He states that the *'Degh Tegh Fateh'* legend was first used by Ranjit Singh, an assertion which is obviously incorrect. However, in his book *Coins of Dal Khalsa and Lahore Darbar* he states that the first couplet is generally known as Gobind Shahi and the second as Nanak Shahi, but no where does he explain the reasons for the choice of these names.[111]

Bikramjit Hasrat in his book *Life and Times of Ranjit Singh* states that on the proclamation of the investure of sovereignty in the Sarkar-i-Khalsa by Ranjit Singh, a coin called the 'Nanak Shahi' with the legend *'Degh Tegh Fateh'* was struck.[112] Bhagat Singh in his book *Sikh Polity*, written in 1978, states that the Sikh *sardars* after assuming power struck a coin with the *'Degh Tegh Fateh'* legend which was called the 'Gobind Shahi' coinage.[113] G.S. Chhabra in his book *Advanced History of the Punjab* calls the coins struck in 1765 with the legend *'Degh Tegh Fateh'* as the Gobind Shahi.[114] None of these historians has given any historical evidence in support of their contentions and they seem to merely repeat the conclusions from the works of earlier writers. In his book *Coins of the Sikhs*, Hans Herrli offers a fairly elaborate study of the entire period of Sikh coinage; he makes the same distinction between the Gobind Shahi coins having the *'Degh Tegh Fateh'* legend and the Nanak Shahi coins with the *'Sikka zad bar har do alam'* legend, but he also does not give any reason or evidence in support of his interpretation.[115]

Many historians have contradicted each other in characterizing certain coins as Nanak Shahi while others describe the same coins as Gobind Shahi. None of them has given any evidence in support of their contentions. The dies carry the entire legend, whereas the coins, when minted, being smaller in size, do not carry the entire legend. It appears that some coins bear the word 'Nanak' very prominently and other bear the word 'Gobind' very prominently, which might have prompted the merchants to call them Nanak Shahi and Gobind Shahi coins respectively. Had the numismatists examined the entire legend, this mistake could certainly have been detected and avoided.

The picture that emerges from the above discussion is that historians and numismatists have characterized the coins with the *'Degh Tegh Fateh'* legend as the 'Gobind Shahi' and the coins with the *'Sikka zad bar har do alam'* legend as the Nanak Shahi coins. Lepel Griffin and Bikramjit Hasrat classify the coins with the *'Degh Tegh Fateh'* legend as 'Nanak Shahi'. No explanation whatsoever has been given for classifying coins as Gobind Shahi. Even when Rodgers, G.L. Chopra, and Hari Ram Gupta differ from Griffin, they do not give any explanation or justification for their contentions. Such statements, lacking any basis or justification, only add to the existing confusion. The only justification is given by

C.J. Brown, who writes that these coins are called Gobind Shahi because Guru Gobind Singh's name appears on these coins. Brown does not seem to have carried out a proper examination of the Sikh coins, as both the names of Guru Nanak and Guru Gobind Singh appear in both the legends on the Sikh coins, as explained earlier, and are fairy visible on almost all Sikh coins. Hence, on this basis alone, no distinction can be made between Gobind Shahi coins and Nanak Shahi coins.

The givers of the benediction are Guru Nanak to Guru Gobind Singh, i.e. the entire lineage of the Sikh Gurus, and the recipients of their blessings are the entire Khalsa Panth and the Sikh community. In the *Holy Granth*, the Gurus after Guru Nanak appear as the nine incarnations of Guru Nanak and call themselves Nanak. Hence, the benediction given is from all of the Nanaks, and the Sikh coins can only be called 'Nanak Shahi' and cannot be characterized by the name of any other Guru, including Guru Gobind Singh, unless the legend on the coin exclusively bears the name of Guru Gobind Singh. No such coin has come to light so far. The gold and silver coins were struck by the state authorities, while the copper coins were struck by various traders and merchants who paid annual fees to the state government. The legends on the copper coins were in the name of the Gurus but these seem to have been simplified for easy die making and for striking coins of smaller size. Most of these legends on the copper coins are the '*Akal Sahai*', 'Guru Nanak Jee', and even 'Nanak Shahi'. Thus, the use of Guru Nanak's name primarily on copper coins, which appeared much later in time after the gold and silver coins, supports our contention that Sikh coins were Nanak Shahi coins. The accounts of the British government after the annexation of the Sikh state describe the Sikh coinage as 'Nanak Shahi' coinage, which further supports the above-mentioned view. Hence to classify Sikh coins bearing the '*Degh Tegh Fateh*' legend as Gobind Shahi coins is an entirely incorrect statement and deserves outright rejection as it is also in contravention of the Sikh traditions and the Sikh ethos. The Sikh coinage struck in the name of the Sikh Gurus can thus only be called Nanak Shahi and should not be characterized by any other name. One may assume that the second distortion in the nomenclature of Sikh coins occurred due to the first distortion in interpreting the meaning of the legend, which has not been contradicted by later historians who brought out the correct meaning.

Proliferation of Sikh Coinage after 1783

In October 1783, the Sikhs lost one of their great leaders, Jassa Singh Ahluwalia, who had guided the Sikh forces for almost 35 years.[116] Jassa Singh belonged to the caste of Kalals, the distillers of alcohol. Denzil Ibbetson observes that the Kalals are renowned for their enterprise, energy, and obstinancy: 'Death may budge, but a Kalal won't'.[117] After his father Badar Singh died in 1722, his widowed mother and the child Jassa Singh were placed under the protection of Mata Sundari, the acting head of the Khalsa. Kapur Singh came from Amritsar to meet Mata Sundari and took a liking to this ten-year-old lad and offered to adopt him. Jassa Singh was administered *pahul* by Kapur Singh and was placed under the charge of his uncle Bhag Singh.[118] Bhag Singh died and his place was taken by Jassa Singh when he was only 13 years old. Jassa Singh took part in numerous battles and became a seasoned military commander. The Dal Khalsa was formed in 1748 and Kapur Singh appointed Jassa Singh as the leader of that grand assembly.[119]

Jassa Singh fought in almost every Sikh battle and kept the other independent Sikh leaders under his sway due to his leadership abilities. He was a great warrior, a mighty general, and an excellent organizer. He bore twenty scars from the sword and bullet marks on his body.[120] He was physically gaunt, with his arms coming down almost to his knees. He had held the fiercely independent *misls* together and was the main architect of the establishment of the Sikh state in 1765.[121] Jassa Singh died in 1783 after a brief illness.

The death of Jassa Singh was a serious setback to the cause of Sikh unity and the Sikh *misls* were in danger of breaking up. Each *misldar*, though technically independent, now became actually independent; as their mutual jealousies became uncontrollable, internecine warfare amongst them became a common feature. Ganesh Das Badhera, who wrote *Char Bagh-i-Punjab* in the mid-nineteenth century, considered the Khalsa community a mere aggregate of individual *sardars* who were politically active. He writes that it was Jassa Singh and the Bhangi *sardars* who declared the sovereignty of the Khalsa and issued a Sikh coin from Lahore.[122] 'This minting of the coin, however, was not confined to Lahore, for every Sardar established his own mint in the area under his control.'[123] The manifesto of the sovereignty of the Khalsa marked at the same time many an individual *sardar's* sovereign status. Each new ruler established his own administration, using his personal discretion.[124]

V. Jacquemont who visited the Punjab in 1831 describes Amritsar and its numerous bazaars, its rich merchants, and prosperous bankers with their large multistoried houses, and the many Sikh *sardars* who had houses in the city which they used when they visited. At intervals along the streets were gates which were shut at night and which cut off communication between the different parts of the town.[125] Traces of the wall can be seen around each of these quarters. Each one had its own ruler, taxes, jurisdiction, and government, but their ancient divisions are no longer under separate authorities. It confirms that each *sardar* exercised his control over a certain portion of the city where he had established his residence and the people in his area were under his protection for which he levied charges and also collected taxes from the businessmen in his area. The city of Amritsar was an amalgamation of a number of independent portions (*katras*) each under an independent *sardar*. But this state of affairs emerged only during the eighteenth century, and with the coming of Ranjit Singh to power the independent portions were taken over and Amritsar became one city by about AD 1810.

Numismatic investigations show that the minting of Sikh coins began from the Lahore mint in AD 1765/1822 Sambat and was regularly continued till AD 1849/ 1906 Sambat. The coins from this period are available.[126] The minting of Sikh coins from Amritsar is considered to have begun in AD 1775/1832 Sambat as the Amritsar coin of 1832 has been located and its minting continued thereafter.[127] Earlier catalogues show that the first coin from Amritsar was dated AD 1778/1835 Sambat as by then the earliest coin located was dated 1835 Sambat and this series goes on till 1839 Sambat. Some new series started from Amritsar, with the coins for AD 1784/1841 Sambat being distinguishable due to their ornamental and symbolic variations but without any change in the legends on these coins, for instance the series with a dagger on the reverse began in 1841 Sambat and continued till AD 1808/1865 Sambat.[128]

Another series with slight changes commenced from AD 1784/1841 Sambat and continued till AD 1788/1844 Sambat. Another series with larger disks commenced from AD 1794 and continued till AD 1827/1884 Sambat. These series seems to have been adopted by Ranjit Singh as he took over Amritsar in gradual stages in order to avoid a direct confrontation with the *sardars* whose properties were being taken over in the holy city. The process of the consolidation of Amritsar continued till AD 1811, i.e. some more series with distinctive marks commenced in AD 1802/1859 Sambat and continued till AD 1806/1863 Sambat. Sikh coins were also minted from Anandgarh, the name of the main fort in Anandpur, from AD 1784/1841 Sambat to AD 1788/1846 Sambat by the *sardars* who held sway over the Anandpur area.[129] The Bhangi *sardar*, Jhanda Singh, occupied Multan in AD 1779 and issued a Sikh coin dated AD 1772/1829 Sambat and this series continued till AD 1778/1836 Sambat when Multan was taken back from the Sikhs and was occupied by Timur Shah in February 1780.[130]

It is also possible that some series were minted by independent *sardars* and that these have not been located because they were minted in very small numbers or because the dies were identical. A custom common in northern India is to distribute new coins on ceremonial occasions such as weddings and religious rites and festivals. The Patiala state rulers had special coins minted for the *puja* on Dussehra; even unused new coins from the previous years were reminted to ensure their purity as offerings placed before the deities.

From the above accounts it is amply clear that the proliferation of Sikh coins commenced after the death of Jassa Singh Ahluwalia, the long-standing leader of the Dal Khalsa, and thereby slackened the hold of the Dal Khalsa over the individual *sardars*. This proliferation of the minting of Sikh coins seemed to have continued for about a decade or so and with the rise of Ranjit Singh and the consolidation of the Sikh state all these separate types of minting came to an end and the Sikh coins were centrally minted at Amritsar and Lahore. These were also minted at some newly acquired territories of the Lahore Darbar such as Jhang, Multan, Kashmir, Peshawar, and Dehrajat. The conclusions drawn about the proliferation of Sikh coins from 1783 to about 1810 become clearly evident in the examination of the various series of coins struck during this period and which are shown in the following catalogues:

1. *World Coins*, Wisconsin: Krause Publications, pp. 994-5.
2. *South Asian Coins*, Wisconsin: Krause Publications, pp. 111-16.
3. Hans Herrli, *The Coins of the Sikhs*, Nagpur: Indian Coins Society, pp. 59-72 and 100-2.

The identification of the individual *misldars* or *sardars* has not been possible because the mint town in most of these cases was Amritsar. The coins were struck in the name of the Gurus with the prevalent legends. A limited distinction could be made in various series due to some minor distinctive marks made by the die makers but it is not possible to distinguish the *sardar* who got those coins minted, there being no records or accounts in evidence. Although during the period AD 1784/1841 Sambat to AD 1800/1857 Sambat the central political authority of the Khalsa state was weakened, the situation was reversed with the coming to power of Ranjit Singh in AD 1800 and his consolidation of the Sikh state. The *de jure* sovereignty of the Sikh Gurus over the Sikh state remained as it had developed since AD 1710 and there was no weakening of its authority.

The Leaf Motif on Sikh Coinage

In numismatic circles, Sikh coins are described as coins with the leaf motif. With the passage of time the Sikh coins were generally recognized by the leaf motif on their reverse. How and why the leaf motif came to be inscribed on Sikh coins is not recorded. The leaf motif has a characteristic and uninterrupted connection with Sikh coins. Unfortunately, the various opinions on the subject are not supported by any evidence; they are of a speculative nature, based partially on circumstantial evidence. Hence, till such time as we are able to lay our hands on some contemporary records, this issue will remain open for further investigation.

C.J. Rodgers states in an article of 1881 that a leaf along with the name of the mint town appeared on the Amritsar rupee for the first time in 1859 Sambat, i.e. AD 1802 and thereafter it appeared regularly on all coins.[131] He has not been able to trace the origin of this symbol. W.H. Valentine states that the leaf motif is 'a pipal leaf, a favourite sign or mark of the Sikhs', but gives no evidence in support of his contention.[132]

C.J. Brown in his book *Coins of India* (1922) claims that the characteristic Sikh 'leaf' appears on Ranjit Singh's earliest rupee of AD 1800/1857 Sambat.[133] Ram Chandra Kak calls it a betel leaf but without any supporting evidence.[134]

Madanjit Kaur notes that the leaf motif is the *peepal* leaf, a traditional Indian symbol signifying the eternal tree of life.[135] Saran Singh states that the *peepal* tree is considered holy by the Hindus and the Buddhists but not by the Sikhs. He identifies it with the lotus flower, drawing support from the scriptures which state that a true believer of the Sikh religion is always steadfast as the lotus is in water.[136] R.T. Somaiya, an expert on Indian trees, calls it the *ber* or *beri* leaf.[137]

W.H. Valentine is very casual in his description of the *peepal* leaf as a favourite symbol or motif of the Sikhs, since he offers no justification for this claim. C.J. Brown's argument that the leaf motif appeared for the first time in 1853 Sambat also seems to be incorrect as coins bearing much earlier dates with the leaf motif are available. Ram Chandra Kak's explanation that it is a betel leaf cannot be accepted without proper evidence. Likewise Madanjit Kaur's assessment is incorrect on two counts: first, it was not introduced by Ranjit Singh, and second, there is no evidence in support of its being a betel leaf. Saran Singh's reasoning is also not acceptable as there does not seem to be any link between the basis and the placement of the leaf on the coin at a particular point of time. R.T. Somiya's contention that the Sikh Gurus liked trees and hence it is the *ber* leaf cannot be accepted without any evidence from contemporary records.

The introduction of the leaf motif on Sikh coins in 1783 and its continuance and uniform appearance on every Sikh coin and from every Sikh mint thereafter seems to indicate that these developments must have been taken on the basis of some important and collective decision of the Khalsa. Had this been the whim of some odd *sardar*, it would soon have ended and would not have been uniformly and universally adopted.

The leaf motif on Sikh coins is widely inscribed on the Amritsar coin of 1845 Sambat, i.e. AD 1788.[138] It is quite likely that the leaf motif first appeared in the early 1740s but these coins have not been traced so far. Thereafter, it appeared universally on all Sikh coins from all the Sikh mints until the annexation of the Sikh state in 1849. Since no documented evidence in support of this is readily forthcoming it seems logical that some important event was responsible for the adoption of the leaf symbol. Further, the leaf symbol appears on long-running series. It can be said with reasonable certainty that the leaf motif first appeared on the series which was produced by the main Sikh mint as it continued to be minted from 1841 Sambat without any change.

R.T. Somaiya states emphatically that the leaf motif on Sikh coins is the *ber* leaf which was based on the actual *ber* tree in the *parikrama* of the Darbar Sahib in Amritsar popularly called the *Dukh Bhanjani*, i.e. remover of sorrows; Somaiya rejects the claim that the motif represents the *peepal* leaf, which quite a few scholars argue is the most logical explanation since the *peepal* tree is widely worshipped as a holy tree by the Hindus.[139] Somaiya further argues that the *ber* tree is part of the folklore of northern India. The *ber* tree grove was selected by Nar and Nariana (Hindu gods) for their stay in the Himalayas. He contends that the so-called symbol of the branch on the Moran Shahi coins is, in fact, a *ber* branch bearing the *ber* fruit. Somaiya's arguments cannot be accepted as proper numismatic investigation or even as historical analysis since they are not based on any contemporary evidence.

Around 1841 Sambat/AD 1784 there was no serious political upheaval and the Sikh *misls* were in possession of their lands and had even made incursions into the Gangetic plain for plunder or for levying the *rakhi* as the situation demanded.[140]

A major event of this period was the prolonged famine of 1783 popularly called the 'chalisa' famine. In 1781, 1782, and 1783 the monsoons completely failed in north India. The drought was most acute in 1783 and resulted in one of the severest famines, known as *chalisa kal* as it occurred in the Bikrami year 1840.[141] The famine affected the whole of northern India but it was particularly severe in the Punjab. Ponds, tanks, and wells went dry. Cattle perished by the thousands and many people died. According to a contemporary observer, Harcharan Dass of Delhi, thousands died in Delhi alone in five to six days. In south-eastern Punjab, the whole countryside was devastated.[142] There was no rain in 1783 and the populace was decimated, peasants abandoned their villages, and thousands died from hunger and disease. The abandoned villages of Patiala were taken over by the neighbouring *sardars*. The faminestricken territory stretched from Multan to Bengal and brought untold misery to all living souls.

In Hissar district, the helpless people died in their villages or perished from hunger and exhaustion in attempting to move south and east. People escaping from Bikaner died in Haryana in a vain endeavour to reach Delhi. Tales are told of parents who devoured their children but it is likely that the children were sold for some measure of grain.[143] The Hazara district was nearly depopulated during the famine, and grain was sold 3 to 4 *seers* per rupee.[144] In the Punjab and Delhi the high prices were beyond the reach of the common people, who also suffered from lack of employment.

During the famine of 1783, most of the Sikh chiefs continued their *langars* or free dining halls to feed the poor and the needy. Some of them spent all their money for this purpose. Describing a Sikh chief of Montgomery district, a report notes: The famine of AD 1783 occurred in Budh Singh's time. He is said to have sold all his property, and to have fed the people with grain from the proceeds.[145] Mohan Singh Sakarchakia gave 100 grams of dried grain to each person daily.[146] Regarding the Rawalpindi area, Shahamat Ali states that before the country was conquered by the Sikhs there was a great famine, from which it rapidly recovered under the good administration of Milkha Singh.[147]

The Sikhs, who had risen from *ryots* to become rulers in only a couple of decades, had deep roots in the land and hence looked after their people. Further, the Sikh tradition of *langar* and sharing established by the Sikh Gurus was very strong and hence the Sikhs were greatly affected by this *chalisa* famine. Since the saviours of the Sikhs are their Gurus, it is presumed that they might have sought their Gurus' blessings for the end of the drought. The rains began in March 1784 and slowly the drought conditions improved. Since the Sikhs minted their coins in the names of their Gurus and since they had great reverence for their coins, it is quite likely that they sought their Gurus' blessings by placing the leaf on their coins as a symbol of fertility and prosperity. Even otherwise in northern India, green leaves are tied at the door of a house where the birth of a baby is expected; it is a symbol of fertility and prosperity. Although this presumption is based on circumstantial evidence drawn from the *chalisa* famine, it is plausible that this horrific event and its memory led the grateful Sikhs to place the leaf motif on the Sikh coins on a permanent basis as a token of their thanksgiving. However, the subject remains open for further speculation. Still, this conjecture has drawn the support of Hans Herrli who writes:

Various Leaf Motifs on Sikh Coins

The following selection of leaves occurring on the coins of Amritsar, the mint where the leaf symbol originated, shows clearly that in many or even in most of the cases the Sikh die-cutters did not at all try to show the leaf of a particular botanically classifiable plant, but simply the general idea of a leaf. The extremely varying forms of the leaf may support an interpretation of the mark proposed by Surinder Singh. He sees in the leaf a general fertility symbol adopted after one of the great famines that regularly afflicted North India.[148]

The Place of Akal Takht in Sikh Polity
as Observed from Sikh Coins

Guru Arjan Dev completed the *Granth Sahib* in August 1604 and summed up the essence thereof as:

In this dish are placed three things—Truth, Harmony and Wisdom. These are seasoned with the name of God which is the basis of all. Who ever eats and enjoys it shall be saved.[149]

Guru Arjan had anticipated the coming of difficult times in the near future. He had started living, advocating the spiritual life and worldly living as two aspects of a single reality. He erected lofty buildings, wore fine clothes, kept fine horses, and maintained retainers in attendance. The Sikhs venerated the Guru to such an extent that he was called Sacha Padshah.[150] In April 1606 Guru Arjan was summoned to Lahore by Jahangir who wanted to convert him to Islam, or otherwise close down his organization.[151] He was accused of various crimes and made to undergo extreme forms of physical torture. Shortly before his demise as a result of this torture, Guru Arjan sent a message to his Sikhs regarding his son Hargobind: Let him sit fully armed on his throne and maintain an army to the best of his ability.[152]

At the time of the ceremony of succession, Guru Hargobind wore two swords, one on each side, declaring that one represents 'mirī', his temporal kingdom, and the other represents 'pīrī', his spiritual kingdom.[153] Thus, 'mirī' and 'pīrī', a new organizational concept of placing both the spiritual and the temporal aspects in the same person yet dealt with separately, came into existence. This institution was further developed under Guru Gobind Singh; at the time of his demise he placed 'pīrī', his spiritual sovereignty, in the *Granth*, hereafter called the *Guru Granth Sahib*, and his 'mirī', i.e. his temporal sovereignty, with the Khalsa, hereafter called the Khalsa Panth.[154] Guru Hargobind inherited 52 body guards, 700 horses, 300 horsemen, and 60 gunners.[155] In 1606, in front of the Harimandir, Guru Hargobind raised a 12-foot-high platform, named the Akal Takht, i.e. God's throne, on the lines of the Mughal throne.[156] It was constructed by Bhai Buddha and Bhai Gurdas with all reverence.[157] The sanction of such a throne and the maintenance of an army have been expressly mentioned in the last message of Guru Arjan as stated above, and the allegation that Guru Hargobind brought about a complete transformation of a passive religious sect to a militant religious sect is not correct. The latter had come into existence when the need for it arose due to the hostile attitude of the ruling emperor towards the Sikh community and its Gurus. Guru Hargobind also introduced the custom of beating the drum as an attribute of his sovereignty, a practice which was prevalent among the Mughals. He treated the Harimandir as the seat of his spiritual sovereignty and the Akal Takht as the seat of his temporal sovereignty. As the Sikh community developed, it adopted quite a few Mughal traditions and practices, but their essence has been according to the Sikh faith and ethos and hence remained radically different from the characteristics of the Mughal institutions.

Early every morning he used to go to the Harimandir, heard the '*Jap Jī*' and the '*Asa Di Var*', and thereafter preached to his Sikhs. In the afternoon he would sit on the Akal Takht, where he administered justice like a king in court, accepted presents, awarded honours, and gave out punishments. Stories of deathless bravery were narrated and ballads of unrivalled courage were sung: the most famous bard was Abdullah.[158] In his first *hukamnama* Guru Hargobind called upon his followers to bring offerings of arms and horses. Thus, the Guru created a government of his own like that of Mughals. The Sikhs came to occupy a kind of separate state within the Mughal state, the position of which was securely established by the fiscal policy of Guru Amar Das and Guru Arjan and his own system of a regular standing army.[159] Guru Hargobind fought six fairly fierce battles (1633 to 1638) with the Mughal officials. Finding no end thereto insight, and these battles being a great strain on his resources of both men and material, he moved to a place near present-day Bilaspur, named it Kiratpur, and spent the rest of his days there till his demise in 1649.[160] Nihar Ranjan Ray very correctly summed-up that Guru Nanak laid down the main planks of the platform on which the edifice of Sikh society was to be built. The later Gurus walked on these planks and few of them—Guru Arjan, Guru Hargobind, and Guru Gobind Singh—strengthened them by buttressing and adding new dimensions to them.[161]

By the time of Guru Gobind Singh, the Sikh community had been all but transformed from a purely religious group to a highly organized body of men and women within the Punjab, militant in spirit, and determined to meet any challenge to their faith and their society, a challenge that came not only from the Mughals but also from the Hindu rajas, perhaps more from the latter.[162] The integration of the temporal and spiritual aspects seems to have been the most significant contribution of the Sikh Gurus to the Sikh way of life.

From 1644 onwards, Guru Hargobind's successor Gurus did not stay in Amritsar and spent their time mostly in the Shivalik Hills, i.e. from 1644 till 1704, when Guru Gobind Singh had to leave Anandpur Sahib, after a long siege by the combined forces of the Mughal governors and Hindu hill rajas in 1704. The Akal Takht, popularly called Akal Bunga, remained unused and dormant for almost a century till the Sikhs were able to assert themselves again against the might of the Mughals and the Afghans. The period from the death of Guru Gobind Singh till the permanent occupation of Lahore in 1765 is marked by instances of the extreme torture of Sikh men, women, and children. All sorts of inhuman and tortuous methods were adopted by the Mughal rulers with the intent to literally annihilate them by either conversion to Islam or by execution. But the spirit breathed in his Sikhs by Guru Gobind Singh gave them exemplary and death-defying courage, tempered with compassion for the weak. This period from 1708 to 1765 is the golden period of the struggle and development of Sikh society into a Sikh nation under extremely trying circumstances. Certain institutions were developed in the midst of persistent enemy attacks. For instance, Sikhs facing extreme pressure and persecution by Samad Khan, Zakariya Khan, Muin-ul-Mulk, and other Mughal officers, moved out from their villages and towns and sought refuge in the Lukhi jungles and the Malwa desert.[163] Since their women and children were not spared, they took them to their hideouts. With the passage of time, they were able to hold their own with their defence-oriented guerrilla tactics and successfully planned intrusions into the Mughal territories. A popular saying sums up the situation: the government rules by the day and the Khalsa rules by the night.[164]

The Sikhs were firmly established in their areas after the close of the first quarter of the eighteenth century. They were regular visitors to Amritsar during Baisakhi and Diwali. They used to meet each other, discuss their common problems and even mutual animosities, which could be sorted out in a soothing atmosphere or by the intervention of other *sardars*. They would then assemble at the Akal Takht, where after some religious ceremony they would choose the senior and the most respected *sardar* as the leader and pass certain resolutions, called *gurmatas*. This assembly has been variously called the general assembly, national council and so on. These *gurmatas* were invariably passed unanimously and without any vote of dissent. Some noteworthy features of the assemblies at the Akal Takht were: (i) All those who attended the assembly were equal to each other and each had an equal right to participate in the deliberations; (ii) All private animosities ceased among those assembled at the Akal Takht and those who willingly sacrificed their personal feelings at the altar of the general good after the *gurmata* was passed; (iii) Every one, irrespective of whether he had spoken for or against the issue when it was debated, considered it his religious duty to abide by it. There is not a single case known where this was not done and some *sardars* did not participate in the fight against the Mughals or the Afghans.[165] European travellers such as John Malcom and George Forster have given detailed accounts of the independence of expression among the participants and noted that after the passing of the *gurmata*, they forgot their private feuds and rendered service to the commonwealth with extreme devotion.[166]

A few important *gurmatas* are noted below:

(a) In 1733, conferring the title of nawab on Kapur Singh.
(b) In 1745, to recognize 25 organized groups of Sikhs to resist persecution and to carry on raids against the Mughal strongholds.
(c) In 1747, *gurmata* passed to erect the fort Ram Rauni in Amritsar.
(d) In 1748, *gurmata* passed to establish the Dal Khalsa and to choose Jassa Singh Ahluwalia as the leader of the Dal.
(e) In 1753, *gurmata* passed to recognize the system of *rakhi* that had been instituted by the *misls*.[167]

A very important *gurmata* was passed in 1765 on Baisakhi. The jubilation over their victory and the festivities of Baisakhi went on for about a month; thereafter the *sardars* sat down at the Akal Takht to attend to the common problems faced by the community. The *gurmata* unanimously passed declared their complete independence and the assumption of sovereignty. They resolved to regain their old territories and acquire new ones wherever possible. They also decided to issue a coin in the name of the Gurus as a mark of their sovereignty.[168] The Sikhs decided to occupy the capital city of Lahore and the Bhangi chiefs Lehna Singh, Gulab Singh, and Sobha Singh marched to Lahore and occupied the city without any serious resistance and parceled the town amongst themselves in May 1765.

It may be noted here that Guru Gobind Singh while at Nanded realized the hostility of the entire Mughal court towards him and the helplessness of the emperor to take any action against Wazir Khan, the *faujdar* of Sirhind.[169] He also realized that it might not be possible for him to leave for the Punjab. Banda Bahadur, a Bairagi, became his ardent disciple and the Guru sent him to the Punjab with his directions; Banda Bahadur was assisted by five senior Sikhs as advisers and about two dozen soldiers to reorganize the depressed Sikh community and to strive to wrest back the lost territories.[170] He defeated Wazir Khan and occupied the entire *faujdari* of Sirhind and the surrounding territories where he established his own *thanas* and set up the initial Sikh state.[171] The Sikhs made a seal for the state and also issued silver rupee coins as a symbol of their sovereignty. The legend on the seal was: '*Deg Teg Fateh O Nusrat Baidrang, Yaft Uz Nanak Guru Gobind Singh*', meaning that *Degh* the economic resources, *Tegh* the strength of sword arm, with unrestrained help, *Yaft Uz*, received from Guru Nanak to Guru Gobind Singh.[172] This seems to be based on the couplet of Guru Gobind Singh's writings: '*Degh Tegh Jug Me Dohon Chalen, Rakh Lo Moi Aaap Awar Na Dalen*.' This means that both my free kitchen and my sword should prevail in the world, preserve me my Lord, and let none trample me.[173] The coin bore the legend:

Obverse   *Sikka Zad Bar Har Do Alam Teg-i-Nanak Wahib Ast,*
            Fateh Gobind Singh Shah-i-Shahan Fazl Sacha Sahib Ast.
Reverse   *Zarb Ba Aman-ul-Dahar Masawarat Shahr-i-Zinat,*
            Al Takht Khalsa Mubarak Bakht.[174]

Meaning a coin has been struck in both the worlds herein and hereafter under the guarantee of Guru Nanak's double-edged sword, the victory of Guru Gobind Singh, King of Kings, has been achieved with the grace of Sacha Sahib. Minted at a place of perfect peace, picture of a beautiful city where the illustrious throne of the Khalsa is to be located.

After the occupation of Lahore, the Sikhs issued a coin dated AD 1785/1822 Sambat. The legend for the obverse was taken from the Khalsa seal made in the time of Banda Bahadur.

Obverse   *Deg Teg Fateh O Nusrat Baidrang,*
            Yaft Uz Nanak Guru Gobind Singh

Since there was no reverse on the Khalsa seal, they took the existing legend as on the reverse of the Mughal coins, i.e. *Zarb Dar-ul-Salatnat Lahore Jalus Maiminat Manoos*, meaning Capital City of Lahore Auspicious and Prosperous Reign. After about 10 years, the Sikhs were able to locate a rupee coin of Banda Bahadur from somewhere in Amritsar. They brought out a Sikh coin from Amritsar with the legend:

Obverse   *Sikka Zad Bar Har Do Alam Shah Nanak Wahib Ast,*
            Fateh Sahi Guru Gobind Singh Shah-i-Shahan Fazl
            Sacha Sahib Ast.
Reverse   *Zarb Sri Amritsar Jioe Takht Akal Bakht Jalus Maiminat*
            Manus.

Meaning coined at Sri Amritsar Jioe, Reign of Illustrious Akal Takht Auspicious
and Prosperous. The Sikhs found that the legend on the reverse of the coins of
Banda Bahadur could not be used as such, as they had a proper city from where
it was being minted, the city of Amritsar being the most sacred city for the Sikhs.
In place of the Takht Khalsa, they gave this honour and authority to the Akal
Takht, which was a place revered next to the Harimandir Sahib. This legend was
continued by Ranjit Singh and his successors on the Sikh coins issued from
Amritsar till the annexation of the Sikh state in 1849 by the British (see Plate II).
It is to be noted that the Sikhs gave the place for the Khalsa Takht to the Akal
Takht, a place higher in constitutional hierarchy to the temporal rulers. It was
this authority of the Akal Takht, inscribed on the reverse of the Sikh coins, under
which Maharaja Ranjit Singh was called upon to appear before the Akal Takht
over some social misdemeanor and was awarded a punishment which he accepted
in complete humility.[175]

Mughal Coins Countermarked
with the Sikh Khanda Ensign

Countermarked Mughal and Suri coins have come to notice. C.H. Biddulph states
that the countermarks were Persian in origin and had been affixed to particular
coins to mark the periods of occupation of either Kabul or Qandahar by their
commanders, following encounters with the Suris in the period when the Mughal
Emperor Humayun had been defeated and had lost his kingdom to Sher Shah
Suri.[176] The countermark was generally in the form of an embossed word *Raij*
within an incuse circle. *Raij* denotes the prevalence of the coin as legal tender.[177]
    The countermark on the Durrani coins invariably has the mark *Raij* on them,
with a date or the regnal year. In a few cases, the word '*Sahib*' (correct, true,
sound, genuine) has been used. These countermarks are contained in cartouches
of different shapes. These are smaller and neater in execution than the countermarks
on Mughal coins. These appear to have been fixed by the Durranis themselves
or by their allies, primarily the Rohillas. They issued coins in the name of the
Durranis even after the Durranis had left India.[178] Similarly, the cis-Sutlej states of
Patiala, Nabha, Jind, and Malerkotla continued to strike coins pertaining to the
fourth year of Ahmad Shah Abdali.[179]
    The Kashmir Valley remained cut off from the rest of the world during the
winter months when the mountain passes were blocked with heavy snow until
the nineteenth century. Coins were in vogue from Ashokan times onwards for

PLATE III: MUGHAL COINS COUNTERMARKED WITH THE SIKH *KHANDA* ENSIGN

| OBVERSE | REVERSE | | OBVERSE | REVERSE |

ENLARGED VERSIONS

AURANGZEB COIN
AD 1698

SHAH ALAM I COIN
AD 1709

taxes levied on winter industries.[180] According to Whitehead, Kashmir rupees were countermarked by the rulers due to the discrepancies in the regnal and the Hijri years and to assure the people of the authenticity of the coins and to guarantee their unrestricted circulation.[181]

Countermarked Sikh coins both copper and silver are available in Kashmir. It is presumed that these were countermarked in Afghanistan at the time when merchants were being taxed on the money carried through the country. Another likely explanation is that these were countermarked by the Sikhs when they took their currency into the Kashmir Valley in 1819 AD and where it remained in use for many years. Sikh copper coins from Dera Ghazi Khan and Dera Ismail Khan (Derajat) had the word 'raij' inscribed on the coin at the minting stage.[182]

The Sikhs seem to have countermarked the Mughal coins with their symbol of *khanda* and not with the prevalent symbols of the *raij* and *sahib*. These countermarked silver rupee coins of the later Mughals are available in Peshawar and the surrounding areas. Bernd Becker, a coin collector who has given me photocopies of these coins in his collection, considers them to have been countermarked by Banda Bahadur before he could issue his own Sikh coinage. There are no accounts available as to who, when, and where these Mughal coins were countermarked by the Sikhs with their *khanda* symbol. The Sikh coins were issued from Peshawar for a few years by Prince Naunihal Singh, grandson of Maharaja Ranjit Singh, who was commanding the Sikh forces under the general guidance of Hari Singh Nalwa for few years, i.e. AD 1833 to 1835. The Sikhs, however, had invaded Peshawar in 1772 and thereafter occupied it for various spells. It is presumed that the Sikhs might have countermarked the Mughal coins with *khanda* between 1772 and 1833 in order to treat it as Sikh currency (see Plate III). The smudge mark on the reverse is due to the pressure used in the marking of the *Khanda* sign.

Since these coins are available in and around the Peshawar area, it appears more likely that the Sikhs before they struck their own coins from Peshawar may have been stamping the Mughal coins in order to treat them as Khalsa coinage.

NOTES

1. Ganda Singh, *Life of Banda Singh Bahadur*, Amritsar: Khalsa College, 1935, pp. 80-5.
2. *Akhbar-i-Darbar-i-Mualla*, old historical records, Jaipur, Newsletter dated 9 January 1711, translated and edited version available in *Panjab Past & Present*, vol. XVIII (II), October 1984, Patiala: Punjabi University, p. 51.
3. Ganda Singh, *Banda Singh Bahadur*, op. cit., pp. 90-9.
4. William Irvine, *Later Mughals*, pp. 98-9.
5. Hari Ram Gupta, *History of Sikhs*, vol. II, p. 17.
6. Elliot and Dowson, *The History of India*, vol. VII, pp. 423-4.
7. Hari Ram Gupta, *History of Sikhs*, vol. II, op. cit., p. 22.
8. Elliot and Dowson, op. cit., vol. VII, pp. 456-7.

9. Ganda Singh, *Banda Singh Bahadur*, op. cit., p. 205.

10. (i)   Ibid., p. 233
    (ii) Hari Ram Gupta, op. cit., p. 35.
    (iii) William Irvine, *Later Mughals*, op. cit., p. 319.
    (iv) Khafi Khan, *Muntakhab-ul-Lubab*; Elliot and Dowson, *History of India*, Delhi: Low Priced Publications, p. 457.

11. M.L. McGregor, *History of Sikhs*, vol. I, Allahabad: R.S. Publishing House, 1979, pp. 113-14.

12. J.D. Cunningham, *History of Sikhs*, New Delhi: S. Chand & Co., 1972, p. 80; Bhagat Singh, *History of Sikh Misls*, Patiala: Punjabi University, 1993, p. 33; Hari Ram Gupta, *History of Sikhs*, vol. III, 1978, p. 40.

13. Hari Ram Gupta, *History of Sikhs*, op. cit., p. 44.

14. Ibid., p. 44.

15. Ibid., p. 45.

16. Ibid., p. 47.

17. (i) Rattan Singh Bhangu, *Prachin Panth Prakash*, edited by Bhai Vir Singh, Amritsar: Wazir Hind Press, pp. 210-17.
    (ii) Hari Ram Gupta, op. cit., p. 47.

18. (i) Ibid., pp. 217-18.
    (ii) Giani Gian Singh, *Shamsher Khalsa*, Sialkot: Alharuf Guru Khalsa, 1892, pp. 120-1.

19. Hari Ram Gupta, *History of Sikhs*, vol. II, p. 54; George Forster, *A Journey from Bengal to England*, vol. I, Punjab: Languages Department, rpt., 1980, p. 313.
    The Sikh force appeared in arms at the period of Nadir Shah's return from Delhi, when the Persian army, encumbered with spoil, and regardless of order, was attacked in the rear by detached predatory parties of Sikh cavalry, who occasionally fell upon the baggage guards, and acquired a large plunder.

20. Teja Singh and Ganda Singh, *A Short History of the Sikhs*, Patiala: Punjabi University, 1952, p. 118.

21. Hari Ram Gupta, *History of Sikhs*, vol. II, op. cit., p. 72.

22. Ibid., p. 79.

23. Ibid., p. 78.

24. Ibid., p. 82.

25. Ibid., p. 88.

26. Ibid., p. 94.

27. Ibid., pp. 110-11.

28. Ibid., p. 115.

29. (i) Ali-ud-din Mufti, *Ibratnama*, Sikh History Research Library (SHR), Accession no. 1277, Amritsar: Khalsa College, 112 (a).
    (ii) Teja Singh and Ganda Singh, *A Short History of the Sikhs*, op. cit., p. 140.

30. (i) Hari Ram Gupta, *History of Sikhs*, vol. II, p. 121.
    (ii) Indu Banga, *Agrarian System of the Sikhs*, New Delhi: Manohar, 1978, p. 29, note 79.

31. (i) Hari Ram Gupta, *History of Sikhs*, vol. II, p. 131.
    (ii) Bhagat Singh, *History of Sikh Misls*, Patiala: Punjabi University, 1993, p. 43.

32. Ibid., p. 183.

33. Ibid., p. 192.

34. Hari Ram Gupta, *History of Sikhs*, vol. II, op. cit., p. 174.

35. Tahmas Khan Miskin, *Tazkira-i-Tahmas Miskin*, 1780, as quoted by Hari Ram Gupta, *History of Sikhs*, vol. II, op. cit., p. 169.

36. Hari Ram Gupta, op. cit., p. 171.

37. Ibid., p. 173. Hari Ram Gupta bases this on the authority of Miskin, Khushwaqt Rai, and Ali-ud-din.
38. Ibid., pp. 40 and 306.
   Aqil Das of Jandiala was the guru of the dissenting sect of the Niranjanis, whose ancestors were Sikhs, but he was vehemently opposed to the Sikhs and had always aided the enemies of the Sikhs. He invited Ahmad Shah and gave away the location of the Sikh camp to the Afghans.
39. Sohan Lal Suri, *Daftar*, I, pp. 46-7, as quoted by Hari Ram Gupta, op. cit., p. 174.
40. James Browne, *History of the Origin and Progress of the Sikhs* (India Tracts), London: East India Company, 1788, p. vii. Reprint *Indian Studies Past & Present*, vol. II, Calcutta 1960-1, p. 555.
41. Both Hari Ram Gupta and Ganda Singh state that Budh Singh and Ajaib Singh were natives of Lahore and the authors of *Risala-i-Nanak Shah* written in Devanagari. Browne met them in Delhi in 1783 and persuaded them to let him have a translation of this manuscript in the Persian language, abridging it as much as possible without injuring its essential purpose. Browne considered it extremely defective in the regular continuation of dates and thus not deserving the name of a historical account.
42. James Browne was sent by Warren Hastings, in 1782, to Lucknow to meet Nawab Wazir Asaf-ud-Daula and thereafter proceed to the Mughal court at Delhi, with his recommendations to watch the interests of the British East India Company. Warren Hastings left India in February 1785 and immediately thereafter Browne was recalled by the acting Governor-General. It was during his stay of about three years in India that Browne came in contact with Budh Singh and Ajaib Singh and wrote his account *The Sikhs upto March 1785* and this was published in 1787.
43. Malcolm, *Sketch of the Sikhs, their Origin, Customs and Manners*, Chandigarh: Vinay Publishers, 1981, p. 75; Mountstuart Elphinstone, *An Account of the Kingdom of Kabul*, vol. II, London, 1815, p. 289; J.D. Cunningham, *A History of Sikhs*, New Delhi: S. Chand & Co., 1972, p. 89; Muhammad Latif, *History of Punjab*, Ludhiana: Kalyani Publishers, 1989, p. 230; G.C. Narang, *Transformation of Sikhism*, Lahore: New Book Society, 1945, p. 236.
44. Hari Ram Gupta, op. cit., pp. 144, 145 and 175. He cites a number of Persian sources in support of this claim.
45. Hari Ram Gupta, 'The First Sikh Coin of Lahore', *Proceedings of the Indian History Congress*, Modern Section, 1938, p. 430.
46. Ibid., pp. 1678, based on the accounts of Ali-ud-din, Sohan Lal Suri, Shamsher Khalsa, and others.
47. Ghulam Ali Khan Azad, *Khazana-e-Amira*, Kanpur: Newal Kishore Press, 1871, p. 114.
   The Sikh nation residing in the Punjab, who from the earliest times have been a source of mischief and trouble, are bigoted enemies of the Musalmans. It is observed that in spite of the fact that Shah had so many times overrun India, these people lacking in foresight have raised the standard of rebellion and disturbance and have killed his viceroy at Lahore. They raised a person named Jassa Singh from amongst themselves to the status of a King, and like a demon, they made him sit on the throne of Jamshid, and blackened the face of the coin with his name. Having taken possession of the city of Lahore and its vicinity, they molested God's creatures in general and Muslims in particular. Hearing this news, Shah Durrani, according to his established practice, again moved towards India.
48. Ganda Singh, 'History of Origin and Progress of the Sikhs by James Browne', *Indian Studies, Past and Present*, vol. II, 1960-1, p. 555. .
49. Ibid., p. 555.

50. Ibid., 581; N.K. Sinha, *Rise of Sikh Power*, Calcutta: A. Mukherjee & Co., 1973, p. 55.

51. Hari Ram Gupta, 'The First Sikh Coin of Lahore', op. cit., pp. 428, 432.

52. Ibid., p. 431, footnote: 'Dr. Sinha, without consulting any of the works quoted above in this connection, jumps to the conclusion that these coins were not struck at all, and refers to no authorities on whom he bases his statement at page 94 of *The Rise of the Sikh Power*.'

53. N.K. Sinha, *Rise of the Sikh Power*, op. cit., p. 55:
It must be admitted that it is difficult to deny the fact of coinage, and I have nowhere done it. But even if these coins were struck, would it be proper to assert that they were authorised official issues of the Sikh commonwealth?

54. Hari Ram Gupta, 'The First Sikh Coin of Lahore', op. cit., p. 431.

55. Ibid.

56. S.S. Bal, 'The Sikh Struggle for Independence and the Place of Sovereignty in Sikh Polity, *The Mediaeval Indian State*, Chandigarh: Panjab University, 1968, p. 128; G.S. Chhabra, *Advanced History of Punjab*, vol. I, Jullandhar: New Academic Publishing Co., 1968, p. 39.

57. N.K. Sinha, op. cit., p. 55.

58. *Akhbar-i-Darbar-i-Mualla*, Old Historical Records, Jaipur Account, dated 6 July 1710, p. 39.

59. *Hadiqat-al-Aqalim* by Murtaza Hussain, Aligarh: Aligarh Muslim University, p. 148.

60. The seal imprint bears the legend '*Degh Tegh Fateh*' adopted on Sikh coins in 1765 and onwards. The legend on the few rupees traced so far is that of '*Sikka Zad bar har do alam*', adopted on the Amritsar rupee of 1775 and onwards.

61. *Khazana-e-Amira*, see note 47 above.

62. Ganesh Das Badhera, *Char Bagh-i-Punjab* (ed. Kirpal Singh), Amritsar: Khalsa College, 1965, pp. 130-1.

63. Khushwaqt Rai, *Kitab-i-Tarikh-i-Punjab*, folio 104, quoted by Hari Ram Gupta, op. cit., p. 177.

64. Ahmad Yadgar, *Tarikh-i-Salatin-i-Afghana*, p. 173, as quoted by Hari Ram Gupta, op. cit., p. 177.

65. Ganda Singh, *Sardar Jassa Singh Ahluwalia*, Patiala: Punjabi University, 1990, p. 110.

66. Lepel Griffin, *Rajas of the Punjab*, Punjab: Languages Department, 1970, p. 461.

67. Brigadier Sukhjit Singh in his letter dated 20 May 1980 (in reply to my letter dated 21 March 1980 regarding the presence of Jassa Singh's coin with the Kapurthala royal family).

68. Hari Ram Gupta, op. cit., p. 167.

69. Hans Herrli, *The Coins of the Sikhs*, Nagpur: Indian Coin Society, 1993, p. 168. Hans Herrli has stated that the complete *sikka zad bar simno-tilla Shah Shujah Armini, Nur-i-Chashan Lord Burnes Khak-i-pa-i-kampani* by Sultan Muhammad Khan bin Musa Khan Durrani has been taken by him from an article in *JRASB*, vol. LVII, no. 1 (1888) by C.J. Rodgers.

70. Jatti Ram Gupta, 'Dussehra Festival in the Punjab during Sikh Rule 1800-1849', *Sikh Review*, 1970, pp. 41-3.

71. N.K. Sinha, op. cit., p. 54.

72. Ibid., p. 55.

73. Khushwant Singh, *History of the Sikhs*, vol. I, Delhi: Oxford University Press, 1987, pp. 152-3.

74. N.K. Sinha, *Rise of the Sikh Power*, op. cit., p. 54.

75. Ibid., p. 227.

76. Khushwant Singh, *History of the Sikhs*, vol. I, op. cit., pp. 160-1.
77. K.S. Thapar, 'Gurmata, Democracy in Practice', *Panjab Past & Present*, vol. IX, pt. II, October 1975, Patiala, pp. 284-9.
78. (i)   Hari Ram Gupta, *History of Sikhs*, op. cit., p. 227.
    (ii)   K.S. Thapar, 'Gurmata', Patiala: P.P.P., vol. IX, October 1975, p. 289.
    (iii) Harjinder Singh Dilgeer, *Hukmnamas of the Akal Takht*, Punjab History Congress, March 1982, Punjab University, Patiala, p. 175.
    (iv)   C.J. Rodgers, 'On the Coins of the Sikhs', *Journal of the Asiatic Society of Bengal*, Calcutta, vol. L, 1881, p. 79.
    (v)   G.C. Narang, op. cit., p. 251.
    (vi)   Muhammad Latif, op. cit., p. 287.
    (vii) J.D. Cunningham, op. cit., p. 93.
79. Hari Ram Gupta, *History of Sikhs,* vol. II, op. cit., pp. 228-9.
80. (i)   Ibid., p. 230.
    (ii)   J.D. Cunningham, *History of Sikhs*, p. 94.
    (iii) G.C. Narang, *Transformation of Sikhism*, op. cit., p. 251.
    (iv)   Muhammad Latif, *History of Punjab*, op. cit., p. 287.
    (iv)   N.K. Sinha, *Rise of Sikh Power*, op. cit., p. 45.
    (v)   G.L. Chopra, *Punjab as a Sovereign State*, Hoshiarpur: V.V. Research Institute (VVRI), op. cit., p. 153.
    (vi)   C.J. Rodgers, 'On the Coins of the Sikhs', op. cit., p. 79.
81. William Irwine, *Later Mughals*, op. cit., p. 110.
82. Hari Ram Gupta, 'The First Sikh Coin of Lahore', *Proceedings of the Indian History Congress*, Modern Section 1938, p. 428.
83. (i)   C.J. Rodgers, 'On the Coins of the Sikhs', op. cit., p. 80.
    (ii)   Ken Wiggins and Stan Goron, 'Gold and Silver Coinage of Sikhs', Inaugural Address, International Colloquium, I.J.R.N.S., Anjaneri, Nasik, 1984, p. 128.
84. (i)   J.D. Cunningham, *A History of Sikhs*, op. cit., p. 94.
    (ii)   Muhammad Latif, *History of Punjab*, op. cit., p. 287.
    (iii) G.C. Narang, *Transformation of Sikhism*, op. cit., p. 251.
    (iv)   G.L. Chopra, *Punjab as a Sovereign State*, op. cit., p. 153.
85. J.D. Cunningham, *A History of Sikhs*, op. cit., Appendix IX, p. 312, Appendix XII, p. 315.
86. H.R. Gupta, *History of Sikh Gurus*, op. cit., 1973 p. 182.
87. (i)   Max Arthur Macauliffe, *The Sikh Religion*, vol. V, op. cit., p. 311.
    (ii)   Dharam Pal Ashta, 'Poetry of Dasam Granth', Ph.D. thesis, Chandigarh: Panjab University Library, p. 26.
88. H.R. Gupta, *History of Sikh Gurus*, op. cit., p. 190.
89. Ibid., p. 180.
90. Dharam Pal Ashta, 'Poetry of Dasam Granth', op. cit., p. 26..
91. Ganda Singh, *Hukmnamas*, Patiala: Punjabi University, 1985, p. 149.
92. Foreign Department, General Report, *Administration of Punjab Territories, 1849-51*, Calcutta, 1856, p. 34.
93. Surinder Singh, 'Nabha State Coinage and Patiala State Nazrana Coins', *Panjab University Research Bulletin*, April 1990 and October 1990.
94. William Irwine, *Later Mughals*, op. cit., p. 110.
95. Hari Ram Gupta, *History of Sikhs*, vol. II, op. cit., p. 230.
96. Bikramjit Hasrat, *The Punjab Papers*, Hoshiarpur: VVRI, 1970, p. 147.
97. H.R. Gupta, *History of Sikh Gurus*, op. cit., pp. 237-8.

98. *History of the Punjab and the Rise, Progress, and Present Conditions of the Sect and Nation of the Sikhs*, London: Allen & Co., 1846 (based on the memoirs of Captain Murray), p. 236.

99. William Irvine, *Later Mughals*, op. cit., p. 110.

100. Bhagat Singh, *Sikh Polity*, New Delhi: Oriental Publishers & Distributors, 1978, p. 200. As the tradition goes, once his Prime Minister Dhian Singh told the Maharaja that as he was their ruler he should not tie a cloth round his waist like the humble servants. The Maharaja inquired, 'In whose name is the coin struck?' Dhian Singh told it was in the name of Guru Nanak. The Maharaja smilingly told him that the ruler was the one in whose name the coins were struck and Ranjit Singh was only the humble servant of the Guru. . . . He considered himself to be the 'Kakur' (dog) at the door of the Gurus and the Panth. He is also said to have called himself a 'rapita' (reporter cum watchman).

101. (i)   M.A. Macauliffe, *The Sikh Religion*, vol. V, op. cit., p. 245.
     (ii) Gulshan Lall Chopra, *The Punjab as a Sovereign State*, op. cit., p. 153.
     (iii) S.S. Grewal and S.S. Bal, *Guru Gobind Singh*, Punjab University, 1967, p. 239.
     (iv) Parmeshwari Lal Gupta, *Coins of India*, New Delhi: National Book Trust, 1969, p. 147.
     (v)   N.K. Sinha, *Rise of Sikh Power*, op. cit., p. 56.
     (vi) Patwant Singh, *The Sikhs*, New Delhi: Harper Collins India, pp. 75, 91, 105.

102. J.D. Cunningham, *A History of the Sikhs*, op. cit., p. 94.

103. Lepel Griffin, *Rajas of Punjab*, Punjab: Languages Department, rpt., 1970, vol. II, p. 466.

104. C.J. Rodgers, 'On the Coins of the Sikhs', op. cit., p. 79.

105. C.J. Rodgers, *Catalogue of Coins in the Government Museum Lahore*, Calcutta, 1891, p. 1.

106. C.J. Brown, *Coins of India*, Heritage of India Series, London: Oxford University Press, 1922, pp. 106-7.

107. Gulshan Lall Chopra, *The Punjab as a Sovereign State*, op. cit., p. 153.

108. Hari Ram Gupta, *History of Sikhs*, vol. II, op. cit., p. 2302.

109. I had the privilege of meeting the late Hari Ram Gupta many times at his residence in Ferozepur and at my residence in Jullandhar from 1980 to 1984. During this period I received from him valuable guidance in my understanding of Sikh history. But Hari Ram Gupta had not seen and studied Sikh coins and hence expressed his ignorance of them from a numismatic angle.

110. Parmeshwari Lal Gupta, *Coins of India*, The Land and the People Series, New Delhi: National Book Trust, 1969, p. 147.

111. Parmeshwari Lal Gupta and Sanjay Garg, *The Coins of Dal Khalsa and Lahore Darbar*, Chandigarh: Punjab Government, 1989, p. 17.

112. Bikramjit Hasrat, *Life and Times of Ranjit Singh*, Hoshiarpur: VVRI, 1977, p. 42.

113. Bhagat Singh, *Sikh Polity*, New Delhi: Oriental Publishers & Distributors, 1978, p. 83. In my meeting with him he stated that his study of Sikh coins was restricted to written accounts and did not extend to actual coins.

114. G.S. Chhabra, *Advanced History of the Punjab*, Jullandhar: New Academic Publishing Co., 1968, vol. II, p. 453.

115. Hans Herrli, *The Coins of the Sikhs*, Nagpur: Indian Coin Society, 1993, pp. 31-2.

116. Ganda Singh, *Jassa Singh Ahluwalia*, Patiala: Punjabi University, 1990, p. 203. As Jassa Singh travelled to Amritsar from Fatehabad for the Diwali celebrations, he made a halt at the village of Bundela. Here he ate a piece of watermelon and while riding his horse developed a stomach ache and became unconscious. On his way to Amritsar

he passed away. It was 7 Kartik, 20 October 1783, Diwali being five days ahead on 25 October.

117. Denzil Ibbetson, *Punjab Castes*, Delhi: Low Priced Publications, 1993, p. 325.

118. Ganda Singh, *Jassa Singh Ahluwalia*, op. cit., p. 8.

119. Ibid., p. 36.

120. Ibid., p. 204.

121. Ibid., p. 160.

122. Ganesh Das, *Char Bagh-i-Punjab* (ed. Kirpal Singh), Amritsar: Khalsa College, 1965, p. 130.

123. Ibid., p. 132.

124. Ibid., p. 133.

125. Victor Jacquemont, *The Punjab Hundred Years Ago*, Punjab: Languages Department, rpt., 1971, p. 50.

126. Hans Herrli, *Coins of the Sikhs*, op. cit., p. 130.

127. Ibid., p. 16.

128. *Standard Guide to South Asian Coins and Paper Currency*, Wisconsin: Krause Publications, 1st edn., p. 113.

129. Hans Herrli, *Coins of India*, op. cit., p. 65.

130. Ibid., pp. 210-11.

131. C.J. Rodgers, 'On the Coins of the Sikhs', op. cit., p. 91.

132. W.H. Valentine, *Copper Coins of India*, New Delhi: Inter-India Publications, vol. II, p. 135.

133. C.J. Browne, *Coins of India*, op. cit., p. 107.

134. Ramchandra Kak, *Archaeological and Numismatic Section, Sri Pratap Museum, Srinagar*, Calcutta: Spink & Co., 1923, p. 152.

135. Madanjit Kaur, 'A Study of Sikh Numismatics with special reference to the Coins of Ranjit Singh', in *Maharaja Ranjit Singh*, edited by Fauja Singh and A.C. Arora, Punjabi University, Patiala, 1984, p. 337.

136. Saran Singh, 'The Formation of Sikhism and the Coins of the Sikhs', *Journal of Malaysian Numismatic Society,* Newsletter, vol. XI, nos. 3-4, 1980, p. 24.

137. R.T. Somaiya, 'Sikh Coins', Nagpur: Indian Coin Society, Newsletter no. 25, March 1994.

138. Hans Herrli, *Coins of the Sikhs*, op. cit., p. 62.

139. R.T. Somaiya, 'Sikh Coins', op. cit., Newsletter no. 25, March 1994.

140. Hari Ram Gupta, *Sikh History*, vol. II, op. cit., p. 127.

141. Hari Ram Gupta, *History of the Sikhs*, vol. III, op. cit., pp. 174-5.
    The famine of 1783: 'In April 1783, as ever famine broke out in the Punjab. In 1781 and 1782 there had been little rain and so the harvest was poor: and the winter rain of 1782-83 completely failed. Hence there was no rabi crop of April 1783. The drought which had been raging for the past two years, and had become most acute in that year became known as the Chalisa because it occurred in the year 1840 of Bikrami Sambat. So terrible was the visitation that thousands of persons died due to absolute starvation. The contemporary Harcharandas says that in April 1784 (it should be 1783), thousands of persons were lost.'

142. *Punjab Gazetteer*, Lahore, 'The san chalesa famine', 1884, p. 14.

143. *Hissar Gazetteer, 1883-4*, Lahore, 1884, p. 13.

144. Hari Ram Gupta, *History of Sikhs*, vol. IV, op. cit., p. 241.

145. Ibid., p. 355.

146. Ibid., p. 527.
147. Ibid., p. 124.
148. Hans Herrli, *The Coins of the Sikhs*, op. cit., p. 41.
149. Mansukhani, Gobind Singh, *The Quintessence of Sikhism*, Amritsar: SGPC, 1965, p. 248.
150. *Dabistan-i-Mazhab*, Mohsin Fani, tr. David Shea and Anthony Troyar, Paris, 1843, pp. 233, 234.
151. *Tuzak-i-Jahangiri* (tr. by Rodgers and Beveridge), 1996 edn., New Delhi: Munshiram Manoharlal, p. 72.
152. Max Arthur Macauliffe, *The Sikh Religion*, vol. III, New Delhi: S. Chand & Co., 3rd rpt., 1985, p. 99.
153. Macauliffe, op. cit., vol. IV, p. 2.
154. A.C. Banerjee, *The Sikh Gurus and the Sikh Religion*, New Delhi: Munshiram Manoharlal, 1983, pp. 327-8.
155. *Dabistan-i-Mazhab*, op. cit., pp. 235-6.
156. Tarlochan Singh, *Guru Tegh Bahadur*, Delhi: Gurudwara Parbandhak Committee, 1965, p. 12, fn. 16.
157. Ibid., p. 12.
158. H.R. Gupta, *History of Sikh Gurus*, New Delhi: U.C. Kapoor & Sons, 1973, p. 110.
159. Ibid., p. 110.
160. Macauliffe, *The Sikh Religion*, op. cit., p. 214.
161. Nihar Ranjan Ray, *The Sikh Gurus and Sikh Society*, New Delhi: Munshiram Manoharlal, 1975, p. 57.
162. Ibid., p. 25.
163. J.B. Cunningham, *A History of Sikhs*, New Delhi: S. Chand & Co., 1972, p. 80.
164. H.R. Gupta, op. cit. p. 45.
165. K.S. Thapar, 'Gurmata', op. cit., p. 287.
166. Ibid., p. 287.
167. K.S. Thapar, 'Gurmata: Democracy in Practice', *Punjab Past & Present*, Patiala: Punjabi University, October 1975, p. 289.
168. (i) Ibid., p. 289.
    (ii) H.R. Gupta, *History of Sikhs*, op. cit., p. 227.
169. H.R. Gupta, *Sikh Gurus*, New Delhi: Munshiram Manoharlal, 1994, p. 320.
170. Ibid., p. 321.
171. H.R. Gupta, *History of Sikhs*, vol. II, op. cit., pp. 12-14.
172. *Hukmnama* dated 12th December 1710 and another addressed to Bhai Dharam Singh, undated, reproduced in *Hukmnama*, edited and compiled by Ganda Singh, Patiala: Punjabi University, 1985, pp. 92-5.
173. Dharam Pal Ashta, 'Poetry of Dasam Granth', Ph.D. thesis, Chandigarh: Panjab University, p. 26.
174. Surinder Singh, 'Study in Sikh Coinage', Ph.D. thesis, Calcutta: Rabindra Bharati University, p. 106-7.
175. Ibid., p. 191 (Gulshan Lall Chopra, K.K. Khullar, C.J. Rodgers, Fauja Singh, Waheed-ud-din have given different accounts.)
176. C.H. Biddulph, *Journal of the Numismatic Society of India*, vol. XXV, pt. II, 1963, p. 39.
177. Ibid., p. 39.
178. Ibid., p. 40.

179. R.C. Temple, 'The Coins of the Modern Chiefs of the Punjab', *Indian Antiquary*, vol. XVIII,.
     Bombay, 1889, pp. 22-41.
180. *Rajatarangini of Kalhana*, tr. Ranjit Sitaram Pandit, New Delhi: Sahitya Akademi, Tranga III,
     1990, 103.
181. C.H. Biddulph, op. cit., p. 43.
182. Hans Herrli, *The Coins of the Sikhs*, Nagpur: Indian Coin Society, 1993, pp. 114, 158.

CHAPTER III

Sikh Coinage during the Lahore Darbar: The Period of Ranjit Singh AD 1800-1839

In the defence and recovery of their country the Sikhs displayed a courage of the most obstinate kind, and manifested a perseverance, under the pressure of calamities, which bear an ample testimony of native resource, when the common danger had roused them to action and gave but one impulse to their spirit. Should any future cause call forth the combined efforts of the Sikhs to maintain the existence of empire and religion we may see some ambitious chief led on by his genius and success, and absorbing the power of his associates, display from the ruins of their commonwealth the standard of monarchy. . . . Under such a form of government, I have little hesitation in saying that the Sikhs would be soon advanced to the first rank amongst the native princes of Hindustan, and would become a terror to the surrounding states.

GEORGE FORSTER[1]

Historical Developments upto AD 1800

The prophetic remarks in George Forster's letter of March 1783 addressed to Lord Cornwallis, the Governor-General, made during his journey from Bengal to England came true within a period of less than two decades, one such ambitious chief, Ranjit Singh, came to occupy a large part of the Punjab, including the capital Lahore in July 1799. Within two decades he had consolidated his position and held sway over the entire trans-Sutlej territories of the Punjab, Kashmir, Peshawar, Derajat, and the frontier areas.

Kanehiya Lal, a *munshi* in the pay of the British, states that Ranjit Singh held a *darbar* in AD 1800 in which he ordered the minting of silver rupee coins, with a Persian couplet in praise of the Gurus on the obverse and his own image along with the date and the place of striking on the reverse. The next day hundreds of such coins were distributed amongst the poor and the needy.[2] However, this account is incorrect. The *darbar* was held in April 1801 and it was ordered that the existing Sikh coin, with the '*Degh Tegh Fateh*' legend, should continue to be minted from Lahore.[3]

Another Sikh historian, Prem Singh Hoti, states that Ranjit Singh had a great love for his religion. Before taking important decisions, he would seek guidance from the *Guru Granth*. Ranjit Singh waived his right to issue coins in his own name in favour of Guru Nanak. 'It is supreme proof of his love for his religion that the maharaja issued the "Nanak Shahi" rupees and the "Nanak Shahi" *mohar*. On one side of these coins was Guru Nanak's figure and on the other the year of striking the coins.' Prem Singh states in a footnote, 'Specimens of these coins can be seen in the Lahore Museum.'[4]

However, this statement about the coins allegedly struck by Ranjit Singh and their being available in the Lahore Museum is not correct. My visit to the Government Museum, Lahore in 1988 revealed no such coin in the collection of Sikh coins, nor any reference in the various catalogues in the Lahore Museum to any such coins bearing the figure of Guru Nanak, as stated by Prem Singh. There is no evidence to support such a claim in the various historical and numismatic accounts of the coins struck by Ranjit Singh nor is there any such coin in the government collections nor with private collectors.

Some historians describe the ceremony of his coronation as a *darbar* but this characterization is incorrect. Ranjit Singh never took the title of Maharaja, although he was at times addressed as such. He was generally called Singh Sahib, Sarkar Khalsa, Noble Sarkar, and so on. He did not sit on a throne. He did not put his name on anything. The fort he constructed in Amritsar was called Gobind Garh and the palace he erected in Amritsar was called Ram Bagh. He did not adopt any of the formal symbols of sovereignty which the contemporary Indian rulers were then using, and this view is confirmed by most of his historians who have commented on this aspect of his governance. The theocratic zeal and democratic spirit among the Sikh masses was far too deeply rooted to allow any individual to adopt such a highly objectionable measure in those times.

Ranjit Singh consolidated his position by taking over the territories of the various *misldars*. He closed the mints run by them, and continued the minting of Sikh coins from the Lahore and Amritsar mints under his direct control. In the first decade of his rule, he brought the Sikh *sardars* under his control by persuasion, fraud, and even by force where necessary; and in the next decade he subdued the Hindu and Muslim chieftains of the hill states of Jammu, Kangra, Derajat, Qasur, Jhang, Multan, Kashmir, Peshawar, and Hazara. New mints were opened in Multan, Kashmir, Derajat, and Peshawar, but the main Sikh mints remained those located at Amritsar and Lahore. Ranjit Singh spent the next two decades consolidating his state and brought about unprecedented prosperity by encouraging commerce, trade, and agriculture.

Among the many trading centres in the Punjab were Lahore, Amritsar, Multan, and Peshawar. Amritsar was known as the commercial emporium of northern India. The Punjab exported grains, pulses, sugar, rice, *ghee*, oil, salt, silk, woollen fabrics, shawls, paper, and gold and silver articles. From Afghanistan, Central Asia, and the hill areas, the Punjab imported dry fruits, carpets, and ornamental woodworks.[5] Town duties, customs, and transit duties fetched annually a sum of 24 lakh rupees.

The big merchants did not carry money but instead issued *hundis*. Almost all the Sikh *sardars* kept their money with bankers in large towns such as Lahore, Amritsar, and Multan, and issued *hundis* whenever they needed money.[6] Before Ranjit Singh set up his treasury, he kept his money with the banker Rama Nand Sahu of Amritsar. The daily production of coins was about 8,000 rupees.[7] A hundred rupees was equal to 98½ rupees of metal and one and a half rupees was kept for expenses and profit. The annual profit of the Lahore mint was about 30,000 rupees. There were also other currencies such as the Shah Shujah rupee in Dera Ghazi Khan, the Mehrabi in Leia, the Chilki rupee in Multan, and the Zaman Shahi. These currencies were of the value of 12 to 14 *annas* of the Nanak Shahi rupee of 16 *annas*, which was of pure silver.[8]

The Myth of Moran's Coins

Ranjit Singh's personal valour, his meteoric rise to power, his mighty army, the grandeur of his court, and his conquest of large areas ruled by the Afghans have been universally acclaimed as achievements comparable with those of Mehmat Ali and Napolean Bonaparte.[9] While his courage, his simplicity, his intuitive understanding of men and matters, and his sense of justice and compassion have been widely praised, his personal life has been the subject of loose gossip and adverse comments by his historians, both European and Indian. Descriptions of his drinking bouts, his *nautch* girls, and his Muslim concubines occur in various historical accounts of the mid-nineteenth century. The Oriental princes and their aristocrats, both Muslim and non-Muslim, commonly availed of the company of singing and dancing girls, and their drinking bouts were the main source of royal entertainment.[10]

Many historians have recorded Ranjit Singh's affair with Moran and the alleged minting of coins in the name of Moran, without offering any evidence or justification of this claim. It seems fairly certain that a dancing girl called Moran attracted the attention of Ranjit Singh and he took her under his patronage. In the absence of any autobiographical accounts and other chronicles by court historians, opinions are bound to differ over the extent of Moran's hold on Ranjit Singh and her place in the affairs of the Lahore Darbar. But the alleged striking of the coins in Moran's name is a claim which could be and should have been satisfactorily established or disproved on the basis of the numismatic information which is fortunately available to us. But unfortunately no such study has been attempted except an inadequate account by C.J. Rodgers. The long period of Muslim rule in India had established certain court traditions and customs for the local princes and aristocrats. The Lahore Darbar under Ranjit Singh was no exception. The court etiquette and customs, the entertainment by singing and dancing girls, and the use of alcohol and opium were closely modelled on the customs of the Mughal court. The main entertainment then revolved around wine, and women. All the Mughal rulers and their aristocrats maintained harems; the women were grouped into various categories, such as singing and dancing girls.[11] The consumption of opium was widely prevalent.[12] The practice of unnatural love with unbearded boys called *gunchas* and *londas* was common among the Muslims.[13] Concubinage was very common among the royalty and the nobility. Courtesans, concubines, and dancing girls had a well-defined place in society and their patrons spoke very highly of them and did so without any inhibitions.[14]

Ranjit Singh was not a much-married man according to Oriental standards.[15] He had two primary wives, Mehtab Kaur and Raj Kaur. He had married about a dozen girls who had caught his fancy and who were the daughters of petty *sardars* and *zamindars*. He married a few widows of *sardars* in accordance with the *karewa* ceremony out of political necessity and social custom. He had about a couple of hundred singing and dancing girls who entertained his courtiers, *sardars*, and guests.[16] These women were also attached with European officers to keep a watch on their activities.

Moran caught Ranjit Singh's fancy sometime around 1802, and he is said to have taken a great liking to her. Historians called her by various names such as Bibi Moran, Moran Sarkar, and Maharani Moran. Syed Waheed-ud-din describes Ranjit Singh's wedding to Moran as having been conducted in accordance with the customs of courtesans, with the procession of the bridegroom's party stretching from the Lahore Fort to the Shalimar Garden, a distance of several miles.[17] The account is apparently a fanciful tale instead of historical account. Muhammad Latif states that Moran was married to Ranjit Singh according to Muslim rites and the nuptials were celebrated with great pomp and show in a *haveli*, especially purchased for her, and located between the Shahabin and the Lahori Gates.[18] This account too appears to be pure fiction. Ranjit Singh, a shrewd politician as yet not fully established and still in the first decade of his reign, was hardly likely to marry an unknown dancing girl according to Muslim rites in Amritsar, a city where the Sikh religious leaders of the Akal Takht were fairly independent of the ruler; indeed they were said to have questioned the Maharaja on some social or religious misdemeanour and were said to have even awarded a suitable punishment to him. K.K. Khullar states that during a victory feast to celebrate the conquest of Multan, Moran, a fabulous dancer of that area, performed an erotic dance to charm the victor. Ranjit Singh fell for her and she was asked to leave the vicious brothel of Multan to decorate the Maharaja's palace, and within a few months he married her.[19] However, there is no corroborating evidence to support this claim; Multan was conquered in 1818 while Moran was discarded by Ranjit Singh in 1811.[20] In all probability, the so-called marriage, if at all it took place, would have been performed in a private ceremony for sheer fun and gaiety as was done in the case of Gul Begum; here official orders were issued to Dhian

Singh, the prime minister, that none of the *sardars* and court attendants were to be present at the bungalow where singing, dancing, and drinking were the main attractions.[21] Such marriages did not give any rights to these women except the right to maintenance.

The Maharaja was very fond of celebrating Holi, and he moved about in the streets of Lahore with Moran and other such women who sat with him on his elephants while he played Holi with his subjects.[22] The people appreciated the Maharaja's way of life, but the Akal Takht authorities were said to have taken strong exception to such conduct, and summoned him before the Akal Takht and asked him to explain his behaviour. Ranjit Singh pleaded guilty to the charge and was awarded some fine as punishment. We have different accounts of this episode; some historians say that he was fined a heavy sum, which was later reduced on his protestation.[23] The actual date of this incident has not been mentioned anywhere. Whether it is true or not is debatable, but one fact emerges that the Akal Takht authorities had the right to question any violation of the religious norms, even by so exalted a personage as the Maharaja. Moran seems to have suddenly vanished from the scene within a few years and there is no mention of her anywhere thereafter. In 1836 Baron Charles Hugel, a European visitor to the Lahore Darbar, stated that Moran had been carried off to Pathankot in 1811, never to be heard of again.[24]

Most contemporary Indian chroniclers and scribes are silent about the Moran affair. Sohan Lal Suri, the court chronicler, states that in 1831, when Ranjit Singh saw William Bentinck helping Lady Bentinck out of a boat at Ropar, the Maharaja is said to have been reminded of his somewhat similar affection for Bibi Moran. Suri does not mention the Maharaja marrying Moran or striking coins in her name.[25] An account by Diwan Amarnath written in 1836-7 notes the Maharaja's great love for Moran and his having struck coins in her name at places which he had conquered.[26] There is no account of Moran by any other contemporary Indian chronicler or newswriter such as Khushwaqt Rai, Bute Shah, Mufti Ali-ud-din, Ganesh Das Badhera, and the various news writers of the Lahore Darbar.

Among the contemporary European visitors to the Punjab, Baron Charles Hugel and Henry T. Princep state that Ranjit Singh had struck coins in Moran's name, an act of great importance in India. Hugel, however, belittles the significance of the act by stating that it was done in jest against the Company Sarkar, which was generally represented as the common wife, the widow, or the mistress of the King of England.[27] In the translated work of Jacquemont, H.L.O. Garret states that Ranjit Singh married Moran and even struck coins in her name.[28] J.D. Cunningham mentions the Moran affair and states that Ranjit Singh caused coins or medals to be struck bearing her name.[29] He further states that Moran once laid a wager, as Empress Nur Jahan had done, that she would get her name engraved on the rupees. Lepel Griffin states that Ranjit Singh struck coins with her name and made an effigy in caricature of the East India Company, which in popular

Indian belief was a woman.[30] Gulshan Lall Chopra, in his note on Sikh coins, states that Ranjit Singh struck coins in Moran's name from Amritsar for the years Sambat 1861, 1862, 1863, and 1866 (i.e. AD 1804, 1805, 1806, and 1809) and her mark or symbol in the shape of a peacock tail was allowed to be inscribed on the coins.

Another feature peculiar to the alleged Moran Shahi rupees is that the first letter *alif* of the word '*Akal*' is left out.[31] Bikramjit Hasrat states that in 1803 Moran persuaded the Maharaja to commemorate their love by striking a new coin. These coins, minted at Lahore during Sambat 1860-6, i.e. AD 1803-9, bear on the reverse the effigy of a dancing girl, and the word 'Moran' in the shape of a peacock tail is imprinted on them. These were called the Moran Shahi rupees as distinguished from the Nanak Shahi rupees, and remained current till Sambat 1884, i.e. AD 1827.[32] Hasrat also states that Ranjit Singh got tired of Moran in 1809 and two years later sent her to Pathankot.[33] Muhammad Latif states that Moran obtained great ascendancy over Ranjit Singh, and under his sanction money was coined at Lahore bearing the inscription of Moran as the favourite queen of Ranjit Singh.[34] Khushwant Singh states that Ranjit Singh met Moran, a Muslim courtesan, in 1803 at a *nautch* party and fell passionately in love with her. He took her into his harem and had a coin minted in her honour, with the figure of a peacock.[35] Waheed-ud-din states that Ranjit Singh struck a coin in her name which bore the figure of a peacock in keeping with the queen's name, which is the plural of the Punjabi word for that bird and which she acquired because of her style of dancing.[36] K.K. Khullar states, 'Maharaja Ranjit Singh married Moran and commemorated the occasion by striking a gold coin in her honour and the said coin bore the figure of a she peacock on its back.'[37] Gopal Singh states that in Sambat 1861, 1862, 1863, and 1866 coins were struck which were popularly called the Moran Shahi coins, named after, it is said, Moran, the Muslim singing girl who had captivated the heart of Ranjit Singh during the early days of his reign.[38]

Besides the above-mentioned historians, a few numismatists have also stated that coins were struck in the name of Moran by Ranjit Singh. C.J. Rodgers, who was the Principal of the Normal Teachers Training College at Amritsar for over a decade after the annexation of the Lahore Darbar, carried out a study of Sikh coins. He states that the Maharaja struck coins in the name of Moran by inscribing the peacock tail as her mark. Further, the letter *alif* in the Moran Shahi rupees had been left out in the word '*Akal*' which is apparently a mint masters' error and not due to its association with Moran. These coins pertain to the years Sambat 1861, 1862, 1863, and 1866 of the Amritsar mint.[39] Rodgers also mentions Moran's coins in the *Catalogue of Coins in the Government Museum Lahore* which he prepared in 1891.[40]

C.J. Brown states that during Sambat 1861-3, first a peacock's tail and then a thumb mirror (*arsi*) appeared on the Amritsar rupees, which bear reference to

Ranjit Singh's favourite dancing girl, Moran.[41] Parmeshwari Lal Gupta similarly states that the peacock tail and the thumb mirror are symbols which represent the coins struck in Moran's name during Sambat 1861-3.[42] However, while preparing the catalogue of Sikh coins with the Sheesh Mahal Museum, Patiala, P.L. Gupta revised his opinion and considers that the so-called Moran Shahi coins were issued by some *misldar* at Amritsar and not by Ranjit Singh. He relies on Cunningham's date for the Moran affair as AD 1810, but this claim is incorrect as well; the earliest coins with the double branches pertain to Sambat 1861 and not to Sambat 1858, as stated by him. However, he states that the coins said to be Moran's coins allegedly issued by Ranjit Singh are the issues of some Sikh *misldar* of Amritsar.[43] The *Standard Guide to South Asian Coins and Paper Money Since 1556 AD* shows the 1862 rupees with the double branch as Moran's coins.[44]

Madanjit Kaur, while mentioning Moran's coins as described by C.J. Rodgers, suggests the possibility that the peacock symbol could be the symbol of Durga, the Hindu goddess representing Shakti, and hence it is possible that the legend of Moran is not correct. However, she does not satisfactorily explain the reasons behind such a conclusion nor has she established that the peacock symbol was introduced by Ranjit Singh.[45] More recently, Ken Wiggins and Stan Goron have carried out a detailed examination of Sikh coins. They also share the views of Cunningham and Rodgers regarding the alleged Moran Shahi coins.[46] From the above account, it becomes apparent that those historians who accept the claim that the Moran Shahi coins were struck by Ranjit Singh differ among themselves over the question of whether these coins were struck at Amritsar, Lahore, or Multan. Coins were said to have been struck in her name in places conquered by Ranjit Singh, either on account of his love for Moran or as a jest against the English East India Company.

The mint towns are variously mentioned as Amritsar and Lahore and the coins are said to have carried Moran's name and effigy or a mere symbol by way of the peacock tail or the *arsi*. The gold coin is stated to bear the figure of a shepeacock (peahen) on its reverse. As the above accounts indicate, over a score of historians have written about Moran's coins without either analysing the information available or even without examining the coins when these coins were readily available all along.

The origin of the Sikh coins as initially struck in AD 1710-12 and thereafter regularly from AD 1765 onwards has already been examined in detail in earlier chapters. All these coins were in the names of the Sikh Gurus, bearing the legends that had existed on Banda Bahadur's seal and coin. The names of the rulers, in accordance with the general practice then prevalent, could not be placed on the Sikh coins; due to their sacrosanctity, being in the names of the Sikh Gurus. The rajas of Patiala had minted gold and silver coins for *puja* purposes in the names of the Gurus, but these coins were not state issue for public purposes.[47] The rajas of Nabha had minted gold and silver coins in the names of the Gurus both for public issue as well as issue to the gurdwaras.[48] With the passage of time, British currency became the currency for public purposes, and these *nazrana* coins popularly called the Guru Sahib coins remained in religious use as late as 1948 till Patiala and Nabha were merged with the Union of India. The coins issued by the trans-Sutlej states of the Lahore Darbar were in the names of the Gurus and not in the names of any rajas.[49]

Ranjit Singh was a great general and a greater statesman. His main ambition was to raise a great Sikh Empire and he worked untiringly towards his goal. He was very fond of exchanging repartee with dancing and singing girls. According to a popular story, Moran, his favourite courtesan, once asked him where he was when God was distributing good looks. He is said to have replied that he was busy securing his kingdom.[50] This story may be apocryphal but it does reveal the primary aim of Ranjit Singh. Once his prime minister, Dhian Singh, asked him why he wore a cloth around his waist like a humble servant when he was the maharaja. Ranjit Singh told him that the coins of the state were struck in the names of the Gurus and hence the Gurus were the rulers and he was their mere humble servant.[51] A person of this self-effacing and modest temperament was not likely to carry out such a sacrilege as to mint coins in the name of a concubine whom he eventually discarded after a few years. The attachments of nobles with such women invariably lasted for short durations, whereas their attachment to their faith and their kingdoms was of an abiding nature. In these circumstances, whatever may have been the failings of Ranjit Singh, it does not seem logical for him to have struck coins, otherwise considered sacrosanct, in the name of a concubine. Had the news that Ranjit Singh had struck coins in Moran's name been generally known to the traders of Amritsar, this information could not have remained hidden from the Akal Takht authorities, and it is certain that they would have taken due notice of such a blatant transgression of Sikh religious teachings.

Even the pictorial coins allegedly struck by Ranjit Singh in 1836, when he was at the height of his power, depicting him seeking the blessings of Guru Nanak were only sample coins, which evidently were not finally minted for general issue, lest these coins may be deemed to violate Sikh traditions.[52] Hence, the alleged existence of Moran's coins is a figment of some fertile imagination, which caught the fancy of certain people who mattered, and the rumour continued to circulate more so after the death of Ranjit Singh; it has been repeated by historians who have not cared to confirm the veracity of this claim.

The Moran Shahi coins are said to have been minted at Amritsar and Lahore during the years Sambat 1861, 1862, and 1863.[53] These coins were selected by C.J. Rodgers in 1881. Thus, the coins under dispute are at sr. nos. 1 to 8 pertaining to the years Sambat 1861, 1862, and 1863, i.e. AD 1804, 1805, and 1806 (see Plate IV). Eight representative coins from these years produced by the

PLATE IV: MORAN'S COINS

AMRITSAR MINT 1861-1863 SAMBAT

NO.1 1861 S

NO. 2 1861 S

NO. 3 1862 S

NO. 4 1862 S

NO. 5 1862 S

NO. 6 1863 S

NO. 7 1863 S

NO. 8 1863 S

LAHORE MINT 1860-1863 SAMBAT

NO. 1 1860 S.

NO. 2 1861 S.

NO. 3 1862 S.

NO. 4 1863 S.

Amritsar mint and four coins from the Lahore mint are shown in Plate IV. It may be clearly seen that these coins from both the Amritsar and Lahore mints do not bear the name Moran or her effigy as contended by various historians. It is likely that the twin branches or the twin leaves depicted on these coins are a variation of the leaf motif rather than a depiction of the peacock tail. The peacock tail is a fanlike object and the craftsman would certainly have made it fairly representative of the actual tail had this indeed been the intention of Ranjit Singh. The figure in sr. no. 6 is more like the top of a jewelled ring rather than an *arsi*, which is a small mirror worn on the thumb ring which permitted its female wearer to discreetly examine her face whenever she wished. The craftsman who made the die for the coin could have made an *arsi* as well if that had indeed been the intention.

The Sikh *sardars* were supposed to mint coins in the name of the Gurus for which a selected legend was already prescribed. They were morally restrained from placing their names on the coins but there were no restrictions on the depiction of ornamentation and figurative symbols. Hence, it is possible that the symbols depicted on these coins are neither a peacock's tail nor an *arsi* but instead are certain ornamental figures as well as the extension of the leaf motif into branches. The change in the style of ornamentation occurred due to the proliferation of Sikh coins after the death of Jassa Singh Ahluwalia, as already explained in an earlier chapter.

Since so many historians and numismatists have characterized them as Moran's coins and since there are no mint records available to us, it is necessary to examine the various facts concerning these coins, i.e. the dates and mint names on the coins, the year in which Ranjit Singh became infatuated with Moran, and the year when Ranjit Singh occupied these towns. The coins pertain to the Amritsar and Lahore mints for the years Sambat 1861, 1862 and 1863, i.e. AD 1804, 1805, and 1806. The affair of the Maharaja with Moran was recorded by Diwan Amarnath on the occasion celebrating the first invasion of Multan by Ranjit Singh in 1802.[54] Khushwant Singh states that coins were issued in the name of Moran.[55] Waheed-ud-din in dates the affair as occurring in the twenty-second year of Ranjit Singh's life, i.e. 1802.[56] Muhammad Latif dates it to 1802, on Ranjit Singh's return to Lahore.[57] Bikramjit Hasrat dates the affair to 1802, on Ranjit Singh's return to Lahore.[58] Griffin dates it to 1806.[59] Cunningham dates it to 1811, which is obviously incorrect as by that time the affair was over and Moran was said to have been sent away to Pathankot.[60] Historians generally agree that the affair occurred in 1802-3.

There is, however, some disagreement regarding the date of the occupation of Amritsar by Ranjit Singh. Diwan Amarnath dates it as 1802,[61] after which Ranjit Singh went to Haridwar to bathe in the Ganga during the Kumbh Mela. Kanehiya Lal states that Amritsar was occupied after Ranjit Singh's bath in the Ganga at the Kumbh Mela, which occurred in 1806.[62] Ahmad Shah Batalvi states that Ranjit

Singh occupied Amritsar in 1805.[63] Cunningham dates the occupation of Amritsar in 1811.[64] Henry T. Princep dates the occupation of Amritsar in 1802 and Ranjit Singh's visit to Haridwar in 1805.[65] C.J. Rodgers also dates the occupation of Amritsar in 1802.[66] N.K. Sinha states that there is some difference of opinion about the date of the conquest of Amritsar, but he relies on Sohan Lal Suri for the sequence of events and hence dates it as 1805.[67]

Sohan Lal Suri, the court historian, states that Amritsar was occupied by Ranjit Singh in 1805.[68] Bhagat Singh gives the date of the occupation of Amritsar as 24 February 1805.[69] J.S. Grewal and Indu Banga date the occupation of Amritsar in 1806.[70] It has been variously stated that after the occupation of Amritsar, Ranjit Singh went to Haridwar to bathe in the Ganga on the occasion of the Kumbh Mela in AD 1806, and hence his occupation of Amritsar may safely be assumed to have occurred in 1805 and not 1802. C.J. Rodgers dates the occupation of Amritsar in 1802 and hence committed the mistake of treating the coins dated Sambat 1861, 1862, and 1863, i.e. AD 1804, 1805, and 1806 as Moran's coins. Had he taken the correct date of the occupation of Amritsar, it is quite likely that his conclusion would have been different, as well as that of a number of historians who relied on his account.

Amritsar at the time when Ranjit Singh occupied the city in 1805 was a combination of several autonomous sections (katras) clustered around the core of the town where the Golden Temple is located. Each katra was a walled area and had only one gate. The traders and residents paid ground rent and a cess for chowkidari to the chief.[71] Ranjit Singh occupied the Lohgarh Fort and Katra Bhangian in 1805 and subdued and occupied the areas of the other sardars in due course. Once the whole city came under his control, Ranjit Singh fortified it with a surrounding wall with 12 gates in 1810 and built the Gobindgarh Fort.[72] Ganesh Das states that the minting of the Sikh coins was not restricted to Lahore and that every sardar had established his own mint in the area under his control. The manifesto proclaiming the sovereignty of the Khalsa meant that at the same time many an individual sardar also claimed to enjoy a sovereign status.[73]

The facts enumerated above establish that Ranjit Singh's affair with Moran occurred in 1802-3 and the coins allegedly struck in her name pertain to AD 1804, 1805, and 1806. These coins are said to have been struck in Amritsar, but large sections of the city were not under Ranjit Singh's control and hence he could not have ordered the minting of Moran's coins from Amritsar; therefore the story of Moran's coins having been struck by Ranjit Singh is most improbable. The distinctive nature of these coins is due to the fact that Amritsar was a conglomeration of a number of independent sections before the city was occupied by Ranjit Singh, and each sardar had his own mint. This fact is established from the Sikh coins shown in the Standard Guide to South Asian Coins wherein about a score of different types of the Amritsar rupee coins are shown to have been in vogue at the same time.[74] Ganesh Das states that Ranjit Singh continued to use the old legends on his coins. But he kept up only the mints of Lahore and Amritsar and closed down all the other mints.[75] This conclusion is drawn from the fact that no further distinctive coins were minted after the occupation of Amritsar by Ranjit Singh.

From the accounts described in the preceding pages which examine this matter from various angles, namely, political, social, religious, and numismatic, it is reasonably certain that there was no likelihood of Ranjit Singh issuing any coins in the name of a concubine, when these coins issued in the names of the Sikh Gurus were considered sacrosanct, and Ranjit Singh did not make any changes to this well-established tradition during his long reign. The so-called Moran coins were issued from one of the mints in Amritsar when Ranjit Singh had not yet completely occupied the city. The so-called peacock tail is probably linked to the extension of the leaf motif in the form of branches and leaves, and the so-called *arsi* is a form of ornamentation which also appears on later coins, and hence it cannot be treated as being exclusive to Moran's coins. The claim that Moran's coins were struck by Ranjit Singh is pure and simple fiction, totally divorced from any reality. It is very strange that many learned historians readily accepted this story for granted without analysing its veracity or accuracy in the light of the existing historical and numismatic evidence.

The Fallacy of Hari Singh Nalwa's Coins

Hari Singh Nalwa was the bravest Sikh general, who not only subdued the north-western Afghan tribes but also instilled in them an awe of his invincibility. For generations after him Afghan women would hush their unruly children by saying, '*Chup shore, Hariya raghla de*', meaning 'Stop making noise, Hari Singh is coming.'[76] During Alexander Burnes's visit to Persia in early 1830, his companion Mohan Lal was asked by Abbas Mirza, the Shah of Persia, whether the Sikh army could compare in courage and discipline with his army. Mohan Lal replied that if Hari Singh Nalwa, Ranjit Singh's commander on the Afghan frontier, was to cross the Indus, His Highness would soon be glad to make good his retreat to his original home in Tabriz.[77]

Hari Singh participated in almost all the important battles fought by Ranjit Singh. It was during the fourth invasion of Multan in AD 1810 that Hari Singh was very seriously wounded, and the Maharaja became greatly worried. A Muslim saint of Multan, who came to meet the Maharaja, called him the *nalwa* of Multan (*nalwa* means the victor). Ranjit Singh, pointing the wounded Hari Singh, stated that Hari Singh was the real *nalwa* of Multan and not he, the Maharaja. Since then Hari Singh came to be known as Hari Singh Nalwa. This incident became part of the family folklore of the famous *sardar*. Lt. Gen. B.S. Nalwa, a descendant of Hari Singh Nalwa, recently recounted this incident to me.

Various biographers and historians have recorded that Hari Singh struck coins in his own name from Kashmir and Peshawar. An examination of a few hundred Sikh coins struck in Kashmir during the period of Sikh rule, now with private collectors and with the Sri Pratap Museum, Srinagar, does not reveal any coin that was struck in the name of Hari Singh. It is a great irony that historian after historian has written a *'Gult-ul-am Darust'*, meaning 'a wrong fact repeatedly called correct', without ever caring to actually examine the coins which were and are readily available. The perpetuation of this fallacy is examined here with reference to the relevant historical accounts, the tenets of the Sikh polity, and the study of the actual coins struck during this period.

In a detailed biography of Hari Singh Nalwa written in 1937, Prem Singh Hoti states that Ranjit Singh greatly appreciated the administration of Kashmir by Hari Singh, and bestowed on him the singular privilege of striking coins in his own name from Kashmir. While expressing his gratitude for the honour, Hari Singh also expressed his disinclination for exercising this privilege. Ranjit Singh appreciated Hari Singh's humility, yet he desired his wishes to be carried out. Hari Singh struck coins in Sambat 1878, i.e. AD 1821, with 10 *mashas* pure silver, and the value of the coin according to the currencies then in circulation was 8 *annas*. On its obverse was the legend *'Akal Sahai'* in the Persian script, and on the reverse the legends *'Hari Singh'* and *'Yak Rupaiya'*. He is also stated to have struck bronze coins called the Hari Singh paise.[78] Prem Singh Hoti further states that Griffin called these rupees Harisinghee rupees, which were legal tender all over the Punjab. Maulana Mohammad Din is also stated to have recorded the above facts in his book *Mukammal Twarikh-i-Kashmir*, i.e. the Complete History of Kashmir. Prem Singh Hoti states that Ranjit Singh also authorized Hari Singh Nalwa to strike coins from Peshawar. These coins weighed 8½ *mashas*.[79]

A.S. Sandhu states that Hari Singh struck a coin after his own name at Srinagar, and that this coin remained current in Kashmir and the Punjab till AD 1849. It was a base coin, of two-thirds the value of the common *sicca* rupee. Hari Singh also struck a coin after his own name at Peshawar in 1834.[80] S.S. Johar who wrote a biography of Hari Singh Nalwa in 1982 is very restrained with footnotes and references. Johar states that Hari Singh sought the Maharaja's permission to strike coins in his own name as this was necessary to uphold the authority of the state. Ranjit Singh readily agreed to the proposal, and a coin was struck which contained 10 *mashas* silver and 6 *mashas* bronze. The coin was known as Hari Singh's rupee. It was equal to 50 paise. Besides the rupees, paisa coins were also minted. The legend thereon was *'Sri Akal Sahai'*, Sambat 1878 on the obverse, and the likeness of Hari Singh and the legend *'Yak rupayia'* on the reverse.[81] These accounts give incorrect amounts for the weight and value of the coin as all rupee coins were of 11 g. only and not 16 g., and 10 g. silver itself was worth 12 *annas* and not 8 *annas*, as stated by Johar and others.

Gulcharan Singh states that Hari Singh Nalwa had the distinction of being the governor of two provinces, and at both the places he had the honour of

FIGURE III: HARI SINGH NALWA

striking coins in his own name. The rupee thus coined was known as the Harisinghee after the general's name. On one side of the coin were the words 'Sri Akal Jio' and on the other side 'Hari Singh' in the Gurmukhi script. This coin was in use in Kashmir till 1890.[82] Kanehiya Lal states that after occupying large areas of Kashmir, Hari Singh Nalwa struck a coin in his own name, which was called the Hari Singhia rupia in the Valley. This rupee was worth 8. *annas* and was prevalent in Kashmir and the Punjab.[83] G.M.D. Sufi states that there is another kind of rupee associated with Hari Singh Nalwa which is called the Hari Singhee; on obverse side of the coin is 'Sri Akal Sahai' and on the reverse side 'Hari Singh'. It was worth 12 *annas* and all taxes, rents, and custom duties were paid in this coin.[84] Ghulam Hassan also shares the views expressed by G.M.D. Sufi regarding the coins struck by Hari Singh Nalwa in his own name.[85]

D.C. Sharma, while explaining the various currencies prevalent in Kashmir, states that in 1821 Hari Singh Nalwa, the Sikh governor of Kashmir, struck a new coin at the mint in Srinagar known after him as the 'Hari Singh *rupaiya*'. It was coined from an alloy of silver and copper in equal proportion of 6 *mashas* each. Its value in proportion to the Nanak Shahi rupee was 10 to 11 *annas*. The coin bears the legends 'Sri Akal Jio' on the obverse and 'Hari Singh Yak Rupayia' on the reverse.[86] D.C. Sharma refers to Major Leach's description of the Hari Singh *rupaiya*. R.K. Parmu states that Hari Singh reformed the currency evidently with the aim of demonetizing the Afghan currency on the grounds that it was foreign, and instead he circulated new coins inscribed with the Sikh legend to commemorate Sikh sovereignty. The new coin weighing 12 *mashas* was made of an alloy of silver and copper in equal proportions. It was named the 'Hari Singh *Rupaiya*' and was valued at 8 *annas* in the open market.[87] This coin remained in circulation as late as AD 1885. R.K. Parmu based his account on Major Leach's description of Hari Singh's *rupaiya*. Major Leach in his report *Revenue of Kashmir for the year 1836-37* describes the Sikh rupee as follows:

Obverse   *Shri Akal Jio*
Reverse   *Hari Singh, Yak Rupaiya.*[88]

N.K. Sinha states that there was another kind of rupee associated with the name of Hari Singh and as such it was called the Harisinghee. On one side of this coin was written 'Sri Akal Jio', and on the other 'Hari Singh'. It was worth 12 *annas* and rents, taxes, and custom duties were paid in this coin.[89] Bikramjit Hasrat states that Hari Singh replaced the old currency in Kashmir by a newly minted currency which bore the inscription of his own name.[90] Bhagat Singh states that there were various currencies then prevalent in Kashmir in the early nineteenth century, viz., Mughal, Bahawalpur, Shikarpur, Khairpur, Zaman Shahi, Murshidabadi, and Nanak Shahi. Another currency called the Harisinghee was minted in Kashmir by Hari Singh Nalwa. On one side was written 'Sri Akal Jio' and on the other side '*Hari Singh*'. It was worth 12 *annas* and was called the small rupee.[91] G.T. Vigue states that he does not know how long Hari Singh was governor of Kashmir, but he coined the rupee that bore his name; it was two-thirds the value of the common *sicca* rupee.[92] He further states that the Harisinghee rupee, which is about the same value as the Kabul rupee, was coined by Hari Singh, and subsequent governors had attempted to impress their names thereon but the coins always retained their original name.[93]

Madhavi Yasin states that Hari Singh Nalwa demonetized the Afghan currency as being foreign, and issued a new coin, the Hari Singh *rupaiya*, to commemorate the inauguration of the new regime.[94] Shahamat Ali, who did not visit Kashmir himself, states that Hari Singh Nalwa was appointed governor of Kashmir and that he established a new rupee of base value which still bears his name.[95] G.S. Chhabra states that Ranjit Singh, pleased with Hari Singh's work in Kashmir, granted him the unique honour of striking coins in his own name. These coins had the words '*Sri Akal Jio*' and '*Sambat 1878*' on one side and '*Hari Singh Yak Rupaiya*' on the other.[96] Gopal Singh also states that Hari Singh Nalwa issued his own coins in Kashmir with '*Shri Akal Jeo*' on one side and '*Hari Singh*' on the other.[97] Ganeshi Lal, who visited Kashmir in 1846 alongwith a British mission, persistently refers to the Kashmir rupee as the Harisinghee rupee; he claims that almost all transactions in grains, saffron, and various cottage industries, as well as the payment of all duties were carried out in this rupee. He states that the total duty, including land revenue in 1846, came to 2,400,000 Harisinghee rupees.[98] He further states that the government charged 5 rupees per 100 rupees coined in the mint. Half the quantity of the alloy is mixed with pure silver to coin the Harisinghee rupee, and the total income from these was 60,000 rupees per annum.[99]

Walter Lawrence, the settlement commissioner in Jammu and Kashmir in AD 1846, treats the figure of Rs. 2,600,000 as revenue given by Gholam Muhyi-ud-din (1841-5) as being equivalent to 1,300,000 imperial rupees, meaning thereby that in the 1840s the Kashmir currency called the Harisinghee rupee was worth 8 *annas* of the British rupee. He refers to Moorecraft's statement made in 1823 that 3,800,000 Kashmir rupees were equal to 2,900,000 *sicca* rupees, meaning thereby that the Kashmir rupee was then worth 11 *annas* of the *sicca* rupee.[100] Sita Ram Kohli states that the Kashmir or Harisinghee rupee, first struck in Kashmir during the *nizamat* of Hari Singh Nalwa in the early 1820s, was equal to 10 *annas* of the standard Nanak Shahi coin.[101] Hans Herrli also gives Major Leach's description of the 'Harisinghee Rupaiya'. Herrli, who carried out an extensive cataloguing of Sikh coins, states that a description matching this rupee has never been published, and as the striking of such a coin by one of Ranjit Singh's governors would have been tantamount to an act of rebellion, its very existence seems highly improbable.[102] Although there exist about forty historical accounts stating that Hari Singh Nalwa struck coins in his own name, there does not exist even a single historical account which disputes this claim or which even entertains any doubts regarding its veracity. In his thesis on the Sikh polity, Bhagat Singh has established that sovereignty belonged to the Gurus and that coins, being an important symbol of this sovereignty, were struck only in the names of the Gurus, yet Bhagat Singh also states that Hari Singh Nalwa struck coins from Kashmir bearing his name, evidently without noticing the contradiction in these two assertions nor offering any authenticated reference in support of this claim.

Hari Singh was in Kashmir for about one year, i.e. from the close of 1820 to the close of 1821. During the first half of this period, the Valley had little or no contact with the outside world since the passes became snow bound in the winter months. Ranjit Singh would obviously need some time, say about a year or so, to appreciate the work of Hari Singh in his capacity as governor of Kashmir before deciding to award him this special privilege—that of striking coins in his own name—which had not been awarded to any other governor or even to a minister. Hence, the claim that Hari Singh Nalwa struck coins in his own name in Kashmir is highly improbable, more so when there is no recorded evidence in support of it.

Prem Singh Hoti has not given any authenticated reference explaining why Ranjit Singh insisted that Hari Singh Nalwa should strike coins in his own name, when the Maharaja himself had not struck any coins in his own name. Ten *mashas* silver was worth about 14 *annas* as the rupee weight had all along been about 11 *mashas*, and pure silver rupees were worth 16 *annas*. Hence, coins with 10 *mashas* silver could not be worth 8 *annas*.' Likewise, neither A.S. Sandhu nor S.S. Johar have given any authentic reference regarding Hari Singh's attempt to seek the concurrence of the Maharaja to strike coins in his own name. The contention that these coins were 10 *mashas* silver and 6 *mashas* copper is also incorrect, as is the claim that the likeness of Hari Singh was inscribed on the reverse of these coins. The impression given by most of these historians that Hari Singh Nalwa was the first to strike Sikh coins in Kashmir is not correct as the coins were duly struck by two of his predecessors (see Plates V and VI).

Kanehiya Lal is incorrect in saying that Hari Singh, after occupying large areas of Kashmir, struck a coin in his own name. During his year-long stay in Kashmir, Hari Singh did improve the administration, but he did not conquer any new area of Kashmir; he administered the territory that had already been under the occupation during the tenure of his predecessors. Kanehiya Lal has made a similar mistake in the case of Ranjit Singh. He states that in AD 1800 Ranjit Singh, after his *raj tilak* ceremony, got coins issued from the Lahore mint, inscribed with the existing Sikh legend on the obverse and his name on the reverse; however, this claim is neither borne out by the evidence of these coins nor was any *darbar* held in AD 1800. The chapter on banking and currency in D.C. Sharma's book *Kashmir under the Sikhs* devotes a few pages to the legends inscribed on

Sikh coins. This chapter is reproduced without any changes in D.C. Sharma's annotated edition of *Kashmir under Maharaja Ranjit Singh* by Charles Baron von Hugel. The above accounts give the impression that D.C. Sharma had carried out a numismatic examination of these coins but in fact he does not seem to have actually examined any Sikh coins struck in Kashmir. The English rendering of the legend is also incorrect. He is mistaken in stating that Ghulam Hassan and Ganeshi Lal had confused the Hari Singh rupee with the Nanak Shahi rupee. Moorecraft, who visited Kashmir in 1823 after Hari Singh had left, estimates the value of the Hari Singh rupee as worth 11 *annas*. It was during the governorship of Mihan Singh that silver and copper were mixed in equal quantities and the value of the Sikh rupee fell to only 8 *annas*. Madhavi Yasin is also incorrect in stating that Hari Singh demonetized the Afghan currency on the grounds that it was foreign and that he issued a new coin as the Hari Singh *rupayia* to commemorate the inauguration of the new regime. There was no system of demonetization in that period, and neither was Hari Singh the first Sikh governor of Kashmir and nor was he the first person to issue Sikh coins from Kashmir.

Ganeshi Lal and Walter Lawrence have discussed the relative value of the Sikh currency vis-à-vis the British rupee and the Nanak Shahi rupee, but they have not discussed the legends inscribed on these coins, and they are thus not party to the propagation of the claim regarding the fictitious 'Hari Singh' legend on the reverse of the coins.[103] In the late 1840s, the Sikh currency issued from Kashmir was popularly called the Hari Singhee rupee although Hari Singh was in Kashmir for only one year during 1820-1. The above assessment clearly reveals the existence of contradictions in the various historical accounts and the complete absence of any authentic references from contemporary records regarding the legend as well as the lack of an actual examination of the coins in question; hence, these historical accounts cannot be taken at their face value. Of all the many historians who have described the legend in the name of Hari Singh not even one mentions the existence and the actual physical examination of such a coin.

One conclusion that clearly emerges from this discussion is that the Sikh currency was popularly called the Harisinghee currency although Hari Singh was the governor of Kashmir for only one year, i.e. during 1820-1. So great was the impact of Hari Singh's firm and constructive administrative measures on Kashmir that it eclipsed the contributions of his predecessors as well as sidelining the efforts of his successors.

The confusion over its value resulted from the fact that the coins minted between 1819 and the early 1830s had about a two-thirds silver content and were valued at 11 to 12 *annas*, and that the coins minted at a later date during the Mihan Singh's governership had a 50 per cent silver content and were valued at 8 *annas*. The decision to have a lower silver content for the Kashmir coin was based on the need to maintain its parity with the prevalent Kabul rupee, which in 1819 was worth about 9 *annas* of the Company *sicca* or the Nanak Shahi rupee. The Lahore Darbar was well aware of the reduced value of their Kashmir currency as Ranjit Singh, while fixing the revenue due from Gulab Singh of Jammu, specifically recorded that the sum was to be paid in the Nanak Shahi rupees from the Amritsar mint.[104]

The place of Sikh coinage in the Sikh polity has already been explained in detail in a preceding chapter. In his inaugural address to the special seminar on Maharaja Ranjit Singh held at the Punjabi University, Patiala in 1984, Bhagat Singh stated most emphatically that Ranjit Singh used his immense power not in his own name, nor in the name of his family, but on behalf of and in the name of the Khalsa or the Sikh commonwealth which was a potent force in those days.[105] At the same seminar, in his paper on 'Trade and Commerce under Ranjit Singh', Bhagat Singh stated that the Harisinghee rupee current in Kashmir had on one side the words '*Sri Akal Jio*' and on the other side '*Hari Singh*',[106] without taking into account the position which he had already stated. Even Ranjit Singh, the mighty ruler, would not dare to assume any symbol of sovereignty in his own name. The power and prestige of the Sikh commonwealth was a very strong deterrent to the pretensions of any over-ambitious ruler. It is inconceivable that one of Ranjit Singh's generals would dare to strike coins in his own name, i.e. take on the most striking symbol of Sikh sovereignty on his own volition or even with the Maharaja's concurrence without provoking strong protests from the Sikh religious authorities at Akal Takht, etc.

Hari Ram Gupta shares the views on Sikh sovereignty and states that coins, one of the most visible and widely recognized symbols of sovereignty, were struck in the names of Guru Nanak and Guru Gobind Singh and not in the name of any *sardar* or ruler.[107] Elsewhere Hari Ram Gupta states that Hari Singh Nalwa had introduced a new silver coin in his own name called the Harisinghee Rupaiya.[108] Although many writers state that Ranjit Singh allowed Hari Singh to strike coins in his own name as a gesture of appreciation, Hari Ram Gupta states that William Moorecraft in an unpublished document accused Hari Singh of extracting twenty-five lakh rupees from the silk traders of Srinagar, an action for which he was transferred to Hazara as a punishment. Hari Ram Gupta has not given any evidence in support of his account. He further states that Ranjit Singh himself struck coins in the names of the Sikh Gurus, and by the end of his reign he had closed the mints in Kashmir and Multan. This contention is incorrect, and these mints continued to operate till the annexation of the Lahore Darbar in 1849.[109] This incident clearly reveals that historians have not given proper attention to the study of Sikh coinage in their accounts and have based their descriptions on incorrect information, and have thus contributed to the distortion of Sikh history.

Hari Singh Nalwa himself was a devout Sikh, devoid of the general vices of the day.[110] He was one of the most upright *sardars* of the Khalsa Panth, who laid down his life in serving the cause of the Sikh commonwealth. He was opposed to the appointment of Kharak Singh as heir apparent by Ranjit Singh.[111] Presumably on that account Ranjit Singh kept him occupied on the frontiers and never brought him to his court, even though he was amply qualified for a position at the *darbar*. He was not awarded any title and was made a general only in 1836; and even then he was the twenty-eighth and the last among 28 such generals.[112] The question then arises: under the circumstances described above regarding the nature of the Sikh polity and the individual standing of Ranjit Singh and Hari Singh Nalwa and the differences between them, could Ranjit Singh have awarded as an honour or conceded to the request for the right to strike coins in his own name by Hari Singh Nalwa from Kashmir in 1822 and from Peshawar in 1834? Could Hari Singh on his own have indulged in the provocative act of striking coins in his own name? Could he have taken over the symbol of sovereignty invested with the Khalsa and the Sikh Gurus? Could he have dared to commit such an act of extreme sacrilege? Why did the Khalsa, who were very jealous about safeguarding the sovereignty of the Sikh commonwealth, not object to these coins which were in circulation in Kashmir and the Punjab? As the above discussion reveals, the claim regarding the existence of Sikh coins issued in the name of a Sikh governor, that too Hari Singh Nalwa, is unacceptable and is totally outside the realm of possibility. But since a negative deduction from the available historical evidence does not constitute a positive proof, the direct physical examination of the coins in question becomes essential. Fortunately, enough coins struck during the period of Sikh rule in Kashmir are readily available.

The victorious Sikh army was led into Srinagar by Misr Diwan Chand in July 1819 and he was made the governor of Kashmir. Within a few months, in late 1819, he was replaced by Diwan Moti Ram. Diwan Moti Ram's eldest son Ram Dayal was killed in Hazara in 1820, and the heartbroken father sought to retire and spend the rest of his life in penance at Banaras.[113] Hari Singh Nalwa was sent in his place in late 1820, and he remained governor of Kashmir till late 1821, when he was recalled to undertake a more difficult task in Hazara. Historians have given different dates for his departure, ranging from 1822 and even 1823, but it is well established in the historical record that he left Kashmir in November or December 1821 as he fought the Afghan tribals in December 1821 on his way back from Kashmir. About 20,000 to 30,000 Afghan tribals blocked his way at the Mangali Pass near Mansehra and he routed them with a small force of only 7,000 troops. Hence, Hari Singh Nalwa was governor of Kashmir only from late 1820 to late 1821.

C.J. Rodgers, who carried out a study of Sikh coins in the late nineteenth century, wrote an article on Sikh coins in 1881.[114] In this article he refers briefly to Sikh coins struck from Kashmir. However, he mentions about a dozen silver coins from Kashmir, including those struck in AD 1819, i.e. Sambat 1876, and some copper coins in the *Catalogue of Coins*, now with the Government Museum, Lahore.[115] He does not comment on Hari Singh's role in connection with these coins. A proper study of Sikh coins from Kashmir appeared only in the 1990s. Ken Wiggins and Stan Goron studied these coins in 1983.[116] Hans Herrli has also studied these coins in recent years.[117] For a proper examination of the Hari Singh coins, the drawings of 15 representative coins pertaining to the years 1819 to 1822 from Kashmir and two coins for the years 1835 and 1836 from Peshawar are given in Plate V.

The legend on the obverse of Sikh coins is the same as the one which appears on the Sikh coins from Lahore in 1765 and 1801, i.e. *'Degh Tegh Fateh, O Nusrat Baidarang, Yaft uz Nanak Guru Gobind Singh'*. The legend on the reverse is also some what similar is contents, except with minor alterations. Silver coins have always been of rupee value only, and very few half-rupee or quarter-rupee coins are forthcoming.[118] Copper coins had also been struck, but these seem to have been minted under licence by private traders as had been the practice in the rest of the Sikh state. These coins are rather crude in form and varied in size.

The striking of Sikh coinage in Kashmir was in continuation of the existing policy of striking coins in Kashmir due to its peculiar geographical location and the Sikh policy of striking coins from conquered territories on assuming the responsibility of their administration, as had been the case in Lahore, Amritsar, and Multan. The issuing of Sikh currency appears to have been started immediately following the Sikh occupation of Kashmir for the payment of taxes, rents, and custom duties.[119] During less than half the year of AD 1819, i.e. Sambat 1876, three different coins and for the year AD 1820, i.e. Sambat 1877, four different coins were issued.

Wiggins and Goron consider the mark 'Ha' on the coin at sr. nos. 5 and 7 (right side of the central double twig) to be the mark of Hari Singh Nalwa.[120] Herrli considers these marks to be merely the distortions of a flowery pattern.[121] The interpretation offered by Goron and Wiggins cannot be treated as correct; it is contrary to the views held by other historians as well, that is, Hari Singh Nalwa was allowed to mint coins in his own name as a gesture of appreciation by the Maharaja for his commendable work in Kashmir. Such an assessment by the ruler could not have been carried out at so early a stage in Hari Singh's term as governor. No such mark exists on the coins at sr. nos. 9 and 10 which pertain to the next year, i.e. AD 1821 or Sambat 1878, which pertains to Hari Singh's tenure as governor.

The coins at sr. nos. 11 and 12 for the year 1821 have the word *'Har'* in the Gurmukhi script imprinted boldly on the centre of the obverse, above the names of the Gurus. Wiggins and Goron as well as Herrli treat this word as the representation of Hari Singh Nalwa's coins and consider that the coins were struck by him in his own name.[122] They have committed a serious error in their

PLATE V: KASHMIR COINS
1876-1879 SAMBAT

NO. 1 1876 S

NO. 6 1877 S

NO. 2 1876 S

NO. 7 1877 S

NO. 3 1877 S

NO. 8 1878 S

NO. 4 1877 S

NO. 9 1878 S

NO. 5 1877 S

NO. 10 1878 S

(contd.)

PLATE V (contd.)

NO. 11 1878 S

NO. 14 1879 S

NO. 12 1878 S

NO. 15 1879 S

NO. 13 1879 S

PESHAWAR COINS
1892 AND 1893 SAMBAT

NO. 16 1879 S

NO. 17 1879 S

assessment for want of a proper understanding of Sikh ideology. The word '*Har*' does not represent Hari Singh but rather it represents the name of God, as may be seen from the words and phrases Harimandir, the Golden Temple at Amritsar, and Har ki Pauri, the steps at the back of the Golden Temple from where every devotee takes a sip of the holy water from the tank. '*Harjee Harimandir awenge*', i.e. 'God will come to his temple', is often sung at Sikh congregations. Likewise, Haridwar in Uttaranchal and Hari Parbat in Srinagar also denote the name of God. Out of the about 56,000 couplets in the *Holy Granth*, about 2,200 start with the word '*Har*'.[123] Furthermore, it should be noted that no Sikh will place his name above the names of his Gurus no matter how great might be the temptation to place his name on a coin. This would constitute such a serious act of sacrilege that it would neither be tolerated by the Khalsa nor be accepted by the individual's own conscience. Moreover, Sikhs do not resort to abbreviating their names as they are very proud of their surname 'Singh' given to them by Guru Gobind Singh. Hence, it is totally incorrect to presume that the word '*Har*' stands for Hari Singh Nalwa's name.

Hari Singh Nalwa left Kashmir in November or December 1821, but the coins for the year 1822 at sr. nos. 13 and 14 also bear the words '*Har*' and '*Harjee*' in the Devanagari script. Moti Ram, who was a general senior to Hari Singh, became governor of Kashmir for a second term immediately after Hari Singh. He was thus in the most reliable position to know and understand the reason for the placement of '*Har*' on the state coins by Hari Singh. Indeed, if Moti Ram had even the slightest inkling that these words were meant to denote Hari Singh's name, it is certain that he would never have allowed these words to continue to appear on the coins struck during his tenure. He seems to have simply followed the practice of Hari Singh and put '*Har*', '*Harji*', '*Om Shri*', and '*Sri Ram*', in the Devanagari script, on the state coins during his second term. This clearly establishes that the word '*Har*' appearing on the Sikh coins issued during Hari Singh's period was not meant to represent his name by his immediate successor Moti Ram, who was in the best position to correctly understand the situation. So pervasive has been the influence of these historical accounts on the numismatists studying Sikh coins that it led Wiggins and Goron to suggest that Hari Singh's stay in Kashmir might have been extended to early 1822 in order to cover the coins at sr. nos. 13 and 14.[125] Herrli argues that although Hari Singh left Kashmir in 1821, it was possible that some mixup of the dies of 1821 and 1822 might have taken place.[126] Such speculation cannot be accepted as an analytical study or as a proper numismatic investigation of Sikh coinage. The coins at sr. nos. 16 and 17 struck from the Peshawar mint do not give any indication whatsoever that these had been struck in the name of Hari Singh Nalwa. The command of the Peshawar expedition was with Prince Nau Nihal Singh, although Hari Singh Nalwa was his principal general.

Taking into consideration the various contradictions in the historical accounts of the coins in question, the clear position regarding the place of Sikh coins in the Sikh polity and in the concept of Sikh sovereignty, along with the incontrovertible evidence of the legends on these coins, it stands fully established that Hari Singh Nalwa never struck any coins in his own name, neither on his own volition nor with Ranjit Singh's appreciation concurrence or sanction. Historians have made a serious error in repeatedly stating this contention without offering any authentic contemporary evidence or any numismatic findings in support of their claim.

Sikh Pictorial Coins

C.J. Rodgers has shown a Sikh pictorial coin which bears on the obverse the Sikh legend, 'Degh Tegh Fateh, Nusrat Baidarang, Yaft uz Nanak Guru Gobind Singh', with the date Sambat 1993 i.e. AD 1836. On the reverse it bears the effigies of two persons, with the mint name Lahore and the frozen date Sambat 1885. Rodgers identifies these figures as those of Guru Nanak and his Muslim disciple Mardana.[126]

In 1892, C.J. Brown mentioned the coin as a curious rupee of Lahore, Sambat 1885, displaying the figures of Guru Nanak and his Muslim follower Mardana.[127] Gulshan Lall Chopra in his 1928 thesis, 'The Punjab as a sovereign state', examined the Sikh coins in the Government Museum, Lahore and the British Museum, London. He mentions a Sikh coin in the British Museum, London which has the usual inscription on the obverse and the figures of Guru Nanak and his Muslim fellow-wanderer Mardana on the reverse.[128]

Madanjit Kaur referred to the same coin in 1984, citing C.J. Rodgers's collection. She also considers the figures depicted on the coin as representing Guru Nanak in a meditative pose and Mardana fanning him with a chaur (flywhisk).[129] The drawings, however, show this object to be a lotus flower and not a fly whisk. Jai Parkash Singh in his Observations on Sikh Temple Tokens, mentions the same coin, and offers a similar explanation that the two figures represent Guru Nanak and Mardana.[130]

Stan Goron and Ken Wiggins made a fairly detailed presentation on Sikh coins in 1984 at the Institute of Research in Numismatic Studies, Anjaneri. By that time a second similar coin had been located in the British Museum, London, and the drawings of the two pictorial coins are given in Plate VI. These drawings are taken from the manuscript received from Goron. Goron and Wiggins argue that both these coins depict the Sikh legend on the obverse, and show Guru Nanak, with a pennant in the background, receiving an offering of flowers from Mardana, on the reverse.[131] They have attempted to link the striking of these pictorial coins with the wedding of Prince Nau Nihal Singh, when to celebrate the occasion a rupee each was distributed to all the inhabitants of Attari town. The explanation that these coins were struck for public distribution on the prince's wedding does not seem to be plausible as these coins were struck in

PLATE VI: SIKH PICTORAL COINS
1885-1893 SAMBAT

OBVERSE

REVERSE

DRAWING BY C.J. RODGERS   (Enlarged)

DRAWING FROM PHOTOGRAPHS   (Enlarged)
RECEIVED FROM BRITISH MUSEUM

early 1836 and the wedding took place in March 1837.[132] Further, in case a large number of these coins had indeed been struck, we would have had many of them available even today, as coins such as these, bearing the effigies of the revered Guru and Mardana, would most certainly have been preserved and passed on from generation to generation as family heirlooms of good omen and would never have been destroyed (see Plate VI).

A closer examination of the drawings of these coins and the interpretation given by various historians reveals that their observations appear to be somewhat out of context with the timehonoured Sikh traditions. Guru Nanak has invariably been shown as sitting under a tree, flanked by his disciples Bala and Mardana. Further, Mardana, the musician, has invariably been shown holding his *rabab*. His being shown as offering flowers to Guru Nanak strikes a discordant note. Guru Nanak has never been depicted with a flag (pennant) as shown on the coin, nor is there any mention of a flag used by Guru Nanak in the *Janam Sakhis*, and this depiction raises further doubts. Since the explanation given by the historians and numismatists has only been speculative, without any authentic evidence in support of the claim. A serious doubt arose in my mind. I felt that there is something more than what has been recorded. I launched a search to locate some reliable evidence regarding this puzzle or to find the correct interpretation if there was any.

Sohan Lal Suri, a descendent of a family of scribes working for the Sikh *misls*, was one of the most respected court historians of the Lahore Darbar; he had extremely intimate relations with the *sardars* of the Lahore Darbar and also enjoyed good relations with the British agents. He also had personal contacts with the Maharaja. His Persian treatise *Umdat-ut-Tawarikh*, about 7,000 pages long, covering the period AD 1812 to 1850, has been treated as a fairly authentic record of the activities of the Lahore Darbar.[133] While examining this long treatise in order to understand and appreciate the account of the Maharaja and his court, I incidentally noticed a passage giving an altogether different interpretation about the above-mentioned coin. Sohan Lal Suri refers to a conversation between Ranjit Singh and Baron Charles von Hugel on AD 13 February 1836 in which the matter regarding the closing of a mint and the preparation of a new diestamp was discussed. Hugel suggested the minting of a new coin with the existing legend as such inscribed on the obverse, and on the reverse the representation of the effigies of the Maharaja and Guru Nanak to be placed in such a way that the Maharaja is depicted with folded hands before Guru Nanak, seeking his blessings. Ranjit Singh was quite pleased with the suggestion, and thus the issuing of the coin under discussion was sanctioned. The translation of the Persian text is given by V. Suri as follows:

Right in the presence of Doctor Sahib mention was made about the closing up of the mint and [the] preparation of a new diestamp. Dr. Sahib said, 'The legend should be on one side and on the other side there should be the effigies of the Maharaja and Baba Nanak in such a way that the Sarkar be presented with folded hands before the Guru Sahib.'

The Maharaja approved of this suggestion which was considered to be proper and auspicious.[134]

Sohan Lal Suri mentions that on the second day of Magh Sankrant, i.e. AD 13 January 1836, Nur-ud-din and Chet Singh were appointed to escort Baron Hugel and Vigne Sahib, who presented themselves before the Maharaja, with Mackeson Sahib.[135] Baron Hugel also mentions in his *Travels in Kashmir and Punjab* that the Maharaja could not meet him on 12 January because this was a Sikh holiday. On 13 January 1836, Faqir Aziz-ud-din brought with him three elephants to conduct them to the palace. Mackeson was also invited.[136]

The actual year of the coin was Sambat 1893, i.e. AD 1836 and this coincides with the visit of Baron Hugel. The authenticity of the facts recorded in the *Umdat-ut-Tawarikh* regarding Baron Hugel's visit to Maharaja Ranjit Singh on 13 January 1836 is clearly established from the account of Baron Hugel. There is, however, no reference to the conversation regarding the design of the coin in Baron Hugel's account, perhaps because he did not consider the incident as worth recording. Sohan Lal Suri's account giving an altogether different picture is apparently very plausible, and is in contradiction to the drawings given by the numismatists. The actual photographs of these coins with the British Museum, London have been secured through the good offices of the British Museum authorities, and the drawings have been made on the basis of these photographs.[137] The figures in the photographs leave no doubt at all that the effigies on these coins are those of Ranjit Singh seeking blessings from Guru Nanak. The drawings of the photographs are given in Plate VI.

Lt. William Barr was a member of the mission led by Lt. Col. C.M. Wade to the Khyber Pass in early 1839, which passed through the Punjab and was received by Ranjit Singh. William Barr gave a very detailed account of the mission in a paper which appeared in the *United Service Journal*, July 1842, and which was later published as a separate book. While visiting the Lahore Fort on 21 February 1839, he noticed the Hall of Justice whose exterior was covered with paintings in oil in very extravagant detail. He writes:

Another picture represents the Maharaja in the presence of Baba Nanak, the founder of the Sikh sect; the holy father being most splendidly robed in a suit of embroidered gold, and sitting. Whilst his disciple, who has done so much to extend the domains of his followers, is dressed in bright green silk, and standing, with his hands joined in a supplicatory manner. Behind the Baba, keeping guard, is an Akali with a drawn sword, with but very little covering. A third represents a similar scene, with the single exception of Ranjit Singh being in a still more reverential position on his knees. A few drawings of flowers, which separate these compartments one from another, are extremely well done and true to nature.[138]

Bikramjit Hasrat stated in 1977 that 'these two paintings in oil, rare specimens are now lost'.[139] I also failed to get any information about these paintings from the authorities in Lahore during my visit to the city in 1988. Barr's account of the paintings on the walls of the Hall of Justice further contributes to the evidence supporting the claim that the coins depict Guru Nanak and Ranjit Singh.

Ranjit Singh considered the British to be greatly advanced in various scientific fields, including medicine, but he was very suspicious of their conduct. Like rulers everywhere, Ranjit Singh also took every precaution against any attempt to poison him by his enemies. While Ranjit Singh sought the opinions of European medicinemen, he would rarely take their medicines unless these were expressly approved by his own physicians and were even tested on someone with a similar ailment. While Ranjit Singh may be accused of being a hypochondriac, it is debatable whether there existed any effective medicine or cure at the time to prevent brain strokes and the resultant paralysis of limbs. Hugel was perhaps aware of this lack of medical knowledge in the Punjab at the time and was also aware of the Maharaja's belief that he had received an extra lease of life by the grace of God, to which end he gave thanks by resorting to prayers, giving grants to various religious endowments, and performing other acts of piety. Perhaps these factors prompted Hugel to suggest the striking of a coin in which Ranjit Singh would be shown seeking the blessings of Guru Nanak. The suggestion *prima facie* appeared very pleasing and was immediately approved by Ranjit Singh. For a person battling for his life, who cherished a firm belief that divine grace could extend his years, this was a godsent suggestion. The paintings on the walls of the Hall of Justice also show Ranjit Singh's definite approval of the suggestion put forward by Hugel. The suggestion, however, had a flaw since Hugel was ignorant of the principles of the Sikh polity based on teachings of Sikh Gurus.

The appearance of only two solitary coins and that too immediately after the annexation of the Punjab gives the impression that these coins were not minted and were only sample coins which did not secure final approval. There are instances where we have only an odd coin from a particular period, but even on the basis of this scanty evidence we cannot construe that certain coins were not struck. However, in the case of the coins minted during the reign of Ranjit Singh, there is no shortage, and coins are available from almost all the years of his reign. Hence, the nonexistence of these coins does give the distinct impression that they were not ultimately minted. This view is further strengthened by the fact that had these coins been minted, the people of the Punjab would certainly have preserved them as family heirlooms and these would have been available to us today.

A very vital aspect of the Sikh polity based on the Sikh ideology is that sovereignty belongs to the Gurus and not to any individual, and that coins are one of the essential symbols of this sovereignty.[140] While all contemporary coins bore the names of the rulers, only the Sikh coins were struck in the names of the Sikh Gurus. The Sikhs, especially the Akalis, were very particular about the observation of this tradition. Ranjit Singh was a very wise and astute ruler who could foresee the future with reasonable accuracy. It may be safely assumed that he realized that the Sikh community would not approve of the striking of such coins which showed a ruler seated along with Guru Nanak, no matter whether he is depicted seeking the blessings of the Guru. Perhaps this realization made him change his mind. He may also have been aware of the views of his community as shown in similar paintings depicted on the walls of the Hall of Justice, and therefore he may have changed his mind. The belief that Sikh sovereignty belongs to the Gurus and that coins are an essential symbol of that sovereignty seems to have been the guiding principle in the nonissue of these pictorial coins. It is therefore possible that these pictorial coins, although informally approved at an early stage when their striking was first suggested by Hugel, were not eventually issued, lest their appearance may hurt the feelings of the Sikhs, who deeply cherished the concept of the sovereignty of the Gurus and the Khalsa Panth.

NOTES

1. George Forster, *A Journey from Bengal to England*, vol. I, Punjab: Languages Department, 1970, p. 339.
2. Kanehiya Lal, *Tarikh-i-Punjab*, Patiala: Punjabi University, 1987, p. 38.
3. Hari Ram Gupta, *History of the Sikhs*, vol. V, New Delhi: Munshiram Manoharlal, p. 32.
4. Prem Singh Hoti, 'Character of Maharaja Ranjit Singh as an individual and as a ruler'. The original article being in Punjabi, its English translation is done by Gurbachan Singh, Khalsa College, Amritsar, in Chapter XI of *Maharaja Ranjit Singh First Death Centenary Memorial*, Punjab: Languages Department, 1970, p. 216.
5. Bhagat Singh, 'Trade and Commerce under Ranjit Singh', in *Maharaja Ranjit Singh*, ed. Fauja Singh and A.C. Arora, Patiala: Punjabi University, 1984, p. 173.
6. Jati Ram Gupta, 'Trade and Commerce under Ranjit Singh', in *Maharaja Ranjit Singh*, edited by Fauja Singh and A.C. Arora, Patiala: Punjabi University, 1984, pp. 190-2.
7. Bhagat Singh, op. cit., p. 183.
8. Foreign Department, *Secret consultations dated 18th November, 1843*, nos. 18-19, New Delhi: National Archives of India.
9. William Murray, *History of the Punjab—The Sikhs*, vol. II, London: H Allen & Co., 1846; Punjab: Languages Department, rpt., 1970, p. 174.
10. K.S. Lal, *The Mughal Harem*, New Delhi: Aditi Prakashan, 1985, p. 202.
11. Ibid., p. 27.
12. Ibid., pp. 162-5.
13. Ibid., p. 172.
14. J. Ovington, *Voyage to Surat in the Year 1689*, London, p. 46.
15. Bikramjit Hasrat, *Life and Times of Ranjit Singh*, Hoshiarpur: V.V. Research Institute, 1977, p. 214.
16. Waheed-ud-din, *The Real Ranjit Singh*, Karachi: Art Press, 1965, p. 169 and pp. 175-8.
17. Ibid., p. 172.
   Ranjit Singh's favourite queen, however, was Moran, a dancing girl of Amritsar, with whom he fell violently in love at first sight, when he was twenty-two. Before he could win her father's consent to her marrying him, he had to agree to a rather awkward condition. It was customary amongst the families of courtesans in Amritsar for the bridegroom to build,

light and blow ablaze with own breath a fire in his fatherinlaw's house. Moran's father, boggling at the idea of marrying his daughter outside his class, made the observation of this custom a condition, hoping that it would frighten the royal suitor away. Ranjit Singh unhesitatingly accepted the condition. It was, however, actually fulfilled in the house of Moran's godfather, Mian Samdu, a wealthy citizen of Amritsar, instead of in her father's house. The wedding was celebrated with great eclat. The bridegroom's party, which formed a procession of elephants, horses, *palkis* and people on foot stretching from Lahore Fort to Shalimar Garden, a distance of several miles, went all the way to Amritsar. The bride was given away by Mian Samdu with a dowry of several lakhs of rupees worth of jewellery, clothes and household effects, as if she was a princess.

18. Muhammad Latif, *History of Punjab*, Ludhiana: Kalyani Publishers, rpt., 1989, p. 358.
19. K.K. Khullar, *Maharaja Ranjit Singh*, New Delhi: Hem Publishers, 1980, p. 107.
20. (i) Baron Charles Hugel, op. cit., p. 384.
    (ii) Gulshan Lall Chopra, *Punjab as Sovereign State*, Hoshiarpur: V.V. Research Institute, 1960, p. 154, fn. 2.
21. (i) Bikramjit Hasrat, op. cit., p. 212.
    (ii) Sohan Lal Suri, *Imdat-ut-Twarikh, Dafter*, III, tr. V.S. Suri, Chandigarh: Punjab Itihas Prakashan, 1974, *Dafter*, III, p. 150. (The Raja Kalan was given a royal order that none of the glorious chieftains or the *khidmatgars* should be present in the bungalow.)
22. Baron Charles Hugel, op. cit., pp. 310-11.
23. (i) Gulshan Lall Chopra, op. cit., p. 154.
         Moran was afterwards discarded owing to unpopularity of Ranjit Singh with the priests of the Golden Temple. These priests showed their resentment first by refusing his offerings to the temple, and then by summoning him before their assembly at Amritsar; and the conqueror of Punjab, with folded hands and bare feet, acknowledged his sin and asked for forgiveness. A propitiatory fine of Rs. 125,000 was levied, but the wily culprit pleaded poverty, and got off by paying Rs. 5,000.
    (ii) K.K. Khullar, *Maharaja Ranjit Singh*, op. cit., p. 71.
         He (Phula Singh) denounced the Maharaja in open assembly. He even ordered that Ranjit Singh be punished. The Maharaja, who was guilty only of taking Moran, his Muslim wife, on a horse ride on the pillion, did not object. It is said he was tied with a rope to a tamarind tree and ordered 100 lashes. But before the punishment could begin, it was waived off.
    (iii) C.J. Rodgers, 'On the Coins of the Sikhs', *Journal of Asiatic Society of Bengal*, vol. L, Calcutta, 1881, p. 85.
    (iv) Fauja Singh, *Some Aspects of State and Society under Ranjit Singh*, New Delhi: Master Publishers, 1982, p. 61.
    (v) Waheed-ud-din, *The Real Ranjit Singh*, op. cit., p. 20.
24. Baron Charles Hugel, op. cit., p. 384.
25. Sohan Lal Suri, *Umdat-ut-Twarikh, Dafter*, III, op. cit., p. 99.
26. Amarnath, *Zafarnama-e-Ranjit Singh*, tr. and ed. Kirpal Singh, Patiala: Punjabi University, 1983, p. 20.
27. (i) Baron Charles Hugel, op. cit., pp. 283-4.
    (ii) Henry T. Princep, *Origin of Sikh Power in Punjab*, Punjab: Languages Department, rpt., 1970, p. 67.
28. V. Jacquemont, *The Punjab Hundred Years Ago*, tr. H.L.O. Garret, Punjab: Languages Department, rpt., 1971, p. 55.
29. (i) J.D. Cunningham, *History of the Sikhs*, New Delhi: S. Chand & Co., 1972, p. 159.

(ii) Gulshan Lall Chopra, op. cit., p. 154.

30. Lepel Griffin, *Maharaja Ranjit Singh*, Punjab: Languages Department, rpt., 1970, p. 109.
31. Gulshan Lall Chopra, op. cit., pp. 154-5.
32. Bikramjit Hasrat, op. cit., p. 46.
33. Ibid., p. 46.
34. Muhammad Latif, *History of Punjab*, op. cit., p. 358.
35. Khushwant Singh, *Ranjit Singh*, Bombay: George Allen & Unwin, 1982, p. 53.
36. Waheed-ud-din, *The Real Ranjit Singh*, op. cit., p. 173.
37. K.K. Khullar, *Maharaja Ranjit Singh*, op. cit., p. 107.
38. Gopal Singh, *History of Sikh Peoples*, New Delhi: World Sikh University Press, 1979, p. 450.
39. C.J. Rodgers, 'On the Coins of the Sikhs', op. cit., pp. 85, 91.
40. C.J. Rodgers, *Catalogue of Coins in the, Government Museum Lahore*, Calcutta, 1891, pp. 92-5.
41. C.J. Brown, *Coins of India*, Heritage of India Series, Calcutta: Association Press, 1922, p. 107.
42. Parmeshwari Lal Gupta, *Coins of India*, New Delhi: National Book Trust, 1969, p. 147.
43. Parmeshwari Lal Gupta and Sanjay Garg, *The Coins of Dal Khalsa and Lahore Darbar*, Chandigarh: Government of Punjab, pp. 46-7.
    'The coins are of the same type as type G and are said to have been issued from Sambat 1858 to 1861 only for three or four years. Here the peepal leaf on the reverse is replaced by a two-pronged twig or spray. Due to the resemblance of this symbol with the tail of a peacock, a legend has sprung out of it. It is said that it is the illusion to the Kashmiri Muslim girl, named Mora or Moran, who had gained favour with Ranjit Singh. She got these coins struck for herself. As such these coins are called Mora-Kanchan-Shahi or simply Mora-Shahi'.
    'Those who believe this story never cared to know that Ranjit Singh's love affair with this girl is dated by Cunningham in AD 1810 (Sambat 1867). If by any reason this date is not relied, even then there is no denial that Amritsar was not occupied by Ranjit Singh at any date earlier than Sambat 1862-3. Whereas the earliest date on the coins of this type is Sambat 1858. Ranjit Singh was not in a position, at this date, to issue any coins from Amritsar by his own authority. It is quite apparent that the coins were issued only in the period of the Dal Khalsa. They might have been issued by some *misl*, stationed at Amritsar, other than that which had introduced the symbol of peepal leaf earlier. This is equally true to the types of J & K that are mentioned next'.
44. *Standard Guide to South Asian Coins and Paper Money Since 1556 AD*, Wisconsin: Krause Publications, 1st edn, p. 113.
45. Madanjit Kaur, 'A Study of Sikh Numismatics with Special Reference to the Coins of Maharaja Ranjit Singh', in *Maharaja Ranjit Singh: Politics, Society and Economy*, ed. Fauja Singh and A.C. Arora, Patiala: Punjabi University, 1984, pp. 329-30.
46. Ken Wiggins and Stan Goron, 'Gold and Silver Coinage of the Sikhs', Inaugural Address, International Colloquium, Nasik: Indian Institute of Research in Numismatic Studies, 1984, p. 132.
47. Surinder Singh, 'Patiala State Coinage', *Research Bulletin*, Chandigarh: Panjab University, vol. XXI, no. 2, 1990, p. 207.
48. Surinder Singh, 'Nabha State Coinage', *Research Bulletin*, Chandigarh: Panjab University, vol. XXI, no. 1, 1990 April 1990, p. 169.
49. (i) Muhammad Latif, *History of Punjab*, op. cit., p. 353.

(ii) Gulshan Lall Chopra, op. cit., p. 154.

(iii) Amarnath, *Zafarnama-e-Ranjit Singh*, op. cit., p. 14.

(iv) Bikramjit Hasrat, *Life and Times of Ranjit Singh*, op. cit., p. 42.

(v) Khushwant Singh, *Maharaja Ranjit Singh*, op. cit., p. 47.

50. (i) Bikramjit Hasrat, op. cit., p. 33.

(ii) Khushwant Singh, *Maharaja Ranjit Singh*, op. cit., p. 7.

51. Bhagat Singh, *Sikh Polity*, New Delhi: Oriental Publishers & Distributors, 1978, p. 200.

52. Surinder Singh, 'Ranjit Singh's Effigy on Sikh Coins', *Journal of the Oriental Numismatic Society*, Newsletter no. 123, Surrey, U.K., April 1990.

53. C.J. Rodgers, 'On the Coin of the Sikhs', op. cit., Plate IV.

54. Amarnath, *Zafarnama-e-Ranjit Singh*, op. cit., p. 20.

55. Khushwant Singh, *Maharaja Ranjit Singh*, op. cit., p. 53.

56. Waheed-ud-din, *The Real Ranjit Singh*, op. cit., p. 172.

57. Muhammad Latif, *History of Sikhs*, op. cit., p. 358.

58. Bikramjit Hasrat, op. cit., p. 45.

59. Lepel Griffin, *Ranjit Singh*, op. cit., p. 109.

60. J.D. Cunningham, *History of Sikhs*, op. cit., p. 159.

61. Amarnath, *Zafarnama-e-Ranjit Singh*, op. cit., p. 21.

62. Kanehiya Lal, *Tarikh-i-Punjab*, op. cit., p. 154.

63. Ahmad Shah Batalvi, *Tarikh-i-Punjab*, tr. Gurbux Singh, Patiala: Punjabi University, 1969, p. 68.

64. J.D. Cunningham, *History of Sikhs*, p. 118.

65. Henry T. Princep, *Origin of the Sikh Power in Punjab*, 1970, pp. 43, 45.

66. (i) Muhammad Latif, op. cit., p. 358.

(ii) Lepel Griffin, op. cit., p. 163.

(iii) C.J. Rodgers, op. cit., p. 83.

67. N.K. Sinha, *Ranjit Singh*, Calcutta: A. Mukherjee & Co., 1975, p. 16.

68. Sohan Lal Suri, *Twarikh-e-Punjab, Dafter*, II, op. cit., p. 65.

69. Bhagat Singh, 'Emergence and Dissolution of Bhangi Misal', *Panjab Present*, vol. XVIII, no. 1, Patiala: Punjabi University, April 1984, p. 45.

70. J.S. Grewal and Indu Banga, *Maharaja Ranjit Singh and His Times*, Amritsar: Guru Nanak Dev University, 1980, p. 80.

71. Anand Gauba, 'Amritsar in the Early 19th Century', in *Maharaja Ranjit Singh and His Times*, Amritsar: Guru Nanak Dev University, 1980, p. 187.

72. Bikramjit Hasrat, op. cit., p. 380.

73. J.S. Grewal and Indu Banga, *Early 19th Century Punjab*, Amritsar: Guru Nanak Dev University, 1975, p. 16.

74. *Standard Guide to South Asian Coins*, op. cit., pp. 112-13.

75. J.S. Grewal and Indu Banga, *Early 19th Century Punjab*, op. cit., p. 17.

76. (i) *Peshawar Gazetteer*, op. cit., p. 70.

(ii) Prem Singh Hoti, *Life of Hari Singh Nalwa*, Ludhiana: Lahore Book Shop, 1937, p. 275.

77. Mohan Lal, *Travels in Punjab, Afghanistan and Turkistan*, Punjab: Languages Department, 1970, p. xix.

78. Prem Singh Hoti, op. cit., pp. 123-4.
(English translation, *Sher-e-Punjab*). 'Maharaja Ranjit Singh regularly received information about the progress in Kashmir, the exalted Maharaja was so pleased with the administration of Hari Singh Nalwa that through a special order he bestowed on Sardar Hari Singh the

high privilege of minting a coin in his name. On receiving the extremely joyful order of
the Maharaja, Sardar Hari Singh held a darbar for thanksgiving. He submitted very respectfully,
that in the rightness of things, a coin can be struck only in the name of the exalted
Maharaja and for persons like him, the Maharaja's appreciation was worth millions. The
Maharaja was still more pleased at the truthfulness, sacrifice and humility of Hari Singh and
wrote back that he (the Maharaja) was heartily pleased to issue that order and would feel
happy to see that order carried out. Sardar Hari Singh, therefore, struck a coin in his name
in Kashmir. Its silver content was 10 *mashas*. Compared with the current (1912) coins it
was worth 8 *annas*. On one side of the coin was inscribed "Sri Akal Sahai" in Persian script
and Sambat 1878. On the other side was written "Hari Singh" with the words "Yak rupai"
under it. Sir Lepel Griffin writes that the Hari Singh rupee is wellknown in Kashmir up to
now (Sambat 1890). He adds that this coin called the Hari Singhia rupee is legal tender all
over Punjab. Maulana Muhammad Din writes in his *Mukmal Twarikh-i-Kashmir* (Complete
History of Kashmir) that Hari Singh struck a coin in his name. It was known as the Hari
Singhia rupaiya. Its value was equal to the present-day 8 annas piece. Those who have
seen the Hari Singhia paisa and the Hari Singhiya rupaiya, are living upto this day (Sambat
1952). Besides silver coins, a bronze coin was also struck. It was called the Harisinghee
paisa.'

79. Ibid., pp. 240-1.
80. A.S. Sandhu, op. cit., pp. 17, 73, 113.
81. S.S. Johar, *Hari Singh Nalwa*, New Delhi: Sagar Publication, 1982, p. 171
82. Gulcharan Singh, *Ranjit Singh and his Generals*, Jullandhar: Sujlana Publishers, 1976,
    pp. 108-9.
83. Kanehiya Lal, *Tarikh-i-Punjab*, Patiala: Punjabi University, 1987, p. 268.
84. C.M.D. Sufi, *History of Kashmir*, vol. II, New Delhi: Light and Life Publications, 1974,
    p. 730.
85. D.C. Sharma, *Kashmir under the Sikhs*, Delhi: Seema Publishers, 1983, p. 230.
86. (i) D.C. Sharma, op. cit., p. 231.
    (ii) D.C. Sharma, Chapter on Banking and Currency included in the annotated translation
         by him of *Kashmir under Maharaja Ranjit Singh* by Charles Baron von Hugel, New
         Delhi: Atlantic Publishers & Distributors, 1984, pp. 70-1.
87. R.K. Parmu, *History of Sikh Rule in Kashmir*, Srinagar: J&K Govt. Publication, 1977,
    p. 122.
88. Major Leach, *Survey 1837*, Foreign Department, Secret Consultations, no. 22, 1843, New
    Delhi: National Archives of India.
89. N.K. Sinha, *Ranjit Singh*, Calcutta: A. Mukherjee & Co., rpt., 1984, p. 152.
90. Bikramjit Hasrat, op. cit., pp. 134, 296.
91. Bhagat Singh, 'Trade and Commerce under Ranjit Singh', in *Maharaja Ranjit Singh:
    Politics, Society and Economy*, ed. Fauja Singh and A.C. Arora, Patiala: Punjabi University,
    1984. p. 182.
92. G.T. Vigne, *Travel in Kashmir, Ladakh and Iskardu*, London: Henry Colburn Publishers,
    1842, p. 57.
93. Ibid., p. 123.
94. Madhavi Yasin, *Kashmir under Ranjit Singh*, op. cit., p. 2, n. 58.
95. Shahamat Ali, *Sikhs and Afghans*, Punjab: Languages Department, rpt., 1970, p. 53.
96. G.S. Chhabra, *Advanced History of Punjab*, vol. II, Jullandhar: Parkash Brothers, 1976,
    p. 75.
97. Gopal Singh, *History of Sikh People*, New Delhi: World Sikh University Press, 1979,
    p. 476.

98. Ganeshi Lal, *Siyahat-i-Kashmir*, March 1846, translated and annotated by V.S. Suri, Simla, 1955, pp. 23, 28, 32, 34 and 39.

99. Ibid., p. 38.

100. Walter Lawrence, *The Valley of Kashmir*, Henry Frowde, London: Oxford University Press, 1895, p. 235.

101. Sita Ram Kohli, 'Land Revenue Administration under Maharaja Ranjit Singh', *Journal of Punjab Historical Society*, vol. VII, no. 2, 1919, p. 90.

102. Hans Herrli, *The Coins of Sikhs*, op. cit., p. 225.

103. Abstract of intelligence report from Kashmir, dated 13 August 1836, nos. 57-9, National Archives of India, New Delhi. 'The old coin has been discontinued and a new one circulated . . . the old rupee was valued 11 *annas* but it has been reduced to 9 *annas* old'.

104. Sita Ram Kohli, op. cit., p. 82.

105. Bhagat Singh, Inaugural address, in Fauja Singh and A.C. Arora (eds.), *Maharaja Ranjit Singh: Polity, Society and Economy*, Patiala: Punjabi University, 1984, p. 2.

106. Ibid., p. 182.

107. Hari Ram Gupta, *History of Sikhs*, vol. II, New Delhi: Munshiram Manoharlal, 1978, p. 229.

108 Hari Ram Gupta, *History of Sikhs*, vol. V, New Delhi: Munshiram Manoharlal, 1991, p. 131.

109 Ibid., p. 506.

110. A.S. Sandhu, *General Hari Singh Nalwa*, op. cit., p. 102.

111. J.D. Cunningham, *History of Sikhs*, op. cit., p. 173.

112. Bikramjit Hasrat, op. cit., p. 268.

113. Lepel Griffin, *Maharaja Ranjit Singh*, op. cit., p. 185.

114. C.J. Rodgers, 'On the Coin of the Sikhs', op. cit., p. 91.

115. C.J. Rodgers, *Catalogue of Coins in the Government Museum Lahore*, Calcutta, 1891, pp. 99 and 125.

116. Wiggins and Goron, 'The Sikh Coinage of Kashmir', *Journal of Oriental Numismatic Society*, Surrey, U.K., Information Sheet no. 25, March 1983.

117. Herrli, *The Catalogue of Sikh Coins*, op. cit., pp. 124-6.

118. Wiggins and Goron, op. cit., pp. 2, 3.

119. Herrli, *The Coins of the Sikhs*, op. cit., p. 123.

120. Wiggins and Goron, op. cit., p. 3.

121. Herrli, op. cit., p. 108.

122. (i) Wiggins and Goron, op. cit., p. 5.
 (ii) Herrli, op. cit., p. 108.

123. Akali Kaur Singh, 'Gur Shabad Rattan Parkash', Patiala: Languages Department, Punjab, p. 111.

124. Wiggins and Goron, op. cit., p. 6.

125. Herrli, op. cit., p. 108.

126. Dual dating has been resorted to in Oriental coinage for various reasons to show different eras or the years of the reign of a ruler along with the particular year. Ranjit Singh has used frozen dates of 1884 and 1885 Sambat, the years in which he had had serious paralytic attacks. The exact reasons for this have not been ascertained so far.

127. C.J. Brown, *Coins of India*, Heritage of India Series, Calcutta: Association Press, 1922, p. 107.

128. Gulshan Lall Chopra, op. cit., p. 155.

129. Madanjit Kaur, 'A Study of Sikh Numismatics with Special Reference to the Coins of Maharaja Ranjit Singh and his Successors', in *Maharaja Ranjit Singh: Politics, Society and Economy*, ed. Fauja Singh and A.C. Arora, Patiala: Punjabi University, 1984, p. 331; Madanjit Kaur, an unpublished Manuscript on Sikh Coins, p. 25.

130. Jai Parkash Singh, 'Observations on Sikh Tokens', *Numismatic International Bulletin*, Dallas, Texas, USA, vol. XVI, no. 12, Dec. 1982, pp. 363-4.

131. Goron and Wiggins, 'Gold and Silver Coinage of the Sikhs', paper presented at the Institute of Research in Numismatic Studies, Anjaneri, Nasik, 1984, p. 15.

132. Sohan Lal Suri, *Imdat-ut-Twarikh*, tr. V. Suri, *Daftar*, III, op. cit., p. 337.

133. Ibid., pp. xxiii-xxv.

134. Ibid., p. 298.

135. Ibid., p. 267.

136. Charles Baron von Hugel, op. cit., pp. 283-5.

137. The photographs of these coins have been received through the good offices of Ken Wiggins and Joe Cribb of the British Museum, London, vide their letter dated 22 January 1990.

138. William Barr, *Journal of a March from Delhi to Kabul*, Punjab: Languages Department, 1970, p. 57.

139. Bikramjit Hasrat, op. cit., p. 436.

140. Bhagat Singh, *Sikh Polity*, op. cit., p. 201.

CHAPTER IV

Sikh Coinage of the Lahore Darbar:
The Post Ranjit Singh Period
AD 1839-1849

It is said that once Maharaja Ranjit Singh was shown the map of India by one of the Christian officers. Ranjit Singh was an illiterate sovereign. He did not know why the map was coloured red, green, blue and yellow, etc. He requested the Christian officer to explain the meaning of the different colourings in the map. The officer explained that the red colour represented the territories of India which had passed into the hands of Christian merchants of England constituting the East India Company. Ranjit Singh immediately exclaimed, 'Sab lal ho jaega', i.e. the whole map of India will become red coloured. There was a ring of prophecy in his explanation. Hardly had twenty years passed after his death, when his words came to be verified to the very letter for the Christian merchants became masters of almost the whole subcontinent of India and the map of the country became coloured red all over.[1]

Historical Developments during 1839-1849

The Sikh state had indeed reached its apogee. Its past achievements might have impressed the casual observer but those who were well informed were quite aware of its impending fate. The three factors which had already become manifest—namely, the evertightening circle of British power and influence around this kingdom, the contending parties in the Lahore Darbar, and, worst of all, the well known incapacities of the heirs of Ranjit Singh—unmistakably indicated the hastening of the end of Sikh independence. Ranjit Singh had been a 'state in person', and his government was personal and not based on any definite norms or established institutions. His death inevitably proved disastrous for the state.[2]

Ranjit Singh expired on 27 June 1839, and a few days later his son Kharak Singh, aged 38 years, succeeded to the throne without any opposition. Prince Sher Singh made some half-hearted attempt to claim the throne but finding no support for his claim, he gave up his intrigues and remained neutral. Kharak Singh had many vices which had impaired both his health and mental reflexes. As his confidant he chose Chet Singh, who was greatly hostile to Dhian Singh, the minister. Nau Nihal Singh, who had returned from Peshawar and who was keen to assume the supreme authority, was won over by Dhian Singh, and various intrigues began to surface; British diplomacy also became very active in the arena of Sikh politics. Disturbances arose in various areas, such as Una, Muzaffarabad, Darband, and Punchh and the *kardars* and provincial governors started defalcating state funds.[3] Kharak Singh became ill in July 1840; it was suspected that he had been administered a slow-acting poison and the likelihood of his early death was anticipated. Kharak Singh died on 5 November 1840.[4]

After the funeral of Kharak Singh, when Nau Nihal Singh, along with Dhian Singh and his son Udham Singh, was entering Hazuri Bagh, the parapet of the gate of the fort wall crashed down. Udham Singh died on the spot, Nau Nihal Singh was greviously wounded and expired within a few hours, and Dhian Singh was slightly hurt. Nau Nihal Singh's death is a controversial subject since the fall of the parapet seems to have been an accident rather than the outcome of a conspiracy. This tragedy struck at the very roots of the Sikh kingdom. The whole Sikh nation was shocked; people in the provinces would not believe it at first, and when the news was confirmed, it caused extreme consternation. The country faced an awkward dilemma: with Nau Nihal Singh's death ended the legitimate line of Ranjit Singh.[5]

There were major differences amongst the parties, especially between Chand Kaur, widow of Kharak Singh, and Sher Singh, but ultimately Sher Singh ascended the throne on 20 January 1841 in the presence of rajas and sardars in an open *darbar*. The Sindanwalia *sardars* did not accept Sher Singh's rule and continued hatching their schemes to disrupt and undermine his regime. In the meantime, disorders occurred in the once-disciplined Sikh army and the troops engaged in loot and plunder. Mutiny in the army broke out in Mandi (Kullu), Multan, Derajat, Peshawar, and Kashmir where the rebellious Sikh army killed the governor, Mihan Singh. The foreign officers also started leaving their posts. The Sikh troops who were loyal to Dhian Singh turned against him due to the atrocities committed against the Sikh troops in Kashmir by his uncle Gulab Singh. The widow of Nau Nihal Singh gave birth to a stillborn child which further queered the pitch between Sher Singh and the Sindanwalia *sardars*.[6] On 9 June 1842 Chand Kaur was made to drink poison and was later stoned to death by her maids. When the maids were punished by the cutting off of their hands, they accused Dhian Singh and Sher Singh for the death of Chand Kaur.

On 15 September 1842, while carrying out an inspection of the troops, Sher Singh was shot dead by Ajit Singh Sindanwalia. Sher Singh's son Kanwar Pratap Singh was slaughtered by Lehna Singh when the young boy was conducting Ganesh *puja*. Dhian Singh, while entering the fort, was cornered by Ajit Singh and his men and was killed and cut into pieces. Thus, in the course of a few hours, the Maharaja, his son, and the minister were slaughtered by the Sindanwalias.[7] These crimes sent a wave of horror through Lahore. The Sikh army *panchayats* decided to punish the malefactors, surrounded the fort, and killed Ajit Singh along with about 600 of his troops.

Dalip Singh, the child prince, was proclaimed Maharaja on 16 September and Heera Singh became his minister. The machinery and the functions of the government were all deranged. The army on which Heera Singh was constrained to depend was an unruly and insatiable monster, which he found in the end impossible to appease. Heera Singh depended on Pandit Jalla, who was against Suchet Singh, uncle of Heera Singh, and in a battle on 27 March, Suchet Singh was killed. The party opposing Heera Singh comprised Kashmira Singh, Peshora Singh, Attar Singh Sindanwalia, and Rani Jindan. Within a few months the two camps met in a fight in which Heera Singh, Pandit Jalla, Mian Sohan Singh, son of Gulab Singh, and their companions were killed. Gradually Jindan took over the functions of the court with the help of Jawahar Singh, her brother, as *wazir* and Lal Singh as commander of the army. The army killed Jawahar Singh on 21 September 1845 and took over the administration of the state.[8] By this time the British had finally decided to take over the Punjab and a large assembly of British troops was poised on the Punjab frontier. Rani Jindan, Lal Singh as the minister, and Tej Singh as commander of the forces did not make any preparations and both her advisers, besides many others, were in the pay of the British. But the *panchayats* in the cantonments were prepared for the battle with the British. The war began on 18 December 1845 and within three days the British were badly beaten by the evening of 21 December. Lal Singh who came with fresh Sikh troops, seeing the situation, withdrew his forces to save the British from total defeat. Thus, the British won the First Anglo-Sikh War with the subversion of the Sikh generals and the Punjab came under British occupation.[9] The Treaty of Lahore in December 1846 made the Lahore Darbar surrender large areas of territory to the British, who then sold off Kashmir to Gulab Singh. Further, The Treaty of Lahore was further revised in favour of the English by the Treaty of Bhairowal on 16 December 1846. The revised Treaty of Bhairowal gave all administrative control so far held by the Regency Council to the British Resident.[10] The Second Anglo-Sikh War was manoeuvred by the British, and the Sikh state was annexed to the British territories in March 1849.

Influence of Sikh Coinage on the Coinage of the cis-Sutlej States

The Phulkian or the cis-Sutlej states emerged as a result of the consolidation of the landholdings of the descendants of Phul in the mid-seventeenth century. The states of Patiala, Nabha, Jind, Faridkot, and Kaithal were ruled by the Malwa *sardars*, who were independent in the administration of their states, yet they stood on an altogether different footing than the Majha *sardars* across the Sutlej. The Sikh *misldars* in the Rachna, Bari, and Jullandhar *doabs* refused to entertain any understanding with the Mughal rulers and the Afghan invaders in spite of repeated suggestions and inducements of *jagirs* and shares in war booty.[11] Their spirit of fierce independence and deep-rooted Sikh teachings and identity prevented them from accepting the overlordship of any authority other than that of their Gurus and the Khalsa Panth. In 1783, when Delhi was administered by Sardar Baghel Singh, it became near impossible for the court officials to arrange a meeting between the *sardar* and the emperor because of Baghel Singh's refusal to make the customary bow before the emperor, it being against the tenets of the Sikh religion.[12] Various rules of protocol were waived in arranging a meeting between the *sardar* and the emperor at the time of Baghel Singh's departure from Delhi in December 1783, during which Mughal mace bearers and courtiers made the customary bows to the emperor on behalf of the fully armed *sardar*.[13]

On the other hand, the rajas of Patiala, the leading cis-Sutlej state, willingly presented themselves and submitted to the Mughal rulers and the Afghan invaders, accepted their overlordship, became their vassals, and paid annual tributes and *nazrana*.[14] They never wholeheartedly joined the mainstream of the Sikh struggle against the tyranny of the Mughals and the invasions of the Afghans. Whenever the Dal Khalsa tried to chastize them for their servile conduct, they managed to save themselves through the good offices of Jassa Singh Ahluwalia, the strongest leader of the Majha *misls* at the time, to whom both Ala Singh and Amar Singh paid a fixed annual tribute.[15]

The Sikhs had been raiding Lahore and its suburbs at every opportunity and finally occupied it in 1765.[16] They issued coins in the name of their Gurus as a symbol of their sovereignty.[17] Amar Singh, the raja of Patiala, also struck coins in 1767, called the Durrani currency since it was issued in the name of Ahmad Shah Abdali.[18] The other cis-Sutlej states also followed the example of the Patiala rulers and started striking Durrani coinage as vassals of the Afghan ruler.[19] These states continued to strike Durrani coins even after the threat of an Afghan invasion had become totally non-existent. The Nabha state broke away from this tradition some time around 1835 and started striking coins in the name of the Sikh Gurus,[20] while the other cis-Sutlej states continued to strike Durrani coins till the British currency became the prevalent currency during the latter half of the eighteenth century and the state currencies died their natural deaths due to excessive debasement and loss of value.

The house of Patiala is said to have been blessed by the Sikh Gurus,[21] but its rulers, although being Sikh *sardars*, had a somewhat diluted and superficial faith in the true spirit of the Khalsa and the Sikh ideology. Their dominant interest was self-preservation and the extension of their territories. They were oblivious to the concept of Sikh sovereignty and the notion that coinage was an essential expression of this sovereignty. Phul's grandson Ala Singh became the chief on his father's murder in 1716. Within a couple of years, he had avenged his father's murder, consolidated his position, and took up his residence at Barnala in 1720, which had to be virtually rebuilt.[22] Ala Singh further consolidated his position by subduing the neighbouring chiefs and annexing Sanawar and other adjoining areas. He founded Patiala and built a mudfort there in 1753.[23] By 1757 he was able to defeat the neighbouring Bhatti chiefs and was looked upon as one of the rising Sikh chiefs. Ala Singh fought against both the Muslims as well as the Sikhs. He joined the Sikhs against the Muslims when it suited his purpose and accepted the suzerainty of the Mughals and the Afghans when it was in his interest to do so. In fact, his religious fervour was greatly tempered by his political ambitions and his desire to avoid an unequal fight with the Afghans.

Ala Singh had three confrontations with the Afghans during Ahmad Shah Abdali's invasions of India, the first in March 1761.[24] When Ahmad Shah reached Sirhind, Ala Singh presented himself bearing costly gifts and promised to pay an annual tribute. Ahmad Shah received him warmly and awarded him a robe of honour (khilat). He also directed the governor of Sirhind to consider Ala Singh's possessions as being separate from his territories. The Sikhs, who hated the Mughals, had no love for the Afghans. In fact, they had their own ambitions and could not resist the temptation of looting the immense baggage train of Ahmad Shah and harrassing his troops on their return. As soon as Ahmad Shah turned his back, the Sikhs started ravaging the Punjab and defeated his army sent under Nur-ud-din, and occupied Lahore. Ahmad Shah made his sixth invasion in February 1762 and in a pitched battle near Barnala killed about 20,000 Sikhs. Ala Singh, who had in fact vacillated in fighting for the Sikhs, was arrested by Ahmad Shah and was eventually released on the payment of a ransom and a promise to pay annual tribute.[25] But as soon as Ahmad Shah turned his back, the Sikhs again started harassing his governors and looting their territories. In early 1774 the Sikhs reached Sirhind, killed Zen Khan, pulled down the fort, and named the place Fatehgarh Sahib.[26] During his seventh invasion in December 1764-March 1765 Ahmad Shah saw Sirhind in total ruin. Ala Singh presented himself, bearing costly presents and sought the governorship of Sirhind. Ahmad Shah realizing the inability of the Muslim governors to resist Sikh attacks, conferred on Ala Singh a khilat, kettle drums, and banners, and installed him as an independent chief of Sirhind for an annual subsidy of three and a half lakh rupees. Ala Singh died soon thereafter on 22 August 1765.[27] He was succeeded by his grandson Amar Singh.

In March 1767 Ahmad Shah again reached Sirhind and called for Amar Singh and after receiving tribute granted him a robe of honour, the subedari of Sirhind, and the superlative title of Raja-e-Rajagan.[28] The rulers of Patiala were authorized to mint Durrani coins as a privilege in recognition of their being independent chiefs.[29] However, historians differ as to whether the coins were initially struck by Ala Singh in 1765 or by Amar Singh in 1767. The study of the coinage of the cis-Sutlej states was initially carried out by General R.C. Taylor, agent to the Lt. Governor of the cis-Sutlej states, in 1869 and his study has been relied upon by Lepel Griffin,[30] and the Patiala state authorities.[31] These authorities believe that the Patiala state mint was established under the orders of Ahmad Shah Abdali and that the initial coins were struck by Maharaja Amar Singh and are current in the family of Amar Singh at Patiala. The succeeding rulers to the throne issued the same coins and considered themselves the subjects of the Durrani emperor.[32] The Hussain Shahi account, written in 1778 within thirty years of the initial issues, makes no reference to the striking of the coins by Ala Singh, and lends support to the view that the coins were initially struck by Amar Singh.

R.C. Temple carried out a detailed study of the coinage of the cis-Sutlej states in 1889.[33] The cis-Sutlej states, which were ruled by Sikh *sardars* except for the Malerkotla state which was under a Muslim ruler, were actually under the suzerainty of the Afghan ruler Ahmad Shah Abdali and his successors. Hence, they all minted Durrani coinage and therefore the study of their coinage has not been taken up in this investigation. The rulers of Patiala, the largest state, while reporting to their Durrani overlords, dismissed the trans-Sutlej Sikhs as 'contemptible wretched troops and infidel armies destined for utter destruction'.[34] The Patiala rulers maintained their rule from 1729 to 1948, when the state was merged into the Indian Union. The Durrani state coinage, popularly called the Raja Shahi coinage, deteriorated due to the mismanagement of successive rulers and its value gradually fell to only 8 *annas*; it was discontinued around 1893 and was replaced by the British Indian currency. [35]

Maharaja Bhupinder Singh ruled Patiala from 1900 to 1938. He was a very capable and clever ruler but his lifestyle was very lavish and extravagant and the state fell into perpetual financial difficulties.[36] He kept the British authorities in good humour by expressions of his loyalty, extravagant entertainments, and assistance in the war effort. The British ignored his drawbacks, but had to place a financial expert, Sir Fredrich Gauntlet, former accountant general, as his finance minister to rescue the rapidly decaying economy of the state.[37] Bhupinder Singh was very fond of celebrating Dussehra and other festivals in regal style and used to offer gold and silver coins especially minted on the occasion for *puja* and for distribution among his household staff and the state officials.[38] The exact date of the issue of these coins could not be ascertained since the complete record is not available with the Punjab State Archives. Being the most important Sikh ruler after the fall of the Lahore Darbar, the Sikh legend was adopted on the *puja* coins, which were called the Guru Sahib coins. The tradition of the distribution of *nazrana* coins continued even after the death of Bhupinder Singh by his son and successor Maharaja Yadvindra Singh. Regular correspondence exists regarding the assessment of the financial requirements with Sardar Sahib Deodhi Mualla. Tenders were solicited from the various *sarafs*, and by and large the work of minting these coins was awarded to Bajramal Bhagirath Mal and Chowdhury Abdul Hakim, who were perhaps the leading *sarafs* in Patiala. The coins which remained undistributed were melted and were recast the following year when the prices of gold and silver had increased to an unusually high rate.[39] The last such correspondence is a letter no. 957 dated AD 22 August 1943 from Sardar

Sahib Deodhi Mualla addressed to the finance minister in which it was stressed that coins once used in *puja* by the august master could not be reused, since this practice was violative of the *shastras*. It was also stressed that the reduction in the number of coins for use in the various ceremonies would also amount to the reduction in the prestige and honour of the *shastras*. Thus, it is evident that the ceremonies continued to be performed by Maharaja Yadvindra Singh till the accession of the state to the Union of India.[40]

There are with the Sheesh Mahal Museum, Patiala about a dozen gold coins and about 1,500 silver coins with the '*Degh Tegh Fateh*' legend. Recently an examination of the large number of Sikh coins in the Sheesh Mahal Museum was carried out by Parmeshwari Lal Gupta and Sanjay Garg under the aegis of the Indian Institute of Research in Numismatic Studies, Anjaneri, Nasik. They have drawn up a catalogue of *The Coins of the Dal Khalsa and Lahore Darbar* on behalf of the Government of Punjab. They describe some coins as problematic coins.[41] The rulers of Patiala, although Sikh, had also conducted certain traditional Hindu *pujas* during Dussehra. They had used both gold and silver coins especially minted for these occasions, as is abundantly clear from the state records. The mark of an arrow appears to be that of Maharaja Bhupinder Singh in the early years of his reign and that of a rifle during his later years, presumably after World War I. The readily available coins pertain to 1958, 1993, 1994 Sambat, i.e. AD 1901, 1936, 1937, all from the period of his rule. These coins bear the Sikh legends (see Plate VII)[42]:

Obverse   *Degh Tegh Fateh-o-Nusrat Baidarang*
            Yaft uz Nanak Guru Gobind Singh
Reverse   *Jalus Maiminat Manus Zarb Sirhind.*

The theory that dual coinage was used by Ala Singh to appease the Durranis as well as the Dal Khalsa, as proposed by Parmeshwari Lal Gupta, is apparently a fanciful assertion as is shown by the definite evidence available in the Punjab State Archives. Walter Hamilton's suggestion that these coins were connected with religious ceremonies stands established and is endorsed by the government records and the coins in the Government Museum.[43] No such coins are forthcoming from the local *sarafs*, which further establishes that these coins were not legal tender and were used for *puja* purposes only. It is understood that most of these coins were exchanged with the prevailing currency from the state treasury. These coins were melted and reminted afresh for *puja* year after year so that the religious ceremonies continued to be carried out with fresh coins every year. The coins available with the Sheesh Mahal Museum are in mint condition. These facts clearly establish that these coins are no longer problematic coins, but were instead the *nazrana* coins used by the Patiala rulers for *puja* as distinct from the regular currency and were not regular issues for public use. There is no mention of Guru

PLATE VII: GURU SAHIB COINS
PATIALA STATE

DATE NOT CLEAR

VS (19)58

VS (19)94

Sahib coins in the Note on the Patiala State Currency, which also establishes that these coins were only for the personal use of the ruler during the Dussehra *puja* ceremonies and were not state issues for general use (see note 31).

The second state that came under the influence of the Sikh ethos and the system of Sikh coinage was Nabha, the second largest Sikh state, and that too to a much larger extent as compared with the Patiala state. Griffin states categorically that Hamir Singh was the first Nabha chief who established a mint, basing his contention on General Taylor's report, *Cis-Sutlej State Mints*. R.C. Temple, who produced a fairly detailed study of the coins of the modern native states of the Punjab, states that in the year AH 1164 or AD 1751, being the fourth year of his reign, Ahmad Shah Durrani raided the Punjab and over-ran the greater part of it, and in that year, he granted to the chiefs of Patiala, Nabha, Jind, and Malerkotla the right to mint Durrani coins in their respective states.[44] Temple further states that Hamir Singh established a mint, but the details were not known to him, nor could he secure a coin of Hamir Singh.[45] None of these historians, however, has given any contemporary historical evidence in support of his contention that Hamir Singh had established a mint. Temple has also not given any historical evidence to prove that Ahmad Shah had given the right to strike coins in 1751 to all these states.

It is recorded in *Husain Shahi*, written in AD 1798, that the coin of Ahmad Shah is current in the family of Amar Singh, the raja of Patiala, and there is no mention in this manuscript about the minting of such coins by the Nabha and Jind states.[46] General Taylor, the agent of the Lt. Governor of the cis-Sutlej states, in his study of the coinage of the cis-Sutlej states in 1869, states that the Patiala mint was established by the order of Ahmad Shah Durrani when Patiala was ruled by Raja Amar Singh. Griffin relies on General Taylor's report.[47] The same view is held in a Note on the Patiala State Currency prepared by the state government.[48] Temple, however, holds the view that the right to coin was given by Ahmad Shah to Raja Ala Singh in 1765.[49]

Historical evidence testifies to the existence of contacts between Ahmad Shah and the Patiala chiefs, but no evidence has come to notice indicating that Ahmad Shah had also made contacts with the rulers of Jind and Nabha and that he had treated them at par with the house of Patiala. As Muslims, the Malerkotla rulers were on a different footing; nor had they embarked on a confrontational course with the Durranis. In his study Temple has shown 46 representative coins of Patiala, Jind, Nabha, Kaithal and Malerkotla. Dates are not given on the coins of all these states except for Nabha; the Nabha coins are almost all dated.[50] Hence, the practice of giving dates on the coins existed only in the Nabha state, and the earliest known date of the Nabha coins is 1877 Sambat, i.e. AD 1820.[51] We are, therefore, of the opinion that Ahmad Shah did not give the right to strike coins to all the cis-Sutlej states in 1751, as stated by Temple; the Nabha state mint was not established by Hamir Singh, as stated by Griffin and Temple, but it appears to have been established sometime during the long reign of Raja Jaswant Singh from AD 1783 to 1840 as a symbol of royalty and with the aim of equating Nabha with the house of Patiala. A certain degree of rivalry always existed between the states of Patiala and Nabha.

Almost all the rulers of the cis-Sutlej states, being apprehensive of the designs of Ranjit Singh, sought the protection of the British, except the house of Nabha which had shown an inclination time and again to side with the mainstream of the Sikhs and against the British. Raja Jaswant Singh was not initially inclined to seek British protection and wanted to side with the Lahore Darbar, but on comprehending the ambitions of Ranjit Singh, he also came under British protection.[52] His successor, Raja Devinder Singh, being an orthodox Sikh, was inclined to transfer his friendship from the British to the Lahore Darbar.[53] In the First Anglo-Sikh War, Devinder Singh did not effectively support the British cause. He was deposed and about one-fourth of the Nabha state territories were confiscated.[54] His son, Bharpur Singh, aged seven, was made the chief under the guardianship of Rani Chand Kaur and four administrators chosen by the British. Bharpur Singh helped the British with great zeal and sincerity in the 1857 upheaval and was duly rewarded.[55] Raja Ripudaman Singh was also deposed in the 1923 upheaval for his leanings towards the Singh Sabha movement and his minor son Pratap Singh was made the chief.[56] When Raja Pratap Singh attained majority, his powers were greatly curtailed as compared to the other rulers of the cis-Sutlej states.[57] The Nabha state stands on a somewhat different footing in its relations with the British paramount power vis-à-vis the other cis-Sutlej states, and its rulers expressed their sympathies with the mainstream of the Sikhs from time to time. It was the only cis-Sutlej state which discarded the Durrani legend and adopted the Sikh legend for its coinage.[58]

Temple was able to collect the earliest coin with the Sikh legend pertaining to the year AD 1850 or Sambat 1907. Hence, he argued that the change in the system of coinage took place during the reign of Bharpur Singh.[59] However, Temple is wrong in this assessment, as the Nabha coins with the Sikh legend pertaining to the earlier period are also available. The coin for the year Sambat 1892 or AD 1835 is available with the Government Museum, Lahore.[60] Another such coin, pertaining to the year Sambat 1893 or AD 1836, is available with the Sheesh Mahal Museum, Patiala.[61] Hence, the discarding of the Durrani coinage in favour of the Sikh coinage was carried out by Raja Jaswant Singh in the later part of his reign when the Durranis had completely disappeared from the Indian scene. The Nabha Sikh legend runs as follows (see plate VIII):

Obverse   *Degh Tegh Fateh, Nusrat Baidarang*
             Yaft Uz Nanak Guru Gobind Singh
Reverse   *Jalus Maiminat Manus, Zarb Nabha*

PLATE VIII: NANAK SHAHI COINS
NABHA STATE COINAGE

OBVERSE

REVERSE

VS 1836 AD

VS 1860 AD

DATE NOT CLEAR

VS 1869 AD

VS 1859 AD

VS 1871 AD

This legend first appeared on Banda Bahadur's seal and then on the coins of the *misls* and the Lahore Darbar, which had become synonymous with the Sikhs and with the concept of Sikh sovereignty. It was adopted by the Nabha rulers and it continued till the end of the state coinage system. The coins pertaining to the period of Bharpur Singh for the years AD 1850, 1851, and 1853 and those of Hira Singh for the years AD 1871 and 1872 have been shown by Temple in his study. With the annexation of the Lahore Darbar territories and increasing British influence, the British currency became the prevalent currency even in the cis-Sutlej states in the latter half of the nineteenth century. The state coins were minted only on special occasions for the needs of the state government or, to be more precise, for the needs of the ruling houses rather than for the general public.[62] The state currency was also devalued due to the mixing of more and more alloy vis-à-vis the British currency which maintained its standard purity.[63] After the annexation of Punjab, the prevalent currencies were sent in bulk to the British mints at Calcutta and Bombay and within a few years the Nanak Shahi and other currencies were rendered obsolete.[64] Although the cis-Sutlej states continued to hold the right to mint coinage, this privilege was in name only and not in actual practice.

Brahminical Influence on Sikh Coinage

During the reign of Ranjit Singh, Sikh coinage as a symbol of Sikh sovereignty continued with almost the same purity as it had when it was first launched by the Sikhs in 1710. Ranjit Singh continued with the system from AD 1800 onwards without introducing any change in the legends or any other parts of the coinage.[65] The only transgression in the system of Sikh coinage occurred in Kashmir where some governors inscribed the names of Hindu deities on the coins and thereafter also introduced their own initials on the obverse of the Sikh coins in the middle of the legends in praise of the Sikh Gurus. The system of Sikh coinage in Kashmir is dealt with later in this chapter.

After the death of Ranjit Singh, the Lahore Darbar soon collapsed. The intrigues at court, the imbecility of the rulers, the treachery of the ministers, the disloyalty of the Dogras and other *sardars*, the complicity of the *purbia* generals Lal Singh and Tej Singh with the enemy, the rulers' trust in the Brahmins rather than in the strength of their own arms, and the total chaos in a formerly well-administered state, all these factors contributed to its downfall and laid the grounds for the annexation of the province by the British in March 1849. Osbourne wrote in 1838, 'It is a melancholy thing to contemplate the future probable state of this beautiful country.'[66] The state had, in fact, reached the point of its highest development.[67]

Although Ranjit Singh used to consult astrologers and Brahmins regarding his health and although he gave large sums of money and jewellery in his *sankalps*, he never sought their help in matters of state. When taking serious decisions, he

PLATE IX: BRAHMINICAL SYMBOLS
ON SIKH COINS

NO. 1 1897 S

NO. 7 1902 S

NO. 2 1898 S

NO. 8 1903 S

NO. 3 1899 S

NO. 9 1903 S

NO. 4 1900 S

NO. 10 1904 S

NO. 5 1900 S

NO. 11 1904 S

NO. 6 1900 S

NO. 12 1905 S

would put two chits, one for and the other against, in the pages of the *Guru Granth* and ask someone to pull out one chit and would act accordingly. He sought the counsels' assistance and the grace of the Sikh Gurus through the *Guru Granth* and not through any Brahminical ritual or consultation.

Ranjit Singh's entire family as well as the family of his *wazir*, Dhian Singh, were eliminated in just a little over five years in the internecine warfare that followed the Maharaja's death. Similarly eliminated were the few Sikh *sardars* who had held some viable positions in the Khalsa Darbar. During this time, selfish and unscrupulous ministers such as Dina Nath who had no loyalty to the state and *purbias* such as Lal Singh and Tej Singh prospered. The Brahminical influence in rituals did creep in, especially under Pandit Jalla's time. This Brahminical influence affected the system of Sikh coinage as is seen in the inscription of Hindu motifs on the obverse of the coins along with the legends of the Sikh Gurus.

Hindu symbols and names such as the *Trishul, Om, Chattar, Sat, Shiv,* and even Ramji were inscribed on the Sikh coins which were struck in the name of the Sikh Gurus. This process seems to have started around 1840 and continued till 1849. Some of these coins are shown in Plate IX.

The inclusion of Brahminical symbols on the obverse of the Sikh coins was a blemish on and an aberration of the concept of Sikh sovereignty. But then at a time when Sikh sovereignty itself was under attack and the Sikh brotherhood was being put to the sword, this symbolic violation becomes somewhat meaningless.

Nimak Shahi Coinage

C.J. Rodgers was the first to notice a Sikh coin dated 1905 Sambat, i.e. AD 1848 which was said to be from Pind Dadan Khan, the central township of the Salt Range; the mint town on the coin is shown as Zarb Nimak.[68] Numismatists have explored the reasons why the Sikhs named these coins Nimak or Nimak Shahi. These coins appear to have been minted in 1904 Sambat, i.e. AD 1847 and 1905 Sambat, i.e. AD 1848, the last years of the Lahore Darbar, and coins from these two years are readily available. Wiggins and Goron conjecture that it is possible that these coins were issued locally in some connection with the salt trade. Since Pind Dadan Khan was the main town in the Salt Range, it was felt that currency meant for local circulation was named Nimak Shahi during the turbulent years of 1847 and 1848.[69] Herrli opines these coins were part of another special issue of the Nanak Shahi coins of the Amritsar mint, issued during the very last and troubled years of the Sikh state[70] (see Plate X).

Jyoti Rai, who has written about these coins, explores the following questions:

(a) The existence of a mint at Pind Dadan Khan.
(b) The reason for establishing the mint.
(c) Pind Dadan Khan was also known as Nimak.[71]

PLATE X: NIMAK SHAHI COINAGE
1905 AND 1906 SAMBAT

The views expressed by Jyoti Rai regarding questions (a) and (b) are by and large shared as these are based on the existence of recorded facts and historical evidence. But we disagree with her assertion that Pind Dadan Khan was also called Nimak during the regime of the Lahore Darbar as per the entry in the *Jhelam Gazetteer* (1904).

The history of Pind Dadan Khan goes back to ancient times. The battle between Alexander and Porus in the summer of 326 BC was fought at Bakhuphala, close to Pind Dadan Khan, which is located on the right bank of the Jhelam 8 km. from the Khewa salt mines. It consisted of three townships located close to each other, namely Kot Sultan, Kot Sahib Khan, and Pind Dadan Khan.[72] The tribes in and around Pind Dadan Khan gave a lot of trouble to Muhammad Ghauri and his generals in 1097. They, however, accepted Islam under great pressure by the close of the twelfth century. Muhammad Ghauri was slain by a Gakkhar of Pind Dadan Khan.[73] The whole district was the scene of perpetual warfare. Tribe fought against tribe, chief warred against chief, and village clashed against village. Daily life was marked by treacherous murders and thievish forays; in some villages, watch towers still exist where watch men beat the alarm drum on the approach of an enemy. Hari Singh Bhangi subdued the local chief of Pind Dadan Khan in 1764 and took tribute from him. Afterwards this tract was occupied by Charat Singh Sukharchakia. The Sikhs were able to introduce a rude and imperfect order over these unruly tribes.[74] Ranjit Singh invaded Pind Dadan Khan and took over the fort, the city, and the salt mines. The annual yield of the Khewa salt mine was 3,20,000 quintals with an annual income of 16 lakh rupees and 2½ lakh rupees from duties. Later in the 1830s Ranjit Singh farmed out the salt mines, including Pind Dadan Khan, to Raja Gulab Singh. Pind Dadan Khan was returned to the Lahore Darbar in 1847.

Mohan Lal, as a companion of Alexander Burnes, visited Pind Dadan Khan on 24 February 1832. In his memoirs, he records that he was received by a Rajput *sardar* sent by Gulab Singh with sweets and gifts. This account confirms that in 1832 the salt mines were with Gulab Singh and that the town was called Pind Dadan Khan.[75] Mohan Lal's account gives the details of the town, its architecture, the working of the salt mines, the nearby Katas Hindu temple, and the fort where he stayed.

There is no evidence regarding the establishment of a Sikh mint at Pind Dadan Khan prior to 1847, although there are numerous accounts about Pind Dadan Khan giving details about its people, places, and salt mines by independent sources. There is no mention of a Sikh mint prior to 1847. With the signing of the treaty of December 1846, all powers were taken away from Prince Dalip Singh, then a child, and were exercised by the British Resident and the Regency Council.

The Nanak Shahi coins along with the other earlier currencies were in use all over the Punjab. But with the large-scale minting of the Nanak Shahi coinage during a long period of peace and prosperity, this had become the dominant coinage in circulation and the other earlier currencies fell out of circulation in the main towns and cities and prevailed only in the distant tribal belts and villages. The tribal areas of Hazara, Rawalpindi, Peshawar, Bannu, the Salt Range, Leia, and Derajat used the earlier coinages, namely Goondah, Mughal, Durrani, Zaman Shahi, Mohamudi, Bahawalpuri, Shujahwala, Furrukhabadi, and Shikarpuri along with the Nanak Shahi coinage. The British officials posted at Lahore with the Resident and at various places in the tribal areas conceived of a scheme to withdraw all old currencies which were both short weight and short value and melt these to mint a uniform Nanak Shahi coinage to facilitate the public and the government and to eliminate the role of greedy money changers.

Jyoti Rai has analysed the correspondence on the issue of establishing different mints at Pind Dadan Khan, Abbotabad, Rawalpindi, Peshawar, Dera Ismail Khan, and other towns. The correspondence between various officials of the British Residency and the Lahore Darbar went on till late 1847. In the meantime, old coins were also sent to Amritsar in great quantities for them to be recoined into new Nanak Shahi coins.[76] It appears that at this stage the British scheme for the annexation of the Punjab came in for serious consideration and the scheme of opening new mints was perhaps shelved. The order for the formal closing of the mint at Peshawar was issued on 21 May 1849.[77] This is corroborated by the fact that but for the Sikh coins (Nimak Shahi) from the Pind Dadan Khan mint, the coins from the other proposd mints are not available and do not seem to have been minted at all.

The mint at Pind Dadan Khan appears to have had an early start and on 21 October 1847 orders were issued for sending Muhamad Shahi, Zaman Shahi, Goondah, and Mehrabi rupees to the Pind Dadan Khan mint for conversion into Nanak Shahi rupees.[78] A detailed account of the functioning of the mint at Pind Dadan Khan has been given by Andrew Fleming of the Punjab Geological Survey.[79]

The position regarding the questions raised by and replied to by Jyoti Rai is as follows:

(a) The existence of the mint at Pind Dadan Khan stands established but it was set up in late 1847 and closed in late AD 1848. There is no account of a Mughal or Afghan mint having been operated from Pind Dadan Khan during the periods of their rule nor of any Sikh mint having been operated at Pind Dadan Khan from AD 1765 to 1846.

(b) The reason for the establishment of mints at Pind Dadan Khan and other towns in the tribal belt was to introduce a uniform system of coinage in the form of the Nanak Shahi coins, and a regular correspondence exists on this subject.

(c) The assertion that Pind Dadan Khan was also known as Nimak does not appear to be correct. Jyoti Rai relies on the location of an entry in the

Punjab Gazetteer which states: 'Pind Dadan Khan in the period preceding its annexation was under the name of Nimak or salt, a Sikh mint town.'[80] However, this entry does not indicate when and why the name of the settlement was changed and by whom. In fact, there is overwhelming historical evidence that before the Sikh period, during the Sikh period, and even after the Sikh period the town was called Pind Dadan Khan. There is no suggestion in the Sikh records to open a mint at Pind Dadan Khan.

Pind Dadan Khan appears to have been named after a tribal chief called Dadan Khan. In the tribal genealogy available, the first Muslim name is the 71st and the present generation is the 84th. Taking 20 years for each generation would bring the total number of years to about 300, and this would be the time of the hold of the Gakkhar tribe over the Pind Dadan Khan area. There is no evidence that the Lahore Darbar changed the town's name to Nimak. The local tribes would most likely have protested the change of the town's name since it had been based on the name of their ancestor for several centuries.

The name Pind Dadan Khan has all along been used as such in the records of foreigners passing through that area during the Sikh period, viz.:

(i)   Mohan Lal, as a companion of Alexander Burnes in 1832, had used only the name Pind Dadan Khan.[81]

(ii) Hari Singh Bhangi on his return from his campaign against Dera Ghazi Khan and Dera Ismail Khan in 1764 attacked Pind Dadan Khan and received a tribute of four thousand rupees.[82]

(iii) Imam-ud-din Hussain stated in 1796 that Pind Dadar (Datan) Khan was under the Sikhs and that the income from salt amounted to 2½ lakh rupees annually.[83]

(iv) Hari Ram Gupta has given a detailed account of Pind Dadan Khan along with Kot Sultan and Kot Sahib Khan. He also states that Ranjit Singh occupied Pind Dadan Khan in 1797.[84]

(v)   The Sikh forces won the Battle of Haidru on 9 July 1813 against Dost Mohamad. Ranjit Singh got the news of this battle on 12 July 1813 from a letter sent from Pind Dadan Khan by Sukh Dayal, an agent of Ram Nand Sahu, stating that the battle was fought on 9 July. Diwan Amarnath says that the Afghans lost 2,000 men in this battle.[85] Elsewhere he states that the Jhelum district consisted of Jhelam, Chakwal, and Pind Dadan Khan.

(vi) Sohan Lal Suri, the court chronicler, states that Gulab Singh in August 1846 reported to Maharaja Ranjit Singh that due to excessive rains the Jhelum had been flooded upto Pind Dadan Khan and that salt worth six lakh rupees had been washed away. He sought some relief for this loss.[86]

In view of the facts stated above, the name of Pind Dadan Khan does not appear to have been changed to Nimak during the Sikh period, and the entry in the *Gazetteer*, on which Jyoti Rai relies for her conclusion, appears to be incorrect. It is not clear how, why, and by whom Nimak or Nimak Shahi came to be written on the Sikh coins. This question requires further investigation, and the conclusions drawn by Jyoti Rai are not based on any authentic evidence.

Sikh Coinage from Kashmir

Kashmir remained under Sikh occupation from July 1819 to November 1846 when the province was ceded from the Sikh state and was given to Gulab Singh by the British for the sum of 75 lakh rupees.[87] The following men were the Sikh governors who ruled the valley during the period of the Sikh occupation:[88]

1.	Misr Diwan Chand	July 1819 to end 1819 (Sambat 1876)
2.	Diwan Moti Ram	End 1819 to end 1820 (Sambat 1876)
3.	Hari Singh Nalwa	End 1820 to end 1821 (Sambat 1877-8)
4.	Diwan Moti Ram	End 1821 to mid 1825 (Sambat 1878-82)
5.	Diwan Chunni Lal	Mid 1825 to end 1826 (Sambat 1882-3)
6.	Diwan Kirpa Ram	End 1826 to mid 1830 (Sambat 1883-7)
7.	Bhima Singh Ardali	Mid 1830 to mid 1831 (Sambat 1887-8)
8.	Sher Singh	Mid 1831 to mid 1834 (Sambat 1888-91)
9.	Colonel Mihan Singh	1834-41 (Sambat 1891-8)
10.	Sheikh Gholam Muhyi-ud-din	1841-5 (Sambat 1898-1902)
11.	Sheikh Imam-ud-din Amir-ul-Mulk Bahadur	1845-6 (Sambat 1902-3)

(Representative coins of the periods of the above-mentioned governors are given in Plate XI.)

After consolidating his position in the Punjab, Ranjit Singh set his eyes on further expansion towards the north-west as he was prevented by the British from taking over the cis-Sutlej states.[89] He made forays into Multan and Kashmir. He marched to Poonch in 1814 and advanced on the Valley but his forces were repulsed by the hostile hill rajas and the equally hostile weather.[90] This is the only major expedition which Ranjit Singh lost in his military career. Better prepared the next time, he moved his forces towards Kashmir after having fully subdued the hill rajas of Poonch and Rajouri. His forces, under the command of Misr Diwan Chand, now wiser after the experience of the 1814 debacle, reached Shaopian on 5 July 1819, where the Afghan Governor Jabbar Khan had taken his position.[91] In a sharp engagement, the Afghans were defeated, Jabbar Khan fled to Kabul, and the Sikh army entered Srinagar on 15 July 1819.[92]

The Kashmir Valley has historically been occupied, exploited, and farmed

PLATE XI: KASHMIR COINS
1881-1903 SAMBAT

NO. 1 1881 S

NO. 7 1886 S

NO. 2 1882 S

NO. 8 1886 S

NO. 3 1882 S

NO. 9 UNDATED

NO. 4 1883 S

NO. 10 1887 S

NO. 5 1884 S

NO. 11 1888 S

NO. 6 1885 S

NO. 12 1888 S

(contd.)

PLATE XI (contd.)

NO. 13 1890 S

NO. 19 1895 S

NO. 14 1890 S

NO. 20 1896 S

NO. 15 1891 S

NO. 21 1897 S

NO. 16 1892 S

NO. 22 1898 S

NO. 17 1892 S

NO. 23 1898 S

NO. 18 1893 S

NO. 24 1899 S

(contd.)

PLATE XI (contd.)

NO. 25 1900 S

NO. 28 1903 S

NO. 26 1901 S

NO. 29 1892 S

NO. 27 1902 S

NO. 30 1892 S

JARAB KASA

MIRA SRI A

KAL PURUKHJI

Note: Hans Herrli has incorrectly read the legend (Persian) on the reverse of Mihan Singh period coins. The same is not very clear on some coins but the same legend in Gurmukhi script is very clear on the 1892 coin. This establishes that Mihan Singh did not place his name on the Sikh coins struck during his governorship as has been done by some other governors.

for taxes by the rulers of India and Afghanistan. The Mughals, the Afghans, and the Sikhs all treated the region as an occupied territory for the maximum extraction of revenue. The Valley is surrounded by high mountains on all sides, with a number of passes which are snow bound in the winter. Hence the Valley was cut off during the winter months from the rest of the country, and its inhabitants adopted cottage industries such as *shawl* making and wood carving. An elaborate system of taxation had evolved over the production of all sorts of commodities and their sale. Since the rulers were bent on extracting the maximum revenue to please their masters in Delhi, Kabul, and Lahore, it was essential to ensure the continuous availability of currency. Hence, the Kashmir mint was forever in the process of minting coins for the collection of taxes and trade.

Various currencies minted from time to time were prevalent in the province. The Mughal currency struck in Kashmir was still in circulation. It was called the Mohammad Shahi, and was valued at 13 *annas* of the Nanak Shahi rupee. The Afghan currency was worth about 11 *annas*. The Kabul rupee was worth about 9 to 10 *annas*. Likewise, the currency issued by the Sikhs was also about 12 *annas* to a rupee, perhaps to maintain uniformity with the prevailing currencies. Its value remained constant, with slight variations, till 1835 and thereafter its value was reduced to 8 *annas* of the Nanak Shahi rupee and this value remained consistent up to 1846.

The legend on these coins from 1819 to 1846 was the same as that on the earlier Sikh coins.

Obverse   *Degh Tegh Fateh O Nusrat Baidarang,*
            Yaft uz Nanak Guru Gobind Singh.

Meaning, 'the kettle to serve the sword, the might of its arms and victory with spontaneous help'. *Baidarang* mean 'spontaneous or unrestrained help received from Nanak to Guru Gobind Singh'.

Reverse   *Zarb Khitta Kashmir, Jalus Maiminat Manus.*

Mint land of Kashmir Sambat (year) auspicious and prosperous reign.[93]

It has already been explained (in Chapter III) that Hari Singh Nalwa placed the word '*Har*' (God's name) on the obverse of the coin. His successor Moti Ram changed the Gurmukhi script of the *Har* into the Devanagari script. He also changed the word *Har* into *Harjee, Om Shri*, and *Sri Ram*.

During the governorship of Diwan Chunni Lal from Sambat 1882-3, only a flower mark and a flag on another issue had been placed on the obverse. There is no indication as to why Moti Ram's use of the Devanagari *Har, Harjee, Om Shri*, and *Sri Ram* had been left out and why these had been replaced with a flower or a flag. Hence, during the period of Diwan Chunni Lal as governor there was no embellishment on the obverse of the coin.

However, on a second issue of 1883 Sambat there is an Urdu letter 'K' placed on the obverse of the coin and the 'K' is considered to be the first letter of the name of the next Governor Kirpa Ram, whereby God's name was replaced by the governor's name. The letter 'K' appears on the obverse of the coins for the years: Sambat 1883: 1 issue; Sambat 1884: 5 issues; Sambat 1885: 2 issues; Sambat 1886: 3 issues; Sambat 1887: 2 issues. One issue that does not bear any date has K. Ram in the Persian script written on the obverse.

In mid 1887 Sambat, i.e. AD 1830, Bhima Singh Ardali became governor and it is possible that the coin with only the flag and without the letter 'K' was his first coin. The first letter 'Bh' of the name Bhima Singh is placed on the 1888 Sambat coins on the obverse in a manner similar to the placing of the letter 'K' on the four issues; in one issue the letter 'Bh' in the Gurmukhi script is also placed on the reverse of the coin.

During 1889 Sambat and 1890 Sambat, i.e. AD 1831 and 1832 only a *katar* was placed on the obverse during the governorship of Sher Singh. In one issue there is a figure of a tiger on the reverse and no embellishment on the obverse.

From 1891 Sambat to 1898 Sambat, i.e. AD 1834 to 1841, Colonel Mihan Singh was the governor of Kashmir. He placed a sword and a shield on the obverse of the coin, i.e. on the legend, and on the reverse, in place of *Jalus Maiminat Manus'* he placed the words *'Akal Purakh'*. There was no other change through the rest of his term of seven years, and there is no indication of his name being placed on the coins as was done by his predecessors.

Hans Herrli errs in reading the couplet on the reverse of the coin struck during the period of Mihan Singh; Herrli incorrectly identifies this as 'San (Year) Sri Akalpur Kashmir'.[94] He is also incorrect in stating that Mihan Singh and his successors called the mint town Sri Akalpur.[95] The correct rendering of the legend on the reverse is 'San Sri Akal Purukh Kashmir'. This becomes very clear from the legend in Gurmukhi on the coin struck in 1892.[96] Hence, Mihan Singh's name does not appear in any coin struck during his period.

The next two governors, Sheikh Ghulam Mohyi-ud-din and Sheikh Iman-ud-din, placed the first letter 'Sh' of Sheikh on the obverse of the coins during the period from 1898 Sambat to 1903 Sambat, i.e. AD 1841 to AD 1846.

From the above analysis of the Sikh coins issued from Kashmir, it emerges that the first embellishment of the Sikh coins, the symbol of Sikh sovereignty and issued in the name of the Sikh Gurus, was done in the time of Moti Ram who brought in the Devanagari script and the words related to the Hindu deities such as *Om Shri* and *Sri Ram*. Hence, in the light of this evidence it is possible to argue that these marks are the representations of God's manifestation as also seen on earlier coins; this can only be deemed as a Brahminical influence and should not be regarded as a serious infringement of the concept of Sikh sovereignty.

The second embellishment came with the placing of the letter 'K', the first letter of the name of Kirpa Ram, and in one coin without date the name 'K.

Ram'. Bhima Singh Ardali put the first letter of his name on the coin; he was obviously aware of what Kirpa Ram had done and followed in his footsteps. The cases of both Kirpa Ram and Bhima Singh constituted serious infringements of the concept of Sikh sovereignty. There were no embellishments by the next two governors, Sher Singh and Mihan Singh. The last two governors were Muslims, and hence it is possible that they did not comprehend the implication of the embellishment on the face of the coin. However, this too is an infringement of the concept of Sikh sovereignty.

Taking stock of the entire period, it appears that the embellishment of Sikh coinage had been started by Moti Ram, the son of Diwan Mokkam Chand, the most trusted general of Ranjit Singh, and his son Kirpa Ram who placed his name with the names of the Sikh Gurus, and lastly by Bhima Singh Ardali and the two Sheikh governors who also followed in their footsteps. These actions of the Sikh governor of Kashmir were a distinct infringement of the concept of the sovereignty of the Khalsa. Why and how it did not come to the notice of the Sikhs, and even in case it did come to their notice, why no action was taken are questions which cannot be answered till some contemporary record becomes available. The Kashmir coinage was the only base coinage of the period of Sikh rule and it was not welcomed in the markets of Amritsar and Lahore where pure silver Nanak Shahi currency was in vogue. Further, the Kashmir currency was mainly confined to the province itself and the infringement may not have come to the notice of the Lahore Darbar.

NOTES

1. B.D. Basu, *Rise of Christian Power in India*, Calcutta: R. Chatterjee & Co., 1931, p. 17.
2. Barkat Rai Chopra, *Kingdom of the Punjab 1839-45*, Hoshiarpur: V.V. Research Institute, 1969, p. 7.
3. Ibid., pp. 55-8.
4. Ibid., p. 69.
5. Ibid., p.92.
6. Ibid., p. 195.
7. Khushwant Singh, *History of the Sikhs*, vol. II, New Delhi: Oxford University Press, 1963, pp. 27, 28.
8. Ibid., pp. 38, 39
9. Ibid., p. 54.
10. Ibid., p. 59.
11. Hari Ram Gupta, *History of Sikhs*, vol. II, New Delhi: Munshiram Manoharlal, 1978, p. 49.
12. Hari Ram Gupta, op. cit., vol. III, p. 169.
13. Ibid., p. 170.
14. (i) Lepel Griffin, *The Rajas of Panjab*, Punjab: Languages Department, 1970, p. 26.
    (ii) Hari Ram Gupta, op. cit., vol. IV, p. 156.
15. (i) Lepel Griffin, op. cit., p. 25.
    (ii) Hari Ram Gupta, op. cit., vol. II, p. 220.
16. Hari Ram Gupta, op. cit., vol. I, p. 227.

17. Ibid., p. 230.
18. Hari Ram Gupta, op. cit., vol. IV, pp. 157-8.
19. Lepel Griffin, op. cit., vol. II, pp. 285, 382.
20. Surinder Singh, 'Nabha State Coinage', *Panjab University Research Bulletin* (Arts), vol. XXI, no. I, April 1990, p. 172.
21. Lepel Griffin, op. cit., vol. I, p. 6.
22. Hari Ram Gupta, op. cit., vol. IV, p. 145.
23. Ibid., pp. 147-8.
24. Ibid., p. 161.
25. Lepel Griffin, op. cit., p. 24.
26. Ibid., p. 25; Hari Ram Gupta, op. cit., vol. II, p. 202.
27. Hari Ram Gupta, op. cit., vol. II, p. 220.
28. Ibid., vol. IV, p. 157.
29. Ibid., vol. IV, p. 157.
30. Lepel Griffin, op. cit., vol. II, p. 286.
31. 'Note Regarding Patiala State Currency', prepared by Patiala State authorities, Punjab State Archives, is reproduced by Surinder Singh in Patiala State Coinage, Annexure A, *Panjab University Research Bulletin*, vol. XXI, October 1990, Chandigarh, pp. 204-9.
32. Hari Ram Gupta, op. cit., vol. II, p. 244.
33. R.C. Temple, 'The Coins of the Modern Chiefs of Punjab', *Indian Antiquary*, vol. XVIII, Bombay, 1989, pp. 21-41.
34. B.R. Grover, 'An Analysis of Contemporary Durrani Revenue Documents and Correspondence Pertaining to Patiala Chieftainship (Zamindari) During the Latter Half of the 18th Century', *Panjab Past & Present*, vol. XXIV-1, Patiala, April 1990, pp. 227-8.
35. Note on Patiala State currency prepared by the Prime Minister of Patiala on 15.7.1919. This note is in a bundle of a dozen files of the Patiala State and Finance Department in the Patiala State Records in the Punjab State Archives, Patiala, without any number.
36. Gur Rattan Pal Singh, *Tribune*, Chandigarh, 22 July 1990.
37. Karan Bir Kaur, 'Maharaja Rajinder Singh of Patiala', *Panjab Past & Present*, vol. XIX, Patiala: Panjabi University, 1985, pp. 128, 167.
38. The minting of *nazrana* coins for special royal ceremonies and *puja* during Dussehra and Diwali. Extract from letter no. 2556 dated 10.5.1992 S from the Treasury Officer, Patiala to the Accountant General, Patiala: Panjab State Archives.
    Adverting to the correspondence resting with my letter no. 2164 dated 18.4.92 I have the honour to state that as intimated vide this office letter no. 554 dated 4.2.1992, the total quantity of gold required for the whole year 1992 for making Patiala Mohars, half Mohars and Puja Coins was 3100 tolas but as some Mohars and half Mohars were credited into the Treasury by the main Marriage Committee and the Deorhi Mualla Department, Mohars and half Mohars required for Guru Puja and *Saloono* were supplied out of the coins credited by the above department and now the total quantity of gold required can be reduced to 2400 tolas out of which purchase of 500 tolas has already been sanctioned by the Finance Minister. Request you to kindly obtain sanction of the Finance Minister to the purchase of 1900 tolas of gold more and 260 tolas of silver and request him to auction a contract for the total quantity of 2400 tolas of gold and 260 tolas of silver at one and the same time.
39. Extract from letter no. 1809 R dated 25.3.2000 S from the Accountant General, Patiala addressed to the Finance Minister, Patiala.
    Last year these silver and gold coins were prepared by melting old *puja* coins. As the time is still not favourable and rates of silver and gold are still too high, I request that similar

procedure may kindly be allowed to be adopted this year too, to meet the requirement of *puja* coins.

40. Extract from the letter no. 957 dated 16.5.2000 S, i.e. AD 22.8.1943 from Sardar Sahib Deorhi Mualla to the Finance Minister, Patiala: Panjab State Archives.

With reference to your letter no. 3595 dated 27.7.1943 I have the honour to state that though the coins, once used in *puja* by the August Master cannot be used again according to the injunctions of the Shastras, but keeping in view the high rates of gold and silver, I have no objection if these are minted after melting down the old coins which are lying in the Reserve Treasury.

Regarding your query about further reduction in the use of gold and silver during war time, I would like to point out that this cannot be done without reducing the Sarishtas observed on the various occasions and it is not within my competence to do so.

41. Parmeshwari Lal Gupta and Sanjay Garg, *The Coins of Dal Khalsa and Lahore Darbar*, Chandigarh: Government of Punjab, 1989, pp. 178-9.

The collection has about 1500 silver coins of the above type. Had they not some peculiarities of their own on the reverse, they would well have been mistaken as the Nabha coinage. Here, some of the coins have a spear pointed downward and some others have a rifle with bayonet placed vertically. The coins having the spear symbol have the figures 58 and those with rifle have the figure 94 by the right of these symbols. The mint name on these coins is Sirhind. There are a few gold coins (1/3 Mohar) (not in this collection). With the above reverse showing spear with figure 58 and rifle with figure 94. The reverse of these coins and that of the Durranis are exactly the same as adopted on the Patiala coins. Along with these facts, the fact that large numbers of these coins belong to the Sheesh Mahal collection make it certain that these coins would have been issued only by Patiala. They pose the question as to why Patiala, which had always associated itself with the Durrani rulers and issued its coins of their type, issued these particular coins adopting the Sikh obverse pattern?

Walter Hamilton has suggested that these coins were used in connection with the religious ceremonies at Dussehra and Diwali. But this seems unlikely. Dussehra has nothing to do with the Sikhs. Only Diwali has some importance for them. They hold the Sarbhat Khalsa meeting on this day. But then, it is to be noted that Patiala always had been indifferent to these meetings. There seems no reason as to why Patiala would issue these coins on these occasions. It should not be lost sight of that the coins bear two different symbols with two different figures, which seem to be some dates. If so, they would be representing Sambat [18]58 (AD 1796) and [18]94 (AD 1737) and thus they mean that they were issued on two different occasions. Only these figures would provide some clue to answer the question. It strikes to our mind that Patiala house, from the very outset, from the time of Alha Singh, had adopted the dual policy to side with the Durranis and at the same time to woo the leaders of the Dal Khalsa. Not unlikely these coins might have been issued to appease the Dal Khalsa at these dates. But what was the necessity to do so, we are unable to anticipate. It is a matter of investigation for the historians of this period.

42. Lepel Griffin, *Rajas of Panjab*, op. cit., p. 382.
43. Ibid., pp. 288-9.
44. R.C. Temple, *Indian Antiquary*, op. cit., pp. 321-2.
45. Ibid., p. 330.
46. Hari Ram Gupta, *History of Sikhs*, vol. II, op. cit., p. 244.
47. Griffin, *Rajas of Panjab*, op. cit., p. 286.
48. Note, Patiala State Currency, Panjab State Archives, Patiala.

49. Temple, *Indian Antiquary*, op. cit., pp. 32-4.
50. Ibid., pp. 335-41.
51. Ibid., p. 340, no. 39.
52. Griffin, *Rajas of Panjab*, op. cit., p. 385.
53. Ibid., pp. 410-11.
54. Ibid., p. 417.
55. Ibid., p. 433.
56. Proceedings, Panjab History Conference, March 1982, p. 264.
57. Ibid., p. 265.
58. Griffin, p. 288; Temple, p. 331; *Catalogue of Coins*, Lahore Museum, 1981, p. 120.
59. Ibid., p. 331.
60. *Catalogue of Coins in the Government Museum Lahore*, p. 120.
61. *Catalogue of Sikh Coins*, Patiala: Sheesh Mahal Museum, p. 180.
62. Griffin, *Rajas of Panjab*, op. cit., p. 289.
63. Accountant General's Note dated 26.6.1935, Panjab State Archives.
64. Foreign Department, General Report, *Administration of Punjab Territories, 1849-51*, Calcutta, 1856, p. 34.
65. Gulshan Lall Chopra, *The Punjab as a Sovereign State*, op. cit., p. 154.
66. W.G. Osbourne, *The Court and Camp of Ranjit Singh*, London, 1840, p. 52.
67. Sohan Lal Suri, *Imdat-ut-Tawarikh, Daftar,* III (tr. V.S. Suri), Chandigarh, 1974, p. 430.
68. C.J. Rodgers, *Catalogues of Coins in the Government Musuem Lahore*, 1891, p. 98. Coin no. 122

    Obverse: '*Sikka Zad Bar Har Do Alam*' legend
    Reverse: '*Zarb Nimak*', part of the R and B of the Zarb is readable. It can safely be observed that the word *Zarb* is there. After *Nimak*, part of the word S is visible and hence it can be taken as Shahi but not with complete certainty. Rodgers further states that *Nimak* here is placed for Pind Dadan Khan, the chief emporium of the salt trade.

69. Ken Wiggins and Stan Goron, 'Gold and Silver Coinage of Sikhs', Inaugural Address, Nasik: Indian Institute of Research in Numismatic Studies, 1984, p. 147:
Some Sikh rupees allegedly bear the word 'Nimak' as the place of minting. No such place will be found in the Punjab. In Persian and Urdu 'Nimak' means salt. The name is said to have been put on the rupees struck at Pind Dadan Khan, a town on the right bank of the Jhelum river, which was noted as the main emporium of salt, extracted in the hills behind the town.
70. Herrli, *The Coins of the Sikhs*, op. cit., p. 107.
71. Jyoti Rai, 'Unidentified Sikh Mints: Proof of the Existence of Nimak', *Journal of the Oriental Numismatic Society*, Newsletter no. 143, Surrey, UK, 1995.
72. (i) Captain Abbot, *Journal of the Asiatic Society of Bengal*, Calcutta, vol. XVII, 1848, p. 619; and vol. XXI, p. 214.
    (ii) Vincent Smith, *District and State Gazetteer Punjab*, vol. I, Delhi: Low Priced Publications, 1993, p. 292.
73. Ibid., p. 302.
74. Ibid., p. 309.
75. Fauja Singh, 'Trade and Commerce in Punjab', in Fauja Singh and A.C. Arora (eds.), *Maharaja Ranjit Singh: Politics Society and Economy*, Patiala: Punjabi University, p. 210.

76. Jyoti Rai, 'Unidentified Sikh Mints', op. cit., Newsletter no. 143.
77. Ibid., p. 2.
78. Ibid., Newsletter no. 143, p. 2.
79. Ibid., Appendix A.
80. *District and States Gazetteer Punjab*, vol. I, op. cit., p. 291.
81. Mohan Lal, *Travels in Punjab, Afghanistan, and Turkistan*, Punjab: Languages Department, rpt. 1971, pp. 24-45
82. Hari Ram Gupta, *History of Sikhs*, op. cit., p. 207.
83. Ibid
84. Ibid., p. 77.
85. Ibid., pp. 101 and 336.
86. Sohan Lal Suri, *Umdat-ut-Twarikh, Dafter,* III, op. cit., p. 203.
87. J.D. Cunningham, *A History of Sikhs*, op. cit., p. 288.
88. Herrli, *The Coins of the Sikhs*, op. cit., p. 119.
89. J.D. Cunningham, *A History of Sikhs*, op. cit., p. 126.
90. Ibid., p. 139.
91. Khushwant Singh, *History of the Sikhs*, vol. I, Delhi: Oxford University Press, 1987, p. 255.
92. Ibid., p. 255.
93. Herrli, *The Coins of the Sikhs*, op. cit., pp. 123-4.
94. Ibid., p. 135.
95. Ibid., p. 120.
96. Ibid., p. 139.

CHAPTER V

Sikh Coins as a Symbol of
Sikh Sovereignty: An Assessment

The broad features of Sikh coinage that have long remained buried under the debris of historical fiction, have been unravelled in this study. These are as follows:

The study of Sikh coinage has not received the attention that it deserves from its historians and numismatists. The comments of historians are often not supported by sufficient historical evidence and are often not based on a proper investigation and analysis of even those coins that are readily available. Both historians and numismatists have considered Sikh coinage as being merely a part of the currencies of the native states which were initially copied from Mughal coinage during the period of its decline and later from British Indian coinage. The native states were carved out by capable leaders during and after the downfall of the Mughal Empire. The native states were thus not formed as a result of the participation of the people in shaking off an alien rule, but merely by ambitious local chiefs, most of whom were subordinates and allies of the Mughal rulers. The Sikh state was the result of a long-drawn-out struggle by the Sikhs lasting for almost two centuries till they secured their absolute rule over north-western India by defeating the Mughal governors and repulsing the Afghan invaders. The currencies of the native states were merely a means to carry out daily transactions among the common people and were meant as a symbol of the sovereignty of their rulers only, whereas for the Sikhs their coins were also the symbol of the sovereignty of their Gurus, whom every Sikh held in great respect and reverence. Hence, the treatment of Sikh coinage as part of the coinage of the native states has led to an inadequate and incorrect assessment of its importance. This basic misunderstanding of the true nature of Sikh coinage has resulted in distorted and inaccurate accounts.

Many scholars of Sikh history, both European and Indian, have contributed to our knowledge of the Punjab. Chronicles of Mughal and Afghan history have also briefly mentioned the Sikhs and their role albeit in brief sections. Most of these writers refer to Sikh coins and their related histories and accounts. Most historians have written about Sikh coins without actually examining them; this negligence is in total violation of the requisite norms of numismatic investigation, which were otherwise diligently observed with regard to the study of the coins of the ancient and medieval periods. Sikh historians such as Hari Ram Gupta, Ganda Singh, Bhagat Singh, Gopal Singh, and Bikramjit Hasrat, with whom I have had an opportunity to discuss some aspects of Sikh history connected with Sikh coinage, stated that they had not actually examined Sikh coins while writing about them. They have also not given any contemporary historical evidence in support of their inferences and assertions about these coins.

British and other European travellers passing through the Sikh territories made comments on Sikh coins, often based on rumour, bazaar gossip, and hearsay. Unfortunately, these accounts have been taken by later historians as authentic historical evidence. Thus, the writings on Sikh coins based on hearsay and the absence of the actual examination of these coins has led to a mis-understanding of the historical facts and consequently to serious distortions of Sikh history. In this study a number of such fallacies have been exposed in order to gain a correct and proper understanding of Sikh coins and their role in the interpretation of Sikh ideology and Sikh history. These distortions have also affected another aspect of Sikh history, i.e. the concept of Sikh sovereignty, which has not been given due attention by its historians in examining its development as a crucial aspect of the Sikh psyche. Since coins are the most important and primary symbol of sovereignty, any distortion of their history and significance results in the distortion of the concept of sovereignty. For instance, historians such as Baron von Hugel, Henry T. Prince, V. Jacquemont, J.D. Cunningham, Lepel Griffin, C.J. Rodgers, G.L. Chopra, Bikramjit Hasrat, Khushwant Singh, Muhammad Latif, F.S. Waheed-ud-din, Amarnath, K.K. Khullar, and Gopal Singh state that Ranjit Singh struck coins in the name of one of his courtesans called Moran. It has been established from a detailed analysis of the historical facts and from numismatic investigation of the coins in question that no such coins were struck in the name of Moran.

Richard Feynman, a leading Nobel laureate in Physics of the late twentieth century, states that whereas religious philosophy prospers on the basis of faith, scientific and analytical study thrives on doubt which a thinking mind entertains over the data made available and the facts as recorded by others, which could bear the burden of truth. Hence, the doubts raised over the issue of Moran's coins led to the detailed examination of both historical and numismatic evidence, viz., the place of concubines in the contemporary society, any instances of coins being struck in the name of a concubine close to the ruler, the dates of the issue of these coins, the places from where these coins were issued, the examination of the actual legends on these coins, and any marks or figures helping to establish such an issue, the concept of sovereignty and its place in the statecraft of the ruler and the ideology of the state. All these aspects besides others relevant to the subject have been examined here and only thereafter has it been concluded that no such coins were struck by Ranjit Singh in Moran's name and that the entire subject is based on hearsay and bazaar gossip. Unfortunately, a galaxy of seasoned and learned historians and numismatists did not follow the well-established conventions of historical research and methodology nor the rigorous procedures of numismatic investigation in this matter. Perhaps they took the juicy bazaar gossip as adding to the already colourful lifestyle of the Sikh maharaja. Their reasons for recording this alleged incident remain a matter of speculation. However, the uncritical acceptance of this story by later historians has resulted in the distortion of Sikh history.

In a somewhat similar manner, many historians have recorded that Hari Singh Nalwa, while governor of Jammu and Kashmir in AD 1820-1, had struck coins in his name on his own authority or with the concurrence of Ranjit Singh. Among these historians are Prem Singh Hoti, A.S. Sandhu, S.S. Johar, Kanehiya Lal, C.M.D. Sufi, Ghulam Hussain, D.C. Sharma, N.K. Sinha, Bikramjit Hasrat, Bhagat Singh, G.T. Vigne, R.K. Parmu, Madhavi Yasin, Shahamat Ali, Gopal Singh, Sita Ram Kohli, and Hari Ram Gupta. Some of these historians have also given the legends that allegedly appeared on these Sikh rupee coins as follows:

Obverse   *Sri Akal Jeo*
Reverse   *Hari Singh Yak Rupaya.*

Both an analytical study of the historical facts and a numismatic examination of the relevant coins have been carried out, and it has been established that Hari Singh Nalwa did not strike any coins in his name. Hundreds of Sikh coins in the Sri Pratap Museum, Srinagar as well as the coins in my own personal collection and those held in the collections of some private collectors have been examined, and no coin with the above-quoted legends could be located. Where ever historians and numismatists have considered it desirable to give the legends on the obverse and the reverse of a particular coin, these have invariably been taken from some existing coins. But in this case it appears to have been the invention of some historian and this error was repeated by others. In case it was minted and circulated, the coin would have been available where representative coins of almost all the years are readily available. The claim of the alleged striking of Sikh coins by Hari Singh in his own name is inaccurate. Ironically even various fictions were invented to justify a particular form of disinformation.

Similarly, some of the leading numismatists have carried out incorrect and incomplete numismatic investigations. They have thus contributed to the further spread of disinformation instead of highlighting the proper classification of the existing coins. For instance, John Dyell, a numismatist of international repute, bases his main arguments on the coins struck by Banda Bahadur as described in *Tazkirat-i-Salatin-i-Chughtaiya* by Hadi Kamwar Khan, but without actually examining this manuscript. Copies of the document are readily available in various places in India, and a scrutiny reveals that there is no mention of these coins in that manuscript.

In a second instance of careless scholarship, Parmeshwari Lal Gupta, a very eminent Indian numismatist and Director, Indian Institute of Research in Numismatic Studies, Anjaneri, Nasik, also bases his account of the coins struck by Banda Bahadur on the alleged account of Hadi Kamwar Khan. When I requested him to quote the relevant portions for verification, it came out that P.L. Gupta had merely repeated the arguments of John Dyell without himself examining the relevant manuscript or even caring to acknowledge John Dyell as the source. Thus, where certain historians have drawn their conclusions without examining the actual coins, certain numismatists have also drawn their conclusions without examining the actual historical documents.

The existence of different historical accounts and different imprints and faulty drawings of the coins have created ambiguous situations which hampered the scholar from arriving at the correct position. The only two pictorial Sikh coins located so far were first mentioned by C.J. Rodgers and he has given their drawings. The drawings show Guru Nanak and another person in Islamic dress; from this Rodgers inferred that the second figure is that of Mardana, sitting with Guru Nanak. The pictures created some doubts in my mind as these were not in the traditional form, and hence struck a discordant note. Further investigation led to the location of the account describing the decision to strike a pictorial coin, and thereafter photographs of these coins were also secured from the British Museum, London.

After having collected all the relevant material, I adopted the method of dovetailing in order to place the different pieces of information in the correct perspective so that a compact, harmonious, and whole picture could emerge. In this case, the accounts of Rodgers, Sohan Lal Suri, William Barr, the drawings of Rodgers, and the actual photographs of the coins from the British Museum, London, all led to the solving of the puzzle. It is now established that these coins are those of Ranjit Singh seeking the blessings of Guru Nanak.

Banda Bahadur made an official seal with the legend '*Degh, Tegh, Fateh o Nusrat Baidarang, Yaft uz Nanak Guru Gobind Singh*'. This legend was taken up on the Sikh coin struck in AD 1765 to commemorate the occupation of Lahore, the capital of Punjab, by the Sikh armies. This legend reflects the concept of Sikh sovereignty. Its meaning is that the free *langar* and the strength of the sword arm and the resultant victory were the result of the spontaneous help received from Guru Nanak to Guru Gobind Singh. Here the phrase 'Nanak Guru Gobind Singh' means the entire Sikh Gurudom, from Guru Nanak to Guru Gobind Singh, the last living Guru. The ten Gurus are taken as one light, one idea, and this notion of unity has also been propounded by Guru Gobind Singh in *Bachittar Natik*. The recipients are of course the members of the Sikh Panth. A number of historians of the Sikhs such as Macauliffe, Gulshan Lall Chopra, J.S. Grewal, N.K. Sinha, Muhammad Latif, Patwant Singh, and others have incorrectly translated this phrase as 'Guru Gobind Singh received from Guru Nanak'. However, this view is entirely against the Sikh ethos and the psyche traditions, and gives a distorted impression of the institution of Sikh Gurudom and the Sikh concept of sovereignty.

Historians such as Hari Ram Gupta, Lepel Griffin, Colonel Sleeman, C.J. Rodgers, C.J. Brown, Bhagat Singh, and others have called the coins struck with the legend 'Degh, Tegh, Fateh', the Gobind Shahi coins and those struck with the legend 'Sikka Zad Bar Har Do Alam', on the initial Sikh coin, as the Nanak Shahi coins. These historians and even some numismatists have drawn this distinction without giving any evidence or reasoning for their assertion. Since the names of Guru Nanak and Guru Gobind Singh occur in both the legends which appear on the Sikh coins, this coinage can only be called the Nanak Shahi coinage and cannot be identified with the name of any other Guru, unless the legend specifically mentions the name of that Guru only; but this is not the case here. It is our presumption that the second distortion in the nomenclature of Sikh coins occurred due to the first distortion in rendering the meaning of the legend which was not contradicted or clarified by later historians, who succeeded in rendering the correct meaning of the legend. Patwant Singh, a recent writer on Sikh history, describes the legend 'Degh Tegh Fateh' as being the attributes ascribed by Guru Nanak to Guru Gobind Singh. In the next chapter while discussing the coins struck by Ranjit Singh, Patwant Singh gives an altogether different meaning to the same legend, translating 'Degh Tegh Fateh' as 'My largesse, my victories and my fame I owe to Guru Nanak and Guru Gobind Singh'. He does not give any reasoning or evidence to explain why he has given two widely different interpretations of the same legend. He does not appreciate that the legends on the Sikh coins were carefully and reverentially designed by the Sikhs in the early eighteenth century and were the true expression of the Sikh concept of sovereignty. It is such flights of fancy that not only distort Sikh history but also dilute the strength of the unique Sikh institutions. This mistake has also been repeated by J.S. Grewal and Jean-Marie Lafont in their recent writings.

The initial Sikh state carved out by the Sikhs under Banda Bahadur was totally dismantled by 1715 and an intensive drive to literally wipe out the entire Sikh community was carried out by the Mughal authorities, with a heavy price put on every Sikh head, dead or alive. The Sikhs took to the jungles and deserts and practiced guerrilla warfare; within half a century, after making many sacrifices, they re-emerged as a powerful force and were able to occupy Lahore, the state capital, in AD 1765. Since their tactics of warfare were designed to avoid frontal-attacks from Mughal and Afghan forces, they would occupy the main towns but leave them during the Durrani invasions. They would retake them after the main force of the Durrani armies would leave for Afghanistan. The Sikhs occupied Lahore in 1761 for a few days and a rumour went round that the Sikhs had struck a coin in the name of their leader Jassa Singh Ahluwalia, the legend thereon being 'Coin has been struck with the grace of Akal (the timeless) and the country of Ahmad is in the grip of Jassa Kalal'. Although no such coin has surfaced nor has any convincing evidence in support of the veracity of this incident been forthcoming, various accounts both in support of and against its minting have emerged. The eminent Sikh historian H.R. Gupta has vigorously supported the issue of the said coins with quite of few arguments which could not be sustained. The same was only rebutted by N.K. Sinha that sovereignty could not be assumed by any *sardar* how strong he may be. The democratic spirit bequeathed to the Khalsa by Guru Gobind Singh was very strong amongst the Sikh com-munity and they held the temporal sovereignty bequeathed to them by Guru Gobind Singh as a sacred trust and would not let anybody, even their leader, hold any claim to sovereignty. In the absence of any such coin, the controversy is like flogging a dead horse. But the most important conclusion that emerges from this controversy is that the Sikhs cherished with great fidelity and reverence the concept of Sikh sovereignty as a sacred trust bequeathed to them by their Gurus.

During the late eighteenth century, Sikh mints were operated by the Bhangi Sardars from Lahore, Amritsar, and Multan. Jassa Singh Ahluwalia, the veteran leader of a quarter-century-long Sikh struggle, exercised some control over the numerous Sikh *sardars*, who were otherwise independent of each other. Jassa Singh Ahluwalia died in October 1783 and his demise weakened the hold of the coordinating authority over the warring Sikhs, and minor quarrels soon escalated into internecine warfare. Each *sardar* tried to strengthen his hold over the areas under his control and even started striking coins. A number of mints in Amritsar and one at Anandgarh came into existence. But a special feature of these mints was that coins were struck by all in the name of the Sikh Gurus as had been the traditional practice, and no *sardar* put his name on these coins or even changed the legend. This shows that the Sikhs held the sovereignty of their Gurus in very high esteem in spite of their mutual differences and animosities.

There appeared a leaf motif for the first time on the reverse of the Sikh coins struck in the name of the Sikh Gurus from the Amritsar mint in 1841 Sambat, i.e. AD 1784, and thereafter it was universally placed on all the Sikh coins produced by the various Sikh mints till the abolition of Sikh currency in 1849 by the British. All efforts to locate some contemporary historical account have proved futile, and till such time as we are able to unearth some historical account dealing with the placing of the leaf motif on the coins, the issue will remain unresolved.

Historians have called the leaf motif by various names. W.H. Valentine calls it a *peepal* leaf, Ram Chandra Kak calls it a betel leaf, Madanjit Kaur calls it a *peepal* leaf, Saran Singh calls it a lotus leaf, and R.T. Somaiya calls it a *ber* leaf. None of these historians has given any relevant evidence in support of his or her contention, and hence none of these accounts can be taken as authentic.

Our presumption is that some major event/issue would have been responsible for the placing of the leaf motif on the Sikh coins, which continued without any change during the entire period of Sikh coinage, appearing on gold, silver, and even copper coins. The only important event that occurred was the *Chalisa* famine, the famine of the forties, from 1840 to 1844 Sambat, in which the entire region of northern India up to Delhi and its surrounding areas was affected. The Punjab was the worst affected province. Many towns were ruined, people moved to safer areas, and children were sold for food. The Sikh *sardars*, who had recently got their landed estates, spent a great deal of their money on feeding their tenants; some even went to the extent of selling their properties to feed the hungry in a spirit of compassion and sharing preached by the Sikh Gurus. It is our presumption that the Sikhs while seeking the blessings of their Gurus in some gathering in Amritsar might have decided to put a leaf motif signifying fertility on the coin as a prayer to their Gurus.

The Sikh rulers of the cis-Sutlej states were local leaders who did not join the Sikh mainstream, whereas their Sikh subjects were a part of the Sikh Panth. Ranjit Singh's ambitions to bring these states under his rule created a greater rift between him and these lesser rajas, who in reaction aligned themselves with the British.

Nabha state was somewhat of a rebel among the cis-Sutlej states and its rulers had their sympathies with the main Sikh state. Raja Jaswant Singh discarded the Durrani coinage and adopted the Sikh coinage with the legend *'Degh Tegh Fateh'* around 1892 Sambat, i.e. AD 1835, and this coinage continued till India gained independence and the state was merged into the Union. Raja Bhupinder Singh ruled Patiala state from AD 1900 to 1938. He lived very extravagantly and celebrated Dussehra and Diwali with great pomp and splendour. He distributed gold and silver coins to his officials and temple priests during these festivals. He got special coins struck with the legend *'Degh Tegh Fateh'*, popularly called the Guru Sahib coins, which were meant for distribution only on these festive and religious occasions and were not intended for use as state coinage. Sikh coinage did influence the rulers of the Nabha and Patiala states to this limited extent.

After the death of Ranjit Singh and the inability of his successors to meet the challenges of ruling the kingdom, the Sikh state began to decline. The court intrigues, the imbecilic rulers, the treacherous ministers, the disloyal Dogras, the complicity of the *purbia* ministers and rulers, the trust in crafty Brahmins, and the British plans to seek the early dismemberment of the Sikh state, all contributed to the decline of the kingdom. During this period of Brahminical influence, certain Brahminical symbols started appearing on the obverse of the Sikh coins. Brahminical symbols such as the *trishul, Om, chattar, Sat,* and *Shiva* started appearing on the Sikh coins. The appearance of these symbols on the Sikh coins was a disfigurement of the coins and an infringement of Sikh sovereignty. But Sikh sovereignty itself was under severe attack and the Sikh Panth was being put to the sword by its enemies. Under these circumstances, the symbolic violation of Sikh sovereignty becomes somewhat meaningless.

A more serious infringement of Sikh sovereignty took place with the minting of the later Kashmir coinage. While the earlier governors of Kashmir, Hari Singh Nalwa, Moti Ram, and Chunni Lal, had put the name of God as 'Har' in Gurmukhi and then later in Devanagari as 'Harji' and 'Om Shree', etc., the succeeding governors put their initials on these coins. Kirpa Ram put 'K' and on one coin he put 'K Ram'. Bhima Singh put 'Bh' and Sher Singh put the image of a tiger on the reverse by the side of the leaf motif. Mihan Singh did not put his name on these coins, and the last two Muslim governors, Sheikh Gholam Muhyi-ud-din and Sheikh Ghulam Amir-ud-din, put 'Sh' on the obverse of the coins of their periods. The infringement of the principle on which Sikh coinage was based by Kirpa Ram, Bhima Singh, Sher Singh, Sheikh Gholam Muhyi-ud-din, and Sheikh Amir-ud-din constituted distinct distortions of the Sikh coins and violated the Sikh concept of sovereignty. How and why this transgression did not come to the notice of the Lahore Darbar and how and why no objection was raised against this offensive action is not clear as no evidence in this connection is forthcoming.

A very important feature that emerges out of this study is the deep-rooted dedication of the Sikhs to their Gurus and their teachings. The tenth master Guru Gobind Singh, shortly before his demise, abolished the institution of the personal guruship and placed his spiritual sovereignty in the Holy Book, thereafter called the *Guru Granth Sahib*, and vested his temporal sovereignty in the Khalsa, thereafter called the Khalsa Panth. The Sikhs treat the *Guru Granth Sahib* as a living Guru, and the Supreme Court of India has also in a judgement accepted the *Guru Granth Sahib* as a juristic person when lying in a gurdwara. The Sikhs, although vested with temporal sovereignty, still treat their Gurus as temporal sovereigns. The daily salutation, '*Wahe Guru Ji ka Khalsa, Wahe Guru Ji ki Fateh*' means that the Khalsa belongs to the Guru and so does the victory also belong to the Guru. Hence, when the Khalsa became the masters of large areas of Punjab, they struck coins in the name and praise of their Gurus. They thus became the *de facto* temporal rulers and the *de jure* temporal sovereignty still rested with the Gurus. This doctrine has been honoured by the Sikhs throughout their rule of over a century, i.e. from AD 1710 to 1849. Sikh coins are not merely a symbol, but also a mirror image of the concept of Sikh sovereignty.

The concept of Sikh sovereignty, its evolution and development under the Sikh Gurus, and its relationship as well as its application to Sikh coinage is broadly explained in the succeeding portion. The concept of Sikh sovereignty emerged with the development of institutions unique to the Sikh community. This distinct way of life spread all over India over the next two centuries. The ten Sikh Gurus led their disciples step by step towards their ultimate goal, i.e. the development of a self-reliant society that could protect its way of life against all odds. The development of social institutions was simultaneously accompanied by the development of political institutions. Eventually these institutions came to the notice of the imperial authorities, which comprehending the danger, made representations to the central power in Delhi. The imperial authorities in Delhi tried to stem the rise of the Sikhs by persecution and oppression. But the spirit of self-reliance bequeathed by the Gurus to the Sikhs was so strong that the Sikhs successfully resisted the imperial authorities and fought with bravery and courage in order to protect their faith and their institutions.

1. Guru Nanak: April 1469 to September 1539

Guru Nanak, the first Guru of the Sikhs, lived in an age of political instability and social chaos which is most vividly described in his own words:

> The Kal age is a knife;
> the kings are butchers.
> Dharma is on its wings and disappearing.
> The Moon of truth does not appear to rise
> in the dark night of falsehood.[1]

The Sultanate of Delhi had declined and broken up; provincial kingdoms had emerged and the *amirs* and *maliks* of the larger provinces became independent rulers.[2] These rulers had little interest in public welfare, they were careless in financial and administrative matters, they were addicted to the pleasures of the flesh, and they tried to govern mainly by force.[3] The government fell into anarchy, and civil war raged. Internal political instability quite naturally invited foreign invasions.[4] An assignee did not have to apply to a governor or other official to coerce his recalcitrant debtors, but coerced them himself with forces raised at his own cost. The most effective method was to kill the debtors and reduce their families to slavery, a most cruel system of local tyranny.[5] Guru Nanak describes the deep suffering of the common people in four of his verses popularly called the *Babar Vani*:

> Compassion is not exercised by merely beholding a suitor.
> There is no one receiveth or giveth not bribes.
> The king dispenseth justice when his palm is greased.
> He does not move in the name of God.[6]

> Greed and sin are ruler and village accountant.
> Falsehood is master of the mint.
> Lust his minister summoneth and examineth men.
> And siteth in the judgement on them.
> The subjects are blind and without divine knowledge
> And satisfy the judges' greed with bribes.[7]

Babar's invasions caused further hardship to the demoralized people of India, especially the Hindu masses. The invaders destroyed Hindu temples, slaughtered Hindus, and enslaved their women and children. When the Mughals set up their own government, their spirit of intolerance led to the imposition of all sorts of humiliations on Hindus, such as the levying of religious taxes, abolition of religious fairs, social discrimination vis-à-vis Muslims and infidels, and rewards for apostates from Hinduism.[8] Guru Nanak describes Babar's invasions:

> (Babur) has come from Kabul with the marriage party of vice.
> And asks for charity by force.
> Honour and righteousness have hidden themselves.
> Falsehood predominates.
> Not the qazi and Brahman but the devil acts as the performer of the rites of the marriage.[9]
> A kingdom that was a jewel was wasted by the dogs.
> No one will mourn their passing.[10]

Guru Nanak witnessed Babar's attack on Sayyadpur, and the atrocities committed by his soldiers greatly distressed him. He states in his *Bani*:

> The kings are like whores, the courtiers like dogs,
> For they awaken those asleep in God's peace.
> The king's servants tear (the docile subjects) with their nails.
> And like curs lick all the blood they spill.[11]

Hindu society suffered from depression and stagnation as a result of rigid casteism and the ritualistic tyranny of the brahmans. The springs of true religion had been choked by the weeds of meaningless rites, rituals, and superstitions, the selfishness of the priests, and the indifference of the people. The true spiritual nature of Hinduism lay buried under ostentation and sectarianism.[12] Guru Nanak was greatly troubled by the barbaric social and political tyranny of the Islamic rulers and invaders, on the one hand, and the ritualistic dominance of the Brahmins, on the other hand. Guru Nanak taught that the one who inflicts torture and the one who submits to tyranny are both equally guilty in the eyes of God, and he preached the vision of a self-reliant society devoid of fear whose members worship one God with absolute devotion.

The seventy years of Guru Nanak's life may be divided into three well-defined periods:

A. PERIOD OF INWARD STRUGGLE AND ENLIGHTENMENT

ON THE BANKS OF THE KALI BAIN IN 1496

After gaining enlightenment on the banks of the Kali Bain, Guru Nanak resigned his assignment under Daulat Khan and proceeded on his travels saying, 'There is no Hindu and no Musalman', meaning that both Hindus and Musalmans had strayed away from true religion. When some *qazis* posed questions to him, Guru Nanak advised them:

Make kindness thy mosque,
sincerity thy prayer carpet,
what is just and lawful thy Quran.
modesty thy circumcision, civility thy fasting
so that thou be a Musalman.[13]

B. PERIOD OF TRAVEL, PROPAGATION OF FAITH, AND THE ESTABLISHMENT
OF DHARAMSALAS AT NUMEROUS PLACES FROM 1496 TO 1521

I. To south-west Punjab for one year, 1496-7
II. To the Gangetic plains up to Dacca, 1497-1510
III. South India, including Ceylon, 1510-15
IV. To the Himalayas, 1515-17
V. To West Asia, including Baghdad, 1517-21

Guru Nanak's extensive travels included visits to the holy places of the Hindus, Buddhists, Muslims, Sufis, and Sidhs, where he held discourses on his gospel of one God and won over many disciples. *Dharamsalas* were opened at the places he visited, where the *sangat* sang hymns in praise of one God. Bhai Gurdas states that a *dharamsala* was opened in every house and *kirtan* was held as it was an unending Baisakhi festival.[14] Some Western historians believe that Guru Nanak undertook these extensive travels to attain wisdom by practicing penitent meditation, through study, and through an enlarged social intercourse with humankind.[15] This assumption has been refuted by later historians who argue that Guru Nanak's journeys were not in search of truth, but rather were meant to propagate the truth he already knew. In his talks with brahmans, *jogis*, *pirs*, Jain *munis*, and other holy men, Guru Nanak was never a student; he was always the teacher who points out falsehood and indicates the path of truth.[16]

C. SETTLED LIFE IN KARTARPUR FROM 1521 TO 1539

After his long tours of India and beyond, Guru Nanak settled down in Kartarpur in AD 1521. He lived the life of a householder, joined by his wife and two sons, and soon his disciples joined him. In this period he gave practical expression to his ideals, combining the life of disciplined devotion with normal daily activities.[17] Guru Nanak followed the same rules that he had laid down for his disciples, which encouraged equality and democracy amongst them. In the *dharamsala* hymns were sung both morning and evening. The disciples who came from far and near were called the *sangat* or congregation. The *sangat* sat in *pangat*, and partook of the food from the free kitchen called the *langar*. These institutions broke down the barriers of caste and class and all individuals stood before the Guru in perfect equality. Guru Nanak said:

Castes are folly, names are folly.
All creatures have one shelter, that of God.
Man, no matter what his caste or social position may be,
is exalted by devotion.[18]

The lowest of the low castes,
The lowliest of the lowly,
I seek their kinship.
Why emulate the so-called higher ones?
Thy elevating grace is where
the downtrodden are looked after.[19]

Guru Nanak denounced the practices of asceticism and renunciation. A Sikh must work and earn his living and share his savings with others. Exploitation of the labour of others is like eating the forbidden food:

Oh Nanak, he alone realizes the way?
Who eats the fruits of toil,
Sharing with others.[20]

To exploit the rightful due to others,
Is like eating the forbidden.
Cow for one (Hindu) and swine for the other (Muslim).
The Lord vouchsafes for us only if we are not usurpers.[21]

Guru Nanak placed great emphasis on the unquestioning obedience and absolute surrender of the disciple to the Guru. He taught this lesson through the nomination of Lehna, who obeyed the orders of the Guru without any questioning.[22] Guru Nanak said:

If thou desire to play at love with me,
Come my way with thy head on the palm of thy hand.
Put thy feet on this road.
Give thy head and regard not human opinion.[23]

Guru Amar Das said:

Entrust thy body, soul, and wealth to the Guru, and obey his orders, so shall you succeed.

This idea, with the passage of time, became a living force in the Sikh community and was beautifully illustrated when the five beloved Sikhs (the *Panj Piaras*) came forward at the call of Guru Gobind Singh at Keshgarh, with their heads virtually in the palms of their hands.[24]

FIGURE IV: GURU NANAK

The last important aspect of Guru Nanak's work was the nomination of a successor. It has aptly been called the key event in the history of Sikhism.[25] Guru Nanak considered Lehna, one of his most devoted disciples, for this onerous responsibility. Lehna became Angad, literally a part of Guru Nanak's body and metaphorically an extension of his mission. It was the establishment of an effective line of succession of the Gurus which, above all other factors, ensured the transmission of the first Guru's leadership and the cohesion of the newly established religious community. The nomination and formal installation of Guru Angad was the first step in the process that resulted in the founding of the Khalsa and ultimately in the emergence of a Sikh nation.[26]

The uniqueness ascribed to Guru Nanak's position lies in the continuity of his work through his successors. The immediate successor of Guru Nanak was also called Nanak and so were all the other successors. The mingling of 'the light' of Guru Nanak with 'the light' of Guru Angad is in accordance with God's *raza* (will).[27] Guru Gobind Singh is quite emphatic about this unity; in his presentation Guru Nanak becomes Guru Angad and Guru Angad becomes Guru Amardas and Guru Amardas becomes Guru Ramdas. Indeed, only 'the foolish failed to understand that the Gurus were all manifestations of one form and were not distinct from one another'.[28] G.C. Narang writes: 'The sword that carved the Khalsa's way to glory was undoubtedly forged by Gobind, but the steel had been provided by Nanak.'[29] J.D. Cunningham notes: 'It was reserved for Nanak to perceive the true principles of reform, and to lay those broad foundations which enabled his successor Gobind to fire the minds of his countrymen with a new nationality and to give practical effect to the doctrine that the lowest is equal with the highest, in race as in creed, in political rights as in religious hopes.'[30] Ernest Trump argues that the disciples of Guru Nanak would no doubt have soon dispersed and gradually disappeared, as well as the disciples of many other Gurus after Nanak, if he had not taken care to appoint a successor before his death.[31]

Bhai Gurdas conceives of the position of the Guru in terms of sovereignty. The true Guru is the true king. The Guru Panth is his coin.[32] Bhai Gurdas compares the Panth to an eight-metal coin.[33] The Guru as the true sovereign commands exclusive allegiance; those who do not submit to the Guru are rebels.[34] Bhai Gurdas does not make any distinction between Guru Nanak and his successors for they too are the Padshah of both *din* and *dunia*.[35] A.C. Banerjee writes that Guru Nanak created a higher moral force which brought about all the virtues of the Sikh community and enabled it not only to survive but also to create a state in a period of ruthless strife.[36] J.C. Archer notes that there was something positive and realistic in the reforms of Guru Nanak, something that made a religion and a state.[37] Kapur Singh does not share Arnold Toynbee's view that the order of the Khalsa was a contingent phenomenon dictated by the exigencies of the moment, but has been the logical development and entelechy of the teachings of Guru Nanak.[38] Sher Singh writes: 'Who knows that given the means which Guru Gobind Singh had at his disposal, with the work of ten generations which had prepared the ground for him, Nanak would have met the situation in the same way in which the former did in his own time afterwards.'[39] Nihar Ranjan Ray observes that 'to achieve the integration of temporal and spiritual seems to me to have been the most significant contribution of Guru Nanak to the totality of the Indian way of life in medieval India.'[40]

2. Guru Angad 1539-1552

Guru Angad moved out of Kartarpur and set up his headquarters at Khadur Sahib on the advice of Guru Nanak in order to avoid any confrontation with the sons of Guru Nanak over property and other matters.[41] Guru Nanak had rejected the sanctity of Sanskrit, called the *deva bhasha* or the language of the gods. He rejected the authority of the Vedas on which the brahmanical system rested. He used the people's language for developing and propagating the people's religion.[42] Guru Angad beautified the *lande* script and invented the Gurmukhi script. He wrote the hymns of Guru Nanak in the Gurmukhi script.[43] The institution of *langar* for the *sangat* was continued and his wife Mata Khivi gave her personal attention to its proper functioning. Guru Angad passed away in March 1552 at the age of 48 years. Shortly before his demise, he appointed his devout disciple Amar Das as his successor.

3. Guru Amar Das 1552-1574

Where Guru Nanak had laid the elementary basis of the Sikh society, Guru Amar Das carried out a number of institutional developments to make Sikh society more self-reliant and to engender greater cohesion amongst its rapidly growing membership. His major contributions were:

1. The *langar* was made more elaborate and all Sikhs and non-Sikhs were fed. In fact, it was obligatory for all those desirous of meeting the Guru to partake of *langar* food before they could meet him. According to Sikh tradition, even Emperor Akbar had to partake of the food of the *langar* before meeting the Guru.[44] When Akbar offered some rent-free lands for the maintenance of the *langar*, the Guru refused, stating that he received sufficient resources from his creator.[45] This was apparently to prevent being under the obligation of the emperor and to avoid possible interference by the Mughal (temporal) authorities in the affairs of the Sikh spiritual kingdom. Contributions to the Guru's *langar* could only be made by the Guru's disciples. The compulsory partaking of food at the *langar* was also a great social leveller, since it encouraged the abolition of the caste system amongst the Hindus, and the slogan often used was 'Pehle pangat pichhe sangat'.
2. Guru Amar Das laid great emphasis on the physical fitness of his disciples.

3. The Guru abolished the prevailing practice of *sati* (widow burning on the pyre of her dead husband) amongst his disciples.

4. He persuaded the women not to use *pardah* to cover their faces. He composed the 'Anand', a song of joy to be recited at the time of weddings and other occasions of happiness.[46]

5. Guru Amar Das collected the hymns of Guru Nanak, Guru Angad, and his own songs and left this collection in the custody of his son Mohan.

6. The Sikhs were rapidly increasing in number and were spread all over the Punjab and the surrounding areas. Guru Amar Das established separate centres of *sangats* called *manjis* and selected his representatives to address these gatherings. They also collected offerings for the Guru and conveyed these twice a year on Baisakhi and Diwali at his headquarters.[47] The institution of the *manji* (*manji* literally means a cot on which the revered and senior person sits while the others sit on the ground) was later developed into the institution of the *masand* by Guru Arjan Dev and this remained in operation till the end of the seventeenth century, when it was abolished by Guru Gobind Singh its having become self-centred and riddled with corruption and thereby redundant for the growing Sikh society.

7. Guru Amar Das, eager to meet his Sikh disciples, invited them with their families and friends twice a year, on Baisakhi during March-April and on Diwali during October-November. He constructed a large *baoli* at Goindwal where the disciples could recite the *Japji* at each of the eighty-four steps leading to the water's edge.[48] This practice became so well entrenched with the passage of time that the large congregations assembled at Amritsar on these two festivals. He also debarred the Sikhs from performing the usual Hindu ceremonies at cremations, which created much resentment amongst the brahmans who relied on their ritualistic roles at these rites to earn their livelihood.[49]

8. The Udasis were eager to convert to Sikhism. They were ascetics and non-householders.[50] The Guru emphatically declared that there was no room for the Udasis in the Sikh religion.

9. The abolition of useless and meaningless Hindu customs and ceremonies related to weddings and cremations led to the severance of links with the general body of the Hindus. This gave the Sikhs a distinct identity and marked their separate corporate character; as Cunningham writes: 'They were preserved . . . from disappearing as one of the many sects of Hinduism.'

The Guru's growing influence and his rejection of Brahminical customs and traditions annoyed the Brahmins and the Khatris who complained to Emperor Akbar against the Guru, giving out distorted information. Akbar invited Guru Amar Das for a discussion but the Guru refused to personally go to the emperor for this purpose. He, however, sent Bhai Jetha, his son-in-law and the future Guru, who explained to Akbar that the Sikhs had no hostility against the Hindus.[51]

Akbar was convinced and rejected the plea of the Hindus. The regulations made by Guru Amar Das during his long tenure accentuated the differences between the Hindus and the Sikhs which became more pronounced with the passage of time. The Sikhs began to gradually drift away from the orthodox Hindu society and formed a new brotherhood of their own.[52]

Guru Amar Das states:

Even in a gale and torrential rain,
I would go to meet my Guru.
Even if an ocean separates them,
A Sikh would go to meet his Guru.
As a man dies of thirst without water,
A Sikh would die without his Guru.
As parched earth exults after a shower,
A Sikh rejoices on meeting his Guru.[53]

These words of the third master emphasize the great influence of the Sikh Gurus among their followers and underline their strong inner urge to be in constant communion with the founders of their faith.

4. Guru Ram Das 1574-1581

Guru Ram Das became the fourth Nanak. In order to avoid a family feud he moved out of Goindwal and purchased a piece of land next to the one given by Akbar to Bibi Bhani (daughter of Guru Amar Das and wife of Guru Ram Das). This place was later named Amritsar. A tank was dug up under Baba Budha's guidance and the place was called Guru ka Chak. It appears that the digging of the tank started in the time of Guru Amar Das, was, however, completed along with the Harimandir by Guru Arjan.

During the short tenure of Guru Ram Das, Srichand, Guru Nanak's eldest son, visited him. Guru Ram Das received him with great regard. Guru Ram Das, however, did not allow the Udasis to join the Sikhs or the Sikhs to join the Udasis. The Udasis, however, consider themselves to be part of the Sikh community.[54] Guru Ram Das passed away in 1581 after selecting his youngest son Arjan as his successor, that is, as the fifth Nanak. The principle of hereditary succession was taking root, yet the selection was on the old principle of devotion and service to the faith.

5. Guru Arjan 1581-1606

During the quarter century of his Gurudom, Guru Arjan carried out the consolidation of the fledgling Sikh Panth which was now rapidly coming of age. In this task, Guru Arjan faced many difficulties, including the lifelong hostility of his disinherited and embittered elder brother Prithia. Prithia tried to administer poison to the infant Hargobind, founded his own sect called the Minas, started writing his own scripture, aided and abetted Sulahi Khan against the Guru, joined hands with Chandu Shah, the *diwan*, against the Guru, and indulged in similar intrigues and conspiracies against his younger brother. The Sikh community was thus faced with profound sectarianism and deep divisions within the family of the Guru himself. The other threats to the Sikh community were posed by the growing hostility of the orthodox Hindus and the fanatic Naqshbandi Sufi, Shaikh Sayyed Ahmad Sirhindi. Despite these internal schisms and external threats to the survival of the Sikh community, the extraordinary genius of Guru Arjan was able to consolidate the Sikh Panth to a considerable extent.

Guru Arjan's first task was the completion of the city of Ramdaspur, the tank of nectar (Amritsar), and the Harimandir located in the centre of the tank. According to tradition, the foundation stone of the holy temple was laid by the Qadiri Sufi saint Mian Mir of Lahore, but there is no contemporary record to support this claim.[55] Guru Arjan also built his quarters in the precincts of the temple. The tank, the temple, and the psychological integration amongst the Sikhs fostered by Guru Arjan all contributed to one continuous process of consolidation and institutional cohesion.[56]

According to *Dabastan-i-Mazhab*, 'before the fifth period no tribute was exacted from the Sikhs, but presents were given by them according to their own discretion to their Guru'.[57] The voluntary contributions from the Sikhs proved to be insufficient for the various construction works then in progress and the running of the *langar*. Guru Arjan named his agents *masands*, presumably a corruption of the word *musannad* (meaning exalted position), and these *masands* were sent to each town to collect tribute. Each Sikh was asked to donate one-tenth of his income as (*daswandh*) to the Guru every year, and the *masands* were called upon to bring this tribute to the Guru in the month of Baisakh. Although the *masands* were initially supposed to collect funds, they also became missionaries and guides on religious matters. Thus developed a system of tax collection which in later times resembled a system of parallel government. The Guru came to be looked upon by his Sikhs as exercising temporal authority in addition to providing spiritual guidance.[58] Guru Arjan also commenced the construction of a large tank at Tarn Taran and a temple by its side.

The most notable achievement of Guru Arjan was the compilation of the holy book known as the *Adi Granth*. Sikh worship consisted of the singing of hymns composed by their Gurus. The dissident groups made their own selections and also distorted the hymns of the Gurus to suit their ill intentions. Guru Arjan now felt the necessity of laying down rules of conduct for the guidance of his followers in the performance of their daily religious duties and expiatory rites.[59] This would bring about consistency in the practice of the Sikh religion and restrict the entry of divergent beliefs and rituals. Prithia's distortion of Guru

Nanak's hymns was causing anxiety to Guru Amar Das, who ordained that only
the real hymns of the Guru should be recited and revered by the Sikhs. He made
a collection of hymns from the time of Nanak to his own time which he had left
with his son Mohan.[60] Guru Arjan's action was the final step in the direction of
consolidating and authenticating the proper Sikh religious practices. Guru Arjan
needed the earlier collection of hymns from Mohan who was reluctant to hand it
over to his envoys Bhai Gurdas and Bhai Budha. Guru Arjan thereafter personally
went to Mohan and sat singing the hymns outside his house. The Guru's melodious
voice softened the heart of Mohan and he gave the *pothis* to him.[61] When the
collection of hymns was completed, Guru Arjan dictated them to Bhai Gurdas
in a tent set up on a selected spot near Amritsar. The great task was finished in
August 1604 and the sacred volume was deposited in the Harimandir in Amritsar.[62]
The *lok bhasha* thus permanently replaced the *deva bhasha* and religion was
brought to the heart of the masses. There was no need at all for a priest to guide
or misguide and exploit the illiterate or illeducated people. Religion ceased to
be a mystery hiding behind a linguistic curtain, and now became a matter of
daily experience by the individual worshipper.[63]

Guru Arjan began living in a grand style for the inspiration of his disciples.
He considered the spiritual life and worldly living as two aspects of a single
reality. He erected lofty buildings in Amritsar, wore rich clothes, kept fine horses
and elephants, and had retainers in attendance. His personal life was otherwise
very simple. The Sikhs venerated their Guru and called him *Sacha Padshah*.[64]
Guru Arjan encouraged his disciples to take to trade and commerce, and with the
settling of traders Amritsar soon grew into a prosperous city. The number of
Sikhs also greatly increased and, according to Mohsin Fani, in almost all towns in
the country a few Sikhs were to be found.[65]

Abul Fazl writes in the *Akbarnama* that the emperor crossed over the Beas
at Goindwal and called on Guru Arjan on 24 November 1598.[66] Sujan Rai
Bhandari states that Akbar was very pleased to meet Guru Arjan who greeted
him with the recitation of hymns composed by Baba Nanak in praise of God.
Guru Arjan told Akbar that during the stay of his troops the price of grain had
gone up and now that the troops were leaving, the peasants would not be in a
position to pay the enhanced revenue. The emperor ordered that the land
revenue be reduced by one-sixth.[67] Indu Bhushan Banerjee states that the
exemption of land revenue was one-twelfth,[68] and G.C. Narang states that the
remission was for the whole year's revenue.[69]

With the installation of the *Granth Sahib* in 1604, the enemies of the Sikhs
complained to Akbar that it contained some passages offensive to Islam. The
emperor called for the *Granth* and the Holy Book was carried to him by Bhai
Gurdas and Baba Budha. Akbar got the alleged offensive passages read out and
found nothing objectionable, and instead he appreciated the hymns in praise of
God.[70] But with the death of Akbar in 1605, the half century of peaceful co-

existence of the Sikhs with the Mughal government came to a sudden end. During the reign of Akbar, the Sikh Gurus Amar Das, Ram Das, and Arjan had very cordial relations with the emperor who was greatly appreciative of their activities.

The important achievements of these three Gurus were the consolidation and large scale expansion of the Sikh community; the complete separation of the Sikhs from the Udasis and the orthodox Hindu community; the development of Amritsar into a sacred place and the centre of the Panth's authority; and the compilation of the *Granth*. During this period, voluntary contributions from the disciples were made compulsory at the amount of one-tenth of their income (*daswandh*) and the collections were made through authorized agents called *masands*. This was more or less a revolutionary arrangement with far-reaching consequences.[71] The Guru could now arrange the budget with much more certainty as the dues of the Guru were paid more readily and unfailingly than even the collection of Mughal revenues. The large *sangat*, increased resources, palatial buildings, tents, horses, and the splendour and magnificence of the *darbar* all gave it the appearance of a princely court.[72] A state, peaceful and unobtrusive, had been slowly evolved, and the Guru as its head was called the *Sacha Padshah* of the Panth. The Sikhs had already become accustomed to a form of self-government within the empire.[73]

Jahangir, who became emperor in October 1605, was already biased against the Sikh Gurus due to his orthodox Islamic leanings. In his autobiography, Jahangir writes:

In Goindwal. . . , there was a Hindu named Arjan, in the garment of sainthood and sanctity, so much so that he had captured many of the simple-hearted Hindus, and even of the ignorant and foolish followers of Islam, by his ways and manners, and they had loudly sounded the drum of his holiness. They called him Guru, and from all sides stupid people crowded to worship and manifest complete faith in him. For three or four generations they had kept this shop warm. Many times it occurred to me to put a stop to this vain affair or to bring him into the assembly of Islam.[74]

Jahangir was also angered by the cordial treatment accorded to the rebel Prince Khusrau by Guru Arjan. He, therefore, ordered him to be produced before him and his property and family handed over to Murtaza Khan and the Guru to be put to death.[75] Guru Arjan's enemies, Prithia, Chandu Das, and the Naqshbandi Sayyad of Sirhind also became active, and the fanatic and orthodox Farid Bukhari was made governor of the Punjab.

Guru Arjan was arrested and taken to Lahore. He was also fined two lakh rupees and was ordered to remove those hymns in the *Granth* which opposed Hinduism and Islam. Father D. Jarric (a Jesuit monk in the Mughal court) states that some Sikhs intended to intercede on his behalf, but Guru Arjan declined their help and prevented his disciples from raising the required amount for the fine. Fines, he said, were for thieves, adulterers, and slanderers, and men

devoted to religion never paid fines.[76] Guru Arjan was imprisoned in the Lahore
Fort. He was tied to a post in the open, exposed to the hot sun of June, burning
sand and hot water were thrown on his naked body for five days, and he was
next to be sewn into a raw hide. Guru Arjan sought permission to bathe in the
nearby river Ravi. He plunged into the Ravi and never appeared again.[77]

The second part of Jahangir's order concerning Guru Arjan's properties and
family was not implemented, presumably on the intervention of Mian Mir, a
Muslim saint of Lahore. Jadu Nath Sarkar in his short account of the Sikhs has
made some very uncharitable and incorrect remarks. His comments on Guru
Arjan—that he was a common revenue defaulter and that this collision of the
Sikhs with the Mughals in Jahangir's time was entirely due to secular causes—
have been debated threadbare by later historians and thereafter rejected. Indu
Bhushan Banerjee has reacted very strongly to Sarkar's claim that there was
nothing exceptional in the punishment meted out to Guru Arjan and that this was
the usual punishment accorded to revenue defaulters in those days. Banerjee
argues that to call Guru Arjan a revenue defaulter because of his incapability or
refusal to pay the fine and then to justify the tortures inflicted on him on the
grounds of current usage, ignoring all other circumstances connected with his
death, shows a perversity of judgement which can hardly be excused in a
historian of Sarkar's eminence.[78]

6. Guru Hargobind 1606-1644

Guru Hargobind became the sixth Nanak, as decided by Guru Arjan, at the age
of 11 years. Some historians argue that Guru Hargobind brought about the
transformation of the Sikh community from a non-violent religious organization to
a military organization.[79] This is not correct, as it was Guru Arjan who had quite
clearly foreseen the difficult times ahead. During the half-century-long reign of
Akbar, the orthodox Islamic fanatics had been kept under control, but their re-
emergence after the death of Akbar and under the rule of the orthodox Jahangir
had been foreseen by Guru Arjan. He changed the style of his *darbar* from that
of a princely court to a more modest one. He arranged for horses and armed
retainers.[80] He instructed Baba Budha to train his young son Hargobind in the
use of all defensive and offensive weapons, riding, as well as languages, arts,
and sciences.[81] Shortly before his death, he sent word through his Sikhs that his
son Hargobind should sit fully armed on his throne and maintain an army to the
best of his ability.[82] What Guru Hargobind carried out was what had already
been started by Guru Arjan and what he did was in accordance with the instructions of his teacher Baba Budha as directed by Guru Arjan. Hence the work of
Guru Hargobind was merely the continuation of the work of Guru Arjan. Guru
Arjan introduced and imparted military training not only to his son Hargobind and
other boys of his age, but he also employed skilled and accomplished warriors
to build the nucleus of Guru Hargobind's army. According to Bhai Mani Singh,

the concepts of *miri* and *piri* were also introduced by Guru Arjan.

From the very beginning, Guru Arjan had conceived of Sikhism essentially as a state—Halemi Raj—the most significant aspect of Sikh sovereignty, by saying that Nanak had founded a state, a dominion of God, a fortress of truth, based on the indestructible foundation of doctrine.[83] Nihar Ranjan Ray has very correctly concluded that 'Guru Nanak laid the main foundations on which the edifice of Sikh society was to be built. The later Gurus walked on these foundations and a few of them—Guru Arjan, Guru Hargobind, and Guru Gobind Singh—strengthened them by buttressing and expanding them.'[84]

Guru Hargobind at his succession ceremony wore two swords on either side—one symbolizing *miri*, the temporal power, and the other *piri*, the spiritual power.[85] He stated that in the Guru's house, the spiritual power and the mundane power shall be combined, and that his rosary would be the sword belt and that on his turban he would wear the emblem of royalty.[86] He inherited 52 bodyguards, 700 horses, 300 horsemen, and 60 gunners.[87] In front of the Harimandir, he built a 12-feet-high platform in 1606 called the Akal Takht, God's throne, on which he sat in princely attire. The Harimandir was the seat of spiritual authority from where he provided spiritual solace to his disciples. The Akal Takht was the seat of temporal authority from where he dispensed justice like a king in court, accepted gifts, awarded honours, and meted out punishments. Court bards used to sing songs in praise of the great Indian heroes.[88] Thus the Sikhs came to occupy a kind of separate state within the Mughal state, the position of which was established by the independent fiscal policy of Guru Amar Das and Guru Arjan and Guru Hargobinds' system of armed self-protection.[89] Sikh consciousness was based on an unprecedented quest for a sovereign Sikh identity which would establish and strengthen the uniqueness of Sikhism.[90]

No clear account of Guru Hargobind's relations with Jahangir during his reign (1606-27) is available. It is historically true that Guru Hargobind was imprisoned by the Mughals in Gwalior. The reasons for the arrest of the Guru are not clear, nor is the date of his arrest; the period varies in different accounts from 40 days to twelve and a half years. Also not clear is the role of Mian Mir, a revered Muslim saint of Lahore who was also a friend of Guru Hargobind's family, in bringing about a rapprochement between the two leaders. The most reasonable period of confinement seems to have been only a few years. Guru Hargobind is said to have gone to Kashmir with Jahangir. His visit to Kashmir and Baramulla is historically true. Whether and what assignment Guru Hargobind held under Jahangir is once again not clear. It is very unlikely that Guru Hargobind would have taken a minor post as he was quite wealthy, with his own resources, and it is presumed that he merely accompanied Jahangir, as Guru Gobind Singh later accompanied Bahadur Shah in his travels in 1706. Guru Hargobind had also visited Sikh places in what is present-day north-western Uttar Pradesh. Guru Hargobind's good relations with Jahangir are seen from the emperor's handing over of Chandu Shah to the Guru for punishment and also the imprisonment of Shaikh Ahmad Sirhindi in 1619.[91] During this period Guru Hargobind was able to soften Jahangir with diplomatic moves and friendly overtures. However, the details of this relationship between the Guru and the emperor are not recorded.

Actual hostility between Mughal troops and the Guru broke out in the early years of Shah Jahan's reign, based on rather flimsy grounds. Guru Hargobind decided to defy the Mughal authorities and fought six engagements against Mughal officials, from 1633 to 1638. He shifted his headquarters from Amritsar to Hargobindpur, then to Kartarpur, then to Phagwara, and finally to Kiratpur,[92] in order to get away from the plains where more military engagements, even a major attack by Mughal imperial forces, were quite likely. The battles of Jallo in 1633, Sangram in 1633, and Lohara in 1637 were minor ones,[93] but the battles of Amritsar in 1634, Gurusar in 1637, and Kartarpur in 1638 were rather major ones.[94]

1. BATTLE OF AMRITSAR, 1634

A large army was sent against Guru Hargobind who retired to Jhabbal after a short scuffle. After a while Guru Hargobind suddenly attacked the Mughal forces, killing many, including their commander. Macauliffe says that in this battle 700 Sikhs defeated 7,000 Mughals. Latif says that this was the first proper engagement between the Sikhs and the Mughal forces in which the Mughal commander Mukhlis Khan was also killed.[95]

2. BATTLE OF GURUSAR, 1637

Kamar Beg and Lal Beg were sent out against Guru Hargobind who was camping in the Lakhi jungle. The Sikhs ambushed and defeated the enemy but at a heavy cost of 1,200 Sikh soldiers slain.[96]

3. BATTLE OF KARTARPUR, 1638

A force under Painda Khan (a disgruntled former friend of Guru Hargobind) and Mir Badhera was sent against the Guru. More Mughal troops joined at Jullandhar. In a hard-fought battle, the Mughal commanders were killed. In the battle Guru Hargobind's youngest son displayed remarkable skill and he was renamed Tegh Bahadur in recognition of his bravery.[97]

After these battles Guru Hargobind realized that his resources were not adequate for the open defiance of Mughal forces, and hence he decided to retreat into the relative security of the Shivalik Hills at Kiratpur (an establishment set up by Gurditta at the instance of the Muslim saint, Pir Buddan Shah). There were no further confrontations with the Mughals during the last decade of Guru

Hargobind's life.[98] Guru Hargobind gave the Sikhs a new confidence in themselves and he strengthened the organizational structure. He demonstrated the possibility of the Sikhs assuming an attitude of open defiance against the Mughal government, which did occur a little over half a century later when Guru Gobind Singh confronted the Mughals; this attitude ultimately led to the emergence of the Khalsa and the establishment of the Sikh sovereign state in the eighteenth century.[99] During the tenure of Guru Hargobind, Baba Budha expired in 1628 at the age of 120 years and Bhai Gurdas expired in 1637 at the age of 88 years. Guru Hargobind expired in 1644 after nominating Har Rai as the seventh Nanak.

7. Guru Har Rai 1644-1661

Guru Har Rai succeeded his grandfather at the age of 14. In accordance with the advice of Guru Hargobind, he maintained a force of 2,000 armed Sikhs and his court had the pomp of a semi-independent chieftain. When Mughal forces invaded the territory of Raja Tarachand of Kalhur, Guru Har Rai moved further into the interior of the Shivalik Hills and stayed for about twelve years in Nahan.[100] Guru Har Rai took a keen interest in organizational and missionary work. Since many *masands* had become corrupt and indifferent to their missionary work, he entrusted the task of preaching in the east to Bhagat Gir who is said to have established about 360 *gaddis*. Another disciple was sent to the central Punjab. Thus were two *bakshishes* established, and many more were set up during the tenures of the ninth and the tenth Gurus.[101] These agencies reduced the importance of the *masands* and paved the way for their eventual abolition by Guru Gobind Singh.

Aurangzeb summoned Guru Har Rai to his court, but instead the Guru sent his fourteen-year-old son Ram Rai.[102] The Guru is reported to have stated, 'I am not a king who payeth thee tribute, nor do I desire to receive anything from thee, nor do we stand in relationship of priest and disciple to each other, so why has thou summoned me?' In explaining a hymn of Guru Nanak, Ram Rai deliberately misinterpreted a passage to avoid causing annoyance to the emperor. When this transgression of the Sikh religion came to the notice of Guru Har Rai he disowned Ram Rai, considering his offence unpardonable. Guru Har Rai expired at Kiratpur in October 1661 at the young age of 32 years. He had nominated his younger son Harkrishan, a five-year-old boy, while suppressing the claim of Ram Rai to the *gaddi*.

8. Guru Harkrishan 1661-1664

Guru Harkrishan, born in 1656, assumed the *gaddi* as the eighth Nanak and was called a 'child saint'. Since Ram Rai had appealed to the Mughal court against the suppression of his claim to the *gaddi*, Guru Harkrishan was summoned to the imperial court, and Mirza Raja Jai Singh was sent to escort him. Guru Harkrishan refused to meet the emperor on the plea that his father and predecessor had forbidden him to meet Aurangzeb. However, within a short time Guru Harkrishan suffered from a severe attack of smallpox and expired on 30 March 1664. While in a state of delirium, Guru Harkrishan pointed to Baba Bakala as his successor.[103]

9. Guru Tegh Bahadur 1664-1675

Tegh Bahadur became Guru at the age of 43. He was bitterly opposed by dissidents. Dhir Mal attacked him and gunshots scraped his shoulder. He went to Amritsar with his few followers but the temple gates were closed to him by Harji, grandson of Prithia. He went to Kiratpur and his jealous relatives did not let him stay there. The difficulties confronted by Guru Tegh Bahadur at the very beginning of his Guruship indicate that the organizational cohesion based on the Guru's undisputed leadership which had been the glory of Sikhism was now in decline and the movement was weakening.[104] Instead of settling down at one place, Guru Tegh Bahadur toured the Majha and Malwa areas for a year and then returned to Kiratpur. He laid the foundation of a new settlement which grew into the town of Anandpur.[105]

Guru Tegh Bahadur found that the Sodhi relations settled in Kiratpur would not leave him in peace, and he moved towards the east via Prayag and Banaras and reached Patna where he decided to stay. It was at Patna that Mirza Raja Ram Singh met the Guru and persuaded him to accompany him to Assam.[106] On receiving the news of the birth of his son, the Guru returned to Patna. Guru Tegh Bahadur stayed for some time in Patna and on hearing of Aurangzeb's fanaticism towards Hindus and Sikhs he decided to return to the Punjab. He initially moved alone, not sure of the reception that awaited him at the hands of his enemies, but he soon called for his family and finally settled down in Makhowal.[107]

During Aurangzeb's rule, orders were passed to demolish all schools and temples of the infidels and to put down their religious practices and teachings; the magnificent temples of Somnath, Mathura, and Banaras were demolished and *jaziya* was re-imposed.[108] The Sikhs, who were also regarded as infidels, could not expect better treatment than the Hindus. Aurangzeb ordered the temples of the Sikhs to be demolished and the Guru's agents (*masands*) who collected the tithes and gifts from the faithful to be expelled from the cities.[109] Such was the situation when Guru Tegh Bahadur returned to Anandpur. Kashmiri Pandits who were being converted on pain of being put to the sword by the specially appointed governor, Afghan Khan, approached Guru Tegh Bahadur who took up their cause. The Guru took to touring the Malwa area between the rivers Sutlej and Ghaggar. The simple but hardy farmers were cowed down by the Muslim officials during the emperor's stay in the Punjab. Guru Tegh Bahadur worked for the physical and spiritual needs of the people of Malwa. Where fields were barren and dry, he got wells dug. Where there was scarcity of milk, he procured cows and gave them free of cost to the people. For the landless peasants he procured some land and urged them to live courageously as free people. In barren areas he got trees planted.[110]

Distorted and exaggerated reports of the activities of Guru Tegh Bahadur were sent to the Mughal court and the Guru was summoned.[111] While the Guru was on his way to Delhi, he was arrested along with his five companions and was put in an iron cage on the way to the capital. The governor and the *qazi* tried to persuade Guru Tegh Bahadur to embrace Islam but he resolutely rejected their overtures. The companions of the Guru were tortured to death in his presence, and the next day he was beheaded outside the *qotwali* in Chandni Chowk, on 11 November 1675.[112] In the confusion, a Sikh of the Guru took away the head of the Guru and carried it to his son Gobind Singh at Anandpur, and the body was taken by another Sikh to the Rakab Ganj area on outskirts of Delhi where he placed the remains of Guru Tegh Bahadur in his own house and set it on fire, so that the Guru's body was suitably cremated.

10. Guru Gobind Singh 1675-1708

Gobind, born in Patna in 1666, remained in that city under the care of his mother and his uncle Kirpal in the absence of his father Guru Tegh Bahadur. He was brought to Makhowal, a settlement set up by Guru Tegh Bahadur, and at the age of 9 years, in 1675, he succeeded as the tenth Nanak after the execution of his father.[113] The martyrdom of Guru Tegh Bahadur caused great gloom in the Sikh community and deeply saddened his son and successor who was still at a tender age. At the time of his assumption of Guruship, a few months later, on Baisakhi in 1676, the Sikhs were divided into two camps—Kirpal and the devotees of the Guru *versus* the powerful *masands* who were keen that the Guru should move out of Makhowal. Guru Gobind Singh, aided by Kirpal and others, resisted the pressure of the *masands* and decided to stay on in Makhowal. The next nine years were comparatively peaceful, and this period of calm helped Gobind to tide over the initial shock of his father's cruel execution and he grew to manhood a determined person.[114] Kirpal methodically and tactfully went about his work to keep the Panth intact. He prevailed upon the Sikhs and the Guru's family to accept the martyrdom of Guru Tegh Bahadur with philosophical resignation and to avoid giving any offence, at least for the time being, to the hill rajas or to the Mughal administration. At the same time, he encouraged more and more Sikhs to come to Makhowal and give their undivided devotion to the young Guru.[115]

Kirpal arranged to carry out the wishes of Guru Tegh Bahadur regarding Gobind's marriage to Jita, daughter of a businessman of Lahore. The marriage was solemnized at a small settlement raised nearby called Guru ka Lahore to avoid any confrontation with the Mughal rulers at Lahore or the powerful *masands* on the way.[116] A small army soon grew around the Guru, and a more strategic site was selected in 1678 and the settlement established there was named Anandpur. This change was also reflected in the Guru's *darbar*. The Guru would meet his daily congregation in an expensive tent, with elephants and horses as part of his retinue. Guru Gobind sat on a raised platform, wearing princely attire and an aigrette on his turban. The Sikhs called him *Sacha Padshah*, and princes from distant places visited him; the whole setting was that of a royal court.[117] A huge kettledrum called the *Ranjit Nigara* was installed at the gate of Guru Gobind's residence. It was beaten regularly every morning and evening as a symbol of Sikh sovereignty. Bhim Chand, raja of Bilaspur, objected to the use of the kettledrum as being the prerogative of the ruler only but the Guru paid no heed to the raja's protests. Guru Gobind had made great strides in literary studies, excelled in the martial arts, and had grown to full maturity and responsibility. The *masands* had been isolated and made ineffectual. An especially trained elephant was sent by the raja of Assam, and a Sikh from Kabul brought the Guru a costly tent for holding his *darbar*.[118]

A quarrel with Bhim Chand was inevitable. He was a year younger to the Guru but far less mature. Bhim Chand's pride was wounded and he could not tolerate a sovereign state coming up within his state. He attacked the Guru in 1682 but was beaten back.[119] In the meantime, the hill rajas plotted to oust the Guru from their area. Bhim Chand made an alliance with the rajas of Kangra and Guler, and the allied forces again attacked Guru Gobind in 1685 but were beaten back with losses.[120]

Cordial relations had existed with the raja of Sirmaur since the time of Guru Har Rai. Raja Medni Parkash invited Guru Gobind Singh to come to his state. The Guru was not willing to leave Anandpur but under pressure from his mother and uncle Kirpal, he agreed and his camp, consisting of 500 soldiers and a large number of animals, left Anandpur in April 1685 and settled down at Paonta, a place on the banks of the Yamuna about 50 km. equidistant from Nahan and Dehra Dun. The Guru built a fort at Paonta and he and his camp found an open space to stay. The Guru's literary and martial activities flourished during his stay of about three years at Paonta. Sikh disciples brought money, arms, and horses in plenty, and war games and martial exercises were carried out. On the literary front, the Guru had 52 poets in his *darbar* who sang their martial compositions for him.[121] The Guru composed *Var Sri Bhagwati*, *Chandi di Var*, *Krishan Avtar*, and other hymns. He employed Muslim mercenaries who unfortunately deserted him in the time of war, an experience similar to the one that his grandfather had had with Painda Khan.[122]

Guru Gobind soon realized that there was a long-standing feud between Garhwal and Sirmaur lasting for the previous few generations. Medni Parkash chose Paonta for the Guru's camp, which, in fact, was located midway on the route which lay conveniently between the two states. Guru Gobind did not like his headquarters being sandwiched between two rival states.[123] Fateh Shah decided to occupy all the territories that were disputed between Medni Parkash and himself, and to achieve this goal he had to dislodge Guru Gobind from Paonta. At this juncture, the Guru's position became very weak. A large number of armed *masands* had deserted him before the battle. The Pathans, who were also familiar with the Guru's resources, changed sides and joined Fateh Shah.[124] Fateh Shah, aware of the Guru's position, expected only a nominal resistance. But this first major battle fought by Guru Gobind Singh was a marvel of war tactics, and he gained success over the overwhelmingly larger enemy. The Guru chose to meet Fateh Shah on the banks of the rivulet Gir at Bhangani, about 10 miles north of Paonta. Having marked the correct position, he asked Medni Parkash and Budhu Shah of Sandhura to march to Bhangani, and himself occupied a hillock to check the Garhwali army. The bulk of the Guru's troops were hidden behind the hillock, from where the battlefield manoeuvres could be manipulated.[125]

The Pathans who had deserted Guru Gobind now joined the Garhwalis who were in front. Guru Gobind put a major part of his army in the attack against the Pathans, which they could not withstand; as they retreated they put the entire Garhwal army in disorder. By evening, Guru Gobind himself plunged into the battlefield and killed Hari Chand, the best general of the enemy. Fateh Shah and his men fled and the Guru won the battle; Budhu Shah and his men had joined him in the afternoon.[126] Medni Parkash and his troops never moved to the battlefield.[127] Although the victorious Sikhs wanted to pursue the Garhwalis, the Guru in his wisdom took the victorious army to Sandhura and from there sent the soldiers to Makhowal. He moved to Ramgarh and met the Rani of Raipur, through whose intervention he entered into an agreement with Bhim Chand and was back in Anandpur in 1688.[128]

The stay in Paonta gave Guru Gobind an insight into the psyche of the Hindu hill rajas whose mutual jealousies and rivalries went back to many generations. They could not overcome their mutual animosity and put up a joint front against the foreign ruler. They preferred to accept foreign suzerainty. Guru Gobind also witnessed the duplicity and disloyalty of his armed *masands*. He came to the conclusion that he had no place to stay other than Anandpur and that all his energies should be devoted to bolstering his bastion to repulse a combined attack by the Hindu hill rajas and the Mughal forces. The Guru utilized the changed situation and sought the good offices of Bhim Chand to build up his headquarters, which he did with remarkable speed and boldness. He weeded out those who had been unfaithful and had not joined the Bhangani battle.[129] He renewed his contacts with his disciples in Malwa and Doaba. He reorganized his *darbar* and rapidly strengthened his army. He built a chain of forts around Anandpur and garrisoned them with trained musket men and mounted guns on the fort walls.[130]

Around this time, the hill rajas had stopped paying the annual tribute to the

Mughal emperor, and a strong Mughal force was sent to realize the arrears. Alif Khan was sent to Kangra and he built a wooden stockade at Nadaun. Bhim Chand sought Guru Gobind's help and the Guru personally joined him with a Sikh force. But for the Guru's timely help the hill rajas would have been defeated, yet Bhim Chand agreed to pay the tribute and accept Mughal suzerainty, which greatly disillusioned Guru Gobind.[131] Rustam Khan was sent against the Guru by Mian Khan, governor of Jammu. The Sikhs launched a surprise attack against Rustam Khan and drove him away after inflicting heavy losses.[132]

Guru Gobind Singh now asked his disciples not only to come in greater numbers to Anandpur, but also to make Anandpur their home. He gave the large influx of Sikhs suitable training and made them observe a proper code of conduct.[133] The increased strength of the Sikh forces under Guru Gobind unnerved the Kangra *faujdar* as well as some rajas, who now sought Aurangzeb's advice on how best to meet the challenge posed by the rising Sikh power. In November 1693 Aurangzeb directed the *faujdar* to prevent Guru Gobind from assembling his Sikhs.[134] A large expedition was sent under Hussain Khan. Guru Gobind sent a well-armed contingent to the aid of the hill rajas and in the ensuing battle Hussain Khan and some hill rajas were killed. This encouraged the hill rajas not to pay the tribute. In 1694, 1696, and 1697 small forces were sent against Guru Gobind, all of whom failed in their objective. Aurangzeb was a greatly suspicious person, especially of his sons and other relatives who he considered were capable of raising a rebellion against him; he used to keep them at widely dispersed locations and away from the throne. Aurangzeb sent Prince Mauzzam to the north under some scheme of his, and it was rumoured that he had been sent to subdue the hill rajas and Guru Gobind. Actually Mauzzam reached Lahore in August 1696 on his way to Kabul and sent some forces to collect tributes from the hill rajas. The entire force of Mughal wrath fell on the rajas and Guru Gobind's headquarters were left unharmed.[135] Mauzzam's arrival had been a cause of great anxiety to the Guru, and the prince's departure now gave him much relief.

During the next two years, 1697-9, feverish literary activity took place. Still Guru Gobind struggled hard to come to some important decisions. During this outwardly peaceful interval, he abolished the office of the *masand* and instituted the Khalsa on Baisakhi, on 30 March 1699. As a true successor of Nanak, Guru Gobind believed himself to have been chosen by God to establish the Panth of Nanak.

The Divine Guru sent me for religion's sake:

On this account I have come into the world.
Extend the faith every where;
Seize and destroy the evil and the sinful;
Understand this, holy men, in your souls.

I assumed birth for the purpose
Of spreading the faith, saving the saints,
And extirpating all tyrants.[136]

In the fulfilment of his mission, Guru Gobind Singh first tried to set his own house in order. The *masands*, who at one time were the representative agents of the Guru, were an important link between the Guru and a large number of his Sikhs. The organization of the Sikh Panth greatly depended on the performance of their duties by the *masands*, but these *masands* had lost the confidence of the Guru. Guru Gobind Singh had witnessed their insolent attitude at his coronation, their refusal to join the Battle of Bhangani, their ill-treatment of the Sikhs, and their dishonesty and corruption, which have been directly portrayed by the Guru himself in the thirty-three *sanwaiyas*.

If any one serves the *masands*, they will say
Fetch and give us all the offerings.
Those beasts plunder men,
and never sing the praises of the supreme lord.[137]

The intervening role of dishonest and corrupt *masands* between the Guru and his followers was most undesirable because of their influence among a large number of Sikhs. Guru Gobind, therefore, decided to establish a direct connection with the Sikhs through freshly appointed agents and by removing all the *masands* whose integrity or loyalty was questionable.[138] In most of the *hukamnamas* issued by Guru Gobind Singh to the Sikh *sangats* after the Baisakhi of 1699, the Sikhs were asked to send their offerings directly to the Guru through authorized persons (not the *masands*) or to bring these personally to Anandpur.

In the time of Guru Hargobind, the Sikhs who were directly linked with the Guru's household and who had remained his permanent companions were called his Khalsa. The *sangat* of the east was called the Khalsa of Guru Hargobind. Likewise, the *sangat* at Pattan was called the Khalsa of Guru Tegh Bahadur and the *sangat* of Machhiwara was called the Khalsa of Guru Gobind Singh even before the Baisakhi of 1699.[139] It is possible that the term Khalsa for the Sikhs in general was derived from its earlier usage. Guru Gobind Singh could not have chosen a more auspicious occasion than the Baisakhi of 1699 and the *sangats* were asked to come in large numbers. In a dramatic, and soul-stirring speech Guru Gobind Singh selected five Sikhs willing to lay down their lives for the *dharma*. The first man was a Khatri from Lahore, the second was a Jat from Delhi, the third was a Washerman from Dwarka, the fourth was a Cook from Jagannath, and the fifth was a Barber from Bidar. Coincidentally these five men represented five different regions of the country. Guru Gobind dressed them in fine clothes and gave them the *khanda pahul*, sweet water stirred with a double-edged *khanda*, and not by the earlier method of *charan pahul*, water with which the feet of the Guru had been washed. After administering the *khanda pahul* to his five Sikhs, he called the five beloved ones (the *Panj Piaras*). Guru Gobind Singh himself took *pahul* from each of them, thereby merging his person with the persons of his disciples.[140] The Guru thus merged himself in the Khalsa and the whole sect became invested with the dignity of Gurudom.

The oft-repeated phrase '*apai Guru apai chela*' beautifully depicts the communion between the Guru and his Khalsa on the same premise on the basis of which Guru Nanak had selected Angad as his successor; he had touched Angad's feet, giving him the status of the Guru during his own life time. Like the Guru himself, his baptized Sikhs were to wear their *keshas* as well as their arms. The wearing of uncut hair was the most important injunction of the Guru to his Khalsa. The Khalsa thus stood distinguished from the rest of the world. After the five beloved ones had baptized the Guru, the principle that emerged was that any five baptized Sikhs could initiate novice Sikhs into the Khalsa. Thus the Khalsa became the Guru and the Guru became the Khalsa.[141] J.D. Cunningham writes: 'The last apostle of the Sikhs effectually roused the dormant energies of a vanquished people and filled them with a lofty though fitful longing for social freedom and national ascendancy, the proper adjuncts of that purity of worship which had been preached by Nanak.'[142] Contemporary estimates indicate that about 80,000 people were baptized in a few days. Guru Gobind Singh describes his feelings about his Khalsa in one of the *Shabad Hazare*:

> All the battles I have won against tyranny
> I have fought with the devoted backing of these people;
> Through them only have I been able to bestow gifts.
> Through their help I have escaped from harm;
> The love and generosity of these Sikhs
> Have enriched my heart and home.
> Through their grace I have attained all learning;
> Through their help in battle I have slain all my enemies.
> I was born to serve them, through them I reached eminence.
> What would I have been without their kind and ready help?
> There are millions of insignificant people like me.
> True service is the service of these people.
> From top to toe, whatever I call my own,
>
> All I possess and carry, I dedicate to these people.[143]

By instituting the Khalsa, Guru Gobind Singh took the most vital decision of his life, thus reaffirming the faith promulgated by Nanak; he consolidated the panth, and inspired the Sikhs to defend their faith and stand on their own feet. All these preparations were likely to invite the intervention of the Mughal government.[144] A newsletter from the imperial court to the *faujdar* of Sirhind admonished the

Guru.[145] Since the Baisakhi gathering had passed off peacefully, Guru Gobind Singh was not disturbed for a couple of years, during which period he continued to consolidate his position. The large congregations of armed Sikhs which assembled during Baisakhi, Holi, and Diwali were sources of great annoyance to the hill rajas. Bhim Chand, the most powerful hill raja, again asked for tribute from Guru Gobind, which was refused, as had been the case on an earlier occasion. From 1699 to 1703, seven attacks were made on Anandpur by the combined forces of the hill rajas,[146] and at times also supported by Mughal contingents, and even by Wazir Khan of Sirhind during the battle of Barsali. Guru Gobind Singh successfully faced all these combinations, defeated the hill rajas, and maintained his sway over Anandpur and the surrounding villages which came under the Guru's control due to the ever-increasing influx of Sikhs to Anandpur.[147] Ahmad Shah Batalvi states that Guru Gobind Singh was in occupation of territory of about 100 sq. miles around Anandpur and was determined to create a dominion for himself and his Sikhs.[148]

The long-standing conflict between Bhim Chand and the resolute Guru came to a climax in late 1704. Bhim Chand is believed to have made a personal representation to the emperor, giving his point of view and emphasizing the potential danger from the Khalsa. Aurangzeb ordered Wazir Khan, *faujdar* of Sirhind, and other Mughal forces from the nearby areas to extend full assistance to the hill rajas. Thus, a formidable combination was formed against Guru Gobind Singh in this trial of strength between the Khalsa and the Mughal Empire.[149]

The allied forces failed to take Anandpur. The Sikhs emerged from the town and put up a stiff resistance and repulsed the attack. Anandpur was, therefore, placed under a long-drawn-out siege. The allies concentrated all their resources on imposing a complete blockade. After about eight months of the siege, food became very scarce and it became increasingly difficult and unrewarding to make nightly forays into the nearby villages. In the meantime, Wazir Khan and the hill rajas started negotiations with an offer of a safe passage and all sorts of assurances, even on behalf of the emperor.[150] Guru Gobind Singh also faced pressure from his own relatives and the Sikhs. He left Anandpur during the night of 21 December 1704.[151] The hill rajas did not pursue him, but the Mughal forces under Wazir Khan soon caught up with the Guru and his forces in the rear while they were crossing the swollen Sirsa stream. The situation resulted in a disaster for the Guru. Along with his two older sons and some followers he was separated from Mata Gujari, his mother, and his two younger sons who fell into the hands of Wazir Khan. Mata Sundari, his wife, was, however, safely escorted to Delhi by Bhai Mani Singh. Guru Gobind Singh lost most of his brave followers including two elder sons in an unequal fight with the vastly outnumbered Mughal forces at Chamkaur near Ropar. The few surviving Khalsa resolved and directed the Guru to escape. Bowing to their wishes Guru left Chamkaur in the middle of the night.

In early 1705, Guru Gobind wandered from place to place in the Malwa area either alone or with a few followers, with the Sirhindi troops in active pursuit after him.[152] At Jatpura (in present-day Ludhiana district) he received the news of the execution of his two younger sons by Wazir Khan and the death of Mata Gujari who had died of grief.[153] Even though he was passing through a hopeless period of severe set backs and defeat, Guru Gobind responded in a remarkable manner. His immediate need was to establish contact with the Khalsa, who gradually started joining him and moved from place to place in search of a suitable location to establish a settlement. Wazir Khan, who was chasing the Guru, came to know the Guru's location and attacked the Khalsa at Khidrana. The Khalsa fought with such great determination and devotion that the larger force of Wazir Khan was severely defeated and Wazir Khan retreated without any further battle with the Guru.[154]

Guru Gobind Singh now settled down at Talwandi Sabo. Slowly his old disciples started returning to him and a small force was established. During about a year's stay at Talwandi Sabo, the Guru dictated a new recension of the *Holy Granth*. Here Guru Gobind received Aurangzeb's messages in reply to the *Zafarnama* which the Guru had written to the emperor, who was now anxious to meet him in the Deccan. Guru Gobind, with a large number of his followers, moved towards the Deccan via Rajasthan. Near Baghaur, he heard of the death of Aurangzeb and planned to return to the Punjab. Prince Mauzzam had also rushed from Peshawar to Delhi to stake his claim to the throne against his brothers. Guru Gobind Singh, who was heading towards Delhi, met Mauzzam before or after the battle of Jaju. Guru Gobind Singh was given an honourable reception by Bahadur Shah, the new emperor. He was allowed to go fully armed in the emperor's presence and was given lavish and expensive gifts.[155] Guru Gobind Singh informed his Khalsa that his other matters were being settled satisfactorily and that he intended to go to Kalhur and not the Punjab.[156] But it appears that no final decision was taken, and Guru Gobind moved with the emperor to Nander.

Guru Gobind Singh had become aware of the hostility of the court, especially over his dispute with Wazir Khan of Sirhind. At this juncture, the Guru met a *bairagi* who became his ardent disciple, and who was later named Banda Bahadur. The Guru chose him as the commander of the Sikh forces to chastize Wazir Khan and others.[157] How Banda came in contact with Guru Gobind, how the Guru was able to ascertain his capabilities, whether they were previously known to each other are questions shrouded in mystery and no authentic account regarding their veracity is available. But what stands established as historical fact is that there could not have been a better choice for the purpose for which Banda Bahadur was sent. Shortly after Banda's departure for the Punjab, the Guru was attacked, apparently by some hired assassins, and was badly injured. The wound did not heal and after some days, the Guru announced that his end was near.[158]

Guru Gobind collected his Sikhs around him and gave them his parting instructions. He opened the *Granth*, placed 5 *paisas* and a coconut, and bowed before it. He declared that henceforth the Holy Book would be the Guru for all time to come and thus he abolished the institution of personal Guruship. He also composed the following verse:

Agya bhai Akal ki tabhi chalayo Panth,
Sab Sikhan ko hukm hai Guru Manio Granth.
Guru Granth je manyo pargat Guru ke deh.
Jo Prabho to milbo chahe khoj shabad me le.

This verse means that under the order of the Immortal God, the Panth was founded. All Sikhs are enjoined to accept the *Granth* as their Guru. Consider the *Granth* as representing the Guru's body. Those who desire to contact God can find Him in its hymns.[159]

Guru Gobind Singh had earlier said in the *Bichittar Natak*:

Installed on Nanak's throne as Guru tenth,
When assumed the scripture of my sovereignty
I promoted religion to the best of my power.

Guru Gobind Singh states that when he assumed the spiritual sovereignty of Guru Nanak, he served the *piri* aspect, the *dharma*, with all his devotion.[160] He also states, in Bhai Nand Lal's rendering of the Guru's remarks:

The Granth is my second self.
And it should be taken as me.
A Sikh who wants to see me
Should have a look at the Granth.
One who wants to talk to me,
Should read the Granth and think over it.[161]

Guru Gobind placed the temporal aspect of his sovereignty in the hands of the Khalsa. This goal had already been partially achieved with the creation of the Khalsa and when he had selected the five beloved ones and had given them the *khanda pahul*. Thereafter, he personally sought the *khanda pahul* from the five chosen ones, thus merging his Guru person with the Khalsa whereby the Guru and the Khalsa became the one and the same. He states: 'Where there are five Khalsa to take a decision I am present in spirit with them.' He had submitted to the will of the Khalsa against his own personal opinion to give sanctity to the decisions of the Khalsa. When he was asked to leave Chamkaur, he left in submission to the will of the Khalsa against his own desire to lay down his life along with his Khalsa. Now when he was leaving his mortal frame, he placed his temporal sovereignty in the hands of the entire Khalsa. The following verse is said to have been composed by either Guru Gobind Singh or by Bhai Nand Lal:

Raj karega khalsa aqi rahe na koe,
khawar hoe sab milen ge bache sharan jo ho.

Meaning that the Khalsa shall rule, and its opponent will be no more. Those separated will be united and the devotees shall be saved.[162]

Guru Gobind Singh defines his temporal sovereignty in the *Krishan Avtar*:

Great death be thou my protector;
All steel I am thy slave.
Deeming me thy own, preserve me.
Single out and destroy my enemies.
Let both my free kitchen and my sword.
Prevail in the world.
Preserve me and let none trample me.
Be thou my cherisher.[163]

When Guru Gobind Singh gave his temporal sovereignty to his Khalsa, he issued a stern warning to them to preserve Sikh identity in its uniqueness, as stated in the *Sarbloh Granth:*

Jab Lag Khalsa rahie niara,
Tab lag jas dion men sara.
Jab aye gai bipran ke reet,
Man na karun in ke partit.[164]

This means that the Khalsa shall continue to be blessed with all my power, so long as it preserves its identity and uniqueness. But when the Khalsa strays from the path of righteousness, I will not stand by them.

Nihar Ranjan Ray rightly states that the integration of the temporal and the spiritual has been the most significant contribution of Guru Gobind Singh to the way of life which he laid down for his Sikhs.[165] Guru Hargobind and the Sikh community felt that for the development of the Sikh faith they would have to vindicate Nanak's message of resisting the evil of tyranny. Bhai Gurdas refers to the martial response of Guru Hargobind to the martyrdom of Guru Arjan as hedging the orchard of the Sikh faith with hardy and thorny *kikar* trees.[166] The two sovereignties of the Godhead—spiritual and temporal—remained centred in the Guru person up to the time of Guru Gobind Singh, who on the eve of his death bestowed the temporal sovereignty on the Panth and the spiritual sovereignty on the *Granth*. The Panth became the Guru Panth and the *Granth* became the *Guru Granth*. The revealed word as such was formally installed as the eternal Guru, leaving no room for any physical/corporeal Guru in Sikh society.[167] The concept of the sovereignty of the Khalsa provides the motivating spirit for the relentless struggle against the state. It also gives the principle of unity, cohesion, and organization to the Sikh people in the form of voluntary submission to the supreme collective authority of the Guru Panth.

Guru Gobind Singh had made himself the master of the imagination of his followers.[168] His death triggered such an enormous popular response that the first sovereign Sikh state came into existence within two years over the Subah of Sirhind and the surrounding territories. The coins struck and the seal adopted by the Sikh state closely reflect the Sikh concept of sovereignty. As unique symbols of Sikh sovereignty they differed from contemporary coinages and remained unchanged during the entire period of the Sikh state till its annexation by the British in March 1849.

The temporal sovereignty (the sovereignty of the Sikh state) bequeathed by Guru Gobind Singh to the Khalsa Panth at the time of his demise in October 1708 was held as a sacred trust both in victory and in defeat. During the First Anglo-Sikh War in 1845 and the signing of the humiliating treaty in March 1846 the Sikh *sardars* had played a very dubious role. However, the Sikh soldiers, unlike the selfish and disloyal Sikh *sardars* who had allied with the British, continued to profess loyalty to their Gurus and fought bravely for the preservation of Sikh sovereignty. M.L. Ahluwalia states:

As to a crore of rupees of the war indemnity imposed by the British on the Lahore government, an offer was mooted by the 'Panches' representing the Darbar army to deduct one month's pay from the salaries of all the armed personnel of the Darbar for making up the amount of one crore of rupees which the British were accepting from Raja Gulab Singh. . . . The British did not agree to the said proposal of the Darbar.[169]

This shows that even though the Sikh rulers of the Lahore Darbar had lost their respect for the principle of Sikh sovereignty in their self-serving pursuit of their personal gains, the dedication and reverence for Sikh sovereignty was still very much in existence amongst the Sikh soldiers, even in defeat.

NOTES

1. *Sri Guru Granth Sahib*, tr. Gopal Singh, 4 vols., Delhi: Gurdas Kapoor & Sons, 1960-2, vol. I, p. 137.
2. A.C. Banerjee, *Guru Nanak and His Times*, Patiala: Punjabi University, 1984, p. 1.
3. A.B. Pandey, *The First Afghan Empire in India (1451-1526)*, Calcutta, 1956, pp. 243-4.
4. A.C. Banerjee, *Guru Nanak and His Times*, op. cit., p. 2.
5. W.H. Moreland, *The Agrarian System of Moslem India*, Cambridge, 1921, p. 71.
6. *Sri Guru Granth Sahib*, tr. Gopal Singh, op. cit., vol. I, p. 350.

7. Max Arthur Macauliffe, *The Sikh Religion*, 6 vols., New Delhi: S. Chand & Co., rpt., 1985, vol. 1, p. 232.
8. Hari Ram Gupta, *History of Sikh Gurus*, New Delhi: U.C. Kapoor & Sons, 1973, pp. 13-15.
9. *Sri Guru Granth Sahib*, tr. Gopal Singh, op. cit., vol. I, p. 722.
10. Tirlochan Singh, *Selections from Sacred Writings of the Sikhs*, London, 1960, p. 86.
11. *Sri Guru Granth Sahib*, tr. Gopal Singh, op. cit., vol. I, p. 470.
12. G.C. Narang, *Transformation of Sikhism*, Lahore: New Book Society, 1945, p. 31.
13. Macauliffe, *The Sikh Religion*, op. cit., vol. I, p. 38.
14. Bhai Gurdas, *Varan*, tr. Jodh Singh, 2 vols., Patiala: Vision and Venture, Var 1, Pauri 27, 1998, p. 57.
15. J.D. Cunningham, *A History of Sikhs*, New Delhi: S. Chand & Co., rpt., 1972, pp. 36-8.
16. A.C. Banerjee, *Guru Nanak and His Times*, op. cit., pp. 198-9.
17. (i) W.H. McLeod, *Guru Nanak and the Sikh Religion*, Oxford: Clarendon Press, 1968, pp. 277-8.
    (ii) J.S. Grewal, *Guru Nanak in Hisotry*, Chandigarh: Panjab University, 1969, pp. 168-9.
    (iii) A.C. Banerjee, *The Sikh Gurus and Sikh Religion*, New Delhi: Munshiram Manoharlal, 1983, pp. 92-3.
18. (i) Indu Bhushan Banerjee, *Evolution of Khalsa*, 2 vols., Calcutta: A. Mukherjee & Co., 1979, vol. I, p. 94.
    (ii) Macauliffe, *The Sikh Religion*, op. cit., p. 278.
19. J.S. Ahluwalia, *The Sovereignty of Sikh Doctrine*, New Delhi: Bahri Publications, 1983, p. 30.
20. Ibid., p. 43
21. Ibid., p. 42.
22. Macauliffe, *The Sikh Religion*, op. cit., vol. II, p. 26.
23. Ibid., vol. I, p. 382.
24. A.C. Banerjee, *Guru Nanak and His Times*, op. cit., p. 161.
25. J.C. Archer, *The Sikhs*, Princeton, N.J, USA, 1946, p. 109.
26. W.H. McLeod, *Guru Nanak and Sikh Religion*, op. cit., p. 143.
27.. Harbans Singh, 'Guru Nanak', *Preet Lari*, November 1969, p. 14.
28. *Bachittar Natik*, translated and published by M.L. Peace, Jullandhar, undated, p. 12.
29. G.C. Narang, *Transformation of Sikhism*, op. cit., p. 34.
30. J.D. Cunningham, *The History of Sikhs*, op. cit., p. 34.
31. Ernest Trumpp, *Adi Granth* (tr.), New Delhi: Munshiram Manoharlal, 1978, p. lxxvii.
32. Bhai Gurdas, *Varan*, tr. Jodh Singh, op. cit., Var. I, Pauri 45.
33. Ibid., Var 7, Pauri 8.
34. Ibid., Var 26, Pauris 31 and 32.
35. Ibid., Var 39, Pauri 3.
36. A.C. Banerjee, *Guru Nanak and His Times*, op. cit., p. 182.
37. J.C. Archer, *The Sikhs*, op. cit., p. 60.
38. Kapur Singh, 'Baisakhi of Guru Gobind Singh', in *Parasarprasna*, Amritsar: Guru Nanak Dev University, 1989, p. 12.
39. Sher Singh, *Philosophy of Sikhism*, Lahore, 1944, p. 24.
40. Nihar Ranjan Ray, *Sikh Gurus and Sikh Society*, New Delhi: Munshiram Manoharlal, 1975, p. 59.
41. A.C. Banerjee, *The Sikh Gurus and Sikh Religion*, op. cit., p. 152.
42. A.C. Banerjee, *Guru Nanak and His Times*, op. cit., p. 152.
43. Hari Ram Gupta, *History of Sikh Gurus*, op. cit., p. 82.

44. A.C. Banerjee, *The Sikh Gurus and Sikh Religion*, op. cit., p. 162.
45. Ibid., p. 165.
46. Ibid., p. 175.
47. Hari Ram Gupta, *History of Sikh Gurus*, op. cit., pp. 84-5.
48. Ibid., p. 85.
49. Indu Bhushan Banerjee, *Evolution of Khalsa*, op. cit., p. 167.
50. Ibid., p. 162.
51. Ibid., pp. 175-6.
52. Ibid., pp. 181-2.
53. *Sri Guru Granth*, op. cit., *Rag Sohi*, pp. 767-8.
54. Macauliffe, *The Sikh Religion*, vol. II, op. cit., pp. 257-8.
55. A.C. Banerjee, *The Sikh Gurus and Sikh Religion*, op. cit., p. 182.
56. Ibid., p. 183.
57. Mohsin Fani, *Dabistan-i-Mazhab*, tr. Troyar and Shea, vol. I, p. 271.
58. (i) A.C. Banerjee, *The Sikh Gurus and Sikh Religion*, op. cit., p. 185.
    (ii) Hari Ram Gupta, *History of Sikh Gurus*, op. cit., p. 90.
    (iii) Indu Bhushan Banerjee, *Evolution of Khalsa*, op. cit., p. 195.
59. Macauliffe, *The Sikh Religion*, op. cit., vol. III, p. 55.
60. Hari Ram Gupta, *History of Sikh Gurus*, op. cit., p. 85.
61. Macauliffe, *The Sikh Religion*, op. cit., vol. III, p. 57.
62. Ibid., vol. III, p. 64.
63. A.C. Banerjee, *The Sikh Gurus and Sikh Religion*, op. cit., p. 192.
64. Mohsin Fani, *Dabistan-i-Mazhab*, op. cit., pp. 233-4.
65. Ibid., pp. 225 and 233.
66. Hari Ram Gupta, *The History of Sikh Gurus*, op. cit., p. 93.
67. Ibid., p. 93.
68. Indu Bhushan Banerjee, *Evolution of Khalsa*, op. cit., p. 214.
69. G.C. Narang, *Transformation of Sikhism*, op. cit., p. 70.
70. Hari Ram Gupta, *History of the Sikh Gurus*, op. cit., p. 98.
71. Indu Bhushan Banerjee, *Evolution of Khalsa*, op. cit., p. 254.
72. G.C. Narang, *Transformation of Sikhism*, op. cit., p. 76.
73. Ibid., p. 76.
74. *Tuzak-i-Jahangiri* (tr. by Rodgers and Beveridge), 1996 edn., Delhi: Munshiram Manoharlal, p. 72.
75. Ibid., pp. 72-3.
76. A.C. Banerjee, *The Sikh Gurus and Sikh Religion*, op. cit., p. 205.
77. (i) Hari Ram Gupta, *History of Sikh Gurus*, op. cit., p. 104.
    (ii) Muhammad Latif, *History of Punjab*, Ludhiana: Kalyani Publishers; rpt., 1989, p. 254, footnote.
78. Indu Bhushan Banerjee, *Evolution of Khalsa*, vol. II, p. 6.
79. (i) Ibid., vol. II, p. 8.
    (ii) Muhammad Latif, *History of Punjab*, op. cit., p. 25.
    (iii) G.C. Narang, *Transformation of Sikhism*, op. cit., p. 101.
    (iv) Ernest Trumpp, *Adi Granth*, op. cit., p. lxxxii
    (v) Macauliffe, *Sikh Religion*, op. cit., vol. IV, p. 2.
    (vi) J.D. Cunningham, *A History of Sikhs*, op. cit., p. 50.
    (vii) Hari Ram Gupta, *History of Sikh Gurus*, op. cit., p. 108.
80. Hari Ram Gupta, *History of Sikh Gurus*, op. cit., p. 92.

81. Macauliffe, *Sikh Religion*, vol. III, op. cit., p. 50.
82. Ibid., p. 99.
83. J.S. Ahluwalia, *The Sovereignty of Sikh Doctrine*, op. cit., p. 91.
84. Nihar Ranjan Ray, *The Sikh Gurus and Sikh Society*, New Delhi: Munshiram Manoharlal, 1975, p. 57.
85. A.C. Banerjee, *The Sikh Gurus and Sikh Religion*, op. cit., p. 235.
86. Ibid., p. 235.
87. Hari Ram Gupta, *History of Sikh Gurus*, op. cit., p. 100.
88. Ibid., p. 110.
89. Ibid., p. 110.
90. J.S. Ahluwalia, *The Sovereignty of Sikh Doctrine*, op. cit., p. l.
91. Ibid., p. 227.
92. Gupta Hari Ram, *History of Sikh Gurus*, op. cit., p. 116.
93. Ibid., p. 117.
94. Ibid., p. 117.
95. Ibid., p. 118.
96. Ibid., p. 119.
97. Ibid., p. 119.
98. Khazan Singh, *History of Sikh Religion*, Punjab: Languages Department; rpt., 1988, p. 133.
99. Indu Bhushan Banerjee, *Evolution of Khalsa*, vol. II, op. cit., p. 34.
100. Hari Ram Gupta, *History of Sikh Gurus*, op. cit., p. 129.
101. A.C. Banerjee, *The Sikh Gurus and Sikh Religion*, op. cit., p. 245.
102. Ibid., p. 249.
103. Ibid., p. 252.
104. Indu Bhushan Banerjee, *Evolution of Khalsa*, vol. II, op. cit., p. 57.
105. A.C. Banerjee, *The Sikh Gurus and Sikh Religion*, op. cit., p. 255.
106. Indu Bhushan Banerjee, *Evolution of Khalsa*, vol. II, op. cit., p. 56.
107. Ibid., p. 57.
108. Ibid., p. 58.
109. Ibid., p. 59.
110. Tarlochan Singh, *Guru Tegh Bahadur*, Patiala: Punjabi University, 1988, p. 276.
111. A.C. Banerjee, *The Sikh Gurus and Sikh Religion*, op. cit., p. 264.
112. Hari Ram Gupta, *History of Sikh Gurus*, op. cit., p. 143.
113. J.S. Grewal and S.S. Bal, *Guru Gobind Singh*, Chandigarh: Panjab University, 1967, p. ix.
114. Ibid., p. 48.
115. Ibid., pp. 48-9.
116. Ibid., p. 52.
117. Ibid., p. 53.
118. Hari Ram Gupta, *History of Sikh Gurus*, op. cit., pp. 149-50.
119. Ibid., p. 150.
120. Ibid., p. 150.
121. Ibid., p. 153.
122. A.C. Banerjee, *The Sikh Gurus and Sikh Religion*, op. cit., p. 285.
123. J.S. Grewal and S.S. Bal, *Guru Gobind Singh*, op. cit., pp. 70-1.
124. Ibid., p. 78.
125. Ibid., p. 80.
126. Ibid., p. 82.

127. Hari Ram Gupta, *History of Sikh Gurus*, op. cit., p. 155.

128. J.S. Grewal and S.S. Bal, *Guru Gobind Singh*, op. cit., p. 83.

129. *Bachittar Natik*, tr. M.L. Peace, op. cit., Chaupai 37, p. 64.

130. Grewal and Bal, *Guru Gobind Singh*, op. cit., p. 86.

131. Ibid., pp. 89-90.

132. Hari Ram Gupta, *History of Sikh Gurus*, op. cit., p. 158.

133. Grewal and Bal, *Guru Gobind Singh*, op. cit., p. 93.

134. *Akhbar-i-Darbar-i-Mualla*, RAS, vol. I, *1677-1695*, 20 November 1693, news from Sirhind, Gobind declares himself to be Guru Nanak. Faujdars ordered to prevent him from assembling (his Sikhs). See Teja Singh and Ganda Singh, *Short History of Sikhs*, p. 61, footnote 4.

135. Grewal and Bal, *Guru Gobind Singh*, op. cit., p. 100.

136. Macauliffe, *The Sikh Religion*, vol. V, op. cit., pp. 300-1.

137. Ibid., vol. V, pp. 322-3.

138. Grewal and Bal, *Guru Gobind Singh*, op. cit., p. 114.

139. In his introduction to *Prem Sumarag*, 2nd edn. of *The Hukamnamas by Guru Hargobind, Guru Tegh Bahadur and Guru Gobind Singh*, Randhir Singh states that the *sangat* of the East, the *sangat* of Pattan, and the *sangat* of Machhiwara were respectively called their Khalsa.

140. Kapur Singh, 'The Baisakhi of Guru Gobind Singh', in *Parasaraprasna*, Amritsar: Guru Nanak Dev University, 1989, p. 1.

141. Indu Bhushan Banerjee, *Evolution of Khalsa*, op. cit., vol. II, p. 153.

142. J.D. Cunningham, *A History of Sikhs*, op. cit., p. 66.

143. Grewal and Bal, *Guru Gobind Singh*, op. cit., p. 123.

144. Ibid., p. 126.

145. Sri Ram Sharma, *The Religious Policy of the Mughal Emperors*, New Delhi: Asia Publishing House, 1962, p. 146.

146. Hari Ram Gupta, *History of Sikh Gurus*, op. cit., pp. 198-202.

147. Grewal and Bal, *Guru Gobind Singh*, op. cit., p. 136.

148. J.S. Grewal, *From Guru Nanak to Ranjit Singh*, Amritsar: Guru Nanak Dev University, 1982, p. 109.

149. Grewal and Bal, *Guru Gobind Singh*, op. cit., p. 138.

150. Hari Ram Gupta, *History of Sikh Gurus*, op. cit., pp. 204-5.

151. Grewal and Bal, *Guru Gobind Singh*, op. cit., p. 140.

152. Ibid., p. 143.

153. Ibid., p. 143.

154. Ibid., p. 145.

155. Ganda Singh, *Makhiz-i-Twarikh-i-Sikhan*, Amritsar: Historical Society, 1949, p. 82.

156. Ganda Singh, *Hukamnamas* (Punjabi), Patiala: Punjabi University, 1985, p. 186. *Hukam-nama* no. 63, dated 2 October 1701.
Indu Bhushan Banerjee states in *Evolution of Khalsa*, vol. II, p. 145, quoting Ganda Singh's views about the above-mentioned *Hukamnama* of Guru Gobind Singh dated 15 October 1707 to the Sikhs of Dhaul, that Guruji soon expected to return to the Punjab, citing reference to para 11 of *Banda Singh Bahadur* by Ganda Singh. An actual examination of this *Hukamnama* shows that Guruji mentioned coming back to Kahler and not the Punjab. This means that the return of the Khalsa to Kahler was decided and, as mentioned by Ganda Singh and Indu Bhushan Banerjee, the claim that Guruji was returning to the Punjab does not seem to be correct.

157. Ganda Singh, *Life of Banda Bahadur*, Patiala: Punjabi University; rpt., 1990, p. 12.
158. Macauliffe, *The Sikh Religion*, vol. V, op. cit., p. 245.
159. Hari Ram Gupta, *History of Sikh Gurus*, op. cit., p. 237.
160. Macauliffe, *The Sikh Religion*, vol. V, op. cit., p. 303.
161. Hari Ram Gupta, *History of Sikh Gurus*, op. cit., p. 237.
162. Ibid., p. 237.
163. Dharam Pal Ashta, 'Poetry of Dasam Granth', Ph.D. thesis, Chandigarh: Panjab University, p. 26.
164. J.S. Ahluwalia, *The Sovereignty of Sikh Doctrine*, op. cit., p. 48.
165. Nihar Ranjan Ray, *Sikh Gurus and Sikh Society*, op. cit., p. 59.
166. Sunita Puri, *Advent of Sikh Religion*, New Delhi: Munshiram Manoharlal, 1993, p. 219.
167. J.S. Ahluwalia, *The Sovereignty of Sikh Doctrine*, op. cit., p. 81.
168. J.D. Cunningham, *A History of Sikhs*, op. cit., p. 66.
169. M.L. Ahluwalia, *Landmarks in Sikh History* (a fully researched and documented history 1699-1947), New Delhi: Ashok a International Publishers, 1996, p. 169.
     M.L. Ahluwalia has vide his letter dated 18 October 1999 intimated the authority for the Sikh Panches, offering one month's salary for Kashmir to the British. *Lahore Political Diaries*, vol. III, p. 88, National Archives of India, Secret Series.

Sikh Religious Tokens

In order to understand the Temple tokens of India, we must first have an understanding of the history, religions and mythology of India.

MAURICE M. GOULD

The Sikh religious tokens, like other temple tokens, are a field of exonumia of which very little is known and even less is written. Although the subject of Indian temple tokens has been taken up by a number of scholars, there are only two readily available accounts of Sikh religious tokens, viz., *A Guide to Temple Tokens of India* by Brotman,[1] and 'Observations on Sikh Tokens' by Jai Parkash Singh.[2] In both accounts, a fair degree of disregard for and ignorance of the Sikh traditions and religious practices is apparent; the inferences drawn by the authors are incomplete and incorrect to a certain extent. Hence, an attempt is made here to address some of the gaps in the account of Sikh religious tokens.

In Hindu religious practices, which are largely matters of private devotion rather than congregational worship, the icon or the image is a symbol of God, an aid to the mind of the devotee to concentrate on the divine in order to become one with it. The large number of Hindu deities and the uninhibited changes in the rituals and iconography have resulted in the construction of lakhs of shrines, tucked in obscure corners and installed niches in the walls of houses and temples across the land. Hindu worship, to a large extent, is not so much an act of prayer but an act to pay homage to the deity and seek its blessings and the grant of boons.[3] This open attitude has resulted in the proliferation of an enormous variety in the depiction of Hindu deities in stone and metal sculpture and on paintings on walls and on paper. Temple tokens are one such manifestation of Hindu religious practices; they are most handy to keep and carry, enabling the individual devotee to bow his head in reverence and seek blessings from the deity when ever he has a moment to spare or when ever the situation so demands.

The origin of the notion of placing the image of a deity on a coin is as early as the third century BC; Gaja Lakshmi was depicted on an uninscribed coin from Kausambhi. Images of Shiva appear on the coins of Ujjain and the Kushanas in the early centuries.[4] Ramatankas were issued in south India by the rulers of the

Vijayanagar Empire to commemorate the enthronement of Rama along with his wife Sita. These Ramatankas were meant for presentation and had no market value apart from the value of the metal contents. These metal tokens were often worn around the neck or kept in the cash box as a means of placating the gods and ensuring that the till would never be empty. These tokens were manufactured by temple authorities and private agencies and were sold to the pilgrims visiting the holy places. The godman got his *dakshina* and the pilgrim got his deity close to him in the form of the token, resulting in the financial gain of the godman and in the spiritual gain of the receiver of the token.

D.C. Sarkar states that Ramatankas were originally manufactured in Ayodhya,[5] whereas S.B. Ota considers these to have been issued from the Agra mint by the Mughal emperor, Akbar, where he lay sick in AD 1604.[6] Parmeshwari Lal Gupta also notes that mintless coins with the effigies of Rama and Sita had been issued by Akbar during the last years of his reign.[7] Besides showing Rama and Sita, the Ramatankas also show Lakshman and Hanuman carrying the mountain, various *Yantra* types, Radha-Krishna, Gopala-Krishna, Kali, and Lakshmi, among other deities. These Ramatankas are made of silver, base silver, and brass. Their shape is round, the size varying from 2.3 cm. to 2.9 cm., and the weight ranging from 7.4 g. to 11.8 g. The scripts used were Devanagari, Bangla, and Gurmukhi.

The sikh religion was founded by Guru Nanak (1469-1539) and his nine successors, the last being Guru Gobind Singh (1676-1708). The Sikhs did not clash with the Mughal rulers till the fifth Guru, Arjan Dev, was executed in AD 1606. The sixth Guru, Hargobind, took up arms to defend himself and his followers. The ninth Guru, Tegh Bahadur, was executed in Delhi under Aurangzeb's orders, and the tenth Guru, Gobind Singh, converted the ordinary Sikhs into the Khalsa, a marital community fully armed to defend itself against the oppressive Mughal rulers. Guru Gobind Singh fought numerous battles against the armies of the Mughals and the Hindu hill rajas. He expired in AD 1708 at Nander in Maharashtra, succumbing to the wounds treacherously inflicted on him by some Pathan assassins. During his last days, Guru Gobind Singh abolished the institution of the personal Guruship and instructed his followers to henceforth treat the *Granth*, the Holy Book, as their Guru and to follow the *Vani* recorded therein.

Banda Bahadur, a disciple of Guru Gobind Singh, came to the Punjab to fight against the Mughal atrocities against the Sikhs. He defeated the governer of Sirhind and occupied the surrounding districts. He set up a Sikh state, issued coins from AD 1710 to 1712, but was finally defeated by the Mughals and was beheaded along with his followers in Delhi in 1716. Inspired by the spirit infused in them by Guru Gobind Singh and Banda Bahadur, the Sikh rose again and again over the next half century, till they came to occupy most of the Punjab plains by AD 1765. Ranjit Singh occupied the capital city of Lahore in 1799, and within a couple of decades he had become the undisputed monarch of the entire north-western region of India from the Indus to the Sutlej. The Sikh Raj, however, came to an end in 1849, when the incapable successors of Ranjit Singh could not hold their own against the British, and the Sikh state was annexed to British India.

The Sikhs came out of Hindu stock and they brought along with them certain Hindu customs and traditions as a matter of habit. A large section of the Sikhs are Sahajdhari Sikhs, who believe in the Sikh scriptures but who do not keep unshorn hair; they follow certain Hindu customs and rituals as well. A very large section of the Sindhi community believes in Guru Nanak only, in addition to their own faith in the Hindu religion. There are a number of sects founded by the relatives of the Sikh Gurus, which broke away from the Sikh mainstream, and which partially follow the Sikh traditions and partially the Hindu rituals. Although the Sikh religion arose partly in reaction against the excessive ritualism and corruption in Hinduism, yet certain Hindu traditions crept into the Sikh way of life over a period of time and the use of temple tokens is one such tradition.

There are four major seats of the Sikh religion, viz., the Golden Temple in Amritsar in Punjab, Anandpur Sahib in Punjab, Patna Sahib in Bihar, and Hazur Sahib in Nander, Maharashtra. These four authorities have not issued any religious tokens bearing the effigies of the Gurus. The Sikh gurudwaras have been issuing to certain pilgrims a small yellow-coloured turban, a pocketbook of holy verses, and a small *kirpan*. This has been a long-established practice which continues to the present day.[9]

Sikh religious tokens appear to have emanated from Amritsar, where very large numbers of devotees come during the Baisakhi and Diwali festivals. The local *mahants/masands* and traders in ornaments get these tokens manufactured in bulk, then sell them to petty mendicants and *sadhus* who, in turn, sell them to the pilgrims; thus making a substantial profit from the various stages of the transaction. There is a tribe of *bhatras*, part soothsayers and part godmen, who move from place to place, especially religious places during festivals, passing on these tokens to the godfearing pilgrims with their blessings. Thus, a token worth only a few paise is passed on to a pilgrim for a few rupees. To the receiver it may be an act of religious devotion but to the giver it is a means of earning his livelihood. It is understood that tokens bearing the inscription '*Hazur Sahib*' were actually manufactured in privately owned factories in Amritsar and were sent to the traders at Nander for sale to the pilgrims going to Hazur Sahib as though these tokens originated at Hazur Sahib and with the blessings of the Guru. Such tokens were also apparently issued by certain sects outside the Sikh mainstream, such as the Udasis, the Nirmalis, and the Namdharis which were set up by those descendants of the Sikh Gurus, viz., Prithi Chand, Dhir Mal, and Ram Rai, who had separated from the Sikh mainstream and who had created their own sects with rather limited followings. The Udasi *deras* and *darbars* were scattered all over the *doabs* and received state patronage in the form of revenue-free grants and financial assistance from the Sikh rulers.[10] The *Yantra* type token, at no. 5, is an issue of some Udasi sect. The brass tokens have gone out of circulation over the last fifty years, presumably due to the Singh Sabha reform movement. The silver tokens have a very limited circulation at present, and may be obtained from silversmiths but not from the Sikh religious places.

Descriptions of the Representative Tokens

(Drawings of these tokens are shown in Plate XII)

No. 1   *Obverse*: Guru Nanak is seated cross-legged under a tree, flanked by his two attendants, Mardana the Muslim musician playing the *rabab* and Bala the Hindu holding a fly whisk, with a *lota*, the all-purpose utensil, and a pair of wooden sandals in the front. During his wanderings and travels Guru Nanak covered the length and breadth of the Indian subcontinent. He stayed on the outskirts of towns and villages, taking shelter under trees. Hence, he is universally shown in Sikh iconography sitting under a tree along with his two disciples.

Reverse: Guru Gobind Singh sitting *do jami* to the left, resting his back on a bolster or a *masand*. A peacock is perched on the parapet at the back. Guru Gobind Singh wears a princely dress and a bejeweled turban with a halo around his head. He also wears a sword and holds an arrow in his hand. Besides being the religious head of the Sikhs, Guru Gobind Singh was also their temporal head; hence he lived like a prince in regal style. He was a great general and an excellent marksman; such was his excellence in archery that none could shoot an arrow farther than him. His arrows, used in war, were gold-tipped so that the victim could identify his assailant. His death is said to have come about as a result of stretching a very strong bow; the strain caused his raw wounds to be opened and they could not be healed again.[11] In his famous letter called the *Zafarnama* addressed to Aurangzeb, he states:

Ba lachargi darmain amdam
Ba tadbir-i-tir-o-kaman amdam[12]

meaning that 'When the treachery of the foes has made a mockery of their vows, armed with arrows and bows we took the field to send them blows'. Brotman[13] and Jai Parkash Singh[14] are both wrong in stating that Guru Gobind Singh is represented holding a wand or a rod on which a bird is perched. Probably the poor workmanship of these tokens gave these writers such an impression. Guru Gobind Singh, like other Asian princes, used hawks in his hunting expeditions. He was particularly fond of white hawks.[15] Jai Parkash Singh is wrong in assuming that the bird perched on the Guru's hand is a parrot;[16] the numerous historical accounts of this iconographic representation note that the bird in question is a white hawk. Jai Parkash Singh is also wrong in identifying the side with Guru Gobind Singh as the obverse and the side with Guru Nanak as the reverse.[17] Guru Nanak is the principal Guru of the Sikhs, and to give precedence to Guru Gobind Singh over Guru Nanak amounts to an act of sacrilege for the Sikhs.

No. 2   *Obverse*: As in token no. 1
          Reverse: As in token no. 1, except that the date 1723 Sambat, i.e. AD 1666, is the date of the birth of Guru Gobind Singh.

No. 3   *Obverse*: As in token no. 1, except the halo around the Guru's head.

PLATE XII: SIKH RELIGIOUS TOKENS

OBVERSE	REVERSE

NO. 1

DIA. 3.12 cms   WT. 11.57 gms

NO. 2

DIA. 2.77 cms   WT. 11.42 gms

NO. 3

DIA. 2.76 cms   WT. 9.97 gms

NO. 4

DIA. 2.96 cms   WT. 11.65 gms

(contd.)

PLATE XII (contd.)

OBVERSE	REVERSE

NO. 5

DIA. 2.91 cms   WT. 10.12 gms

NO. 6

DIA. 2.71 cms   WT. 5.43 gms

ENLARGEMENTS

NO. 7

DIA. 2.76 cms   WT. 6.35 gms

(contd.)

PLATE XII (contd.)

OBVERSE	REVERSE

NO. 8

DIA. 2.04 cms   WT. 4.01 gms

NO. 9

DIA. 32 mm   WT. 9.5 gms

NO. 10

DIA. 37 mm

Reverse: As in token no. 2, except the legend '*Sat Kartar*' in the Devanagari script, meaning 'God is Truth', and the date 400 which cannot be deciphered for want of any details.

No. 4   *Obverse*: As in token no. 1, with slight figurative variations.

Reverse: As in token no. 1, except the date 1804. The date 1804 Sambat, i.e. AD 1747, has no significance in Sikh history and appears to be a fictitious date; the inclusion of such dates on temple tokens of India has been a general practice.[18]

No. 5   *Obverse*: As in token no. 1.

Reverse: Is a *Yantra* token with a *tantrik* representation of numerical figures in the modern Devanagari arranged in rows in the spaces created by a pair of parallel lines placed at right angles so that the total of any of the three figures in a row—horizontally, vertically, and diagonally—comes to 15 in all cases.[19]

No. 6   *Obverse*: A greatly worn out token, with the clasp having broken due to the wear and tear of many years. The figures are those of Guru Nanak with Bala and Mardana, as in the earlier tokens, although the design of the decoration is somewhat different.

Reverse: is the first verse of the '*Japji Sahib*', also called the *mool mantar*,

'*Aikomkar, Sat nam, Karta Purakh, Nir bhau, Nir ver, Akal murat, Ajuni saib bhang, Gur parsad, Jap, Adh sach, Jugad sach, Habi sach, Nanak, Hosi bhi sach.*'[20]

Means there is but one God. True is his name, creative his personality and immortal his form. He is without fear, sans enmity, unborn and self-illumined. By the Guru's grace, he is obtained. Embrace his meditation. True in the prime. True in the beginning of ages. True he is even now and true he verily shall be, O Nanak.

No. 7   *Obverse*: Guru Gobind Singh sitting *do jami* to the right on a carpet with a bolster at the back, whereas in the token at no. 1 in Plate XII he is depicted sitting to the left. Perhaps this token was made by a craftsman in Austria and the earlier tokens were made locally. Guru Gobind Singh is shown wearing all the fineries befitting a prince. He has a halo around his head and is armed with a sword and a bow. He holds a hawk on his hand. On the top is written 'Guru Gobind Singh' in the Gurmukhi script.

Reverse: contains the *mool mantar* in the Gurmukhi script as in token no. 6. Under the *mool mantar* is written in Urdu, i.e. in the Persian script, the address of the manufacturer and the place of manufacture. The inscription states: 'Raja Darya Mal Devi Dayal of Chowk Darbar, Amritsar got these manufactured from Austria'. The Chowk Darbar area adjoins the Manji Sahib portion of the Golden Temple complex in Amritsar. Darya Mal was probably a *mahant* or perhaps an important trader who got these tokens made in Austria. The workmanship of this token is very fine. The brass token had an original coating of gold wash, which is now almost completely rubbed away.

No. 8   *Obverse*: Bears the figure of a warrior standing to the right, holding a sword in his right hand and a bundle of seven arrows in his left. The legend running along the border is 'PARCRESTOA CONCORDIARES', with the date 1707. The legend in Dutch means 'Through concord small things grow large', and the seven arrows represent the seven provinces of The Netherlands.

Reverse: The Sikh *mool mantar* as in token no. 6 in the Gurmukhi script, but it is written in the manner of the Dutch legend, 'The coin of the United Dutch Provinces according to the law of the empire'. The above legends occur on Dutch gold ducats and there were several mints in The Netherlands making imitation ducats in the eighteenth and nineteenth centuries. This token made of brass is now in the collection of coins of the Babhut Mal Dugar Sardar Shahr, Rajasthan. D.K. Handa states that the token in all probability is the medal issued by the Dutch authorities when Guru Gobind Singh visited Agra at the beginning of 1707.[21] However, this assessment is merely conjectural since Guru Gobind Singh did not hold any position of patronage in Agra so far as the Dutch mission was concerned. There is no evidence of any such medals issued by the Dutch for any person in a position to promote their interests. This token appears to have been made to order in The Netherlands, wherein the *mool mantar* has been correctly laid out although in the Dutch style; but on the obverse instead of Guru Gobind Singh's effigy the obverse of a Dutch ducat dated 1707 has been stamped. This could have been a mistake as such errors often occurred in the minting of coins. Further, the Sikh religious tokens came into existence much later after the time of Guru Gobind Singh.

No. 9 *Obverse*: Is a very finely made bust of Guru Nanak, with 'Guru Nanak' written in the Devanagari script above the head.

Reverse: Is the picture of the Golden Temple in Amritsar, in a pool of water, and the *mool mantar* is recorded in the Gurmukhi script around the temple with a fictitious date 999. The token is of pure silver and may be brought from the silversmiths in northern India today. Its price is eighty rupees, with its metal contents worth about sixty rupees. There are a couple of small private factories in Chandni Chowk, Delhi which manufacture such tokens in bulk. It is a common practice to distribute sweets on weddings and important festivals. Affluent persons present such tokens along with the sweets as a symbol of well-being with the Guru's grace. The recipients preserve these as a blessing. The token mentioned by Brotman is a somewhat similar token and its origin is of recent times.[22]

No. 10 Brotman shows this to be a miscellaneous token.

Obverse: The scene is not identifiable. Perhaps it is Guru Gobind Singh on horseback, with his attendant following, and a dog running behind. In some paintings of Guru Gobind Singh in the Pahari style, he is shown riding a horse followed by some attendants and a dog.

Reverse: The scene is not identifiable. However, the bull is Nandi. The peacocks may be intended as representations of demigods; the peacock is the vehicle of Kartikeya, the god of war, and the son of Shiva. The man standing cannot be identified.[23]

Legend: Illegible, probably in the Gurmukhi script.

The above assessment of Brotman seems to be incorrect. Guru Gobind Singh had prescribed five items of daily wear, viz., 'kesh', hair on the face and the head; 'kangha', a comb to keep the hair tidy; 'kara', a heavy steel bangle to ward off attack; 'kirpan', a sword to defend oneself; and 'kachhera', a pair of breaches in place of the *dhoti*, the daily wear of the Hindu men in those times.

The wearing of the *dhoti* was changed to the *kachhera* by the sixth Guru, Hargobind, when this dress was considered to be a hindrance in fighting against the Mughals. Hence, Guru Gobind Singh or his followers would not be depicted wearing *dhotis*. It could be that the obverse and the reverse of different tokens were mixed up in this token.

NOTES

1. Irwin F. Brotman, *A Guide to the Temple Tokens of India*, Los Angeles: Shamrock Press, 1970, pp. 12-13.
2. Jai Parkash Singh, 'Observations on Sikh Tokens', *Numismatic Bulletin*, Dallas, Texas, USA, vol. XVI, no. XII, December 1982.
3. Brotman, *Temple Tokens of India*, op. cit., p. 9.

4. Ibid., p. 21.

5. D.C. Sarkar, *Studies in Indian Coins*, Delhi: Motilal Banarsidass, 1968, p. 254.

6. S.B. Ota, 'Origin and History of Rama Tankas', *Journal of Numismatic Society of India*, Banaras, vol. XV, 1978, p. 160.

7. Parmeshwari Lal Gupta, *Coins of India*, New Delhi: National Book Trust, 1979, pp. 125, 227, and Plate XXVI.

8. Hari Ram Gupta, *History of Sikh Gurus*, New Delhi: Kapoor & Sons, 1973, pp. 236-9.

9. Baron von Hugel, *Travels in Kashmir and Punjab*, Punjab: Languages Department, rpt., 1970, p. 395.

10. Sulakhan Singh, 'State Patronage to the Udasis under Maharaja Ranjit Singh', in *Maharaja Ranjit and His Times*, ed. J.S. Grewal and Indu Banga, Amritsar: Guru Nanak Dev University, 1980, pp. 103-16.

11. Hari Ram Gupta, *History of Sikh Gurus*, op. cit., pp. 243 and 236.

12. D.S. Duggal, *Zafar Nama*, Jullandhar: Insitute of Sikh Studies, 1980, p. 97.

13. Brotman, *Temple Tokens of India*, op. cit., pp. 142-52.

14. Jai Parkash Singh, 'Observations on Sikh Tokens', op. cit., pp. 359-61.

15. Hari Ram Gupta, *History of Sikh Gurus*, op. cit., p. 243.
    He was always well dressed and well armed. He wore a sword and a shield, bow and arrows. His sword was sparkling and his shield strong. His bow was of green colour and arrows were tipped with gold. Such arrows were used only in the battle field so that the victim could identify his assailant. He wore a plume on his turban and got the appellation of 'Kalghidhar'. He rode generally on a blue horse and was called 'Neelae Ghore da Swar' or the rider of the blue-coloured horse. While on horseback he carried a white hawk on his right hand. The people hailed him as 'chityan bazan walla' or the hunter with the white hawk.

16. Jai Parkash Singh, 'Observations on Sikh Tokens', op. cit., p. 362.

17. Ibid., p. 361.

18. Brotman, *Temple Tokens of India*, op. cit., p. 37.

19. D.C. Sarkar, *Studies in Indian Coins*, op. cit., p. 257.

20. Manmohan Singh (tr.), *Sri Guru Granth Sahib*, English and Punjabi translation, Amritsar: Shiromani Gurudwara Parbandhak Committee, 1981, p. 1.

21. D.K. Handa, *Studies in Indian Coins and Seals*, Delhi, 1989, p. 170.

22. Brotman, *Temple Tokens of India*, op. cit., p. 145.

23. Ibid., pp. 198-9.

Encyclopaedia on Sikkhism: Numismatic Discrepancies

A critique on the entries concerning Sikh coinage in *Encyclopaedia on Sikhism*, edited by Harbans Singh, Patiala: Punjabi University, 1995-8.

1. Entry on Akal Takht

The Akal Takht and the Harimandir had been desecrated and demolished several times during the eighteenth century by Mughal governors and Afghan invaders. In one of the gatherings of the Sarbat Khalsa on the Baisakhi festival of 1765, it was decided to rebuild the Akal Takht and the Harimandir; funds for this purpose had already been set apart from the pillage of Sirhind in 1764. It is stated in the entry on the Akal Takht.

The work was entrusted to Bhai Desraj who was also furnished with Guru Ki Mohar or the Guru's seal to enable him to raise more funds.[1]

An examination of the available *hukamnamas* shows that no Sikh Guru had used a seal or *mohar* on his directions issued to the Sikh *sangat* in the form of *hukamnamas*.[2] Hence, to state that the seal of the Guru was given to Desraj is not correct as no Guru is known to have kept any such seal in his name.

2. Entry on Hari Singh Nalwa

The entry on Hari Singh Nalwa states:

From Maharaja Ranjit Singh, Hari Singh received a special favour when he was allowed to strike a coin in his own name. This coin, known as the Hari Singh rupee, remained in circulation in the valley till the closing years of the 19th century.[3]

The examination of hundreds of Sikh coins from Kashmir, available in the Sri Pratap Museum, Srinagar and in personal and various private collections, has not revealed any Kashmir coin struck in the name of Hari Singh, particularly from among the coins of the period when he was the governor of Kashmir. It is strongly believed that no coin was struck by Hari Singh Nalwa in his own name. This issue is discussed in detail in Chapter III.

3. Entry on Moran

Moran, a Muhammadan dancing girl of Lahore, whom Maharaja Ranjit Singh is said to have married in 1802. . . . Ranjit Singh remained under her spell for a number of years and some say he even had coins of gold and silver struck in her name during 1803-09. They are known as Arsi-wali Mohar or Moranshahi coins. . . . It was resented by the Sikhs and, as the story goes, the Maharaja was summoned to Amritsar by the Jathedar of Shri Akal Takht to explain his conduct and was sentenced to be flogged publicly. Ranjit Singh willingly offered to undergo the punishment, but he was let off on payment of a fine of one lakh twenty-five thousand rupees.[4]

The above entry on Moran gives the impression that Ranjit Singh was summoned and reprimanded by the Akal Takht for striking coins in the name of his concubine. Ranjit Singh willingly offered to undergo the punishment, which means that he accepted the charge and admitted to the striking of Sikh coins in the name of Moran, when all along these coins had been struck in the name of the Sikh Gurus. This position is not correct and the issue is discussed in detail in Chapter III. It has been conclusively established that no coins were struck in the name of Moran by Ranjit Singh.

The references given below the entry are:

(i)   Waheed-ud-din, *The Real Ranjit Singh*;
(ii) Khushwant Singh, *Ranjit Singh*;
(iii) Gulshan Lall Chopra, *The Punjab as a Sovereign State*;
(iv) Bikramjit Hasrat, *Life and Times of Ranjit Singh*.

Khushwant Singh does not mention the appearance of Ranjit Singh at the Akal Takht, but Waheed-ud-din makes a passing reference to this incident, writing: 'On a visit to the Akal Takht, he was adjudged guilty of violating a sacrosanct canon. He at once bared his back for the Akali-in-charge of [the] Akal Takht to lay the whip across.' Gulshan Lall Chopra mentions the appearance of an intoxicated Ranjit Singh in public, with Moran on an elephant.[5] He also refers to Ranjit Singh being summoned to the Akal Takht and being fined one lakh twenty-five thousand rupees.[6] Bikramjit Hasrat states that Ranjit Singh, against all norms of public decorum, went riding on an elephant accompanied by Moran, in a drunken condition. The Maharaja was summoned to the Akal Takht, his offerings were rejected, and he was sentenced to a public flogging, which was later changed to a fine of one lakh twenty-five thousand rupees.[7] The references cited in support of the entry clearly establish that the punishment awarded to Ranjit Singh was not on account of the striking of the coins in the name of Moran, but it was because of his public appearance with Moran while in a drunken state in the bazaars of Lahore.

In addition to these references, there are quite a few more which also refer to Moran's affair with Ranjit Singh and to the summoning of the Maharaja by the Akal Takht. Lepel Griffin in his *Rajas of Punjab*, Baron von Hugel in his *Travels in Kashmir and Punjab*, Princep in his *Origin of Sikh Power*, N.K. Sinha in his *Ranjit Singh*, and J.D. Cunningham in his *A History of Sikhs*, all refer to the public exposure of Ranjit Singh with Moran, but these historians do not deal with his being summoned to the Akal Takht. Hari Ram Gupta in his *History of Sikhs*, vol. V, states that Moran's affair with the Maharaja outraged the Akalis and he was summoned to the Akal Takht. Ranjit Singh begged forgiveness but was declared guilty and was given one mild lash and then forgiven; he also paid one lakh twenty-five thousand rupees as a fine.[8] Bhagat Singh in his *Sikh Polity* states that Ranjit Singh's ride with Moran, a dancing girl, through the streets of Lahore was considered a moral offence. He confessed his guilt and was awarded a sentence of flogging but was let off without any punishment.[9] Hence, the entry in the present form is not correct and requires suitable modifications. Further, there has been no case of flogging of a culprit by Akal Takht authorities, their punishment have been religious and not physical.

4. The Entry on Coins or Numismatics

The entry on Sikh coins or numismatics has dealt with various aspects of Sikh coinage.[10] The account, however, suffers from certain discrepancies and inaccuracies. Some of these are as follows:

(i) It is not correct to state that the first Sikh coin was issued by Banda Bahadur from his bastion of Mukhlisgarh. The small fortress was originally called Mukhlispur, in the name of Mukhlis Khan, who was then the *faujdar* of Sirhind, and not Mukhlisgarh; it was renamed Lohgarh by Banda Bahadur.[11] It was located at a distance of 10 miles from the main Sikh camp and fort at Sadhura. The Sikhs occupied Lohgarh with the aim of using it as a place of tactical retreat from the Mughal forces which overwhelmingly outnumbered the Sikh forces both in men and armaments; the Sikhs would withdraw from Sadhura to Lohgarh and then disperse into the adjoining dense forests. I have visited the ruins of Lohgarh and today the place is not sufficient to support even a moderate-sized village, leave alone a state capital.

The Mughal emperor, Bahadur Shah, attacked Sadhura and in the fierce battle both sides suffered heavy losses, and the Sikh forces withdrew to Lohgarh. The imperial army reached Lohgarh on 9 December 1710 and laid seige to the fortress. After a day's fight, on 10 December, the Sikh forces vanished into the dense jungle during the night, leaving behind a few injured persons.[12] Banda Bahadur reappeared in early 1712 and again occupied Sirhind and Lohgarh. Farrukh Siyar sent the imperial forces in great strength in February 1713. The Sikh forces held back the Mughal armies for a few months at Sadhura and when they could not withstand the pressure any further, they used the same tactic as in

1710 and moved to Lohgarh.[13] After a day's action at Lohgarh where fifty-two rearguard defences were raised, the Sikh forces again vanished into the safety of the dense jungle where the Mughal forces were loathe to follow them. Further, the legend on the reverse of the coins does not give the name of any mint town, but does refer to what the ideal capital of the Sikh state should be in the future. The legend on the reverse is:

Zarb Ba Aman-ul-Dahar, Massawarat,
Shahr-i-Zinat Altakht Khalsa Mubarak Bakht

meaning 'coined at the refuge of the world, a place of perfect peace, picture of a beautiful city where the ornate throne of the Khalsa is located'. The legend has been rendered into English in accordance to the actual words on the coin, including the word '*Khalsa*', which has not been given in the historical accounts (see Plate I). Hence, no coin could have been struck at Lohgarh. Coins could have been struck only at a place where facilities for minting coins were available. This aspect is discussed in detail in Chapter I.

(ii) The legends on the Sikh coin have been incorrectly quoted in the entry. In the legend on the obverse, the word '*Zad*' meaning 'struck' or 'coined' is missing between '*Sikka*' and '*bar*'.[14] In the legend on the reverse, the word '*Khalsa*' is missing from the phrase '*Altakht Khalsa Mubarak Bakht*'. The omitting of the word '*Khalsa*' after '*Altakht*' results in eliminating from the coin a major feature of the concept of Sikh sovereignty, as depicted on Sikh coins. This aspect is discussed in detail in Chapter I.

(iii) The coin alleged to have been struck by Jassa Singh Ahluwalia is a disputed issue among historians, and no such coin has been traced so far. Lepel Griffin's attempt to trace such a coin with the Kapurthala family in 1860 was not fruitful. In fact, he could not contact any individual who had seen the coin in question.[15] The account that the local *qazis* minted such a coin and then sent it to Ahmad Shah Abdali is only a conjecture not based on any evidence.[16] This issue is discussed in detail in Chapter II.

(iv) No Sikh coin appears to have been struck in 1764, as claimed in the entry, after the conquest of Sirhind. No historian has mentioned this event nor has any coin of 1764 been traced so far. Further, classifying a Sikh coin as a Gobind Shahi coin is incorrect and goes against the spirit of the Sikh ethos. All Sikh coins bear only one of two legends, viz., '*Sikka zad bar har do alam*' and '*Degh Tegh Fateh*'. In both these legends the names of Guru Nanak and Guru Gobind Singh appear, and no coin has been traced so far which bears only the name of Guru Gobind Singh. Copper coins, which were not state issue, do have small legends with the name of Guru Nanak, Nanak Shahi, etc. But even among the copper coins, no coin with only the name of Guru Gobind Singh has been traced. Hence, Sikh coins can only be called Nanak Shahi coinage, as was the practice even after the annexation of the Lahore Darbar in 1849. Sikh coinage cannot be characterized as Gobind Shahi coinage. This issue is discussed in detail in Chapter II.

(v) The English rendering of the famous legend 'Degh Tegh Fateh O Nusrat Baidarang. Yaft uz Nanak Guru Gobind Singh' is given in the entry as 'Degh Tegh and unhindered victory Guru Gobind Singh inherited from Guru Nanak'.[17] The correct meaning is Degh (food), Tegh (sword), Fateh (resultant victory), Nusrat (help), Baidarang (spontaneous), Yaft uz (received from) Guru Nanak Guru Gobind Singh, i.e. food, arms, and the resultant victory with spontaneous help were received from Nanak Guru Gobind Singh. Here the recipient is the Khalsa, who received the blessings given by Guru Nanak Guru Gobind Singh. The ten Gurus are treated as one light, one idea and each successor Guru is regarded as the reincarnation of Guru Nanak and was in fact called Nanak. Hence, to say that Guru Gobind inherited from Guru Nanak is incorrect.

(vi) The assertion that gold and silver coins were issued from Amritsar from 1777 onwards, as stated in the entry, is incorrect, as the first coin struck from Amritsar in 1775 is readily available.[18] The legend on the reverse of the Sikh coins from the Amritsar mint is 'Sri Amritsar Jeo, zarb. Sambat. . .Jalus Takht Akal Bakht' (meaning the fortunate throne with Akal's grace). The last line was changed in 1841, with the proliferation of Sikh mints, to 'Jalus maiminat manus Takht akal bakht', meaning 'the throne of prosperous reign with Akal's grace'.[19] The various mints were run by independent sardars in their individual capacity and there is no evidence of a mint having been run at the Akal Takht. No coin giving the mint town as the Akal Takht has been traced so far.

(vii) It has been stated in the entry that the Lahore coins prior to Ranjit Singh's period were called the Gobind Shahi and the coins struck with the coming to power of Ranjit Singh were called the Nanak Shahi coins. Their distinguishing mark was the leaf symbol. This is an incorrect statement made without any supporting evidence. Ranjit Singh held a darbar in April 1801, at which he was given the Raj Tilak along with other honours. He ordered that the existing Sikh coin with the 'Degh Tegh Fateh' legend should continue to be minted from Lahore.[20] This issue is discussed in detail in Chapter III. The leaf symbol on Sikh coins appeared on the coins of the year 1841 Sambat, i.e. AD 1783 and thereafter was adopted on all Sikh coins within a few years. The leaf symbol came into use much before the period of Ranjit Singh. In fact, Ranjit Singh made no change in the legend and other markings of the Sikh coins and he only centralized the issuing of Sikh coins in the Lahore and Amritsar mints to ensure the maintenance of the purity of the metal. This issue is discussed in detail in Chapter III.

(viii) The entry alleges that Ranjit Singh struck coins in the name of one of his courtesans, Moran, and that these coins were called 'Moran Shahi' and 'Arsi de Mohar Wale' coins. This issue is discussed in detail in Chapter III, wherein it is established from various angles that no such coins had been struck and that the entire allegation is based on hearsay without being supported by any historical or numismatic evidence. As regards Sher Singh, his name does not appear on any Sikh coin. When he was the governor of Kashmir from the middle of 1831 to the middle of 1834, the impression of a tiger appeared on the reverse of a coin issued from Kashmir for the year 1890 Sambat, i.e. AD 1833.[21] As regards the legend 'Akal Sahai Sher Singh', this is the likely impression of his personal seal as most of the sardars had their personal seals with the inscription 'Akal Sahai' before their names; indeed the seal of Ranjit Singh was very similar. This could not be the reverse of a state coin.

(ix) It is alleged in the entry that a gold mohar had, besides the usual legends, three lines of 'Wahe Guru Jee' written over its other side. This is not a gold mohar but rather an unfinished token collected from a mint, and was in the possession of C.J. Rodgers. His collection of Sikh coins was purchased by the Punjab Government and is now with the Government Museum, Lahore.[22]

(x) It has been stated in the entry that Hari Singh Nalwa was twice permitted to issue coins in his name, first in 1831 in Kashmir and then in 1834 in Peshawar. This is an incorrect statement. When Maharaja Ranjit Singh could not mint coins in his own name, how could he allow this privilege and honour to one of his generals, moreover a general who was ranked thirty-seventh in the list of thirty-eight generals of the Lahore Darbar? This issue is discussed in detail in Chapter III. Hari Singh did not strike any coin in his own name. He put only the name of God, Har, on the coin of 1878 Sambat, i.e. AD 1821 and not AD 1831 as stated in the entry. The Sikh coins were issued from Peshawar from 1891 to 1894 Sambat, i.e. AD 1834 to 1838.[23] These coins were struck under the orders of Nau Nihal Singh and were not issued in Hari Singh Nalwa's name. This is discussed in detail in Chapter IV. We have not come across any coin struck in the name of Hari Singh Nalwa either from Kashmir or Peshawar despite examining a very large collection of such coins in the Srinagar Museum and the coins in the possession of private collectors. The bibliography shown in the entry, C.J. Rodgers' book *Coins Collections in Northern India*, 1894, reprinted in 1983, New Delhi is a revised version of the author's article 'On the Coins of the Sikhs', *Journal of the Asiatic Society of Bengal*, vol. L, pt. I, Calcutta, 1881. The second source, *Umdat-ut-Twarikh*, Lahore, 1885-9 does not deal with the study of Sikh coinage except for a few casual references. My critique on C.J. Rodgers's account 'On the Coins of the Sikhs' addresses these various inaccuracies and the total lack of understanding of the Sikh ethos and tradition; this article appears in *Panjab Past & Present*, vol. XXV, pt. II, October 1991, Patiala: Punjabi University, pp. 40-55.

Note: I have been requested by the Editor-in-Chief, *Encyclopaedia on Sikhism*, vide his letter no. Ency/477 dated 18 October 1999 to revise the entry in accordance with my findings. The new revised entry is likely to appear in the revised edition of the *Encyclopaedia* in the near future.

NOTES

1. *Encyclopaedia on Sikhism* (4 vols.), ed. Harbans Singh, Patiala: Punjabi University, 1995-8, vol. I, p. 58.
2. Ganda Singh, *Hukamnamas* (Punjabi), Patiala: Punjabi University, 1985.
3. *Encyclopaedia on Sikhism*, op. cit., vol. II, p. 252.
4. Ibid., vol. III, p. 123.
5. Gulshan Lall Chopra, *The Punjab as Sovereign State*, Hoshiarpur: VVRI, 1960, p. 123.
6. Ibid., p. 154.
7. Bikramjit Hasrat, *Life and Times of Ranjit Singh*, Hoshiarpur: VVRI, 1997, p. 44.
8. Hari Ram Gupta, *History of Sikhs*, vol. V, New Delhi: Munshiram Manoharlal, 1991, p. 35.
9. Bhagat Singh, *Sikh Polity*, New Delhi: Oriental Publishers & Distributors, 1978, p. 177.
10. *Encyclopaedia on Sikhism*, op. cit., vol. IV, pp. 136-8.
11. Hari Ram Gupta, *History of Sikhs*, vol. II, New Delhi: Munshiram Manoharlal, 1978, p. 3. Mukhlis Khan, the Governor of Sirhind, often hunted in these jungles. In the heart of a dense forest he built a rest house for himself on the top of a hill in 1677, and called it, after his own name, Mukhlispur. It looked like a small fort, that is why Kahfi Khan calls it a 'Qulachi'. This has been renamed by Banda Bahadur as Lohgarh.
12. Ibid., p. 19.
13. Ganda Singh, *Life of Banda Bahadur Singh*, Amritsar: Khalsa College, 1935, p. 188.
14. Ibid., p. 83.
15. Lepel Griffin, *Rajas of Punjab*, Punjab: Languages Department, rpt., 1970, p. 461.
16. Hari Ram Gupta, *History of Sikhs*, op. cit., p. 178. Ganesh Dass asserts that these coins were minted by the bigoted mullahs of Lahore and were sent to Kabul to excite the spirit of revenge of Ahmed Shah Abdali against the Sikhs (*Risala-i-Sahib-nama*, p. 210). Ganesh Dass does not give any source for this statement. He compiled his account in 1849, nearly one hundred years later. His isolated authority cannot be accepted. Besides, he places this event in 1765, evidently referring to another coin of that year.
17. *Encyclopaedia on Sikhism*, op. cit., p. 137.
18. Hans Herrli, *The Coins of the Sikhs*, Nagpur: Indian Coin Society, 1993, p. 59.
19. Ibid., pp. 57-65 (Amritsar Coins).
20. Hari Ram Gupta, *History of Sikhs*, vol. V, op. cit., p. 32.
21. Herrli, *The Coins of the Sikhs*, op. cit., p. 134.
22. *Catalogue of Coins in the Government Museum Lahore*, compiled by C.J. Rodgers, Calcutta, 1891. This token is shown on p. 92, serial no. 1 of the Sikh Gold Coins.
23. Herrli, *The Coins of the Sikhs*, op. cit., pp. 201-2.

A Critique: 'On the Coins of the Sikhs' by C.J. Rodgers

On 29 March 1849, Henry Elliot read out the proclamation of the annexation of the Punjab at the Darbar held in Lahore.[1] The child Maharaja Dalip Singh was made to attend, put his signature to the document, hand over the Koh-i-noor diamond, and step down from the Sikh throne.[2] The kingdom of Lahore, the Sikh state, ceased to exist. The Nanak Shahi currency was withdrawn and the Company *sicca* was introduced as the symbol of British sovereignty over the Punjab. Shiploads of Nanak Shahi currency units were transported to the Bombay and Calcutta mints for being reissued as British *sicca* rupees.[3] It was the British policy to maintain the Company *sicca* at a slightly higher intrinsic value over the Indian currencies so that it was not melted down and reminted into the local currencies.[4] The Nanak Shahi rupee was valued at 17 *annas* due to the purity of the silver,[5] while the Company rupee was valued at 15½ *annas* due to the 5 per cent alloy used for hardening purposes. This was another reason for the British to remove Sikh coinage from circulation.

The Second Anglo-Sikh War was fought by only part of the Sikh army and the bulk of the *sardars* remained subservient to the British,[6] yet the totally disorganized Sikh army, deceived by its leaders who were in league with the British, deprived of arms and ammunition, even facing shortages of food supplies, gave such a tough fight that the fully prepared British army could win the war by the skin of their teeth. The annexation has been termed as naked lawlessness and a violent breach of trust.[7] Extremely oppressive and discriminating measures were taken to not only subdue but also to crush the valiant spirit of the Khalsa.[8] Large numbers of Hindus, who had embraced Sikhism during the last half century and who could not stand the rigours of the repressive measures, started returning to the Hindu faith.[9] The British started entertaining the hope of the virtual extermination of the Sikh nation.[10] It was an attempt no different from those of Abdus Samad Khan[11] and Muin-ul-Mulk,[12] but with far more sophisticated and dangerous weapons. George Clark, the Governor of Bombay, stated that the sect of the Sikhs would disappear within fifty years.[13] Besides the abolition of the Sikh zamindaris, the extensive disbandment of Sikh soldiers without offering them any alternative appointments, and other discriminatory measures, a calculated attack was also mounted against the Sikh religion as the real strength of the Sikhs lay in their absolute faith in their Gurus and their teachings.[14] To overpower and subdue the Sikhs, it was considered essential to undermine the Sikh doctrines and destroy the Sikh ethos. The charge of the Golden Temple at Amritsar and other historic gurudwaras was given to the deputy commissioners.[15] The *mahants* were given proprietary rights over the Sikh gurudwaras even though they were the most debased and corrupt persons.[16] While Muslim and Hindu shrines were handed over to their representatives, Sikh shrines were given to the Government's henchmen, the *mahants*.[17] The *Guru Granth Sahib* was called a heathen scripture.[18] A bigoted German, Ernest Trumpp, was specially selected to translate the *Guru Granth* and his derogatory remarks on the Holy *Granth* and on the lives of the Sikh Gurus were universally condemned and representations against this were made to the Governor-General.[19]

Macauliffe states that Trumpp's translation was highly inaccurate and un-idiomatic and that furthermore it gave mortal offence to the Sikhs by the *odium theologicum* introduced into it. Whenever he saw an opportunity to defame the Gurus, the sacred book, and the religion of the Sikhs, Trumpp eagerly availed himself of it.[20]

Christian missions were established in Punjab and religious imperialism became no less important than colonial imperialism. Christian missions were established in areas which were densely populated by Sikhs such as Amritsar, Tarn Taran, Batala, Ludhiana, and Lahore, and their discreditable manoeuvres greatly alarmed the Sikhs.[21] One such move was the appointment of C.J. Rodgers as the Principal of the Teachers Training College in Amritsar, a post he occupied for over a decade, and through which he managed to influence the minds of young teachers to disregard the Sikh ethos and the Sikh faith.

Amritsar, besides being the most sacred site of the Sikh religion, was the greatest trade centre in northern India, where about fifty different currencies were exchanged, the premier currency of course being the Nanak Shahi currency.[22] Rodgers was a keen numismatist and found a very fertile area for his hobby for which he used the good offices of his students who hailed from all over the Punjab.[23] Although his main collections included Indo-Greek, Mughal, and Suri coins, during his long stay in Amritsar he also collected Sikh coins, which certainly is the first collection of Sikh coins ever assembled. His entire collection of Sikh coins—gold, silver, and copper—was purchased by the Punjab Government and placed in the Government Museum in Lahore.[24] Rodgers later prepared a catalogue of the coins in the Lahore Museum, in which 13 gold, 157 silver, and 143 copper coins of the Sikhs were listed.[25] Ken Wiggins and Stan Goron have used Rodgers's study as the basis of their articles written between 1981 to 1984.[26] Hans Herrli, who has been studying Sikh coins for almost a decade, is working on a comprehensive catalogue of Sikh coins.[27] We certainly owe our gratitude to Rodgers for assembling the first collection of Sikh coins and to the Punjab Government for acquiring the same and placing it with the Government Museum, Lahore. But Rodgers's treatment of the Sikh Gurus and the Sikh religion is totally atrocious and warrants strong condemnation.

The studies carried out by the above-mentioned numismatists have been in the nature of cataloguing these coins and are not analytical studies. Their main aim has been to ascertain the ruler's name and the date and the place of issue. They have accepted the inferences drawn by Rodgers as a matter of course and they have not made any effort to analyse the authenticity of Rodgers's claims and assertions. Besides these numismatists, numerous historians, in fact almost all the historians of Sikh history from the mid-nineteenth century to the present day, have made brief references to these coins, treating Rodgers's inferences as the gospel truth. Rodgers's inferences suffer from certain serious shortcomings and the uncritical repetition of these statements by a galaxy of historians,[28] who failed to personally examine these coins, has merely spread certain kinds of disinformation leading to the distortion of Sikh traditions and Sikh history. This note is primarily intended to point out the shortcomings in Rodgers's study and some of the incorrect inferences which he drew.

The study of Sikh coins has been the most neglected subject all along, although it has certain very fascinating features which make these coins stand apart from the contemporary coins. The most unfortunate aspect of the study of these coins has been that no scholar conversant with the traditions and the history of the Sikhs took up this study. Coins are the true reflection of the religious, social, political and economic trends of an era and whatever historical data agree with the facts imprinted on the coins get the stamp of authenticity.

The accounts of Sikh history written by British and European scholars including their paid Indian *munshis*, and even some Indian scholars as well, with the single exception of J.D. Cunningham, suffer from a certain bias and prejudice and the accounts written by certain Sikh scholars are too eulogistic. Hence, the coins assume an added importance for a true understanding of Sikh history. Another disturbing factor has been that historians have tried to match Sikh coins with unauthentic evidence rather than testing this information against the testimony of these coins. Rodgers's account also suffers from these shortcomings. Rodgers's account covering 23 pages in the *Journal of Asiatic Society of Bengal*, devotes 8 pages to the historical introduction and the rest explaining 74 drawings, along with two pages covering the chronological data.[29] In his historical introduction, Rodgers shows a distinct bias and prejudice against the Sikh doctrines, the Sikh Gurus, and the Sikhs in general. He was either acting as a willing tool of the British policy to denigrate the Sikh religion, the prime source of their strength, as one of the repressive measures adopted in the post-1849 period or else he had a perverse mind.

We give below some of the views put forward by Rodgers on Sikh doctrine and the Sikh Gurus in his own words as recorded in his above-mentioned article on Sikh coins.

(a) Since 1849 the Sikhs have been nothing more than what they were before the time of Gobind Singh . . . a religious sect when the present generation has passed away, there will be little in Panjab to show that Sikhs were once rulers.

(b) By religiousness (about Sikhs) I do not mean real godliness.

(c) There was very little in the characters of some of the Sikh religious leaders to mark them as teachers of religion. Their lives were loose, as were their doctrines.

(d) They encourage bloodshed, hatred, malice and all uncharitableness where ever and when ever Mohammedans are concerned.

(e) Nanak's disciples (Sikhs were an ignorant rabble . . .). They were his servants and followed him for what they obtained as alms or in the shape of food.

(f) Angad, the second Guru, did not rise above his fellow Sikhs in scholarship. His influence on his sect was nil.

(g) Talking about the *Guru Granth*, he says, 'It was the book in the mother tongue of thousands of unlettered men and women. . . . Its language being three centuries old is not intelligible to the masses.'

(h) Writing about Guru Hargobind he states, 'His movements must have resembled those of a freebooter or an insurgent.'

(i) Joining the regular army, he rendered himself obnoxious by appropriating the pay of the soldiers. He was imprisoned many years for this. He after-wards entered the service of Shah Jahan, but his old propensities woke out afresh, and he left it and became once more a freebooter.

(j) About Guru Har Rai he writes: 'He died in 1660 AD having done nothing worthy of notice.'

(k) About Guru Har Kishan, he writes: 'He died in 1664 AD having accomplished nothing.'

(l) About Guru Tegh Bahadur he writes: 'But as a rule [he] led a roving life of a common faqir. In one of these excursions he was imprisoned at Delhi. But it turns out that this excursion was a predatory one, and as a consequence he was not only imprisoned but executed in AD 1675.'

(m) The moral obliquity of the Sikhs is not to be wondered at. Their surroundings were against all integrity of morals. We are told of this Guru (Guru Gobind Singh) that he was proficient in the science of Kok. . . . His eccentricities are regarded as his religious teachings. His worship of iron, because by its aid he plundered, is one.

(n) Thus we see the last two Gurus, father and son, came to a violent death which resulted from their own wrong doings.

(o) The hatred of Guru Gobind Singh towards Mohammedanism was so great that he prohibited the study of Persian.

(p) Much false sympathy has been bestowed on these two men. But the truth is that were two such men to arise now in India, there is no doubt they would be hunted down.

(q) Commenting on the period AD 1716 to AD 1748 he states: 'During this time Sikhism, in spite of Mohamadan suppressions, had prospered, as all wrong prospers where it is not exterminated.'

(r) Ranjit Singh was in learning a thousand years behind his time. Hence, I suppose he cared little as to what was on his coins.[30]

The above comments are totally unwarranted from an enlightened educationalist brought up in the liberal traditions of the West. He deserves all the condemnation and a point-by-point rebuttal by a serious student of Sikh history. For the purpose of this article, we shall confine ourselves to the examination of his study from the numismatic angle only. Suffice if to say that Rodgers has, deliberately or otherwise, lamentably failed to understand and appreciate the Sikh ethos and this failure reflects in the inferences drawn by him regarding Sikh coins.

An ignorant rabble led by freebooters, with immorality in their lives and malice in their hearts, and a loose doctrine, as made out by Rodgers cannot raise a people's revolution from the depressed and oppressed section of society, the affluent Hindus were always aligned with the Mughal and Afghan rulers,[31] determinedly faced the mighty Muslim armies assisted by the Hindu rajas. They not only established the Khalsa Raj over the entire Punjab, but they also stemmed the centuries-old tide of Muslim invaders, and stationed their sentinels at the Khyber Pass, the gateway of such invasions.[32] But for the strength of Sikh doctrine, the shape and culture of today's India would have been altogether different. It has been no small achievement.

The coins depict the name of the rulers and the place and the year of striking to express the suzerainty of the ruler. Contrary to the prevailing concept of sovereignty which belonged to the ruler, the Sikh coins have been the symbol of Sikh sovereignty, the sovereignty of the Guru Khalsa or the Khalsa Panth, and not of any particular ruler or individual *sardar*.[33] Sikh coins can be properly analysed only with a proper understanding of the concept of Sikh sovereignty. Unfortunately, this was neither appreciated nor understood by Rodgers.

The Sikh doctrine envisages the investment of divine sovereignty, both spiritual and temporal, in the Sikh Gurus.[34] Guru Nanak, the first Sikh Guru, has been called '*Din Duniya da Padshah*', i.e. the king of both the spiritual and the temporal worlds.[35] The basic concept of Sikhism is the worship of one God, through love of His premier creation, the human beings,[36] by earning one's bread with the sweat of one's brow and sharing it with one's less fortunate fellows,[37] thereby living the life of a householder with all the duties and functions in accordance with moral values.[38] The Sikh religion became a way of life, and so strong has been the faith of the Sikhs that resistance to oppression became inevitable,[39] because there is no place for escapism from the demands of the real world in Sikh doctrine, such as the practices of asceticism, monasticism, and celibacy. The Sikh community increased under the successor Gurus through the institutions of the *sangat,* the *pangat,* and the *langar,* each with its own distinct way of social living; they undermined the oppressive attitude of the ruling classes. The oppression of the rulers resulted in a series of martyrdoms commencing with the martyrdom of the fifth master, Guru Arjan Dev, in AD 1604. Guru Hargobind armed his followers to defend themselves and put on the twin swords of '*miri*' and '*piri*'.[40] He built the Akal Takht[41] opposite the Harimandir, from where he exercised his temporal sovereignty, and he attended to the spiritual needs of the Sikhs from the Harimandir. The Sikhs were already formed into a state within a state.[42] The martyrdom of Guru Tegh Bahadur, eventually led to the creation of the Khalsa,[43] by Guru Gobind Singh, who raised an army of '*sant sipahis*', i.e. 'saint soldiers',[44] for the defence of the Panth and the upliftment of the down trodden. Shortly before his demise, Guru Gobind Singh abolished the institution of the personal Guruship,[45] and ordered the Sikhs to seek spiritual guidance from the *Granth,* which thereafter was called the *Guru Granth Sahib,* the repository of the spiritual aspects of divine sovereignty,[46] and the temporal sovereignty was vested in the Khalsa Panth,[47] ordaining that where ever there are five Sikhs the Guru is present amongst them in spirit.[48] This concept of the sovereignty of the Khalsa Panth has ever since then been held most dear to the heart of every Sikh, and every victory has been deemed as the benediction of their Gurus. Guru Gobind Singh made the institutions of the Guru and the Khalsa synonymous when he administered the *khanda pahul* to his five *piaras* and thereafter himself took the same from them, thereby merging the personality of the Guru with those of his disciples. He has aptly been called '*ape Guru ape Chela*', i.e. he is both the Guru and the Disciple.[49]

Another aspect of the Sikh doctrine is its continuity of belief from Guru Nanak to Guru Gobind Singh.[50] It has been deemed as a lamp lighting another lamp and in the *Guru Granth* each successor of Guru Nanak is called Nanak. The most democratic step taken by Guru Gobind Singh was the creation of the Khalsa, which was very similar to the action of Guru Nanak who, after nominating his successor Guru Angad, bowed before him as his first disciple. Thus, real importance has been given to the eternal nature of the doctrine and not to the transitional person of the Guru.[51] The teachings of the ten masters constitute a single light that lit the Khalsa Panth. Indu Bhushan Banerjee states that the investment of the sovereignty in the *Guru Granth* and the Khalsa Panth was the culmination of a process that had started much earlier.[52] G.C. Narang likewise states that the harvest which ripened in the time of Guru Gobind Singh had been sown by Guru Nanak and had been watered by his successors. The sword which carved the Khalsa's way to glory was, undoubtedly, forged by Guru Gobind Singh, the steel for which had been provided by Guru Nanak.[53] Rodgers has miserably failed to understand these aspects of the concept of Sikh sovereignty whose true reflection was symbolized in Sikh coinage.

Within a couple of years after the demise of Guru Gobind Singh, the first physical manifestation of a sovereign Sikh state came into existence with the occupation of Subah Sirhind and the surrounding territories by the Khalsa armies under Banda Bahadur.[54] The legends selected for the Sikh state seal and the Sikh coins were a true reflection of the sovereignty of the Khalsa Panth. These legends are as follows:

(i)   *Degh Tegh Fateh Nusrat Baidrang, yaft uz Nanak Guru Gobind Singh*, meaning that 'An abundance of resources, the sword arm, and the resultant victory with unrestrained patronage has been received by the Khalsa Panth from Guru Nanak Guru Gobind Singh'. The Khalsa Panth as the recipient is implied and the term 'Nanak Guru Gobind Singh' is a poetic phrase depicting the ten masters from Guru Nanak to Guru Gobind Singh as one entity.

(ii) *Sikka zar bar har do alam, Teg Nanak wahab ast, Fateh Gobind Singh Shah-i-shahan, Fazal sacha sahib ast*, meaning that 'coin has been struck in each of the two worlds under the guarantee of Guru Nanak's sword. Victory to Guru Gobind Singh, King of Kings, has been with the grace of Saccha Sahib, the Lord Almighty'.

(iii) *Azmat-i-Nanak Guru ham zahir-o-ham batin ast, Badshah din-o-duniya ap sacha Sahib ast*, meaning that 'the greatness of Guru Nanak is both apparent and intrinsic, the true Lord is the king of both the spiritual and the temporal worlds'.

The first legend is available on the state seal imprints and the second legend on the few coins traced so far. Although mentioned by contemporary writers, no imprint or coin with the third legend has been traced so far.[55] Rodgers was ignorant of the origin of the Sikh coins during the time of Banda Bahadur, which signalled the real start of Sikh coinage. William Irvine wrote about Banda Bahadur's coin at about the same time when Rodgers was studying Sikh coins, i.e. at the close of the nineteenth century.

Rodgers commenced his study with the controversial coin of Jassa Singh Ahluwalia which has not been located so far, and hence it has no numismatic value and is useful only in understanding the concept of Sikh sovereignty in the Sikh polity.[56] The first major mistake Rodgers committed was in calling the 1822 Sambat, i.e. AD 1765 coin as the 'Gobind Shahi' and not the 'Nanak Shahi' (p. 79). There is no such distinction in actual practice as both the legends ascribe the coins to the benediction of Guru Nanak Guru Gobind Singh. It has already been explained that Nanak Guru Gobind Singh is one entity and the fanciful distinctions made by Rodgers are totally incorrect. Rodgers was also unable to give a correct translation of the couplet when he states that Guru Gobind Singh received from Guru Nanak (p. 79). It is incorrect both in spirit as well as in literal translation. Rodgers's error is due to his lack of understanding of the Sikh concept of sovereignty and the fact that in poetic composition certain aspects are left silent for the purposes of rhyme. Guru Gobind Singh has stated in the *Dasam Granth*, '*Deg Teg Jag me duon chalen Rakh lo mohe ap, avar na dalen*', meaning that his prosperity and the might of his armies should be supreme in the world and under God's protection, no power shall be able to defeat him.[57] The recipient in this legend is obviously the Khalsa Panth, seeking the benediction of their Gurus. Sikh currency cannot be given any name other than Nanak Shahi, as for example the religion founded by Christ cannot be called anything other than Christianity. Sikhs were for quite some time called the Nanakpanthis in the initial stages of the growth of the new faith. Rodgers's apprehension about the 1823 and 1824 Sambat coins is also incorrect as the 1823 Sambat coin is in our collection and the 1824 Sambat coin is with the Sheesh Mahal Museum, Patiala.[58] Hence, his inference of an interruption in the coinage in AD 1766 and 1767 is incorrect. The stay of Ahmad Shah Abdali in Lahore in 1766-7 was only for three to four months. He went back disappointed when the Sikhs spurned with disdain his offer of the governorship of Lahore to Sardar Lehna Singh.[59] The Sikhs were quite confident of holding their own against the Afghans. Further, their concept of sovereignty did not permit them to be subservient to any other power.

The earliest Sikh coin from Amritsar pertains to the year 1832 Sambat[60] and not 1835 Sambat, as stated by Rodgers (p. 80). Rodgers was unable to understand the legend due to his lack of knowledge of the Sikh ethos and the Persian language. His characterization of these coins as Nanak Shahi as distinct from the coins bearing the other legend is not only incorrect, but he has also not given any rational basis for his inference. Unfortunately, his inference has been repeated by other numismatists who were equally ignorant of Sikh traditions. The complete couplet could not be accommodated on the coins; this practice was in accordance with the Mughal and Afghan system of coin minting where the die is larger than the coin and only part of the legend can be fitted on to the surface of the coin.[61] This practice cannot be deemed as a draw back in Sikh coinage.

Rodgers's thinking about the Anandgarh coin is most confused, although there is a definite historical background to it. During the lifetime of Jassa Singh Ahluwalia, the leader of the Dal Khalsa, coins were struck from Lahore, Amritsar, and Multan for a few years. These cities were under the control of the Bhangi *sardars*, although most of the *sardars* were independent in their own right. Jassa Singh Ahluwalia commanded their respect and had a hold over them. There came a certain vacuum in the leadership after the death of Jassa Singh in 1840 Sambat, i.e. AD 1783. Various *sardars* started striking their own coinage, but this does not mean that they struck coins in their own names or with their own legends. They were simply striking the coins for their own use with the existing legend in praise of their Gurus. It was customary to distribute the newly struck coins on weddings and on special occasions, and it is equally possible that the only mint in Amritsar could not cater to their increasing needs. Amritsar city consisted about dozen independent *katras*, duly walled and under the control of various *sardars*.[62] From 1840 Sambat, we get about half a dozen series of Sikh coins with slight differences in the flowering, marks, etc., but no indication about the *sardars*.[63] It is quite possible that we have not come across other differing series or perhaps some smaller *sardars* may have borrowed the dies from other *sardars* for the occasional striking of their coins. One such mint was operated from Anandgarh for a few years from 1840 Sambat onwards.[64] 'Ahad' stands for the first year of this series and the Figure 4 in Plate V is a coin struck in the third year, i.e. 1843 Sambat. The slight inaccuracy in the word 'Anandgarh' is understandable. There are about thirty different spellings given by European writers for the simple word 'Sikh'. Rodgers states: 'The Katar and Gurz would seem to indicate that it was to be one of brute force' (p. 86). The absurdity of such a statement would mean that the arms and animals shown on various British coats of arm are a sign of their brutality and animalism.

Rodgers, para 2, p. 81, citing a reference to a passage from J.D. Cunningham's *A History of the Sikhs* is quite confusing and it is not clear what he is trying to infer. In para 2, p. 82, Rodgers' construction of the phrase 'Sacha Shahan' is incorrect. The word 'Sacha' is part of the line 'Fazal Sacha Sahib ast' and the word 'Shahan' is part of the line 'Fateh Guru Gobind Singh Shah-i-Shahan' and 'Sacha Shahan' as such is no word. Rodgers's presumption that between 1846 and 1856 Sambat, there must have been great disorder and chaos all over the Punjab is not correct as a number of coins pertaining to these years, from the Amritsar mint, are available with us and with the Sheesh Mahal Museum, Patiala.[65]

Kanehiya Lal's account (p. 82) is an unnecessary addition. Kanehiya Lal, an employee of the Lt. Governor of the Sirhind Division, chose to write on the life of Ranjit Singh in AD 1872. His account contains a fair amount of fiction and has little historical value. Ranjit Singh scrupulously followed the concept of Sikh sovereignty and the entire coinage struck during his long reign, from all the mints, used the prevailing two legends in praise of the Sikh Gurus.[66] Rodgers's comments on Ranjit Singh's learning and his being unconcerned about the legends on his coins not only shows Rodgers's gross ignorance of the facts but also the existence of mental perversity.

Rodgers has made a serious mistake in the chronological account on p. 83 in giving the date of the occupation of Amritsar as AD 1802.[67] This erroneous date was first given by Princep and was followed by certain European historians. Later historians connected with the Sikh state have given the date of occupation as AD 1805. It stands established that Ranjit Singh occupied the Bhangi portion of the city and the fort in 1805 and occupied the rest of the approximately dozen autonomous *katras* between 1805 and 1809; as and when he occupied the main territories of the various *sardars*, he also took over their territory in Amritsar. After taking possession of the entire city, Ranjit Singh fortified Amritsar with a wall around it and closed all the other mints and retained only one mint. Ranjit

Singh had to be very patient and tactful in bringing about the occupation of Amritsar, as any bloodshed in the holy city would have had unfavourable repercussions for him.

Rodgers waxes eloquently over Ranjit Singh's attachment to one of his courtesans named Moran (pp. 81 and 82). Rodgers bases his contention that Ranjit Singh struck coins in the name of Moran on some bazaar gossip or loose talk that was designed to malign the then rising Sukharchakiya *sardar*. He mentions Cunningham as his source regarding the story that Moran had made a wager to have her name on a Sikh coin just as Noor Jahan had her name on Mughal coins and that the determined courtesean succeeded in her designs. We have perused all the editions of Cunningham's *A History of Sikh* and this incident is not found recorded anywhere. Rodgers further errs in stating that Ranjit Singh discarded Moran under pressure from the Akalis and took up with another courtesan by the name of Gul Bahar. Ranjit Singh's affair with Moran occurred in the early part of his life, and she is said to have been discarded in 1811, whereas Gul Bahar's association with Ranjit Singh commenced in 1831-2 and hence Rodgers's inference is incorrect. The strength and charisma of Ranjit Singh were a puzzle to the British and all sorts of scandalous stories regarding the ruler's character, personality, and actions were propagated by European historians.[68]

Like Jassa Singh's coins, certain coins have been attributed to Moran and hence their direct examination becomes essential. The coins attributed to Moran are said to be the issues from the Amritsar mint primarily for the years 1861 to 1863 Sambat, i.e. AD 1804 to 1806. Historically, Amritsar was not under the control of Ranjit Singh during these years; therefore he could not have issued the coins from this city even if he had any such desire or intention. The leaf motif on Sikh coins first came into use in 1840 Sambat, i.e. AD 1783 and its representations assumed some variations in the form of a double branch, etc., for the short period in the Amritsar mint, and thereafter the symbol reverted to the single leaf. Rodgers has not been able to trace its origin; the same question defies the numismatists even today, although certain historians have identified it as the '*peepal* leaf' but without any evidence in support of their contention. Madanjit Kaur's assessment that it was initiated by Ranjit Singh is incorrect as the leaf motif appeared long before Ranjit Singh came to power. The drawings of the coins with the double branch and the *arsi*, etc., clearly show that these markings do not give any indication of an association with Moran (see Plate IV). Copper coins bearing a lion's figure are attributed to Prince Sher Singh and coins with a peacock were in existence in India; if Rodgers's contention is to be accepted, then Ranjit Singh could have struck such coins from only the Lahore mint with at least the figure of the peacock, but there is no such coin in the entire series of the Lahore coins which are readily available. Ranjit Singh had his faults, but he was a highly religious person and all his actions were in conformity with the concept of Sikh sovereignty. It is also a known fact that Moran had no influence over Ranjit Singh in state affairs[69] and that she was discarded after a few years.[70] In these circumstances, it is preposterous to conclude that Ranjit Singh even thought of undertaking such a sacriligious act. However, many historians continued to narrate this story, as grandmothers construct stories of princes and princesses for their half-sleepy grandchildren, as part of Sikh history. This disinformation started by Rodgers has, whether deliberately or inadvertantly, resulted in the distortion of Sikh history.

Rodgers misunderstood the significance of the coin shown at Figure 23 of Plate VI. In fact, he made an incorrect drawing of the actual coin and hence called these the effigies of Guru Nanak and Mardana. We obtained photographs of these coins from the British Museum, London and noted the following features:

There are two such coins which are sample coins made by Ranjit Singh on the advice of Baron von Hugel in AD 1836 (Plate VI), showing Ranjit Singh seeking blessings from Guru Nanak, but these coins were not actually minted since this depiction was violative of the concept of Sikh sovereignty.[71] Rodgers is also wrong about the Peshawar coin (p. 87). Prince Nau Nihal Singh was the supreme commander of the Khalsa forces of which Hari Singh Nalwa was an important general, and the coins at Peshawar were struck under his orders.[72] The legend on the reverse is 'Zarb Peshawar Jalus - San 1894'. Here 'san' means the year and 'Sanat-i-Jalus' is not an actual word; rather it is an incorrect construction. Rodgers's view on the double dating on Sikh coins for the 1884 and 1885 Sambat series is only a conjecture and is not supported by reliable evidence. The matter requires further investigation.

We have examined the major drawbacks in Rodgers's study of Sikh coins and left out the minor errors as being normal mistakes in such studies, particularly in their initial stages. The most painful and undesirable aspect has been the prejudice and distorted vision of Rodgers regarding the Sikhs and their religious leaders and institutions. It is unpardonable in the case of a historian of any merit.

NOTES

1. C.H. Payne, *A Short History of the Sikhs*, Punjab: Languages Department, rpt., 1970, p. 212.
2. Khushwant Singh, *History of Sikhs*, vol. II, New Delhi: Oxford University Press, 1963, p. 82.
3. Foreign Department, General Report, *Administration of Punjab Territories 1849-51*, Calcutta, 1856, p. 34.
4. Sethi, Bhat and Holkar, *A Study of Holkar State Coinage*, Indore, 1976, p. lxx
5. C.J. Rodgers, 'On the Coins of the Sikhs', *Journal of Asiatic Society of Bengal*, vol. L, Calcutta, 1881, p. 91.
   That the metal is good is shown by the Nanak Shahi rupees being in constant demand for the manufacture of ornaments and from the fact that they sell for 17 *annas* each, on account of the excellent silver they contain.

6. G.S. Chhabra, *Advanced History of Sikhs*, vol. II, Jullandhar: Parkash Brothers, 1976, p. 327.

7. Evans Bell, *Annexation of Punjab*, Punjab: Languages Department, rpt., 1970, p. 6.

8. G.S. Dhillon, *Insights into Sikh Religion and History*, Chandigarh: Singh & Singh Publication, 1991, pp. 125-8.

9. Khushwant Singh, op. cit., p. 96.

10. Ibid., p. 96; *Administrative Report Punjab Territories*, op. cit., p. 81.

11. Hari Ram Gupta, *History of Sikhs*, vol. II, New Delhi: Munshiram Manoharlal, 1978, p. 38.

12. Ibid., p. 115.

13. Khushwant Singh, op. cit., p. 96.

14. G.S. Dhillon, op. cit., p. 126.

15. Khushwant Singh, op. cit., p. 195; G.S. Dhillon, op. cit., p. 12.

16. G.S. Dhillon, op. cit., p. 127.

17. Ibid., p. 127.

18. J.C. Archer, *The Sikhs*, Princeton, NJ, USA, 1946, p. 266.

19. Madanjit Kaur, 'Sikh Reaction to Trumpp's translation of *Adi Granth*', *Panjab History Conference*, Patiala University, 1980, p. 219.

20. Macauliffe, *Sikh Religion*, vol. I, p. vii.

21. G.S. Dhillon, op. cit., p. 128.

22. Jati Ram Gupta, 'Trade and Commerce in Panjab under Ranjit Singh', in *Maharaja Ranjit Singh: Politics, Society and Economy*, Patiala: Punjabi University, 1984, pp. 188-9.

23. P.L. Gupta and Sanjay Garg, *Coins of Dal Khalsa and Lahore Darbar in the Sheesh Mahal Museum, Patiala,* Chandigarh: Punjab Government, 1989, p. iii.

    Attention to Sikh coinage was given earliest by C.J. Rodgers, Principal, Teachers Training College at Amritsar, who was an ardent collector of coins. He had collected coins from all over Panjab with the help of his students who came from all parts of the province. He published a paper in the *Journal of Asiatic Society of Bengal* in 1881. After him, no serious attempt has been made to study this coins series. The few articles that were published during the last thirty years by some Indian scholars are based mostly on Rodgers's paper and contribute little to our knowledge. During the present decade Ken Wiggins and Stan Goron attempted to present some detailed study in their own way based on the coins that they came across. Later Hans Herrli attempted a book on the subject, but it is more in the nature of a compilation. None of these works may be said to be any kind of serious study of the subject.

24. C.J. Rodgers, 'On the Coins of the Sikhs', p. 93.

25. *Catalogue of Coins in the Government Museum Lahore*, Calcutta, 1891, pp. 92-7 and 123-7.

26. Ken Wiggins and Stan Goron, 'Gold and Silver Coinage of Sikhs', Inaugural Address, International Colloquium, Nasik: IIRNS, 1984, p. 121.

    It is just over a hundred years ago that Charles Rodgers in an informative but necessarily fairly brief article, it was somewhat lacking in detail and also not too well structured. Several important points appear to have escaped his notice and in spite of his long residence in the Panjab and his diligent search for coins, some types are not remarked upon. Despite these shortcomings, however, students and collectors of Indian coins have cause to be grateful to Rodgers for his initial study of the Sikh coinage for laying down the path for further investigation.

27. Hans Herrli, 'The Coins of the Sikhs', The manuscript was received from the author for comments on 28 August 1990.

28.	(i)	C.J. Brown, *Coins of India*, p. 107.
	(ii)	Baron von Hugel, *Travels*, p. 283.
	(iii)	Henry Princep, *Origin of Sikh Power in Panjab*, p. 67.
	(iv)	Jacquemont, *The Panjab Hundred Years Ago*, p. 55.
	(v)	J.D. Cunningham, *A History of Sikhs*, p. 159.
	(vi)	Griffin, *Maharaja Ranjit Singh*, p. 109.
	(vii)	Gulshan Lall Chopra, *The Punjab as a Sovereign State*, p. 15.
	(viii)	Bikramjit Hasrat, *Life and Times of Ranjit Singh*, p. 46.
	(ix)	Muhammad Latif, *History of Punjab*, p. 357.
	(x)	Khushwant Singh, *Ranjit Singh*, p. 53.
	(xi)	Waheed-ud-din, *The Real Ranjit Singh*, p. 173.
	(xii)	K.K. Khullar, *Maharaja Ranjit Singh*, p. 107.
	(xiii)	Gopal Singh, *History of Sikh People*, p. 450.
	(xiv)	Amarnath, *Zafarnama-e-Ranjit Singh*, p. 20.
	(xv)	Wiggins and Goron, 'Gold and Silver Coinage of Sikhs', p. 40.
	(xvi)	Hans Herrli, 'The Coins of the Sikhs', p. 62.
29.	C.J. Rodgers, 'On the Coins of the Sikhs', *Journal of Asiatic Society of Bengal*, Calcutta, 1881, pp. 73-96.
30.	Ibid., pp. 71-7.
31.	Hari Ram Gupta, *Sikh History*, vol. II, pp. 74-7.
32.	S.T. Das, *Indian Military: Its History and Development*, New Delhi: Sagar Publications, 1969, p. 73.
33.	S.S. Bal, *The Sikh Struggle for Independence and the Place of Sikh Sovereignty in Sikh Polity 1699-1765 in the Medieval Indian State*, Chandigarh: Panjab University, 1968, p. 131.
34.	(i)	Nanak founded a state, a dominion of God, a fortress of truth based on the indestructible foundation of the doctrine. *Guru Granth*, p. 966.
	(ii)	Jasbir Singh Ahluwalia, *The Sovereignty of Sikh Doctrine*, New Delhi: Bahri Publications, 1983, p. 23.
35.	J.S. Grewal, *Guru Nanak in History*, Chandigarh: Panjab University, 1979, p. 299.
	Bhai Gurdas often conceives of the position of the Guru in terms of sovereignty. The true Guru is the true king. The Guru's panth is his coin.
36.	*Sri Guru Granth*, pp. 1 and 459.
37.	*Sri Guru Granth*, p. 1245.
38.	In pursuing the Divine amid the normal life lies true commerce with God. Guru Nanak in *Siddh Goshti*.
39.	*Sura su pechanie jo larhe din ke hit. Purza purza kat mare kabu na charhe khet. Guru Granth*, p. 1105.
40.	Max Arthur Macauliffe, *The Sikh Religion*, vol. IV, New Delhi: S. Chand & Co., 1985, p. 2.
41.	Ibid., p. 3.
42.	Hari Ram Gupta, *Sikh Gurus*, New Delhi: Kapoor & Sons, 1973, p. 110.
43.	J.S. Grewal and S.S. Bal, *Guru Gobind Singh*, Chandigarh: Panjab University, 1967, pp. 121-6.
44.	Indu Bhushan Banerjee, *Evolution of Khalsa*, vol. II, Calcutta: A. Mukherjee & Co., 1980, p. 156.
45.	Ibid., p. 155.
46.	(i)	Koer Singh, *Gur Bilas Padshahi Das*, Patiala: Punjabi University, 1968, pp. 283-4.
	(ii)	Gian Singh Giani, 'Twarikh Guru Khalsa', '*Guru Gobind Singh Agya bhai Akal ke,*

tabhi chalayo panth, sab sekhon ko hukam hai Guru manio Granth. Guru Granth ji manao pargat Gurau di deh jo Prabhu ko milbo chahe khoj shabad me le'. This means: Under orders of the immortal God, the Panth has been started, all the Sikhs are ordered to accept the *Granth* as their Guru. Consider the *Guru Granth* as representing the Gurus' body. Those who desire to meet God should find him in the hymns of the *Guru Granth*.

47. Jasbir Singh Ahluwalia, *The Sovereignty of Sikh Doctrine*, p. 23.
The vesting of the divine aspect of temporal sovereignty into Society (Khalsa Panth) on the Baisakhi day of the year 1699 at Sri Anandpur Sahib through the baptismal ceremony of Amrit, a process that institutionalised the evolution of the Sikhs from a religious into a political entity as an instrument of history—expressing the will of God.
'The Khalsa is my determinate form. I am immanent in the Khalsa'—Guru Gobind Singh.

48. A.C. Banerjee, *The Sikh Gurus and the Sikh Religion*, New Delhi: Munshiram Manoharlal, 1983, p. 311.
Bhai Gurdas has stated that where there are two Sikhs there is a company of saints, where there are five Sikhs, there is God. Guru Hargobind had almost identified the disciple with the Guru when he said, deem the Sikh who comes to you with the Guru's name on his lips as your Guru.

49. Hari Ram Gupta, *Sikh Gurus*, p. 185.

50. Bhai Gurdas, *Varan*, ed. Bhai Vir Singh, Amritsar, 1962. Bhai Gurdas does not make any distinction between Guru Nanak and his successors, for they too are the Padshah of both *din* and *dunia* (Var 39, Pauri 3). Bhai Gurdas states, 'Nanak struck his coin in the world and instituted a pure panth. He installed Lehna as Guru, blending light with light and changed form, a wonder of wonders beyond everyone's comprehension' (Var 1, Pauri 45).

51. J.S. Grewal, *Guru Nanak in History,* Chandigarh: Panjab University, 1979, p. 301.
For Bhai Gurdas, the office of the Guru is more important than the person. . . . The position of the master and the disciple is interchangeable, precisely because in Bhai Gurdas' conception of the Guru, the office is distinct from the person. Much before the author of the 'Ramkali var, Padshahi Dasven ki' praised Guru Gobind Singh for becoming the chela as well as the Guru (of the Khalsa) the idea had been popularized by Bhai Gurdas (Var 41).

52. Indu Bhushan Banerjee, *Evolution of the Khalsa*, vol. II, p. 119.

53. G.C. Narang, *Transformation of Sikhism*, Lahore: New Book Society, 1945, p. 25.

54. Ganda Singh, *Life of Banda Bahadur Singh*, Amritsar: Khalsa College, 1935, p. 80.

55. The first legend was imprinted on the *Hukamnama* issued by Banda Bahadur to the Sikhs of Jaunpur in 1710.
The second legend is found on three coins located so far with Colonel Charles Panish, John Dyell, and Mrs Norman J. Puddester. The third legend stands recorded in the *Akhbar-i-Darbar-i-Mualla* AD 1710 and the *Hadiqat-ul-Aqalim*, Aligarh: Aligarh Muslim University, p. 148.

56. Hari Ram Gupta, 'The First Sikh Coin', *Proceedings of Indian History Congress*, 1938, Modern Section, pp. 427-33.

57. (i) Max Arthur Macauliffe, *Sikh Religion*, vol. V, p. 311.
(ii) Dharam Pal Astha, 'Poetry of Dasam Granth', Ph.D. thesis, Chandigarh: Panjab University, p. 26.

58. P.L. Gupta and Sanjay Garg, *The Coins of Dal Khalsa and Lahore Darbar*, p. 26.

59. Hari Ram Gupta, *History of Sikhs*, vol. II, p. 239.
He (Ahmad Shah) addressed Lehna Singh a letter offering him Governorship of Lahore

together with a present of dry fruits of Kabul. The latter sent Rahmatullah Beg of Village Modak declining the offer on the ground that in obeying him, he would fall in the eyes of his co-religionists. Lehna Singh returned his fruits also and sent to him instead a quantity of inferior kind of grain stating that the fruits were the food of kings, while he lived on the grain sent to him as a sample.

60. Hans Herrli, 'The Coins of the Sikhs', p. 51.
61. R.C. Temple, 'The Coins of the Modern Chiefs of Punjab', *Indian Antiquary*, vol. XVIII, Bombay, 1889, p. 335.
62. Ganesh Das Badhera, *Char Bagh-i-Pujab*, edited by Kirpal Singh, Amritsar: Khalsa College, 1965, p. 16.
63. *Standard Guide to South Asian Coins and Paper Money since 1556 AD*, Wisconsin, Krause Publication, p. 113.
64. Hans Herrli, 'The Coins of the Sikhs', p. 91.
65. P.L. Gupta, *The Coins of Dal Khalsa and Lahore Darbar*, pp. 39-44.
66. G.S. Dhillon, *Insights into Sikh Religion and History*, Chandigarh: Singh & Singh Publications, 1991, p. 91.
67. Raghubir Singh, 'The Conquest of Amritsar', *Journal of Sikh Studies*, vol. XIV (2), Amritsar: Guru Nanak Dev University, August 1987, p. 124.
68. Surinder Singh, 'Myth of Moran's Coins', abridged edition under publication with Oriental Numismatic Society, Surrey, U.K.
69. (i) Bikramjit Hasrat, *Life and Times of Ranjit Singh*, Hoshiarpur: VVRI, 1977, p. 46.
    (ii) Waheed-ud-din, *The Real Ranjit Singh*, Karachi: Lion Art Press, 1965, p. 173.
    And yet Moran is not known to have played any prominent part in the politics of the court of Ranjit Singh.
70. Baron von Hugel, *Travels in Kashmir and Panjab*, Punjab: Languages Department, 1970, p. 384.
71. Surinder Singh, 'Ranjit Singh's Effigy on Sikh Coins', *Newsletter of Oriental Numismatic Society*, Newsletter no. 123, Surrey, U.K., March-April 1990, p. 4.
72. Surinder Singh, 'Fallacy of Hari Singh Nalwa's Coins', *Studies in Sikhism and Comparative Religion*, New Delhi: Guru Nanak Foundation, 1991, p. 41.

Chronological Data on Sikh History (AD 1469 to 1850) with Spescial Reference to Sikh Coinage

Introduction

The study of coins, especially those pertaining to the recent past, requires constant reference to the recorded events and their dates in deciphering the legends, dates and other facts connected with these coins. Since extensive historical records are available, the dovetailing of these facts with those available on the coins becomes essential for a proper understanding and assessment of these coins. This aspect becomes more important in the case of Sikh coins because these have been struck in the name of the Sikh Gurus and not in the name of the Sikh rulers who issued these coins. At times even the mint names are not clear since the coins do not cover the entire die, and hence their deciphering becomes very difficult.

The concept of Sikh sovereignty is inherent in the Sikh doctrine. Guru Nanak preached resistance against religious and social oppression and this laid the foundation of the sovereignty of Sikh society. Guru Gobind Singh while abolishing the institution of personal Guruship placed spiritual sovereignty with the *Guru Granth* and temporal sovereignty with the Khalsa Panth. Hence, sovereignty has been held by the Sikhs in the name of their Gurus and its most important symbol, the coins, have invariably been struck in the name of their Gurus. This crucial aspect of Sikh coinage has been lost sight of by the European historians and numismatists and hence a number of discrepancies have crept into their accounts and assessment of these coins. It is only when we keep in mind the true concept of Sikh sovereignty that the proper pattern of Sikhs coins falls into place and can be properly understood. The various differences with the existing coinages become clear and the aberrations therein due to human failing become abundantly clear. The concept of Sikh sovereignty is the keynote to the understanding of Sikh coinage.

The Sikh coins bear the Bikrami Sambat whereas most historical accounts have used the Christian era and the conversion of one into the other has constantly to be carried out. Most scholars give some fragmentary accounts of the

Sikhs coins without any actual examination of these coins, even though such coins were readily available in the markets and in various collections, both with individuals and museums. Many inaccuracies have thus crept into the historical accounts. This makes the deciphering of these coins even more complicated and difficult. The chronological data given by the European numismatists, viz., C.J. Rodgers, S. Goron, and K. Wiggins are too meagre for a proper assessment of these coins.

An attempt has been made here to list briefly all the important events and their dates, both in the Bikrami and Christian era, from Guru Nanak to the annexation of the Lahore Darbar in a chronological order, with special reference to its usefulness in the study of Sikh coins. Where there are wider disagreements over certain dates, etc., these have been explained in footnotes. Otherwise the more plausible dates have been taken into account where the differences are of a minor nature. It is hoped that this will serve as a useful ready reckoner to those who are in the initial stage of the study of the Sikh coins.

SIKH GURUS 1469-1708

Sambat   AD
1526-96   1469-1539   GURU NANAK

Born on 15 April 1469[1] at Talwandi (Nankana Sahib).
Married at the age of 15 years.
Served as a storekeeper at Sultanpur for ten years.
Started his long tours at the age of 28 years.
   I. Tour: Panjab and eastern India upto Dacca.
   II. Tour: Southern India, including Sri Lanka.
   III. Tour: Himalayas, Kashmir, Garwal, etc.
   IV. Tour: Middle Eastern countries, including Baghdad.
   V. Tour: Within Panjab.
Guru Nanak visited Tibet, but opinion differ as to whether he went there via the Lahul Spiti route or via the Lachung Lachen (Sikkim) route.[2]
During his tours he visited numerous holy places of various religions, giving discourses and holding discussions with their leaders. He settled down in Kartarpur now in (Pakistan) around 1526 and lived the life of a householder. Guru Nanak started congregational prayers and established a free community kitchen, the institutions of *sangat* and *langar*. Guru Nanak preached the worship of one God (Akal Purakh), with complete participation in the life of a householder, moral and spiritual living, earning one's livelihood and sharing it with one's fellow beings, instead of penance, renunciation and individual salvation as the ultimate end of all religious endeavour. He preached against the religious tyranny of the Brahminical order and its elaborate ritualism and caste distinctions as well as the political tyranny of the Muslim rulers. He developed a new society totally bereft of caste barriers and with a sense of pride in an individual's effort to earn his living and sharing it with his fellow beings with love and without fear.
Shortly before his death, on 22 Sept. 1539, he nominated Lehna, his

most devout disciple as his successor. He named him Angad (literally meaning a limb of his own body) and bowed before him as his first disciple. In this way the spirit of Guru Nanak passed on to Guru Angad as a lamp lights a lamp, and in the same manner, every succeeding Guru passed on the Guruship to his successor, till the institution of personal Guruship was abolished by Guru Gobind Singh. He placed his spiritual sovereignty in the *Granth*, hereafter called *Guru Granth Sahib* and placed his temporal sovereignty in the Khalsa hereafter called Khalsa Panth.

1596-1609	1539-52	GURU ANGAD

Born in 1504, a devout disciple, was awarded the mantle of Guruship by Guru Nanak. He set up his headquarters at Khadur Sahib, improved upon the Gurmukhi script and opened a school for its formal teaching. He improved upon the institution of *langar*, he expired on 29 March 1552.

1609-31	1552-74	GURU AMAR DAS

Born in 1479, the mantle of Guruship was passed on to him by Guru Angad, shortly before his expiry. He set up his headquarters at Goindwal. Guru Amar Das created 22 '*manjis*' (administrative divisions) to attend to the needs of the people of those areas. The in-charge of these '*manjis*' addressed their congregations and collected offerings which were used to maintain *langars*, erect necessary buildings and to help the poor. He established the custom of the gathering of the Sikhs at his headquarters twice a year, i.e. in April on Baisakhi and in October/November on Diwali, after the harvesting seasons, for his disciples to meet him and each other.

Akbar, the great Mughal, is stated to have called on him and partook food in his *langar*. Guru Amar Das expired on 1 September 1574.

1631-8	1574-81	GURU RAM DAS

Born in 1534, he was invested with the mantle of Guruship by Guru Amar Das shortly before his expiry. He was married to Bibi Bhani, daughter of Guru Amar Das.

He set up his headquarters at a new place called Guru ka Chak or Chak Ram Das which later on became known as Amritsar.

He dug up a tank which was later on named the tank of nectar (Amritsar). Sri Chand, son of Guru Nanak, called on Guru Ram Das to join the Sikh mainstream, but Guru Ram Das did not agree to this request as the ascetic lifestyle of the Udasis, the disciples of Sri Chand, was against the basic tenets of Sikhism.

Guru Ram Das expired on 1 September 1581.

1638-63	1581-1606	GURU ARJAN DEV

Born in 1563, the mantle of Guruship was placed on his shoulders by Guru Ram Das shortly before his expiry. He was the youngest son of Guru Ram Das and his elder brother Prithia did not take kindly to his supercession and created all sorts of hindrances.

		Guru Arjan Dev enlarged the tank and constructed the Harimandir in its centre in 1589. This Harimandir, later on called the Golden Temple, has all along played a very vital role in the psyche of the Sikhs and has been the fountainhead of the zeal and spirit of the Sikh nation. He appointed '*masands*' as agents to propagate the Guru's preachings and to collect and pass on the contributions made by the disciples to the Guru at Amritsar. The voluntary contribution came to be known as '*daswandh*', meaning one-tenth of the annual income. The *manji* system, which had lost its utility, was thus replaced by the *masand* system.
1647	1590	Guru Arjan commenced the building of another tank at Tarn Taran, a *baoli* at Lahore, townships at Gobindpur and Kartarpur, a well with six Persian wheels at Chheharta, etc.
1655	1598	Akbar visited Guru Arjan Dev on 24 November 1598 and was deeply impressed by him.
1661	1604	Guru Arjan Dev procured copies of the hymns of the first three Gurus from Mohan, son of Guru Amar Das, and by adding the hymns of Guru Ram Das and his own, he compiled the '*Adi Granth*'. It also contains the hymns of some Sufi Muslim and Hindu saints mostly from the lower castes. The *Adi Granth* became the Holy Book of the Sikhs, like the Vedas for the Hindus, the Bible for the Christians, and the Quran for the Muslims.
		Guru Arjan Dev was arrested under the orders of Jahangir. He was most inhumanly tortured and died on 4 June 1606.
1663	1606	Guru Arjan Dev had encouraged trade and industry amongst the Sikhs. His disciples were too willing to pay the voluntary *daswandh* rather than the compulsory revenue to the Mughals. Costly presents and fine horses came as gifts and the number of buildings, the increased visitors, and the *langar*, etc., all added to the appearance of a princely state. Guru Arjan, however, lived a very simple and pious life and was called '*Sacha Padshah*' by his devotees. The inherent seeds of Sikh sovereignty thus started sprouting.

1663-1701	1606-44	**GURU HARGOBIND**
		Born in 1595, he became the sixth Guru in 1606 on the demise of Guru Arjan Dev.
		When Bhai Buddha, the master of ceremonies, tied the sword belt on the wrong side, the Guru called for another sword to be tied on the other side. He described the two swords as the representative of his '*miri*' (spiritual) and '*piri*' (temporal) powers. He maintained a regular Sikh armed force. Built the Akai Bunga, later on called the Akal Takht, where he sat in princely style, taking administrative decisions, bestowing favours, and even awarding punishments.
1666	1609	He was summoned to Delhi by Jahangir and imprisoned in Gwalior Fort.
		An understanding was reached and the Guru was released. He was responsible for the release of a large number of Rajput princes undergoing imprisonment in Gwalior Fort and has thus been called '*Bandi Chhor*'. The period of imprisonment has been differently stated by various historians as lasting from two to twelve years.[3]
		The Guru visited Srinagar and Baramulla and Sikh gurdwaras were raised there.

1690-1701	1833-44	Built a protection wall around Amritsar and a fort named Lohgarh. Guru Hargobind successfully fought six battles against minor Mughal forces. In the battle of Kartarpur, young Tyag Mal showed great valour and was honoured as Tegh Bahadur. The Guru moved to Kiratpur (Shivalik Hills), an area some what secure from Mughal attacks. Guru Hargobind expired on 3 March 1644.

1701-18	1644-61	**GURU HAR RAI**

Born in 1630, he was given the mantle of Guruship in 1644 by Guru Hargobind shortly before his death. The Guru spent about twelve years in Nahan state and then returned to Kiratpur. He was summoned to the Mughal court in Delhi but he sent his son Ram Rai in his place. He blessed Phul[4] during his visit to Nathana (cis-Sutlej area). Guru Hari Rai expired on 6 October 1661.

1718-21	1661-4	**GURU HARKRISHAN**

Born in 1657, he became the eighth Guru in 1661. Being of tender age, he was called a child saint. He was also summoned to the Mughal court at Delhi and camped with Raja Jai Singh in the Bangla Sahib area. He expired on 30 March 1664 due to smallpox.

1721-32	1664-75	**GURU TEGH BAHADUR**
		Born in 1621, he took over the mantle of Guruship in 1664. He was the youngest son of Guru Hargobind. Spend eight years in Patna and Assam.
1729	1672	Came back to Punjab and settled down at Makhowal (renamed Anandpur). He went to Aurangzeb to save Kashmiri Pandits from forcible conversion to Islam. He was arrested at Agra, taken to Delhi and imprisoned. He was asked to take up Islam, but on his refusal he was inhumanly tortured and executed along with his associates in Chandni Chowk, on 11 November 1675 under Aurangzeb's orders.

1732-65	1675-1708	**GURU GOBIND SINGH**
		Born in December 1666 at Patna, he took the mantle of Guruship in 1675 at the age of 9 years and 3 months.
1742-45	1685-8	Shifted his headquarters to Paonta Sahib. Fought the famous battle of Bhangani, defeating Fateh Shah of Garhwal.
1745	1688	Returned to Anandpur.
1756	1699	Created the Khalsa on 30 March 1699. Abolished the corrupt and debased institution of '*masands*'. Created a small regular army and fortified Anandpur with a ring of smaller fortresses around it.
1761	1704	Attacked by the combined forces of the hill rajas and the Mughal army of Sirhind, Lahore, and Delhi. The situation became critical after a few months' siege. Agreed to vacate Anandpur under agreement of safe passage.

He was treacherously attacked by the Mughal forces. In the various engagements he lost his mother, all his four sons, almost the entire Khalsa army, and most of the religious literature he was carrying. Guru Gobind Singh escaped to the Malwa desert almost all alone.

1762	1705	Settled down at Damdama Sahib, dictated the *Holy Granth*. Wrote the famous letter called *Zafarnama* to Aurangzeb.
1763	1706	Moved towards Deccan to meet Aurangzeb. While in Rajasthan, on his way to the Deccan, he received news of the death of Aurangzeb in March 1706.
	June 1706	Bahadur Shah became the next emperor.
	July 1706	Guru Gobind Singh was received with honour by Bahadur Shah at Agra.
1765	1708	The Guru moved to the Deccan and set up his camp at Nander, near the Mughal camp. He met Banda Bairagi who became his devout disciple. He sent Banda Bahadur to Punjab with an advisory council of trusted Sikhs to chastise the Sirhind ruler and help the Sikh to regain lost territories. The Guru was treacherously attacked by some Pathan agents of the governor of Sirhind or the Mughal emperor.

Shortly before his demise, the personal Guruship was abolished, the Guru advised the Sikhs to henceforth seek spiritual guidance from the *Holy Granth*. He placed his temporal sovereignty in the Khalsa as a whole. The abolition of the institution of personal Guruship appear to have decided in 1699 when the Guru established the Khalsa and after administering the '*Khanda Pahul*' to his five disciples, he himself took *Khanda Pahul* from them in the same manner, whereby the Guru also became the disciple. The personal Guruship stood formally abolished after the death of Guru Gobind Singh. Guru Gobind Singh was a great scholar, a brave warrior, and a great commander. He wrote many compositions which are called the '*Dasam Granth*'. He fought 20 battles in 30 years. He breathed a new spirit in his Khalsa disciples that has been evident in their exemplary courage for the last two centuries. Khushwaqt Rai in his *History of Sikhs* states that Guru Gobind Singh issued a coin with the legend, '*Deg Tegh Fateh, Nusrat Baidarang, Yaft uz Nanak Guru Gobind Singh*'.[5]

Macauliffe states that the Guru spoke the above couplet while breathing his last.[6]

Muhammad Latif states that Guru Gobind Singh used a seal in the Gurmukhi script with the above legend.[7]

It was in the possession of the '*pujaris*'.

No such coin nor the seal imprint has come to notice so far and these accounts do not appear to be correct.

BANDA BAHADUR 1708-1716

1757-73	1708-16	BANDA BAHADUR

Born around 1700 at Rajouri in a Rajput family, he was named Lachhman Das. While still a young man, he become an ascetic (*bairagi*). He went around practicing occult powers and finally settled down on the banks of the Godavari river, near Nander in the Deccan.

1765	1708	Banda came in contact with Guru Gobind Singh and became a devout disciple of the Guru. Historians differ as to whether or not he was baptized into the Khalsa by Guru Gobind Singh. No authentic evidence is available in this regard.
	Sept. 1708	Guru Gobind Singh made Banda Bahadur the commander of the Sikh forces, gave him an advisory council of five trusted Sikhs and about 25 soldiers. 'Hukmnamas' instructing Sikhs to join Banda Bahadur were also given.
1766	Jan. 1709	Banda Bahadur reached Punjab, and Sikhs in large numbers started joining him. The news of the demise of Guru Gobind Singh at the hands of the Pathans had further incited them and about 50,000 Sikhs came under his flag at Sadhaura in a few months' time. Banda ravaged many towns and established his 'thanas', i.e. posts.
1767	13 May 1710	Famous battle of Chapar Cheri fought near Sirhind. Banda Bahadur defeated and killed Wazir Khan, the governor of Sirhind. The town was sacked. Banda Bahadur sacked Saharanpur and renamed it Bhanagar. Banda Bahadur established his camp at Mukhlispur (a small fortress constructed by Mukhlis Khan for camping during hunts in the Shivalik Hills.) Banda Bahadur repaired the fortress and renamed it Lohgarh. Banda Bahadur raised another small fortress for himself and few soldiers on a nearby hillock another 600 ft. higher which was named Sitaragarh from where he watched the troops and issued oral orders which were clearly heard in Lohgarh and the same is clearly heard till date. Banda Bahadur struck coins in the name of Gurus and adopted a state seal also in the Guru's name.

Coin
Obverse:
سکہ زد بر ہر دو عالم ـ تیغ نانک واہب است ـ
فتح گوبند شاہ شاہاں ـ فضل سچا صاحب است ـ

Reverse:
ضرب با امان الدہر مصورت شہر زینت التخت خالصہ مبارک بخت ـ ۰

William Irvine and Ganda Singh refer to the above legend on Banda Bahadur's coins, but neither of them has cited the primary source of their information.[8]

Hadiqat-al-Aqalim states that the Sikhs struck coins with the legend.[9]

عظمتِ گورو نانک ـ ہم ظاہر و ہم باطن است ـ
بادشاہ دین و دنیا ـ آپ سچا صاحب است ـ

A newswriter of Jaipur states that the above legend has been used on a seal and not on a coin.[10]

The actual couplet on the seal of Banda Bahadur that has come down to us imprinted on his *hukmnamas* is: [11]

دیگ تیغ فتح نصرت بیدرنگ ـ یافت از نانک گورو گوبند سنگھ ـ

The coins that have been located so far are three coins with the first legend but with slight modifications.[12] Banda Bahadur is reported to have sent two crore rupees to Sirmaur for safe custody.

	30.11.1710	Mahabat Khan captured the Lohgarh Fort after the Sikh forces withdrew from Sadhaura and Lohgarh. Amir Khan occupied Sirhind.
1768	March 1711	Sikhs assembled near Lahore.
	April 1711	Banda Bahadur reorganized his forces and camped at Kalanaur.
	June 1711	Another fierce battle between Banda Bahadur and Amir Khan, heavy casualties on both sides.
1769	Jan. 1712	Banda Bahadur moved into the Shivalik Hills.
	Oct. 1712	Banda Bahadur recaptured Sirhind, Sadhaura and Lohgarh.
1770	Jan. 1713	Farrukh Siyar became the Mughal emperor.
	June 1713	A fierce battle fought at Sadhaura and after four months' siege, Banda Bahadur withdrew his forces to Lohgarh and from there escaped into the Shivalik Hills.
1772	March 1715	Banda Bahadur again came to Punjab with reorganized forces.
	June 1715	A fierce fight took place between Banda Bahadur and Abdus Samad Khan. Banda Bahadur and his men were besieged in the Gurdas Nangal fortress near Gurdaspur. The siege lasted for six months.
	Dec. 1715	The entire food stock and ammunition with Banda Bahadur was exhausted. The Mughal forces captured Banda Bahadur with 740 men. All taken to Delhi.
1773	10.6.1716	Banda Bahadur and his infant son executed after undergoing great torture. [Banda Bahadur set up a fully sovereign Sikh state, with its own coinage as the symbol of its sovereignty. Although it lasted for a very brief period of a few years, it gave the Sikhs a goal to be achieved and they strove to attain this goal with great devotion and against extreme odds. The struggle lasted for half a century and Sikh sovereignty was once again established over Punjab in 1765.]

EXTREME PERSECUTION OF THE SIKHS 1716-1745

1773-1802	1716-45	Farrukh Siyar ordered the annihilation of the Sikhs in Punjab.
1773	1716	The governors of Lahore, Sirhind and Jammu vied with each other in exterminating Sikhs from their areas. Rs. 20/- fixed as prize money for every Sikh head. Sikhs hid themselves in jungles, hills, and deserts.
1775	1718	Sikhs organized themselves into bands and started looting rich traders and government officials in nearby villages and towns.
1782	1725	Abdus Samad Khan, governor of Lahore, failed to exterminate the Sikhs.
1790	1733	Zakarya Khan failed to subdue the Sikhs, sent a deputation to the Sikhs to accept peace. The Sikhs rejected the peace offer. However, the 'Khilat' was thrust upon a simple Sikh youth, Kapur Singh, who thus became Nawab Kapur Singh with a *jagir*, but without any obligation to attend Mughal court.
1791	1734	Sikhs move into Amritsar.

1792	1735	Budha Dal and Taruna Dal created for defence against Mughal forces. Sikhs resort to guerrilla attacks in spite of Zakarya Khan's peace offer and *jagir*, etc. Zakarya Khan confiscated the *jagir* and mounted pressure against the Sikhs.

Kapur Singh became the leader of the Sikhs.

1796	1739	Nadir Shah invaded India and looted Delhi. Nadir Shah annexed the trans-Indus areas of the Mughal Empire, viz., Afghanistan, the North Western Province, Sindh, Gujarat, and Sialkot to his Persian Empire. Due to the disturbed conditions, the Sikhs again started their guerrilla attacks against state officials, traders and government cash in transit.

Sikhs attacked the rear of Nadir Shah's army and looted his baggage train. Many prisoners were also released. The surprise raids occurred mostly at the time when the Afghans were fording swollen rivers.[13]

1797	1740	After the departure of Nadir Shah, Zakarya Khan again mounted pressure against the Sikhs. Many Sikhs were caught and executed at 'Nikhas' in Lahore, later on named 'Shahid Ganj' by the Sikhs. Sikhs were stopped from gathering at Amritsar. The holy place was given to a debased Muslim, Massa Rangar, who started using it as a place of vice and pleasure.
	1740	Within a month's time, the Sikhs killed Massa Rangar in a daring attack.
1798	1741	Zakarya Khan again tried to persuade the Sikhs to a peaceful existence under his rule.

The Sikhs turned down all such offers.

1802	1745	Zakarya Khan died in 1745.
1803	1746	Yahiya Khan became the governor of Lahore. Jaspal Rai, brother of Lakhpat Rai, was killed in a Sikh raid.

Lakhpat Rai, the Mughal minister, arranged for the great persecution of the Sikhs.

	May 1746	A large Mughal army assembled under the command of Yahiya Khan and Lakhpat Rai. The encounter took place with about 15,000 Sikhs in which about 10,000 Sikhs perished. This is called the 'Chhota Ghalughara'.
1804	March 1747	Yahiya Khan was ousted by his brother Shah Nawaz Khan, and Lakhpat Rai was put in prison.

SIKH MISLS 1745-1799

1802	1745	Sikh bands became fairly well established in various parts of Punjab under their leaders; these groups were called *misls*.[14]

Rise of the Phulkian families in Malwa.[15]

Ala Singh became the premier Malwa Sardar.

1804	1747	The Sikhs built a small fort 'Ram Rauni', near Amritsar.
1804	1747	First invasion of Ahmad Shah.
1805	1748	Ahmad Shah advanced upto Sirhind, was defeated by Mughal forces in March 1748 near Sirhind, and went back to Afghanistan via Lahore.

The Sikhs attacked his rear and baggage train at various places and seized a large booty as baggage, arms, horses, camels, etc.

	March 1748	Sikhs assembled at Amritsar on Baisakhi day.

The entire Sikh force was named the Dal Khalsa under the leadership of Jassa Singh Ahluwalia. Sikhs were constituted into 11 major groups and 65 groups in all, with varying strengths.

	April 1748	Muin-ul-Mulk appointed governor of Punjab. Sikhs called him Mir Manu.
1806	1748-50	Second invasion of Ahmad Shah.
		Mir Manu submitted to Ahmad Shah, ceded certain districts, paid 14 lakh rupees as tribute. Ahmad Shah returned to Qandahar. During the ensuing chaos the Sikhs raided Lahore and occupied Kotwali for a short time.
1807	1750	Mir Manu enraged over the Sikh raids, sent raiding parties against the Sikhs.
		Fixed ten rupees as prize money for every Sikh head.
1808-9	1751-2	Third invasion of Ahmad Shah.
		Ahmad Shah reached Lahore and defeated the Mughal forces. Mir Manu became his vassal. Ahmad Shah conquered Kashmir on his way back and annexed Punjab and Kashmir to his empire. During the ensuing chaos, the Sikhs raided the Bari and Jullandhar Doabs. Collected booty from Hissar and Sonepat.
1809	1752	Ala Singh founded Patiala.
1809-10	1752-3	Mir Manu recommended the persecution of the Sikhs after the departure of Ahmad Shah. About 30,000 Sikhs were killed under sustained pressure, yet the spirit of the Khalsa remained undaunted and could not be subdued.
	Nov. 1753	Mir Manu died of poisoning.
1810-14	1753-7	The weak government was a natural assistance to the Sikhs in commencing their activities once again with increased intensity.
1811	1754	Jassa Singh Tokha rebuilt 'Ram Rauni' and named it Ramgarh. The *misl* got the name 'Ramgarhia'. Charat Singh and Jai Singh entered Lahore and plundered rich merchants.
1811-13	1754-6	The Dal Khalsa ravaged Sirhind and Ambala districts. The Sikhs settled in Batala, Kalanaur and the surrounding areas of Amritsar.
		The Sikhs established a protection system (*rakhi*), taking one-fifth of the produce half yearly after harvesting season. Thus commenced the regular territorial hold of the Sikhs and their regular revenue system, a step towards the establishment of their sovereignty.
1813-14	1756-7	Fourth invasion of Ahmad Shah.
		Ahmad Shah reached Delhi, carried out a systematic plunder of the city. Returned back due to the outbreak of cholera epidemic among his troops.
		Sirhind was annexed to his empire.
1814	1757	Ala Singh of Patiala submitted to Ahmad Shah. Sikhs attacked Timur Shah (his son) at Sunam and relieved him of half of his treasure.
		Sikhs also attacked the rear of the Afghan troops and relieved them of a lot of their loot.
		Ahmad Shah sent an expedition against the Sikhs, destroyed the Harimandir at Amritsar, and filled the holy tank with debris.
		Jahan Khan made governor of Lahore.
	Oct. 1757	Sikhs collected at Amritsar to celebrate Diwali.
		Jahan Khan attacked them repeatedly, in which Baba Deep Singh was killed.
1815	Jan. 1758	Adena Beg with Sikh help started expelling the Afghans from their outposts.
		Abed Khan, Afghan governor of Lahore, was attacked and killed by the Sikhs.
		Complete lawlessness prevailed in Punjab.

	Mar. 1758	Adena Beg invited the Marathas for help against the Afghans. The Marathas invaded Sirhind and defeated Abdus Samad Khan.
		Jahan Khan left Lahore without a fight.
		The retreating Afghans were taken prisoners by the Sikhs and brought to Amritsar to clean the holy tank.
	Sept. 1758	Adena Beg died in September 1758.
		Sikhs occupied almost the entire Punjab.
		The *misls* became well established and numerous mud forts were constructed all over Punjab for their defence.
1871	1760	The Marathas occupied Delhi.
	Nov. 1760	The Sikhs attacked Lahore and plundered part of the city. They took 30,000 rupees for '*Karah Parshad*'.
1817-18	1760-1	Fifth invasion of Ahmad Shah.
	14.1.1761	The Marathas were defeated in the historic Third Battle of Panipat.
		The Maratha confederacy broke up.
		Scindia of Gwalior, Gaekwad of Baroda, and Holkar of Indore owed only nominal allegiance to the Peshwa. Bhonsle of Nagpur became independent.
	Mar. 1761	Ala Singh of Patiala submitted to Ahmad Shah, paid 4 lakh rupees as tribute, and agreed to pay an annual tribute of 5 lakh rupees. Ahmad Shah instructed the governor of Sirhind not to interfere in the territories of Ala Singh, which consisted of about 700 towns and villages.
		The Sikhs greatly harassed Ahmad Shah on his return journey. Many prisoners were got released at the Goindwal ferry.
	June 1761	The Sikhs defeated Mirza Khan of Char Mahal.
		Invaded and devastated Sirhind.
		Attacked and plundered Malerkotla.
	Aug. 1761	Nur-ud-din was sent by Ahmad Shah to crush the Sikhs but was defeated at Sialkot.
		Abed Khan was defeated at Gujranwala, his arms and ammunition looted by the Sikhs.
	Nov. 1761	Sikhs assembled for Diwali at Amritsar.
		The Dal Khalsa under Jassa Singh Ahluwalia attacked Lahore and occupied the fort for some time.
		The Sikhs are alleged to have struck rupee coin from the Lahore mint.[16]
1819	Jan. 1762	Sixth invasion of Ahmad Shah.
		It was primarily against the Sikhs. The Sikhs had besieged Jandiala. Ahmad Shah reached Jandiala by forced marches. In the meantime the Sikhs had moved to Malerkotla.
		Ahmad Shah surprised them at Kup and the two armies met in a straight fight. The Sikhs were encumbered with families and camp followers and lost about 20,000 men. The battle is called 'Wada Gallughara'.
		Ahmad Shah came to Amritsar and once again destroyed the Harimandir and the holy tank.
		Ahmad Shah stayed the entire year 1762 in Panjab to subdue and crush the Sikhs, but he totally failed in the objective.
	May 1762	Sikhs invaded Sirhind and took a heavy tribute.
	Oct. 1762	Sikhs came to Amritsar to celebrate Diwali.
		They were 60,000 armed men under Jassa Singh Ahluwalia.
		Ahmad Shah came from Lahore and the two armies fought for the whole day.

		Ahmad Shah sensing Sikh superiority ran back to Lahore during the ensuing night.
	Dec. 1762	Sikhs made repeated attacks on the flanks and the rear of the retreating Afghan army.
1820	Jan. 1763	The Sikhs reorganized themselves into the Budha Dal and Taruna Dal with younger leaders to defend Amritsar.
	Feb. 1763	The Sikhs attacked Lahore and brought back Afghan prisoners to clean the holy tank.
	May 1763	Kasur was invaded and plundered.
	June 1763	Sikhs subdued almost the entire Jullandhar Doab.
	Nov. 1763	Ahmad Shah's general Jahan Khan was defeated at Wazirabad.
	Dec. 1763	Malerkotla was attacked and looted.
1821	Jan. 1764	Sikhs attacked Kheri, Morindah, Garaundha, Kurali, etc., and plundered these towns.
		Zain Khan was attacked and killed.
		Sirhind was attacked and the city plundered, the walls of the fort were pulled down.
		Lahore attacked and Kabuli Khan subdued and made to pay tribute.
	Mar. 1764	Rohtas Fort captured.
		Sarbuland Khan, governor of Kashmir, came to subdue the Sikhs, but was defeated and kept prisoner in the Rohtas Fort.
		Sikhs under Jassa Singh, Khushal Singh, and Baghel Singh crossed the Yamuna with 40,000 men and plundered Saharanpur, Shamli, Kandlah, Ambi, Najibabad, Deoband, Muzaffarnagar, Muradabad, Chaudausi and Garh Mukteshwar.
		Najib-ud-daula paid Rs. 11 lakhs as hush money to prevent the further devastation of his territories.
	June 1764	The Sikhs under Hari Singh Bhangi marched on to Multan, and plundered the city. They also entered Derajat and plundered its towns.
	Dec. 1764	Sikhs under Jassa Singh crossed the Yamuna again and attacked Nijib-ud-daula's territories.
1821-2	Dec. 1764	Seventh invasion of Ahmad Shah.
	March 1765	Reached Lahore via Eminabad.
		Sikhs attacked his outposts and assembled at Amritsar.
	Jan. 1765	Ahmad Shah advanced on Amritsar but the Sikhs avoided a direct fight. Ahmad Shah destroyed the Harimandir and the holy tank and returned to Lahore.
		Ahmad Shah moved to Jandiala and then to Batala.
		At both places the Sikhs attacked and harassed his flanks.
		Ala Singh again submitted to Ahmad Shah and agreed to pay annual tribute.
	Mar. 1765	Sikhs returned from the trans-Yamuna territories and assembled in Amritsar to face the Afghans. Pitched battles were fought for seven days.
		Heavy casualties were suffered by both sides.
		Sikhs used their guerrilla tactics of running battles and so demoralized Ahmad Shah that he made a hasty retreat to Afghanistan.
	16 May 1765	Sikhs assembled at Amritsar.
		Gurmata passed to regain more territories, occupy Lahore, and strike coins of their own in the name of their Gurus as a symbol of the sovereignty of the Khalsa.

Lahna Singh, Gujjar Singh, and Sobha Singh occupied Lahore and divided the city into three administrative zones each under a *sardar*. Silver rupee struck from the Lahore mint.[17]

دیگ تیغ و فتح نصرت بیدرنگ – یافت از نانک گرو گوبند سنگه
ضرب دارالسلطنت لاهور سکه بت مینت مانوس جلوس ۱۸۲۲ –

	Oct. 1765	Sikhs crossed the Yamuna and plundered Najib-ud-daula's territories. The rival forces met at Shamli. The Sikhs resorted to surprise attacks and greatly harassed Najib-ud-daula.
	Jan. 1766	Sikhs plundered Rewari and certain territories of Jaipur.
1823	Apr. 1766	Najib-ud-daula defeated the Sikhs in a pitched battle at Kamilla Ghat. Sikhs retreated to Punjab.
1823-4	1766-7	Eighth invasion of Ahmad Shah. Ahmad Shah defeated the Sikhs at Rohtas. Sikhs vacated Lahore which was occupied by Ahmad Shah. Ahmad Shah was keen to plunder Delhi, but without fighting with the Sikhs. He offered Sikhs the governership of Lahore as his vassals. Sikhs rejected his offer. Ahmad Shah moved his army to Sirhind. Sikhs attacked his camp at Lahore and Ahmad Shah had to return to Lahore. Ahmad Shah realized his inability to subdue the Sikhs.
1824	Mar. 1767	Amar Singh of Patiala submitted to Ahmad Shah. He was given the title of *Raja-i-Rajgan*, the *subdedari* of Sirhind, and the right to mint Durrani currency.
1824	May 1767	Sikhs ravaged Najib-ud-daula's territories across the Yamuna but were driven back.
1824	July 1767	Ahmad Shah turned back totally disappointed. Sikhs inflicted heavy casualties on his army by surprise attacks on his flanks and rear. The Afghan governor handed over Lahore to the Sikhs immediately after the departure of Ahmad Shah.
1824	Dec. 1767	The Sikhs attacked the Gangetic Doab. They were pushed back by Najib-ud-daula. Najib, however, admitted to being beaten by the Sikhs with their repeated attacks.
1825-6	Dec. 1768-9	Ninth invasion of Ahmad Shah. Ahmad Shah reached Jhelam. Sikhs were hovering on his flanks and rear while avoiding a frontal attack. Ahmad Shah realized his inability to face the Sikhs, and turned back to Afghanistan.
1826-7	Dec. 1769-70	Ahmad Shah came upto Peshawar, but realizing Sikh superiority he turned back. Ahmad Shah's plans to attack India in the succeeding two years, i.e. 1770 and 1771 but it didn't materialize.

	Dec. 1770	Sikhs invaded and plundered Panipat.
1829	1772	Ahmad Shah died on 14 April 1772, the day on which Sikh forces had crossed Indus and plundered Peshawar city.
	May 1772	Jhanda Singh Bhangi invaded and occupied Multan city and fort.

Sikhs issued coins from Multan, in the name of their Gurus as a symbol of the sovereignty of the Khalsa.[18]

دیگ تیغ فتح نصرت بیدرنگ ۔ یافت از نانک گورو گو بندر سنگھ ۔

ضرب دارالامان ملتان سکمت ۱۸۲۹ جمیت مانوس جلوس ۔

1831	May 1774	Sikhs attacked Sirhind, Alikhan, the Mughal governor ran away to Delhi.
1831-2	1774-5	Sikhs plundered Shahdara adjoining Delhi.
		First invasion of Timur Shah.

Crossed the Indus in January 1775, defeated Sikhs at Rawalpindi. Turned back after realizing the strength of the Sikh forces.

1832	Apr. 1775	The Sikhs attacked Deoband and Kanjpura.
	Apr. 1775	Sahib Singh Bhangi, second son of the Gujjar Singh, married to Raj Kanwar, daughter of late Charat Singh. The marriage was arranged by Mihan Singh (father of Ranjit Singh) with great pomp and show. Sikhs issue coin from Amritsar.[19]

سکہ زد بر ہر دو عالم ۔ فضل سچا صاحب است ۔

فتح سچی گورو گو بندر سنگھ ۔ شاہ نانک واہب است ۔

ضرب سری امرتسر جیو ۔ سکمت ۱۸۳۲ جلوس تخت اکال بخت ۔

1833	May 1776	Rahim Khan Rohila attacked Jind.
		Gajpat Singh, ruler of Jind, sought help from the Majha Sardars who defeated Rahim Khan and occupied the Rohila territories of Hissar, Rohtak and Hansi.
	Oct. 1776	Sikhs plundered the crown lands near Delhi in league with Zabita Khan.
1834	Sept. 1777	Zabita Khan defeated by the Mughal army at Ghauspur.
1835	Sept. 1778	Sikhs plundered towns around Delhi as well as the outskirts of Delhi city.
1836	June 1779	Abdul Ahad (imperial minister) invaded the cis-Sutlej states with an army of 50,000 troops. Peace negotiations failed.
		Patiala army defeated.
		Jassa Singh Ahluwalia came with the Majha Sikhs.
		Abdul Ahad retreated to Delhi without fighting the Sikhs army.
		Sikhs greatly harassed the retreating Mughal army.
1822-37	1765-80	The Majha sardars became rich with plunder from the trans-Yamuna areas and differences started developing amongst them. Their combined forces became disunited against the Afghan attacks after 1765. The Afghan inability to subdue the Sikhs also bred complacency and thereafter led to differences amongst the Sikh *sardars*. Armed as they were, these differences developed into internecine warfare amongst the *misls* and thus a fine force began to disintegrate.[20]
1836-7	1779-80	Second invasion of Timur Shah.
		Timur Shah's armies had failed to conquer Multan in 1777 and 1778.

		He personally advanced on Multan, defeated the Sikhs who did not fight well and vacated the fort and the city.
	Feb. 1780	Timur Shah occupied Multan Fort and city on 8 February 1780.
	Nov. 1780	Ranjit Singh born on 13 November 1780.
1837-8	1780-1	Third invasion of Timur Shah.
		Reached Multan, subdued Bahawalpur.
		Returned home.
1838	1781	Sikhs attacked Multan city. Collected *rakhi* from the surrounding areas and returned.
	June 1781	Imperial forces moved under Shafi Khan to subdue the Sikhs.
		The campaign failed against the guerrilla warfare and the diversionary tactics of the Sikh forces.
	July 1781	Zabita Khan arranged peace with the Sikhs. The imperial government accepted Sikh sovereignty over the country west of the Yamuna and their right to claim *rakhi* in the Upper Ganga Doab.
1840	1783	The Raja of Garhwal was subdued and became a tributary of the Sikhs. Likewise, the raja of Nahan and the other smaller hill rajas became Sikh tributaries.
	Feb. 1783	Jassa Singh and Baghel Singh invaded and plundered Farukhabad.
		One-tenth of the plunder was spent on the renovation of the HariMandir Sahib in Amritsar.
	Mar. 1783	The Sikhs ravaged Delhi. The Sabzi Mandi, Malkagunj and Pahari Dhiraj areas were plundered. The Sikhs set up their headquarters at Majnu ka Tilla (on the outskirts of Delhi).
		The Sikhs entered the Red Fort on 13 March 1783.[21]
		Peace arrived at with Sikhs through Begam Samru.[22] Certain major concessions made to Sikhs.
		Baghel Singh controlled Delhi for 8 months during which period he constructed seven historic gurudwaras[23] in Delhi connected with Sikh Gurus.
	Dec. 1783	Baghel Singh's interview with emperor.
		Sikhs received with great honour. 12.5 per cent octroi decided to be sent annually to Baghel Singh at his headquarters at Chhalondi for keeping Delhi city safe from Sikh ravages.
	1783	There had been very little or no rain in 1781, 1782 and 1783 all over northern India, especially in Punjab. The '*chalisa*' famine of great intensity occurred.
		Great destitution and deaths occurred all over northern India.
		Tanks, wells, ponds dried up.
		The famine was followed by pestilence and cholera.
		The 'tittan' insect destroyed all vegetation.
		Great anarchy prevailed all over the country.
		Sikhs *sardars* ran *langars* to feed the poor.[24]
	20.10.1783	Jassa Singh died suddenly on 20 October 1783 while going to Amritsar. His death led to the disintegration of the Sikh confederacy and various *sardars* became independent. They struck coins, and about five different varieties from Amritsar and one variety from Anandgarh (probably Anandpur) are forthcoming but all these coins are not in the name of any *sardar* as sovereignty belonged to the Khalsa Panth and not to any individual ruler.

1841	1789	Warren Hastings expressed concern over the increasing Sikh dominance and contemplated means to restrict their advance.
1842	1785	Ranjit Singh suffered from smallpox.
		His face was disfigured and he lost his left eye.
	Nov. 1785	Fourth invasion of Timur Shah.
		Timur Shah came up to Peshawar. Sought assistance from the Sikhs to march on Delhi.
		The Sikhs refused safe passage.
		Timur Shah returned back from Peshawar.
1845-6	1788-9	Fifth invasion of Timur Shah.
		Crossed Indus at Attock, reached Multan in December 1788, entered Bahawalpur.
		Returned without a fight with the Sikhs.
1847	1790	Mihan Singh died in 1790. Some historians date this event to 1792.
	1790	Ranjit Singh became the head of the Sukharchakiya Misl on 15 April 1790.
1848	1791	Ranjit Singh occupied Akalgarh and Balaki Chak.
1850	1793	Timur Shah died in 1793.
1851	1794	First invasion of Shah Zaman.
		Reached Peshawar in December 1794. Came to Multan and retreated without facing the Sikhs.
1852	1795	Ranjit Singh annexed Bheeckochak and Shakargarh.
1852	1795	Second invasion of Shah Zaman.
		Reached Peshawar in November 1795.
		Occupied Rohtas. Before the Sikhs could put up a unified front, he turned back.
1853	1796	Ranjit Singh married to Mahtab Kaur, daughter of Sada Kaur. Shah Zaman sought safe passage to Delhi, but the Sikhs refused despite a promise of a part of the booty.
	Oct. 1796	Third invasion of Shah Zaman.
		Reached Peshawar in November 1796.
		Entered Lahore in January 1797.
		Sikh *sardars* vacated Lahore and assembled at Amritsar to face Shah Zaman.
		Shah Zaman was defeated at Amritsar and returned to Lahore.
		Sikhs cut off his supply lines.
		Shah Zaman turned back.
1854	1797	Ranjit Singh took control of his estates from his mother and Diwan Lakhpat Rai.
		Ranjit Singh appointed Dal Singh as his deputy.
1855	1798	Ranjit Singh conquered the Rasulnagar Fort and renamed it the Ram Nagar Fort.
1855-6	1798-9	Fourth invasion of Shah Zaman.
		Shah Zaman reached Peshawar in September 1798.
		The disunited Sikhs kept on retreating before his forces.
		Shah Zaman entered Lahore in November 1798.
		Shah Zaman was defeated at Amritsar by Ranjit Singh and other *sardars*.
		Shah Zaman went back to Lahore. The Sikhs cut off his supply lines and plundered his outposts.
		Shah Zaman turned back in January 1799.
1856	Jan. 1799	The Bhangi *sardars* reoccupied Lahore.

RANJIT SINGH 1799-1839

1856	1799	Ranjit Singh occupied Lahore with the help of Sada Kaur and local residents on 7 July 1799.
1857	1800	Ranjit Singh won the battle of Bhasian without any serious fight.[26] Jodh Singh Ramgarhia was defeated at Batala in a minor battle.
	Dec. 1800	East India Company sent its agent Munshi Yusaf Ali to the Darbar of Ranjit Singh.
1858	1801	Ranjit Singh was proclaimed ruler by Sahib Singh Bedi on Baisakhi day, the 12 April 1801. Sardar Ranjit Singh became Maharaja Ranjit Singh but he used the title Singh Sahib, Sarkarwala, etc., and never sat on a throne in respect to the concept of Sikh sovereignty, i.e. sovereignty belonged to the Khalsa Panth and not to any individual. Silver rupee coins were struck in the name of the Gurus. The legend 'Deg Tegh Fateh' of 1765 on the Lahore mint rupees was changed to the legend that existed on the Amritsar coins of 1775 and the coins of Banda Bahadur of 1710.

سکہ زد بر هر دو عالم مضل سچا صاحب است ـ
فتح گوبند سنگ شاه شاهان ـ تیغ نانک واسب است ـ
ضرب دارالسلطنت لاهور سنبت مینت مانوس جلوس ۱۸۵۹

		Ranjit Singh adopted the same couplet and exactly in the same form as it appeared on the 1784 Amritsar coins, without any modification at all in AD 1801.[27]
1857	1801	Ranjit Singh attacked Kasur, defeated Nizam-ud-din, and extracted nazrana. Attacked Jammu, plundered the town, accepted nazranas from various people. Attacked Dul Singh who had sided with the Bhangis, and occupied Akalgarh Fort. Ranjit Singh went in support of Sada Kaur against Kangra. Subdued the Nurpur ruler. Demolished the Sujanpur Fort near Pathankot. Occupied Dharamkot and Behrampur.
1859	1802	Ranjit Singh exchanged turbans with Fateh Singh Ahluwalia as a mark of perpetual friendship. Thus, the resources of the three leading misls—Sukharchakiya, Kanehiya and Ahluwalia—got pooled together. Ranjit Singh took Moran as a concubine in his harem. Prince Kharak Singh was born to Rani Raj Kaur. Ranjit Singh occupied Daska, Pathohar, Chinoit. Ranjit Singh invaded Kasur, Nawab paid nazrana. Pindi Bhatian and Phagwara conquered and given to Fateh Singh Ahluwalia.
1860	1803	First invasion of Multan by Ranjit Singh. Nawab Muzaffar Khan came out of Multan and paid nazrana. Sahiwal subdued and nazrana received. Jhang subdued and nazrana received.
1860	1803	Ranjit Singh marched upto Rawalpindi and subdued various minor principalities on his way and collected nazranas.
1861	1804	Isar Singh born to Rani Mehtab Kaur.

1861	1805	Expedition sent against Sansar Chand. Sansar Chand's forces expelled from Hoshiarpur and Bijwara. Second invasion of Multan by Ranjit Singh. Nawab submitted and paid *nazrana*. Ranjit Singh visited Haridwar on the occasion of the Kumbh Mela. Ranjit Singh marched against the Bhangis in Amritsar on the plea of collecting the Zam Zama gun. Sada Kaur and Fateh Singh helped him in occupying Bhangi estates without any bloodshed.[28] Gurdit Singh Bhangi and his mother Sukhan given minor estates.
1862	Oct. 1805	Jaswant Rao Holkar visited Amritsar seeking Ranjit Singh's help against the British. Various historians, mostly European, have stated that Ranjit Singh struck coins in the name of his courtesan Moran. This is a distortion of history and stands fully disproved.
1863	1806	First Anglo-Sikh Treaty between Ranjit Singh, Fateh Singh and Lord Lake. Ranjit Singh not to help Holkar and the British to respect the territories of Lahore Darbar. Jaswant Rao Holkar left Amritsar disappointed. First expedition of Ranjit Singh in the cis-Sutlej area over a dispute between Patiala and Nabha. Occupied Dalondi, received heavy *nazranas* from the cis-Sutlej chiefs. On his return, conquered Ludhiana, Jagraon and Raikot and distributed these territories amongst his friends. Sher Singh and Tara Singh born to Rani Mehtab Kaur. Gorkhas invaded Kangra. Diwan Maukam Chand appointed C-in-C of the Khalsa army. Ranjit Singh developed an ailment after a bath in the Katas tank and remained in Meanee village for a couple a months till his recovery.[29] It was the first paralytic attack.
1864	1807	Ranjit Singh attacked Kasur on 10 February 1807, as Qutbuddin had sided against Ranjit Singh in the battle of Bhasin. Qutbuddin was caught while running away. Ranjit Singh pardoned him and granted him a *jagir* at Mamdot. Kasur was annexed to the Lahore Darbar. Pasrur town annexed. Third invasion of Multan. Nawab submitted and paid heavy *nazrana*. Second incursion into the cis-Sutlej states over a dispute between Rani Aus Kaur and her husband. Dispute patched up by the parties. Ranjit Singh extracted heavy *nazrana*. Collected *nazranas* from the nearby chiefs. Occupied Wadni, Zira and Kot Kapura.
	Sept. 1807	Ranjit Singh met Charles Metcalfe, the British agent, on 11 September 1807 to draw out the terms of the treaty. Ranjit Singh occupied the estates of Tara Singh Gheba after his death. Widow of Tara Singh put up a minor fight at Rohan but was defeated. Ranjit Singh annexed the territories of the Nakai Misl adjoining Lahore and Kasur. By the close of 1807, Ranjit Singh had occupied most parts of Amritsar.

He closed all the mints operated by the misl chiefs and kept only one mint.

Coins (silver rupee) struck from Amritsar.[30]

1865	1808	Budh Singh Faizullahpuri was attacked by Maukam Chand and Fateh Singh.

Budh Singh escaped to the cis-Sutlej territories. His territories in Jullandhar Doab and Patti annexed.

Sialkot conquered from Jiwan Singh. Gujrat subdued, Sahib Singh became a tributary. Akhnur subdued and heavy *nazrana* received from Nawab Alam Khan.

Sheikhupura attacked and annexed.

Third expedition into the cis-Sutlej states.

Faridkot, Malerkotla, Ambala and Sahabad subdued.

The cis-Sutlej *sardars* sought British help to protect themselves from Ranjit Singh.

1866	1809	Treaty of Amritsar on 2 April 1809 between Ranjit Singh and the British.

Ranjit Singh desired to be the overlord of all the Sikh states.

The British gave protection to the cis-Sutlej states and confined Ranjit Singh to the Sutlej and thus came very close to Lahore. After quite a bit of sabre rattling, Ranjit Singh succumbed to British pressure. It was a major defeat for Ranjit Singh at the hands of the British.[31]

Ranjit Singh withdrew his forces from Faridkot and Malerkotla.

Ranjit Singh moved his troops to the hills areas. Pathankot subdued.

Jasrota, Chamba, and Basoli subdued, became tributaries and paid *nazranas*.

Sahib Singh Bhangi defeated and all his territories in Gujarat occupied.

Sikh troops sent to Kangra to help Sansar Chand against the Gorkhas.

Sansar Chand tried to make his peace with the Gorkhas, but Sada Kaur occupied the Kangra Fort, Haryana and surrounding territories, with Ram Kaur and Raj Kaur, the widows of Baghel Singh, confiscated and occupied by Ranjit Singh.

1866	1809	Shah Shujah expelled from Afghanistan. Elphinstone writes in 1809 that 'Almost the whole of the Panjab belongs to Ranjit Singh, who in 1805 was one of the many chiefs, but when we had passed, had acquired the sovereignty of all the Sikhs in the Panjab.'

1867	1810	Ranjit Singh occupied Wazirabad.

Khushal and Sahiwal areas subdued.

Meeting between Ranjit Singh and Shah Shujah.

Fourth invasion of Multan by Ranjit Singh.

Hari Singh Nalwa seriously injured. Peace made by nawab on payment of Rs. 2.50 lakhs as *nazrana*.

Bahawalpur subdued.

The British established their agency at Ludhiana.

1868	1811	Moran's influence declined and she was sent to Pathankot to remain away from Lahore.

Kotla Fort (between Nurpur and Kangra) annexed.

Ranjit Singh remained mostly at Lahore.

Muhyuddin (surgeon) treated him for certain boils.

1869	1812	Marriage of Prince Kharak Singh with the daughter of Jaimal Singh, the Kanehiya chief.

Orcherlony visited Lahore.

Joint expedition against Kashmir with Fateh Khan. Sikhs were deceived by Fateh Khan but gained knowledge about snow-bound Kashmir.

Shah Shujah secured by Sikhs.

Fifth invasion of Multan.

Nawab subdued and *nazrana* accepted.

Ranjit Singh occupied Attock Fort on an invitation from Jahandad Khan (brother of Ata Khan).

Occupation of Attock was of very valuable and strategic importance.

1870	1813	Second invasion of Kashmir under Diwan Maukam Chand. Sikhs were defeated at Shaupian.

Heavy rain and snow adversely affected them.

Apr. 1813 — Shah Shujah entered Lahore under Sikh protection. Ranjit Singh demanded the Koh-i-noor diamond as promised by Wafa Begum, wife of Shah Shujah.

June 1813 — Shah Shujah grudgingly parted with the Koh-i-noor.

Dost Mohd. did not appreciate the occupation of Attock by the Sikhs and attacked the Sikhs with his best troops. Dost Mohd. was defeated at Chuck and his camp looted at Hazro. It was a decisive victory of the Sikhs over the Afghans.

1871   1814   Shah Shujah escaped into British territories and sought asylum at Ludhiana.

1872   1815   Third invasion of Kashmir by Ranjit Singh.

Agha Khan (Raja of Rajouri) subdued. His fort and town sacked for his duplicity with the Sikh forces in 1813.

1873   1816   Sixth invasion of Multan by the Sikhs.

Nawab submitted and paid heavy *nazrana*.

Ramgarhia territories occupied after the death of Jodh Singh Ramgarhia.

Prince Kharak Singh made heir apparent in a grand *darbar* in Anarkali.

1874   1817   Seventh invasion of Multan.

Bhawani Das, the Sikh general, returned without a fight. He was fined and disgraced.

Ranjit Singh suffered some health problems.

1875   1818   Eighth and final invasion of Multan.

Sikhs had annexed all the surrounding territories of Khushab, Sahiwal, Mitha, Tiwana, Jhang.

Large forces with great preparation were sent, Multan city was occupied, and the fort besieged. The siege lasted six months.

The fort walls were breached and the fort occupied.[32] Nawab Muzaffar Khan died fighting along with his five sons.

Fort was garrisoned with Sikh forces.

Sikh coin struck from Multan.[33] This coin remained under issue till 1848.

Diwan Sawan Mal appointed *nizam* of Multan. The occupation of Multan gave an opening to the Sikhs into the Derajat and Sindh territories.

Peshawar occupied and *nazranas* accepted.

Charge of Peshawar given to Jahandad Khan, ex-governor of Peshawar.

Yar Mohd. expelled Jahandad Khan.

Sikh forces sent against Yar Mohd.

Yar Mohd. paid 50,000 rupees *nazrana* and became a tributary.

1876   1819   Fourth and final invasion of Kashmir.

		Birbal Dhar had given all intelligence about Afghan forces in Kashmir. Large-scale preparations made.
		Large stock of stores and ammunition stocked at strategic places.
		All petty rulers in the Jammu region had been subdued and made tributaries.
		Afghan forces defeated at Pir Panchal and Aliabad.
	May 1819	Sikh army under Misr Diwan Chand entered Srinagar.
		Jabbar Khan defeated at Shaupian and the victorious Sikh army under Misr Diwan Chand entered Srinagar.
		Misr Diwan Chand given title of Fateh-i-Nusrat and made governor of Kashmir.
		Sikh coins struck from Srinagar.[34]
		Diwan Moti Ram replaced Misr Diwan Chand as governor of Kashmir by the end of 1819.
1877	1820	After the occupation of Multan and Kashmir, Ranjit Singh turned his attention to the Derajat areas. Ranjit Singh expelled Zaman Khan from Dera Ghazi Khan and placed it under the nawab of Bahawalpur in return for a large sum of money.
		Ranjit Singh suffered from intermittent fever.
		William Moorcraft visited Lahore.
		Hari Singh Nalwa made governor of Kashmir.
1878	1821	Kanwar Nau Nihal Singh born in February 1821.
		Ranjit Singh invaded Mankera, the territory was annexed, and Nawab Haji Ahmad Khan was given some *jagir* elsewhere. All his territories of Bannu, Tonk, Liya and Kundian came under Sikh occupation.
		Dera Ismail Khan occupied by the Sikh forces and placed under their direct control.
	Dec. 1821	Hari Singh Nalwa defeated 30,000 Afghans with his 7,000 troops at Mangli Pass on his way back from Kashmir.
1879	1822	Allard and Ventura joined the Lahore Darbar.
		Gulab Singh appointed raja of Jammu.
		Minor crisis at Wadni (in the cis-Sutlej area) with the British.
		Hari Singh Nalwa made governor of Hazara.
		Hari Singh Nalwa occupied Mansehra and Deoband and annexed these territories to Hazara.
		Hari Singh Nalwa constructed a fort and town at Haripur (Hazara).
		Dera Ghazi Khan finally annexed.
		A strong fort built at Girang and garrisoned with Sikh troops.
1880	1823	Sikh troops sent towards Sindh on the pretext of subduing the Baluchi tribals. The *amirs* of Sindh paid *nazranas*.
		Sada Kaur imprisoned and asked to retire from public life.
1881	1824	Azim Khan couldn't tolerate his brother Yar Mohd. as a tributory of the Sikhs.
		Azim Khan collected a large Pathan force to expel the Sikhs.
		The Pathans under Azim Khan met the Sikh forces under Ranjit Singh with Hari Singh Nalwa and other *sardars* at Naushera.
		A fierce battle was fought and the Sikh army won a decisive victory over the Afghans, about 4,000 Afghans and 2,000 Sikhs killed.
		Sikh leader Akali Phula Singh was killed in action. Ranjit Singh occupied Peshawar and made it over to Yar Mohd. once again.

Nazranas and tributes collected.

Sansar Chand Katoch died.

Vakils of the *amirs* of Sindh visited Lahore. Ranjit Singh demanded annual tribute that was earlier paid to the Afghan rulers. The *amirs*, however, resisted the demand.

1882	1825	Ranjit Singh and Fateh Singh get estranged.

Misr Diwan Chand died.

Ranjit Singh sent troops towards Sindh but they were recalled due to famine conditions.

Dr. Murry sent to Lahore to treat Maharaja Ranjit Singh who had suffered a severe paralytic attack.

Agent of the Nizam of Hyderabad visited the Lahore court. Diwan Chuni Lal made governor of Kashmir.

1883	1826	No serious military activity due to the increasing ill health of Ranjit Singh.

Dr. Murray stayed for 8 months treating Ranjit Singh for his paralytic attack.

Wahhabi insurgency under Sayad Ahmad emerged in Pathan and Afghan tribal areas.

1884	1827	Diwan Kirpa Ram appointed governor of Kashmir.

Fateh Singh Ahluwalia crossed over to the cis-Sutlej territories.

Capt. Wade, political agent at Ludhiana, visited Lahore.

Deputation of the Lahore Darbar met Lord Amherst, Governor-General, at Simla.

Court and Avitable joined the Lahore Darbar forces.

Hari Singh defeated the Afghans at Saidu.

1885	1828	Dhian Singh given the title of Raja-i-Rajgan.
1886	1829	Ranjit Singh visited Gujarat, Wazirabad, and Sialkot.

Dr. Hornigberger, Hungarian Homeopath, joined the Lahore Darbar services.

1887	1830	Sayyad Ahmad Khan murdered Yar Mohd. and occupied Peshawar and incited the tribals for a *jehad* against the Sikhs. Some writers state that he was being indirectly supported by the British against the Sikhs. Ranjit Singh sent Gen. Ventura and Prince Sher Singh, who defeated Ahmad Khan. Retook Peshawar and Sultan Mohd., brother of Yar Khan, was made governor of Peshawar.

Bhima Singh Ardali made governor of Kashmir.

1888	1831	Alexander Burnes visited Lahore.

Jacuemont and G.J. Vigne also visited Lahore.

Meeting between Ranjit Singh and William Bentinck at Ropar. Ranjit Singh couldn't secure British concurrence for his advances towards Sindh as the British had their own eyes set on Sindh. Prince Sher Singh appointed governor of Kashmir.

1889	1832	Joseph Wolfe visited Lahore.

Ranjit Singh occupied Derajat.

Sikh coins struck from Derajat.[35]

	Apr. 1832	Col. Pollinger signed a commercial treaty with *amirs* of Sindh in April 1832 for throwing open the Indus river to navigation for trade by the British. Ranjit Singh's ambition over Sindh thus thwarted.

Ranjit Singh stated to have taken a concubine, Gul Bahar in his haram.

Alexander Gardener entered the service of the Lahore Darbar.

	26.12.1832	Indus Navigation Treaty.
		Sada Kaur died at the ripe old age of 70 years.
1890	Mar. 1833	Treaty between Ranjit Singh and Shah Shujah. Ranjit Singh to help Shah Shujah regain his throne in Afghanistan and Shah Shujah to relinquish all his claims over territories under Sikh occupation.
1891	1834	Col. Mihan Singh appointed governor of Kashmir.
		Shah Shujah defeated by Dost Mohd. Sikh mission sent to Calcutta.
		Ranjit Singh suffered another attack of paralysis.
		Dr. MacGregor called from Ludhiana.
		Ranjit Singh's speech became hesitant and his sight greatly reduced. He could hardly mount a horse.
		Dogra General Zorawar Singh conquered Ladakh in 1834. The state was, however, annexed in 1842, when the Ladakhi Gyalpo was permanently deposed. Ladakh was under the *de jure* sovereignty of the Maharaja at Lahore but under the *de facto* control of Gulab Singh, raja of Jammu.
	Mar. 1834	Peshawar occupied by Sikhs on 6 March 1834.
		Ranjit Singh sent a force under Hari Singh Nalwa, Ventura, and Court under the nominal command of Prince Nau Nihal Singh. The Pathan chiefs sent their families away as they were aware of the duplicity of Shah Shujah and of Ranjit Singh's intention to occupy Peshawar. They agreed to enhance the tribute but the Sikh army occupied Peshawar on the pretext that the prince wanted to see the town and the Pathan chiefs left the city. Hari Singh Nalwa appointed governor of Peshawar along with the governorship of Hazara.
		The British did not appreciate the Sikh occupation of Peshawar.
		Sikh coins struck from Peshawar.[36]
		Dost Mohd. got greatly agitated over the Sikh occupation of Peshawar and wrote to Ranjit Singh to hand over Peshawar or be prepared to face a war.
		Ranjit Singh sent an equally strong rejoinder.
1892	1835	Dost Mohd. made a religious issue to incite fellow tribals against the Sikhs, made elaborate preparations. Ranjit Singh sent a large force under Hari Singh Nalwa but also played the diplomatic game of breaking away minor tribal chiefs with money and allurements. Gulab Singh and Avitable sent to Kohat and Ventura joined Ranjit Singh at Attock. Dost Mohd. realizing his weakness left the field with bag and baggage during the night of 11 May 1835.
		Nau Nihal Singh marched against Shah Nawaz Khan in Dera Ismail Khan, nawab was imprisoned and his territories annexed to the Lahore Darbar.
1893	1836	Ranjit Singh's claim over Shikarpur thwarted by the British.
		Zorawar Singh conquered Ladakh.
		Hari Singh Nalwa constructed and fortified the Jamrod Fort at the mouth of the Khyber Pass.
1894	1837	Marriage of Kanwar Nau Nihal Singh with the daughter of Sham Singh Attariwalla.
		Henry Fane, C-in-C, represented the British government. The Sikh troops sent away from Jamrod and Peshawar for ceremonial duties.
	Apr. 1837	Akbar Khan, knowing the absence of the troops, attacked Jamrod.
		Hari Singh Nalwa sought immediate assistance from Lahore, but his

request was not deliberately placed before Ranjit Singh by Dhian Singh to make Hari Singh Nalwa's position difficult.

Heavy casualties on both sides.

Sikhs repulsed the Afghans on 30 April 1837 but their leader Hari Singh Nalwa was seriously wounded and died. Ranjit Singh cried bitter tears, as the loss of Hari Singh was too great. The Dogras became supreme as no other *sardar* could checkmate them. Ranjit Singh never fully annexed the frontier but ruled them through Muslim chiefs.

Ranjit Singh built several forts and garrisoned these with his troops and maintained moving columns to keep the tribals under subjection.

These forts were at Nara, Daram, Maru, Salana, Machin and Sikham to protect Peshawar, Khairabad, Jahangira, Shahkadur, Attock, Mansehra, Haripur, and Nawanshahr, etc.

1895	1838	The MacNaughton Mission came to Lahore.
	June 1838	Tripartite Treaty between Ranjit Singh, Shah Shujah, and British. Ranjit Singh was to give 5,000 troops, and the British to give officers and financial assistance to Shah Shujah against Dost Mohd. Ranjit Singh was virtually forced into this treaty by British diplomacy.
		Birth of Prince Dalip Singh.
		Osborne visited Punjab.
		Lord Auckland, the Governor-General, met Ranjit Singh at Ferozepur.
		The British occupied Ferozepur and set up a cantonment there in violation of the Treaty of Amritsar.
	21.12.1838	Ranjit Singh suffered a stroke and severe attack of paralysis. Remained critical for several days. Speech and sight virtually gone.
1896	1839	Ranjit Singh partially recovered was very feeble.
	2.6.1839	Suffered another stroke accompanied by dropsy and fever.
		Dr. Steel sent by the British to treat the Maharaja.
	24.6.1839	Ranjit Singh suffered another stroke.
	27.6.1839	Ranjit Singh breathed his last at 7 p.m. on 27 June 1839, and thus the most brilliant period of Sikh history came to a close.

POST RANJIT SINGH PERIOD 1839-1850

After the death of Ranjit Singh, the stability of the Sikh political system took a nose dive. The three major reasons for this rapid decline were the ever-tightening noose of British power and influence round the kingdom of the Lahore Darbar, the contending rival parties, and the incapacity of the successors of Ranjit Singh.

The Government of Punjab degenerated into chaos. The real power went into the hands of incompetent nominal rulers, who ditched the army and the state, to somehow hold on to what little power or authority they could.

It was a decade of the dirtiest intrigues and murders in which the lion's share was usurped by the clever British government and the crafty Dogra Gulab Singh, on the dismemberment of the once mighty Sikh state, to whom one was a proclaimed friend and the other a privileged servant.

1896	Sept. 1839	Kharak Singh was appointed Maharaja in a succession ceremony on 1 September 1839.

Dhian Singh became the *wazir*.

Chet Singh became Kharak Singh's chief advisor.

Nau Nihal Singh arrived from Peshawar.

Chet Singh started intrigues against Dhian Singh.

Kharak Singh, being ineffective, was not willing to drop Chet Singh.

Dhian Singh murdered Chet Singh, the first of the murder series.

Nau Nihal Singh took over the administration and established a certain degree of coordination with Dhian Singh.

	Nov. 1839	Due to the imbecilic nature and hostile attitude of Kharak Singh, he was not allowed to meet Capt. Wade and General Keene, the British C-in-C. Capt. Wade was shifted to Indore and Clark was appointed the British agent at Ludhiana.
1897	Jan. 1840	Nau Nihal Singh virtually took over all control of the administration from Dhian Singh.

Kharak Singh maintained a very insulting attitude towards Dhian Singh in the Darbar. Dhian Singh retired to Jammu.

	Feb. 1840	Disturbances in Muzzafarabad, Hazara, Hasan Abdal and Poonch. Governors and Kardars slackened in sending cash and the revenue fell into arrears. Dhian Singh was recalled to take over the administration.
	May 1840	Attar Singh Sindanwalia started intriguing against Dhian Singh in the British territories.

Kharak Singh already sick, his condition became serious.

	Nov. 1840	Kharak Singh expired on 5 November 1840.

At the cremation of Maharaja Kharak Singh, Prince Nau Nihal Singh, while walking under an archway, was seriously injured by falling stones. Udham Singh (son of Gulab Singh) walking with him died instantaneously. Dhian Singh who was following them was badly bruised.

Prince Nau Nihal Singh died of the injuries.[57]

Dhian Singh's record is so dark and dirty in intrigues and murders that all historians agree on his capability to carry out evil deed. He even kept away the mother of the injured prince which raises serious doubts about his character and motives.

	9-11-1840	Sher Singh was proclaimed the successor.

Rani Chand Kaur (mother of Nau Nihal Singh) announced the pregnancy of Gilwani, widow of Prince Nau Nihal Singh.

	20-11-1840	Co-regency of Chand Kaur and Sher Singh formed.
	Dec. 1840	Sher Singh left for his estates in Batala greatly disappointed.

Differences developed between Chand Kaur and Dhian Singh.

Dhian Singh left for Jammu.

1898	Jan. 1841	Sher Singh marched on Lahore with his troops.

Chand Kaur decided to defend with the help of Gulab Singh.

	16-1-1841	Unsuccessful attack.

Fort well defended by Gulab Singh and Gardner.

Dhian Singh returned to Lahore.

Sher Singh lost about 5,000 men.

Gulab Singh left the fort and Lahore and carried away great wealth.

	20-1-1841	Sher Singh occupied the fort. Dhian Singh became the *wazir*.

The Sindanwalia *sardars*, hostile to the ruling group, started entering into intrigues.

	Apr. 1841	Sher Singh sought British advice and help to subdue Sikh troops who were becoming more and more rebellious.

		Dhian Singh dissuaded him from calling in British troops.
		Rebellions and upheavals in Kullu, Mandi, Multan, Derajat and Peshawar.
	17-4-1841	Mihan Singh, governor of Kashmir, murdered by mutinous troops asking for the arrears of their salaries. Gulab Singh sent to crush the mutinous troops used very repressive measures.
		Shaikh Gholam Mohyi-ud-din made governor of Kashmir.
	Jun. 1841	Partial order was restored in the state. Chand Kaur made overtures to the British, seeking their help.
	Nov. 1841	Alexander Burnes was murdered by rebellious Afghans in Kabul.
		MacNaughton was made to sign a humiliating treaty and was then murdered thereafter.
		The British retreat became a rout and the rout became a massacre. Only a few persons escaped to narrate the story. The British lost 20,000 lives and 15 millions pounds in this misadventure.
1899	1842	Widow of Nau Nihal Singh gave birth to a still-born child.
		Clark, the British agent at Ludhiana, visited the *darbar* to condole Kharak Singh's death and to congratulate Sher Singh.
	June 1842	Chand Kaur got murdered by Dhian Singh through some maid servants.
	Nov. 1842	Sher Singh attempted to make up with the Sindanwalia *sardars*.
		Released certain leaders friendly towards the Sindanwalias and disliked by Dhian Singh.
1900	1843	Sher Singh lost interest in state affairs, indulged in hunts, drinking bouts, and debaucheries, remaining away from the capital for long periods.
	Aug. 1843	Sher Singh appeared to be siding with the Sindanwalias.
		To counterbalance this new emerging alliance, Dhian Singh sponsored the claim of Dalip Singh.
		Dalip Singh with his mother Jindan was brought to Lahore from Jammu where he was residing.
		Kanwars Kashmira Singh and Pashora Singh were encouraged by the interested parties to further complicate the situation for Sher Singh.
	Sept. 1843	Sher Singh shot dead by Ajit Singh Sindanwalia while inspecting troops on 15 September 1843.
		Prince Partap Singh, son of Sher Singh, also brutally murdered.
		Hira Singh, son of Dhian Singh, escaped from the scene. Ajit Singh got Dhian Singh murdered in the fort. The Sindanwalia *sardars* proclaimed Prince Dalip Singh as the next successor.
	16.9.1843	Hira Singh won the support of the army and stormed the fort.
		Sindanwalia *sardars*, Lehna Singh, Ajit Singh and other conspirators murdered.
		Troops looted Lahore city.
		Bhai Gurmukh Singh and Misr Beli Ram also murdered.
		Dalip Singh, aged 5 years, made ruler.
		Hira Singh became the *wazir* in place of Dhian Singh.
		Some order restored in the capital.
1901	Mar. 1844	Hira Singh marched agent Suchet Singh near Lahore.
		Suchet Singh and Raj Kesri were killed.
	May 1844	Kashmira Singh, Peshora Singh, and Attar Singh Sindanwalia started intriguing against Hira Singh at Bhai Vir Singh's camp.
		Hira Singh despatched his troops who besieged Bhai Vir Singh's camp.
		Bhai Vir Singh, Kashmira Singh and Attar Singh Sindanwalia were killed.

		Peshora Singh submitted to Hira Singh and his life was spared.
	June 1844	Most of the European officers left the service of the Lahore Darbar on their own due to the uncertain conditions and the mutinous troops. Others were sent away due to their being in league with the British.
	Oct. 1844	The Sikhs resented the British upholding the claim of Nabha state over the Moran estate (in the cis-Sutlej territories) against the claim of the Lahore Darbar. The Sikhs also resented the holding back of the treasure found in the house of Suchet Singh at Ferozepur.

June 1844 — Most of the European officers left the service of the Lahore Darbar on their own due to the uncertain conditions and the mutinous troops. Others were sent away due to their being in league with the British.

Oct. 1844 — The Sikhs resented the British upholding the claim of Nabha state over the Moran estate (in the cis-Sutlej territories) against the claim of the Lahore Darbar. The Sikhs also resented the holding back of the treasure found in the house of Suchet Singh at Ferozepur.

The Lahore Darbar finances in very bad shape. Troops clamoured for their salaries. Attempts to realize money from the *sardars* created great resentment.

The Sikh *sardars* started sending large sums of money held by them into British territories for safe custody from exactions by the Lahore Darbar.

Hira Singh's position became very weak.

Rebellions broke out all over the state.

Peshora Singh escaped into British territories.

Hira Singh developed differences with Rani Jindan who had her own ambitions.

Pandit Jhaula, the most confidential adviser of Hira Singh, became very unpopular with the other *sardars*.

Hira Singh also developed differences with Sham Singh Atariwala.

12.12.1844 — Hira Singh attempted to escape to Jammu.

Sham Singh and Jawahar Singh with 6,000 troops caught up with the fleeing Dogras.

Hira Singh, Sohan Singh, son of Gulab Singh, Labh Singh, Pandit Jhaula, Mian Dall Singh, chief of Akhnur, got killed along with other Dogra *sardars*.

28.12.1844 — A regency of ten *sardars* was formed under Jawahar Singh as *wazir* and Lal Singh as C-in-C of the Sikh forces.

1902 Feb. 1845 — The Lahore Darbar became financially bankrupt.

It was decided to invade Jammu to secure the treasures held by Gulab Singh.

Gulab Singh was too clever for the Sikhs. He maintained an elaborate spy network and was able to foil every Sikh move to his own advantage.

22.2.1845 — Rani Jindan attempted to cross over to the British with Dalip Singh but her attempt was foiled by the Sikh army.

March 1845 — Sikh troops marched against Jammu. No coordination amongst the *sardars*. Gulab Singh played one against the other and the movements of the Sikh army were also very slow.

July 1845 — Kanwar Peshora Singh occupied Attock.

Peshora Singh was subdued and killed by the Lahore Darbar troops.

Sept. 1845 — Jawahar Singh became very unpopular.

Rani Jindan abondoned Jawahar Singh.

Jawahar Singh and some of his followers were murdered.

The Sikh army came back from Jammu without achieving its object of securing the treasures of Gulab Singh. The government treasury at Lahore was almost empty. The Gobindgarh treasury at Amritsar was left with about 50 to 60 lakh rupees.

Nov. 1845 — Lal Singh became the *wazir* and Tej Singh became the C-in-C.[38]

The ruling *junta* decided to make the turbulent Sikh army fight the British so that they may retain their position to some extent. The British had all along been keen to dismember the Sikh state and found the most opportune time and were anxious for a fight.

23.11.1845	Sikh troops marched to the Sutlej ferries.
6.12.1845	British troops at Meerut and Ambala moved to Ludhiana.
13.12.1845	Lord Hardinge, the Governor-General, issued the proclamation of war.
18.12.1845	First engagement at Mudki.

Lal Singh ran away in the middle of the battle as already planned with the British.

The British won but suffered heavy casualties.

21.12.1845   Battle of Ferozepur.

The British led the attack at their chosen site. The Sikhs fought bravely. They were not allowed to pursue the British troops at night by their commanders.

Lal Singh ran away with the guns.

Additional forces joined the British troops the next morning and thus defeated the Sikh army.

1903   21.1.1846   The Sikhs attacked and burned down a large part of the Ludhiana cantonment.

Sikhs defeated Harry Smith at Budhowal and captured his baggage.

Harry Smith fought a minor skirmish with Ranjodh Singh at Aliwal.

10.2.1846   Battle of Sobraon.

The Sikh army deprived of ammunition and rations, crossed the Sutlej at Sobraon. The British made three attacks and were repulsed.

Lal Singh and Tej Singh ran away from the field as planned with the British.

Gulab Singh came and started negotiations with the British to the detriment of Sikh interests.

Lal Singh cut off the boat bridge so that the Sikh army could neither get any reinforcements nor could it retreat.

Under such circumstances the British won and the Sikhs lost.

The Sikh army stood defeated and thus came the most inglorious end of the most glorious army of the Khalsa.

9.3.1846   The Treaty of Lahore was signed between the Lahore Darbar and the British:

1. All Sikh territories south of the Sutlej taken over by the British.

2. Jullandhar Doab to be occupied by British troops.

3. An indemnity of Rs. 1½ crores imposed on the Lahore Darbar.

4. All rebellious Sikh troops to be disbanded. Only 20,000 infantry and 12,000 cavalry to be maintained by the Lahore Darbar.

5. Dalip Singh recognized as a minor ruler, with Rani Jindan as the regent and Lal Singh as the *wazir*.

Adequate British troops retained at Lahore to protect the raja.

Henry Lawrence appointed as the British resident.

16.3.1846   Separate treaty made with Gulab Singh at Ambala. Kashmir was sold to Gulab Singh for Rs. 1 crore as part of the indemnity due from the Lahore Darbar.[39]

Lal Singh, the *wazir*, opposed the ceding of Kashmir to Gulab Singh. He was removed and banished from Punjab.

| | 16.12.1846 | Treaty of Bhirowal. |

The British troops were to leave Punjab by the end of December 1846 but they had no intention of leaving Punjab. The British resident managed through some Sikh chief to circumvent Rani Jindan, the regent, to retain British troops till the minor Maharaja Dalip Singh became a major by 1854.

The Lahore Darbar was also made to pay Rs. 22 lakhs per annum for the upkeep of British troops in Punjab. Circumstances leading to the Second Anglo-Sikh War. The Khalsa army regarded their defeat as a matter of chance and due to the treachery of their leaders. The disbanded soldiers felt slighted and humiliated. Lord Dalhousie started the ruthless suppression of the Sikhs. The Sikhs felt cheated because the British gave better treatment to other communities.

Deportation of Rani Jindan to Benaras hurt the pride of the common Sikhs.

Abbot was instigating Muslims into rebellion against Chattar Singh, the governor of Hazara. Mool Raj, the governor of Multan, was asked to pay an exorbitant succession fee and enhanced revenue. His resignation was also not accepted by the resident.

1905   Mar. 1848   The British made up their mind to annex Punjab Fredrick Curie sent as resident to provoke the Sikhs into action so that annexation could be justified.

Kahn Singh sent with British officers to take over from Mool Raj. The British officers who provoked local soldiers were killed.

The British got the chance they were waiting for.

1848   Mool Raj, when he ran short of silver rupees to pay wages to his soldiers, minted a very small gold coin equal in value to the rupee for purposes of disbursement of salaries to the troops. It weighed 0.65 g. and bore the legend '*Sat Guru Sahai*' on the obverse and '*Mundrika*' 1905 Sambat, i.e. AD 1848 on the reverse.

Nov. 1848   The British army assembled at Ferozepur.

Gough attacked Sher Singh at Ramnagar, the battle was indecisive.

1906   13.1.1849   The two armies met at Chhillianwala, tremendous loss on both sides. The Sikhs had an edge over the British.

22.1.1849   Multan fell to the British.

24.1.1849   Chattar Singh joined Sher Singh.

British troops spared from Multan joined their forces.

12.3.1849   The two armies fought at Gujarat. The British had vastly superior artillery. The Sikhs fought valiantly but were routed. Sher Singh and his remaining army surrendered to the British.

29.3.1849   A *darbar* held in Lahore on 29 March 1849. Annexation of Punjab proclaimed. Signed by the British and Dalip Singh. The Sikh state ceased to exist as the soldiers laid down their arms with tears in their eyes, exclaiming '*Aj Ranjit Singh mar Gia*', meaning that on that day the Sikh soldiers felt the death of their beloved Maharaja Ranjit Singh.

1907   1850   Nanak Shahi silver rupees numbering lakhs were sent to Bombay and Calcutta for restriking into British currency and the Nanak Shahi rupee was declares a dead currency.[40]

NOTES

1. Opinions differ and some authors give the date of birth as Oct./Nov. 1469.
2. The special issues of *Sikh Review*, Calcutta, 1969 on Guru Nanak give an account of Guru Nanak's visit to Tibet via Lachung Lachen.
3. Contemporary historian Mohsin Fani gives the period of detention at Gwalior as 12 years, but others state the same to be about two years only. The Guru was released on the recommendation of Mian Mir of Lahore. The detention for a couple of years only seems to be correct as it fits with the rest of the activities of Guru Hargobind.
4. Phul became the head of the Phulkian families, the rulers of the cis-Sutlej states.
5. Khushwaqt Rai, *History of Sikhs*, p. 46.
6. Max Arthur Macauliffe, *The Sikh Religion*, vol. V, p. 245.
7. Muhammad Latif, *History of Punjab*, p. 370.
8. (i) William Irvine, *Later Mughals*, p. 111.
   (ii) Ganda Singh, *Life of Banda Bahadur*, pp. 82, 83.
   The absence of primary references makes it difficult to compare these legends with those on the actual coins which have slight variations.
9. *Hadiqat-al-Aqalim*, Aligargh: Aligarh Muslim University, p. 148.
10. *Akhbar-i-Darbar-e-Mualla*, Jaipur, 1710.
11. *Hukmnama*, AD 12 December 1710, Ganda Singh Collection.
12. One such coin is with the Numismatic Society, New York, and the other two are with European diplomats who made their collections from Delhi coin dealers.
13. Ahmad Shah Batalvi has recorded a conversation between Nadir Shah and Zakariya Khan.
    Nadir Shah—Have you got any troublesome people in the country?
    Zakariya Khan—None except a sect of Hindu faqirs who assemble twice to bathe in a tank. They consider it a place of pilgrimage.
    Nadir Shah—Where are their place of abode?
    Zakariya Khan—Their homes are the saddles of their horses.
    Nadir Shah—These rebels will raise their head again.
    Hari Ram Gupta, *History of Sikhs*, vol. II, pp. 54-5.
14. Important Sikh Misls in 1745:
    1. Ahluwalia Misl under Jassa Singh Ahluwalia.
    2. Bhangi Misl under Hari Singh Bhangi.
    3. Dhallewalia Misl under Gulab Singh.
    4. Faizullahpuria Misl under Kapur Singh.
    5. Kanehiya Misl under Jai Singh Kanehiya.
    6. Karorasinghia Misl under Karora Singh.
    7. Nakai Misl under Hari Singh Nakai.
    8. Nishanwala Misl under Daswandha Singh.
15. The Malwa *sardars* arose from the Phul family of Phul Sandhu Jat. Due to the slackened hold of the Mughal government, these families made their strongholds at Patiala, Nabha, Jind, Kaithal, Faridkot, etc. Ala Singh of Patiala became the premier *sardar*. He was a Sikh and took *pahul*, but never became a part of the Sikh mainstream. He allied with the Mughals and Durrani for the sake of his estate and, whenever the Majha Sikhs tried to punish him, he was able to buy peace through the good offices of Jassa Singh Ahluwalia, the leader of the Majha Sikhs, to whom Ala Singh paid regular tribute.
16. Brown has stated that Sikhs occupied Lahore in 1758 under Jassa Singh Ahluwalia and struck their coin. His account is based on a manuscript received by him which he admits

is defective in dates, etc. Brown's account has been followed by Malcolm, Elphinstone, Cunningham, Latif, G.C. Narang, etc. The eyewitness account of Tahmas Khan Miskin records that Lahore was jointly seized by the Marathas and the Sikhs and was leased to Adena Beg by the Marathas on an annual tribute of 75 lakhs. The question of the Sikhs having struck their coins in 1758 didn't arise.

Ghulam Ali Khan Azad has recorded in *Khazana-e-Amira* that the Sikhs put Jassa Singh on the Mughal throne and struck a coin in April 1765. A Maratha newsletter also mentioned that the Sikhs had created disturbances in Lahore. Lepel Griffin has stated that no such coins were struck at all. Ganesh Das has stated that few coins were minted by bigoted mullahs to malign the Sikhs in the eyes of Ahmad Shah. Giani Gian Singh has stated that coins were struck in 1761. Hari Ram Gupta has opined that coins were actually struck in 1761. From the totality of the data available, it appears that such coins may have been struck by the Sikhs in 1761, probably in small numbers in the first flush of victory. No such coin has been located so far.

The legend thereon is said to be:

Sikka zad dar jehan bafazal-e-Akal
Mulk-e-Ahmad garift Jassa Kalal

17. This coin and those of the succeeding years are readily available with museums and private collections. It remained the prevalent currency till the annexation of Panjab by the British in 1849.
18. The coins issued from Multan in 1722 continued to be struck till 1779, till the city was captured by Timur Shah and the Sikhs were evicted therefrom.
19. The earliest Sikh coin from Amritsar has been traced to 1832 Sambat and the same continued till 2005 Sambat, i.e. AD 1848.
20. George Forster prophesized in 1793 regarding the internecine warfare amongst the Sikh *sardars* that one day an able chief would obtain absolute power on the ruins of the Sikh commonwealth and the same came true within twenty years with Ranjit Singh subduing the rival misls and the Sikh chiefs and the establishment of his kingdom.
21. Jassa Singh Ahluwalia's followers made him sit on the imperial throne, i.e. the Diwan-i-Am, and called him Padshah. Jassa Singh Ramgarhia and other *sardars* protested that sovereignty belonged to the Khalsa and that no *sardar* could attribute it to his own person.
Jassa Singh stepped down from the throne on realizing his indescretion.
22. The peace terms were:
    1. A major part of the Sikh army was to retire to Panjab.
    2. Baghel Singh to remain in Delhi with 4,000 troops.
    3. Sikhs permitted to build seven historic gurdwaras.
    4. Sikhs got 6 *annas* per rupee, i.e. 37 per cent income from octroi duty.
    5. Kotwali in Chandni Chowk placed under Baghel Singh.
23. The seven historic gurdwaras were:
    1. Mata Sundari Gurdwara in Teliwara.
    2. Gurdwara Bangla Sahib where Guru Harkishan stayed.
    3. Gurdwara Majnu ka Tilla where Guru Nanak and Guru Hargobind stayed.
    4. Gurdwara Moti Bagh where Guru Gobind Singh stayed.
    5. Gurdwara and samadhis where Mata Sundari and Mata Sahib Devi were cremated.
    6. Gurdwara Sisganj where Guru Tegh Bahadur was executed.
    7. Gurdwara Rakabganj where Guru Tegh Bahadur's body was cremated.
24. Sikh *sardars* ran free *langars* (kitchens) to feed the poor and the needy.

Mahan Singh provided 100 g. roasted gram to each person.

Budh Singh of Montgomery sold all his properties to feed the poor in his area.

25. There is a difference of opinion amongst historians. Some state that Ranjit Singh was appointed Governor of Lahore by Shah Zaman for salvaging his guns from the Jhelum river. Others state that he was invited by the citizens of Lahore to intervene against misrule by the Bhangi *sardars*. The later account seems to be more accurate as Ranjit Singh occupied Lahore much before he salvaged and handed over the guns to Zaman Shah.

26. Sahib Singh of Gujrat, Jassa Singh Ramgarhia, Jodh Singh of Wazirabad and Nizam-ud-din of Kasur assembled at Bhasian to dislodge Ranjit Singh. They didn't make a cohesive force and wasted their time in fruitless activities. Ranjit Singh also avoided a frontal attack and after some skirmishes and due to mutual differences amongst his opponents, Ranjit Singh came out victorious without a full-scale battle.

27. Certain historians have wrongly stated that Ranjit Singh struck coins with the Sikh legend on the obverse and his name on the reverse and that the first days' coins were distributed amongst the poor. It is also wrong that Ranjit Singh introduced the *peepal* leaf motif on these coins as the leaf motif had appeared on Amritsar coins in 1841 Sambat, i.e. AD 1784 when Ranjit Singh was nowhere in the picture.

28. Certain historians, mainly European and later Indian historians, have treated the occupation of Amritsar as having taken place in 1802 while others, mainly court chroniclers, etc., have stated that the occupation took place in 1805, which seems to be more correct.

29. Some historians have called his ailment a venereal disease. Such an ailment did not require local confinement and the symptoms are not only urinary infection. The ailment seems to be the first attack of a paralysis, which forced him to stay put in Meanee.

30. The coins struck from Amritsar were exactly the same as those struck earlier by the Bhangi misl from 1775 onwards.

31. Terms of the Treaty of Amritsar:
    1. The two Governments to maintain friendly relations.
    2. The British to have no concern, north-west of the Sutlej. Likewise, Ranjit Singh would not interfere in the affairs of the cis-Sutlej states which were under British protection.
    3. Ranjit Singh recognized as an independent ruler.
    4. Neither Government to keep large armies on the banks of the Sutlej.
    5. Ranjit Singh to maintain a minimum force in the 45 parganas in the cis-Sutlej area required for internal peace keeping.
    6. Violation of any part of the treaty by the contracting parties will make the treaty null and void.

32. The Multan fort was constructed on a large mound. Its walls were erected by cutting the sides of the mound and hence while these were 30 ft. high from the outside, these were hardly 3 ft. from the inside. The moat remained dry in summer and got filled up during the rainy season. Hence, the fort had to be subdued before the rainy season. Further, it was very difficult to breach the fort walls with the guns then in existence.

33. The legend on the obverse has been changed to that on the Lahore coin of 1801 and the legend on the reverse remained the same as on the 1772 Multan coin but for the change of the Sambat year to 1875.

34. These coins were regularly struck in large numbers by all the governors of Kashmir till Kashmir was handed over to Gulab Singh in 1846.

35. Coins struck from Derajat from 1889 to 1896 but presumably in small numbers.

36. The coins struck from Peshawar were in small numbers and were struck for a few years only.

37. The death of Nau Nihal Singh is the subject of a serious controversy. Whether the falling of the ramparts at that particular time was a mere accident due to the incessant firing of guns from the walls of the fort or whether it was a deliberate plan of the Dogras to remove the prince, who was trying to become independent, cannot be said with certainty. Cunningham, Griffin, Steinbeck and Charmichael Smith consider the prince's death to the result of the intrigues of Dhian Singh. Ganda Singh supports this explanation.

Prem Singh Hoti calls it a delibeate murder, of which he gives some details.

Muhammad Latif and Honigberger consider it to be the result of the accidental falling of the stones of the archway. Sohan Lal Suri and Clark support his view, which is also shared by Khushwant Singh.

Dhian Singh's record is so dark and dirty in intrigues and murder that all historians agree on his capability to carry out the murder. His keeping even the mother of the prince away from her injured son raises serious doubts about his credibility.

38. Sikh leaders Lal Singh and Tej Singh were in league with the British Government. The Sikh troops were moved to various places in consultation with the British authorities so that British forces would have all the advantages and the Sikh troops would lose their striking power. The Sikh forces were deprived of their guns and ammunition and even food supplies were withheld by the Sikh *wazir* and the C-in-C to ensure the defeat of the Sikh army. The Sikh army of 60,000 was not permitted to attack the 6,000 British soldiers at Ferozepur. The Sikh army was moved away and held back till the British had collected enough strength at the place of their choice for battle. All this not being enough, Lal Singh ran away from the battle field in the midst of the fighting lest the Sikh army should win. In spite of the above handicaps, the leaderless soldiers of the Khalsa army fought with such bravery that the mighty British Government in India was shaken to its very foundations and won the war by the skin of their teeth.

It was the most inglorious victory won by the British—won by deceit and not by valour.

39. Art. IV, Treaty of Lahore: The Sikh state, in place of a cash indemnity of one crore rupees (ten million), ceded all the forts, territories, rights and interests in the hill countries which are situated between the rivers Beas and Indus, including the provinces of Kashmir and Hazara.

On 16 March 1846, Raja Gulab Singh signed the Treaty of Amritsar whereby he became the Maharaja of Jammu and Kashmir and all territories east of the Indus and west of the Ravi.

He was to pay an indemnity of one crore.

The British later decided not to give him Chamba, Mandi, Nurpur, etc., and reduced the indemnity by 25 lakhs.

40. Foreign Department, General Report, *Administration of Punjab Territories 1849-51*, Calcutta, 1856, declaring the Nanak Shahi currency as dead currency.

Genealogical Table: Maharaja Ranjit Singh's Family

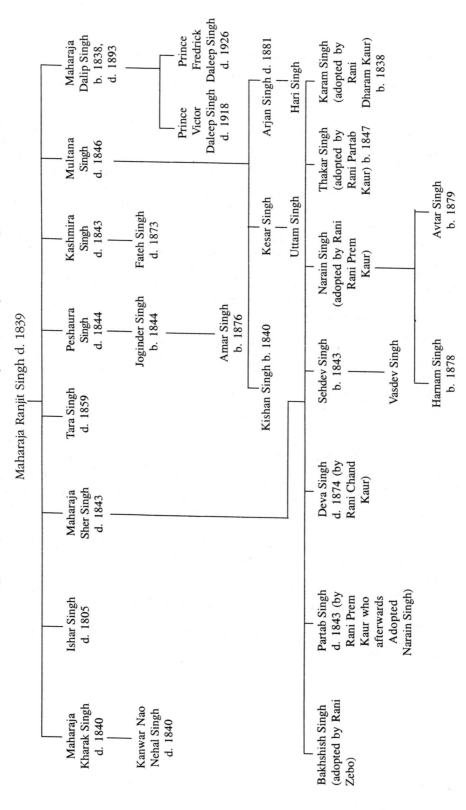

Note: The above Genealogical Table has been taken from Barkat Rai Chopra, *Kingdom of the Punjab 1839-45*, Hoshiarpur: VVRI Publications, 1969, p. 440.

Genealogical Table: Sindanwalia Family

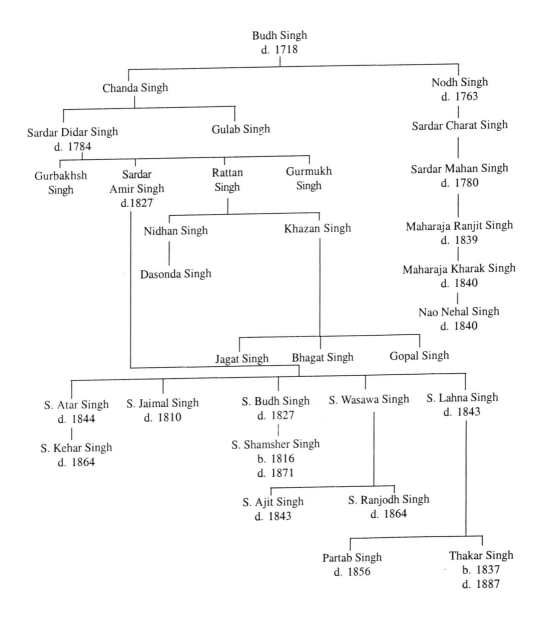

Note: The above Genealogical Table has been taken from Barkat Rai Chopra, *Kingdom of the Punjab 1839-45*, Hoshiarpur: VVRI Publications. 1969, p. 441.

Bibliography

I. PRIMARY SOURCES

A. *Collections of Sikh Coins*

Government Museum, Chandigarh.
Government Museum, Lahore.
Personal collection and some private collections.
Sheesh Mahal Museum, Patiala.
Sri Pratap Museum, Srinagar.

B. *Catalogues of Coins and Gazetteers*

Gazetteers, District and States Gazetteers of Undivided Punjab prior to Independence (4 vols.), New Delhi: Low Priced Publications, 1993.
Gupta, Parmeshwari Lal and Sanjay Garg, *The Coins of Dal Khalsa and Lahore Darbar in the Sheesh Mahal Museum, Patiala*, Chandigarh: Punjab Government, 1989.
Hans, Herrli, *The Coins of the Sikhs*, Nagpur: Indian Coins Society, 1993.
Kak, R.C., *Archaeological and Numismatic Section, Sri Pratap Museum, Srinagar*, Calcutta: Spink & Co., 1923.
Rodgers, C.J., *Catalogue of Coins (Miscellaneous), Lahore Museum*, 1985.
———, *Catalogue of Coins in the Government Museum Lahore*, Calcutta, 1891.
Standard Guide to South Asian Coins and Paper Money Since 1556 AD, Wisconsin: Krause Publications, 1st edn.
Valentine, W.H., *Copper Coins of India* (2 vols.), New Delhi: Inter India Publications, 1914.
Whitehead, R.D., *Catalogues of the Coins of the Punjab Museum, Lahore*, vol. III, Oxford, 1843.
World Coins Standard Catalogues, 21st edn., Wisconsin, Krause Publications, 1994.

C. *Select Articles*

Dyell, John, 'Banda Bahadur and the First Sikh Coinage', *Numismatic Digest*, vol. IV, pt. I, June 1980, Bombay, pp. 59-90.

Gupta, Hari Ram, 'The First Sikh Coin of Lahore', *Proceedings of the Indian History Congress*, Modern Section, 1938, pp. 427-34

Panish, Charles, 'The First Sikh Trans-Sutlej Coinage', *Journal of the Numismatic Society*, vol. XXIX, pt. II, pp. 88-90, Varanasi, 1967.

Rai, Jyoti, 'Rediscovering the Sikh Mint Peshawar, Dera, Rawalpindi', *Journal of the Oriental Numismatic Society*, Newsletter no. 146, Autumn, 1998.

————, 'Unidentified Sikh Mints: Proof of the Existence of Nimak', *Journal of the Oriental Numismatic Society,* Newsletter no. 143, Winter 1995.

Rodgers, C.J., 'On the Coins of the Sikhs', *Journal of Asiatic Society of Bengal*, vol. L, Calcutta, 1881, pp. 71-93.

Singh, Surinder 'Ranjit Singh's Effigy on Sikh Coins', *Newsletter of Oriental Numismatic Society*, Newsletter no. 123, Surrey, UK, April 1990.

Somaiya, R.T., 'Sikh Coins', Newsletter no. 25, Nagpur: Indian Coin Society, March 1994.

Temple, R.C., 'The Coins of the Modern Chiefs of the Punjab', *Indian Antiquary*, vol. XVIII, Bombay, 1889, pp. 21-41

Wiggins, Ken and Stan Goron, *Information Sheet of the Oriental Numismatic Society*, Surrey, UK, nos. 23 to 26 and 92 to 93, Amritsar, 1981; Lahore and Multan, 1982; Kashmir, 1983; Miscellaneous mints, 1984; 'Gold and Silver Coinage of Amritsar', Nasik, 1984.

D. *Travelogues and Accounts by Newswriters*

Ali, Shahamat, *Sikhs and Afghans*, Punjab: Languages Department, rpt., 1970.

Barr, William, *Journal of a March from Delhi to Kabul*, Punjab: Languages Department, rpt., 1970.

Foreign Department, General Report, *Administration of Punjab Territories 1849-51*, Calcutta, 1856, Punjab States Archives, Patiala.

Forster, George, *A Journey from Bengal to England*, Punjab: Languages Department, rpt., 1980.

Garret, H.L.O. and G.L. Chopra, *Events of the Court of Ranjit Singh*, Punjab Government Publication, Punjab: Languages Department, rpt., 1970.

Hornigberger, John Martin, *Thirty Five Years in the East Calcutta, 1852*, Punjab: Languages Department, rpt., 1970.

Leach, Major, *Survey 1837*, Foreign Department, Secret Consultation, no. 22, New Delhi: National Archives of India, 1943.

Moorcraft, W., *Travels in the Himalayan Provinces of Hindustan and Bokhara from 1819-1825*, Punjab: Languages Department, rpt., 1970.

Vigne, G.T., *Travels in Kashmir, Ladakh and Skardu* (2 vols.), London: Henry Calburn Publishers, 1842.

E. *Persian Manuscripts and Documents*

Ashok, Shamsher Singh (ed.), *Prachin Jung Name*, Amritsar: SGPC.

Akhbar-i-Darbar-i-Mualla, The News of the Royal Mughal Court 1707-18. Translated by Bhagat Singh, *Panjab Past & Present*, vol. XVIII, no. II, October 1984, Patiala: Punjabi Univerisity, pp. 1-206.

Ali-ud-din, Mufti, *Ibratnama* (2 vols.), Lahore: The Punjabi Adabi Academy, 1854.

Amarnath, *Zafarnama-e-Ranjit Singh*, translated and edited by Kirpal Singh, Patiala: Punjabi University, 1983.

Badhera, Ganesh Das, *Char Bagh-i-Punjab*, edited by Kirpal Singh, Amritsar: Khalsa College, 1965.

Batalvi, Ahmad Shah, *Tarikh-i-Punjab*, translated by Gurbux Singh, Patiala: Punjabi University, 1969.

Elliot, H.M. and John Dawson, *The History of India as Told by its Own Historians* (8 vols.), New Delhi: Low Priced Publications, rpt., 1990.

Fani, Mohsin, *Dabistan-i-Mazhab*, tr. David Shea and Anthony Troyar, Paris, 1843. Portion on Sikhs, translated by Ganda Singh, in *Panjab Past & Present*, Patiala: Punjabi University, April 1967.

Hadiqat-al-Aqalim (MS), Murtaza Hussain, Aligarh: Aligarh Muslim University.

Ijad, Mir Muhamad Ahsan, *Farrukhsiyar Nama*, OR 25, BM, London (copy with Aligarh Muslim University, Aligarh).

Karim, Abdul, *Tarikh-i-Punjab*, Amritsar: History Research Department, Khalsa College.

Khan, Mohammed Hadi Kamwar, *Tazkirat-i-Salatin-i-Chughtaiya*, edited by Muzaffar Alam, New Delhi: Asia Publishing House, 1980.

Khan, Khafi, *Muntakhab-ul-Lubab* (2 vols.), Calcutta: Mohamad Hashim, 1874.

Lal, Kanehiya, *Tarikh-i-Punjab*, translated by Jeet Singh Seetal, Patiala: Punjabi University, 1968.

Mohyi-ud-din, Gholam (Bute Shah), *History of Punjab*, SHR 1288, Amritsar: History Research Department, Khalsa College.

Mubarakullah, *Tarikh-i-Iradat Khan*, SHR 492, Amritsar: History Research Department, Khalsa College.

Parsad, Debi, *Gulshan-i-Punjab*, translated by Harinder Singh Kohli, Patiala: Punjabi University, 1979.

Qasim, Muhamad (of Lahore), *Ibrat Nama*, SHR 1270, relates to events from 1707 onwards, Amritsar: Sikh History Research Department, Khalsa College.

Qazi, Faqir Mohamad, *Jammah-ut-Tawarikh*, Kanpur: Newal Kishore Press, 1874.

Rai, Khushwaqt, *Twarikh-i-Sikhan*, MS SHR 1275, Amritsar: History Research Department, Khalsa College.

Shah, Ahmad (of Batala), *Tarikh-i-Hind*, SHR 1291, Amritsar: Khalsa College.

Shah, Gulam Hussain, *Siyar-ul-Matakherin*, Kanpur: Newal Kishore Press, 1897.

Steingass, F. *Comprehensive Persian English Dictionary*, New Delhi: Munshiram Manoharlal, 1996.

Suri, Sohan Lal, *Umadat-ut-Twarikh* (5 vols.), Lahore: Arya Press, 1885 (with Punjab States Archives, Patiala).

Tuzak-i-Jahangiri, translated by Rodgers and Beveridge, New Delhi: Munshiram Manoharlal, 1996.

F.   *Urdu Manuscripts and Documents*

Bhadour, Attar Singh, *Twarikh-i-Sidhu Brarahan Khanden-i-Phul*, Amritsar: Sikh History Department, Khalsa College.

Chand, Hukum, *Twarikh Zila Multan*, SHR 1249, Amritsar: History Research Department, Khalsa College, 1884.

Faiz-ul-Haq, *Twarikh-i-Darbar Sahib*, SHR 93, Amritsar: Sikh History Department, Khalsa College, 1869.

Mohammad, Din, *Tarikh-i-Punjab*, SHR 2166, Amritsar: Sikh History Department, Khalsa College, 1849.

Muhamad, Azam Beg, *Tarikh-i-Hazara*, Punjab Govt., Lahore: Victoria Press, 1874.

G. *Punjabi Manuscripts and Documents*

Anonymous, *Guru Hargobind Sahib*, no. 5357, Amritsar: Sikh Reference Library.

Bachitra Natik, translated by Ujjagar Singh Bawa, Washington, USA: Sikh Youth Forum, 1999.

Bachittar Natik, Guru Gobind Singh, translated and published by M.L. Peace, Jullandhar (undated).

Bhai Maharaj Singh, Biography Compiled by Nahar Singh, Patiala: Sikh Lok Itihas Prakashan Sabha, 1989.

Bhangu, Rattan Singh, *Prachin Panth Parkash*, edited by Bhai Vir Singh, Amritsar: Wazir Hind Press, 1962.

Giani, Gian Singh, *Panth Prakash*, Punjab: Languages Department, rpt., 1970.

———, *Tarikh Guru Khalsa* (2 vols.), Punjab: Languages Department, rpt., 1970.

Gurdas, Bhai, *Varan* (2 vols.), translated into English by Dr Jodh Singh, Patiala: Vision and Venture, 1998.

Hoti, Prem Singh, *Life of Hari Singh Nalwa*, Ludhiana: Lahore Book Shop, 1937.

Nabha, Kahan Singh, *Encyclopedia of Sikh Literature* (*Mahankosh*), Punjab: Languages Department, rpt., 1981.

Sena Pat, *Sri Gur Sobha*, edited by Ganda Singh, Patiala: Punjabi University, 1967.

Sewadas, Parchian, *Episodes from lives of the Gurus*. Translated by Kharak Singh and Gurtej Singh, Chandigarh: Institute of Sikh Studies, 1995.

Singh, Gajinder, *Jassa Singh Ahluwalia*, Jullandhar: Prem Harpreet Parkashan, 1979.

Singh, Ganda, *Jassa Singh Ahluwalia*, Patiala: Punjabi University, 1990.

Singh, Harbans (ed.), *Encyclopedia of Sikhism* (4 vols.), Patiala: Punjabi University, 1995-8

Singh, Karam, *Banda Bahadur*, Amritsar: Chief Khalsa Diwan, 1907.

————, *Banda Kaun See*, Amritsar: Amrit Agency, undated.

————, *Maharaja Ala Singh*, Amritsar: Chief Khalsa Diwan, 1915.

Singh, Koer, *Gurblass Padshahi Daswin*, edited by Shamsher Singh Ashok, Patiala: Punjabi University, 1968.

Singh, Satbir, *Guru Hargobind*, Patiala: Punjabi University, 1968.

Singh, Sukha, *Gurvalas Padshahi (tenth guru)*, SHR 2297, Amritsar: Sikh History Research Department, Khalsa College.

Sri Guru Granth Sahib, translated by Gopal Singh (4 vols.), New Delhi: Gurdas Kapoor & Sons, 1960-2.

Sri Guru Granth Sahib, translated by Gurubachan Singh Talib, Patiala: Punjabi University, 1988.

Sri Guru Granth Sahib, translated by Manmohan Singh, Amritsar: SGPC, 1983.

II. SECONDARY SOURCES

A. *English Books and Printed Works*

Ahluwalia, J.S., *The Sovereignty of Sikh Doctrine*, New Delhi: Bahri Publications, 1983.

Ahluwalia, M.L., *Landmarks in Sikh History*, New Delhi: Ashoka International Publishers, 1996.

————, *Looking Across India's North Western Frontier*, New Delhi: Ashoka International Publishers, 1990.

Alam, Mazaffar, *The Crises of Empire in Mughal North India*, New Delhi: Oxford University Press, 1986.

Anand, Balwant Singh, *Guru Nanak*, New Delhi: Guru Nanak Foundation, 1983.

Archer, J.C., *The Sikhs*, Princeton, NJ, USA, 1946.

Ashta, Dharam Pal, 'Poetry of Dasam Granth', Ph.D. thesis, Chandigarh: Panjab University.

Bal, Sarjit Singh, *Life of Guru Nanak*, Chandigarh: Panjab University, 1969.

Bamzai, P.N.K., *Social and Economic History of Kashmir*, New Delhi: Metropolitan Publications, 1987.

Banerjee, Anil Chandra, *Guru Nanak and His Times*, Patiala: Punjabi University, 1984.

————, *Guru Nanak to Guru Gobind Singh*, New Delhi: Rajesh Publications, 1978.

————, *Sikh Gurus and The Sikh Religion*, New Delhi: Munshiram Manoharlal, 1983.

————, *The Khalsa Raj*, New Delhi: Abhinav Publication, 1985.

Banerjee, Indu Bhushan, *Evolution of Khalsa* (2 vols.), Calcutta: A. Mukherjee & Co., 1979.

Banga, Indu, *Agrarian System of the Sikhs*, New Delhi: Manohar, 1978.

Bell, Evans, *Annexation of Punjab*, Punjab: Languages Department, rpt., 1970.

Bhagat, Lakshman Singh, *Guru Gobind Singh*, Punjab: Languages Department, rpt., 1970.

Brotman, Irwin F., *A Guide to the Temple Tokens of India*, Los Angeles: Shamrock Press, 1970.

Brown, C.J., *Coins of India*, Heritage of India Series, Calcutta: Association Press, 1922.

Browne, James, *History of the Origin and Progress of the Sikhs* (India Tracts), London: East India Company, 1788.

Chandra, Satish, *Medieval India*, New Delhi: Har Anand Publication, 1999.

Chhabra, G.S., *Advanced History of Punjab* (2 vols.), Jullandhar: Prakash Brothers, 1976.

Chopra, Barkat Ram, *Kingdom of the Punjab 1839-45*, Hosphiarpur: VVRI, 1969.

Chopra, Gulshan Lall, *The Punjab as a Sovereign State*, Hoshiarpur: VVRI, 1960.

Codrington, O., *A Manual of Musilman Numismatics*, London, 1904.

Court, Major Henry, *History of Sikhs*, Lahore: CMG Press, 1888.

Cunningham, J.D., *A History of Sikhs*, New Delhi: S. Chand & Co., 1972 (original edition, 1948, Chandigarh: Panjab University).

David, Ron, *Land of the Five Rivers and the Sikhs*, Punjab: Languages Department, rpt., 1970.

Deol, G.S., *Banda Bahadur*, Jullandhar: New Academic Publishing House, 1972.

Devahuti, *Problems and Indian Historiography*, New Delhi: D.K. Publication, 1979.

Dhillon, Dalbir Singh, *Sikhism, Origin and Development*, New Delhi: Atlantic Publishers & Distributors, 1988.

Dhillon, G.S., *Insights into Sikh Religion and History*, Chandigarh: Singh & Singh Publications, 1991.

————, *Researches in Sikh Religion and History*, Chandigarh: Sumeet Prakashan, 1989.

Donie, James, *The Punjab, North Western Frontier Province and Kashmir*, New Delhi: Low Priced Publications, 1994.

Duggal, D.S., *Zafar Nama*, Jullandhar: Institute of Sikh Studies, 1980.

Elliot, A.C., *The Chronicles of Gujrat*, Punjab: Languages Department, rpt., 1970.

Fane, H.E., *Five Years in India*, Punjab: Languages Department, 1970.

Forster, George, *A Journey from Bengal to England*, Punjab: Languages Department, rpt., 1970.

Fox, Richard G., *Lions of the Punjab*, New Delhi: Low Priced Publications, 1990.

Franklin, W., *The History of Shah Alam*, New Delhi: Classical Publication, rpt., 1979.

Fredrich, Drew, *Jammu and Kashmir Territories*, New Delhi: Oriental Publishers, 1971.

Gauba, Anand, *Amritsar: A Study of Urban History, 1840-1947*, Jullandhar: ABS Publications, 1988.

Gill, Pritam Singh, *History of the Sikh Nation*, Jullandhar: New Academic Publishers, 1978.

Gordon, John, *Sikhs*, Punjab: Languages Department, rpt., 1970.

———, *The Sikhs,* Punjab: Languages Department, rpt., 1970.

Gough, Charles and Arthur Innes, *The Sikhs and Sikh Wars*, Punjab: Languages Department, rpt., 1970.

Gray, C., *European Adventures of Northern India, 1785-1849*, Punjab: Languages Department, rpt., 1970.

Gregor, M. William, *History of Sikhs*, Punjab: Languages Department, rpt., 1970.

Grewal, J.S. and Indu Banga, *Civil and Military Affairs of Ranjit Singh*, Amritsar: GNDU, 1987.

———, *Early 19th Century Punjab*, Amritsar: GNDU, 1975.

———, *Maharaja Ranjit Singh and His Times*, Amritsar: GNDU, 1980.

Grewal, J.S., and S.S. Bal, *Guru Gobind Singh*, Chandigarh: Panjab University, 1967.

Grewal, J.S., *Guru Nanak in History*, Chandigarh: Panjab University, 1969.

———, *From Guru Nanak to Maharaja Ranjit Singh,* Amritsar: GNDU, 1982.

———, *Guru Tegh Bahadur and Persian Chroniclers*, Amritsar: GNDU, 1976.

———, *Historians of Punjab*, Amritsar: GNDU, 1974.

———, *Ideology, Polity and Social Order*, New Delhi: Manohar, 1996.

———, *In the By-lanes of History: Some Persian Documents from a Punjab Town*, Shimla: Indian Institute of Advanced Studies, 1975.

———, *Medieval India: History and Historians*, Amritsar: GNDU, 1975.

———, *The Sikhs of Punjab*, The Cambridge History of India, New Delhi: Orient Longman, 1990.

Griffin, Lepel, *Maharaja Ranjit Singh*, Punjab: Languages Department, rpt., 1970.

———, *Minor Phulkian Families*, Punjab: Languages Department, rpt., 1970.

———, *Rajas of Punjab*, Punjab: Languages Department, rpt., 1970.

Gupta, Hari Ram, *History of Sikh Gurus*, New Delhi: U.C. Kapoor & Sons, 1973.

————, *History of Sikhs*, vol. II, New Delhi: Munshiram Manoharlal, 1978.

————, *History of Sikhs*, vol. III, New Delhi: Munshiram Manoharlal, 1980.

————, *History of Sikhs*, vol. IV, New Delhi: Munshiram Manoharlal, 1982.

————, *History of Sikhs*, vol. V, New Delhi: Munshiram Manoharlal, 1991.

————, *Jadu Nath Sarkar, Essays*, Chandigarh: Panjab University, 1958.

————, *Jadu Nath Sarkar, Life and Letters*, Chandigarh: Panjab University, 1958.

————, *Marathas and Panipat*, Chandigarh: Panjab University, 1961.

————, *Punjab on the Eve of the First Sikh War*, Chandigarh: Panjab University, 1975.

Gupta, Parmeshwari Lal and Sanjay Garg, *The Coins of Dal Khalsa and Lahore Darbar in Sheesh Mahal Museum, Patiala,* Chandhigarh: Department of Cultural Affairs, Government of Punjab, 1989.

Gupta, Parmeshwari Lal, *Coins of India*, New Delhi: Munshiram Manoharlal, 1969.

Gurdas, Bhai, *Varan* (2 vols.), Translated by Dr. Jodh Singh, Patiala: Vision and Venline, 1998.

Hans, Surjit, *A Reconstruction of Sikh History from Sikh Literature*, Jullandhar: ABS Publications, 1988.

Haroon Khan, Sheriwani, *Muslim Political Thought and Administration*, New Delhi: Adarah-i-Adbiyat-i-Delhi, rpt., 1976.

Hasrat, Bikramjit, *Life and Times of Ranjit Singh*, Hoshiarpur: VVRI, 1977.

————, *The Punjab Papers*, Hoshiarpur: VVRI, 1970.

Hassan, Ghulam, *Tarikh-i-Hassan*, Srinagar: Research Division, Jammu and Kashmir Government, 1954.

Henry, G.A., *Through the Sikh Wars*, Punjab: Languages Department, rpt., 1970.

Hira, Bhagat Singh, *Semitic Religious Thought and Sikhism*, New Delhi: National Book Shop, 1992.

Hoti, Prem Singh, *Life of Hari Singh Nalwa*, Ludhiana: Lahore Book Shop, 1937.

Hutchison, J. and P. Vogel, *History of Punjab Hill States* (2 vols.), New Delhi: Low Priced Publications, 1999.

Ibbetson, Denzil, *Punjab Castes*, New Delhi: Low Priced Publications, 1993.

Irvine, William, *Later Mughals*, New Delhi: Taj Publications, 1989.

Johar, S.S., *Hari Singh Nalwa*, New Delhi: Sagar Publications, 1982.

Kaur, Madanjit, *Golden Temple Past and Present*, Amritsar: GNDU, 1983.

Khan, Waheed-ud-din, *The Real Ranjit Singh*, Karachi: Long Art Press, 1965.

Khilnani, N.M., *Rise of Sikh Power in Punjab*, New Delhi: Independent Publishing Co., 1990.

Khullar, K.K., *Maharaja Ranjit Singh*, New Delhi: Hem Publishers, 1980.

Kiernan, V.G., *Metcalfe Mission· Metealge to Lahore*, Punjab: Languages Department, rpt., 1971.

Kohli, Surinder Singh, *Travels of Guru Nanak*, Patiala: Punjabi University, 1969.

Lafont, Jean-Marie, *Maharaja Ranjit Singh: Lord of the Five Rivers*, New Delhi: Oxford University Press, 2002.

Lal, K.S., *The Mughal Harem*, New Delhi: Aditi Parkashan, 1985.

Latif, Muhammad, *History of Punjab*, Ludhiana: Kalyani Publishers, rpt., 1989.

Lawrence, H.M.L., *Adventures of an officer in Punjab* (2 vols.), Punjab: Languages Department, rpt., 1970.

Lochlin, G.H., *The Sikhs and Their Scriptures*, Lucknow: Lucknow Publishing House.

Macauliffe, Max Arthur, *The Sikh Religion, Its Gurus, Sacred Writings and Authors* (6 vols.), New Delhi: S. Chand & Co., 1985.

Majumdar, R.K. and A.N. Srivastava, *Historiography*, New Delhi: SBD Enterprises, 1988.

Malhotra, D.K., *History and Problems of Indian Currency, 1835-1939*, Lahore: Minerva Book Shop, 1939.

Malik, Arjan Das, *An Indian Guerilla Warfare*, London: John Wiley & Sons, 1975.

Mansukhani, Gobind Singh, *The Quintessence of Sikhism*, Amritsar: SGPC, 1965.

McLeod, W.H., *Evolution of the Sikh Community*, New Delhi: Oxford University Press, 1975.

———, *Guru Nanak and the Sikh Religion*, New Delhi: Oxford University Press, 1968.

———, *The B40, Janam Sakhi*, Amritsar: GNDU, 1980.

Murray, William, *History of the Punjab—The Sikhs* (2 vols.), London: H. Allen & Co., 1846; Punjab: Languages Department, rpt., 1970.

Narang, G.C., *Transformation of Sikhism*, Lahore: New Book Society, 1945.

Nayyar, Gurbachan Singh, *Campaigns of Hari Singh Nalwa*, Patiala: Punjabi Univerisity, 1995.

———, *Hari Singh Nalwa*, Amritsar: Dharam Parchar Committee, 1993.

———, *Sikh Policy and Political Institutions*, New Delhi: Oriental Publications & Distribution, 1979.

Nijjar, B.S., *Punjab under Later Mughals*, Jullandhar: New Academic Publication Co., 1972.

Orlich, L., *Travels in India including Sindh and Punjab* (2 vols.), London, 1845.

Osbourne, W.G., *The Court and Camp of Ranjit Singh*, London, 1840.

Parmu, R.K., *History of Sikh Rule in Kashmir*, Srinagar: J&K Governmental Publication, 1977.

Pearse, Hugh, *Memories of Alexander Gardener*, Punjab: Languages Department, rpt., 1970.

Princep, Henry T., *Origin of the Sikh Power in Punjab*, Punjab: Languages Department, rpt., 1970.

Rangarajan, L.N., *Kautilya's Artha shastra*, New Delhi: Penguin Books, 1987.

Sandhu, Avtar Singh, *General Hari Singh Nalwa*, Lahore: Cunningham Historical Society, 1936.

Sarkar, D.C., *Studies in Indian Coins*, New Delhi: Motilal Banarsidass, 1968.

Sarkar, Jadu Nath, *Fall of Mughal Empire* (4 vols.), New Delhi: Orient Longman, 1971.

————, *Aurangzeb* (5 vols.), Calcutta: M.C. Sarkar & Sons, 1916.

Sethi, R.R., *Lahore Darbar*, New Delhi: Munshiram Manoharlal, 1950.

Sharma, D.C., *Kashmir under Sikhs*, New Delhi: Seema Publication, 1983.

Sheetal, Sohan Singh, *How Fell the Sikh Kingdom*, Ludhiana: Lyall Book Depot, 1970.

Sikhism and Indian Society, Shimla: Indian Institute of Advanced Studies, 1967.

Singh, Avtar, *Ethics of Sikhs*, Patiala: Punjabi University, 1983.

Singh, Bhagat, *History of Sikh Misls*, Patiala: Punjabi University, 1993.

————, *Maharaja Ranjit Singh and his Times*, New Delhi, 1990.

————, *Sikh Polity*, New Delhi: Oriental Publishers & Distributors, 1978.

Singh, Daljit, *Sikh Ideology*, New Delhi: Guru Nanak Foundation, 1984.

————, *Sikhism*, Amritsar: Singh Brothers, 1994.

Singh, Fauja and R.C. Rabra, *City of Faridkot*, Patiala: Punjabi University, 1976.

Singh, Fauja and Rattan Singh Saggi, *Perspectives on Guru Amardas*, Patiala: Punjabi University, 1982.

Singh, Fauja, *City of Amritsar*, Patiala: Punjabi University, 1977.

————, *Historians and Historiography of the Sikhs*, New Delhi: Oriental Publishers and Distributors, 1978.

————, *History of Punjab*, Patiala: Punjabi University, 1990.

————, *Maharaja Kharak Singh*, Patiala: Punjabi University, 1977.

————, *Sarhind Through the Ages*, Patiala: Punjabi University, 1984.

————, *Some Aspects of State and Society under Ranjit Singh*, New Delhi: Master Publishers, 1982.

Singh, Ganda, *Ahmad Shah Durrani*, New Delhi: Asia Publishing House, 1959.

————, *Baba Banda Bahadur*, Sirhind: Sarhind Historical Research Society, 1997.

————, *Hukamnamas*, Patiala: Punjabi University, 1985.

————, *Life of Banda Bahadur Singh*, Amritsar: Khalsa College, 1935.

————, *Sardar Jassa Singh Ahluwalia*, Patiala: Punjabi University, 1990.

————, *Select Bibliography of Sikhs and Sikhism*, Amritsar: SGPC, 1965.

Singh, Gopal, *History of Sikh Peoples*, New Delhi: World Sikh University Press, 1979.

Singh, Gulcharan, *Ranjit Singh and his Generals*, Jullandhar: Sujlana Publishers, 1976.

Singh, Gurmukh Nihal, *Guru Nanak: His Life, Time and Teachings*, New Delhi: Guru Nanak Foundation, 1981.

Singh, Harbans, *Perspectives on Guru Nanak*, Patiala: Punjabi University, 1990.

Singh, Jagjit, *The Sikh Revolution*, Chandigarh: Bahri Publication Pvt. Ltd., 1981.

Singh, Justice Gurdev, *Perspectives on the Sikh Tradition*, Amritsar: Singh Bros., 1996.

Singh, Kanwaljit, *Political Philosophy of the Sikh Gurus*, New Delhi: Atlantic Publishers & Distributors, 1989.

Singh, Kapur, *Parasaraprasana*, Amritsar: GNDU, 1989.

Singh, Khazan, *History of Sikh Religion*, Punjab: Language Department, rpt., 1988.

Singh, Khushwant, *History of the Sikhs*, New Delhi: Oxford University Press (2 vols.), 1987.

———, *Ranjit Singh*, Bombay: George Allen & Unwin, 1982.

Singh, Kirpal, *Historical Study of Ranjit Singh's Times*, New Delhi: National Book Shop, 1994.

Singh, Patwant, *The Sikhs*, New Delhi: Harper Collins India, 1999.

Singh, Puram, *The Spirit of the Sikhs*, Patiala: Punjabi University, 1981.

Singh, Ranbir, *The Sikh Way of Life*, New Delhi: India Publishers, 1982.

Singh, Seva Ram, *The Divine Master, Guru Nanak*, Lahore: Gulab Singh & Sons, 1904.

Singh, Sher, *Philosophy of Sikhism*, Amritsar: SGPC, rpt., 1986.

Singh, Sohan, *Banda the Brave*, Published by Bhai Narain Singh, Mazang, Lahore, 1915.

Singh, Taran, *Sikh, Gurus and Indian Political Thought*, Patiala: Punjabi University, 1981.

Singh, Teja and Ganda Singh, *A Short History of Sikhs*, Patiala: Punjabi University, 1952.

Singh, Wazir, *Sikhism and Punjab Heritage*, Patiala: Punjabi University, 1989.

Sinha, N.K., *Ranjit Singh*, Calcutta: A. Mukharjee & Co., 1975.

———, *Rise of Sikh Power*, Calcutta: A. Mukherjee & Co., 1973.

Smith, G.C., *History of the Reigning Family of Lahore*, Punjab: Languages Department, rpt., 1970.

Steinbach, Colonel, *The Punjab Country of the Sikhs*, Punjab: Languages Department, rpt., 1970.

Sufi, G.M.D., *History of Kashmir*, New Delhi: Light and Life Publications, 1974.

Suri, Sohan Lal, *Umdat-ut-Tawairkh*, vol. II, Punjabi translation by Amarnath Singh, Amritsar: GNDU, 1975.

Talib, G.S., *Guru Gobind Sahib*, Patiala: Punjabi University, 1984.

———, *Guru Tegh Bahadur*, Patiala: Punjabi University, 1976.

———, *The Origin and Development of Religion*, Patiala: Punjabi University, 1997.

Thorburn, S.S., *Punjab in Peace*, Punjab: Languages Department, rpt., 1970.

Thornton, T.H., *History of Punjab* (2 vols.), London: Allen & Co., 1846.

Trumpp, Ernest, *Adi Granth* (tr.), New Delhi: Munshiram Manoharlal, 1978.

Valentine, W.H., *Copper Coins of India* (2 vols.), New Delhi: Inter-India Publications, 1983.

B. *Journals and Periodicals*

Abstract of Sikh Studies, Chandigarh: Institute of Sikh Studies.

Calcutta Review, Calcutta.

Indian Antiquary, Bombay.

Journal of the Asiatic Society of Bengal, Calcutta.

Journal of the History of Sikh Studies, Amritsar: Guru Nanak Dev University.

Journal of the Indian Institute of Advanced Studies, Shimla.

Journal of the Malaysian Numismatic Society, Kuala Lumpur.

Journal of the Numismatic Society of India, Banaras.

Journal of the Punjab Historical Society, Lahore.

Journal of the Punjab University Historical Society, Lahore.

Newsletter of Oriental Numismatic Society, Surrey, UK.

Numismatic Digest, Bombay.

Numismatic International Bulletin, Dallas, Texas, USA.

Panjab Past & Present, Patiala: Punjabi University.

Panjab University Research Bulletin, Chandigarh: Panjab University.

Proceedings of the Indian History Congress.

Proceedings of the Punjab History Conference, Patiala: Punjabi University.

Sikh Review, Calcutta.

Studies in Sikhism and Comparative Religion, New Delhi: Guru Nanak Dev Foundation.

The Spokesman Weekly, Chandigarh.

Index